SO-ATE-781

5681
B2
B462
1993

ANALYSIS OF FINANCIAL STATEMENTS

ANALYSIS OF
FINANCIAL STATEMENTS

Leopold A. Bernstein, Ph.D., C.P.A.

Professor of Accounting
Bernard M. Baruch College
The City University of New York

COLORADO CHRISTIAN UNIVERSITY
LIBRARY
180 S. GARRISON
LAKEWOOD, COLORADO 80226

FOURTH EDITION

IRWIN
Professional Publishing®
Chicago • London • Singapore

This symbol indicates that the paper in this book is made of recycled paper. Its fiber content exceeds the recommended minimum of 50% waste paper fibers as specified by the EPA.

An expanded version of this text is published by Richard D. Irwin, Inc., under the title *Financial Statement Analysis: Theory, Application, and Interpretation, Fifth Edition.*

© RICHARD D. IRWIN, 1978, 1984, 1990, and 1993

All rights reserved. No part of this book may be reproduced in any form or by any means, electronic, mechanical, photocopying, recording, or otherwise, without the prior written permission of the publisher.

This publication is designed to provide accurate and authoritative information in regard to the subject matter covered. It is sold with the understanding that neither the author nor the publisher is engaged in rendering legal, accounting, or other professional service. If legal advice or other expert assistance is required, the services of a competent professional person should be sought.

From a Declaration of Principles jointly adopted by a Committee of the American Bar Association and a Committee of Publishers.

Project editor: Waivah Clement
Production manager: Bob Lange
Compositor: Impressions, a division of Edwards Brothers, Inc.
Typeface: 10/12 Times Roman
Printer: R. R. Donnelley & Sons Company

Library of Congress Cataloging-in-Publication Data

Bernstein, Leopold A.
   [Financial statement analysis. Selections]
   Analysis of financial statements / Leopold A. Bernstein. — 4th
ed.
      p.   cm.
   "An expanded version of this text is published . . . under the title
Financial statement analysis . . ."—CIP t.p. verso.
   Includes bibliographical references and index.
   ISBN 1-55623-930-0
   1. Financial statements. I. Title.
HF5681.B2B462 1993
657'.3—dc20   93–1209

Printed in the United States of America
   6 7 8 9 0 DOC 0 9 8 7 6

Preface

The major objective of this fourth edition, as was that of preceding editions, is to present an up-to-date treatment of the analysis of financial statements as an aid to decision making.

This edition brings into sharper focus the knowledge and skills which are required for the intelligent analysis of financial statements. It reflects a comprehensive updating of authoritative pronouncements on accounting and auditing standards and practices as well as the valuable suggestions of practicing financial analysts, credit analysts, and other users of financial data.

While the analysis of financial statements serves many and varied purposes, its major usefulness is in making investing and lending decisions. Such decisions, and the actions to which they lead, are, of course, at the heart of the free market system.

Investing and lending decisions require the application of thorough analysis to carefully evaluated data. They require, moreover, the ability to forecast—to foresee. Sound information is obtained by an *understanding* of the data from which it is derived as well as by the application of tools of analysis to aid in its extraction and evaluation. Foresight, which is essential to the assessment of opportunity and risk, is also rooted in understanding: understanding of the elements comprising the data and of the factors that can change them. The common denominator is *understanding*. Alfred North Whitehead assured us that foresight can be taught when he wrote: "Foresight depends upon understanding. In practical affairs it is a habit. But the habit of foreseeing is elicited by the habit of understanding. To a large extent, understanding can now be acquired by a conscious effort and it can be taught. Thus the training of foresight is by the medium of understanding."

Thus, the keynote of this work is *understanding*. It focuses on understanding the data which are analyzed as well as the methods by which they are analyzed and interpreted.

Leopold A. Bernstein

v

Contents

6 ANALYSIS OF RETURN ON INVESTMENT AND OF ASSET UTILIZATION
195

Known Uncertainties. Special Reports. Reports on "Compiled" and "Reviewed" Financial Statements. The SEC's Important Role. Implications for Analysis: *Implications Inherent in the Audit Process, Audit Risk and Its Implications.* Implications Stemming from the Standards that Govern the Auditor's Opinion. The Audit Function as Perceived by the Auditor: *Qualification, Disclaimers, and Adverse Opinions.* Questions.

Chapter 1

OBJECTIVES OF FINANCIAL STATEMENT ANALYSIS

THE NATURE OF FINANCIAL ANALYSIS

The process of financial statement analysis consists of the application of analytical tools and techniques to financial statements and data in order to derive from them measurements and relationships that are significant and useful for decision making. Thus, financial statement analysis first and foremost serves the essential function of converting *data,* of which in this age of the computer there are a bewildering quantity and variety, into useful information, which is always in scarce supply.[1]

The processes of financial analysis can be described in various ways, depending on the objectives to be attained. Thus, financial analysis can be used as a preliminary *screening* tool in the selection of investments or merger candidates. It can be used as a *forecasting* tool of future financial conditions and results. It may be used as a process of *diagnosis* of managerial, operating, or other problem areas. It can serve as a tool in the *evaluation* of management. Above all, financial analysis reduces reliance on pure hunches, guesses, and intuition, and this reduces and narrows the inevitable areas of uncertainty that attend all decision-making processes. Financial analysis does not lessen the need for judgment but rather establishes a sound and systematic basis for its rational application.

APPROACHES TO THE SUBJECT

There are a number of possible approaches to a discussion of the tools and techniques of financial analysis. One way, popularly employed in books on the subject, is to describe the analysis of specific financial statements, such as balance sheets, without a concurrent emphasis of objectives to be attained. The approach employed here will be to examine the

---

[1] Walter B. Wriston put it this way: "The incessant production of new data . . . creates a paradox; information, the thing that eliminates uncertainty, now increases everybody's feeling of insecurity because of the failure to convert data into knowledge." See Walter B. Wriston, "The World according to Walter," *Harvard Business Review,* January-February 1986, p. 65.

process of financial statement analysis with emphasis on the major objectives (see Chapter 2, "Building Blocks of Financial Statement Analysis") that they are designed to achieve. In order to do this, we turn first to an examination of the information needs and the specific analytical objectives of the most important categories of users of financial data, namely:

Credit grantors.

Equity investors.

Management.

Acquisition and merger analysts.

Auditors.

Other interested groups.

Objectives of Credit Grantors

Credit grantors are lenders of funds to an enterprise. Funds are lent in many forms and for a variety of purposes.

Trade creditors usually extend very short-term credit. They ship goods or provide services and expect payment within the customary period that forms the terms of trade in their industry. Most trade credit ranges from 30 to 60 days, with cash discounts occasionally allowed for specified earlier payment. The trade creditor does not usually receive interest for an extension of credit. The trade creditor's reward takes the form of the business transacted and the possible profit that flows from it.

An enterprise receives other short-term and longer-term credit or loans from a variety of sources. Short-term credit is often provided by various sources, mainly by banks or by sale of commercial paper. Longer-term credit is provided by banks in the form of term loans and by financial institutions, such as insurance companies, through their purchase of bonds or notes or through private placements. Companies also obtain longer-term funds through the public sale of notes or bonds in the securities markets. Leasing and conditional sales are other forms of long-term financing. The sale of convertible, and generally subordinated, bonds combines the borrowing of money with the added feature of an option to the lender to exchange his or her claim for an equity interest should the lender find it profitable to do so. Similarly, the issuance of preferred stock, which is senior to the common equity but junior to debt, combines the fixed reward features of a loan with the absence of definite principal repayment requirements that characterize equity securities.

One outstanding characteristic of all pure credit extension relationships is the fixed nature of the rewards accruing to the credit grantor. Thus, should the enterprise prosper, the credit grantor will still be limited to his or her contractually fixed rate of interest, or to the profit on the goods supplied. However, should the enterprise incur losses or meet other adversities, the credit grantor's principal may be placed in jeopardy. This uneven nature of the lender's risk-reward ratio has a major effect on the lender's point of view and on the manner in which he or she analyzes the possibilities of credit extension.

The difference in the point of view of the lenders as compared to that of the equity investor results in differences in the way they analyze future prospects and in the objectives they seek. The equity investor looks for reward primarily to future prospects of earnings and to changes in those earnings. The credit grantor, on the other hand, is concerned primarily with specific security provisions of his or her loan, such as the fair market value of assets pledged; and for repayment of principal and interest, the credit grantor looks to the existence of resources and the projections of future flows of funds (The term *funds* refers to cash and to assets very readily convertible to cash, such as cash equivalents) and the reliability and stability of such flows. Equity investors, as a result of the theoretically unlimited nature of their rewards, may be receptive to highly abstract descriptions of "concepts," potentials, and future probabilities. Lenders, on the other hand, require a more definite link between the projections of the future and the resources already at hand as well as the demonstrated ability to achieve operating results. Whereas equity investors look to the rewards of earnings growth, creditors are more concerned with how low earnings will shrink during recessionary periods. Credit grantors generally are more conservative in their outlook and approach and rely on financial statement analysis to an even greater extent than do equity investors, for it serves to reassure them regarding the borrower's demonstrated ability to control the flow of cash and to maintain a sound financial condition under a variety of economic and operating circumstances. The more speculative the loan, the more similar are the lender's analytical approaches to those of the equity investor.

The techniques of financial statement analysis used by lenders as well as the criteria of evaluation used by them vary with the term, the security, and the purpose of the loan.

In the case of short-term credit extension, the credit grantor is concerned primarily with the current financial condition, the liquidity of the current assets, and the rate of their turnover. These considerations are covered in Chapter 3.

The evaluation of longer-term loans, which includes the valuation of bonds, requires a far more detailed and forward-looking inquiry and analysis. Such an analysis includes projections of cash flows and fund flows and the evaluation of the longer-term earning power of the enterprise as the ultimate source of assurance of an enterprise's ability to meet the fixed charges arising from its debt as well as from its other commitments under a variety of economic conditions. This subject is examined in Chapter 5.

Since the profitability of an enterprise is a major element in the lender's security, the analysis of profitability is an important criterion to the credit grantor. Profit is viewed as the primary source for interest payments and as a desirable source of principal repayment.

Credit analysis, whether long term or short term, is concerned with capital structure because it has a bearing on risk and on the creditor's margin of safety. The relationship of equity capital to debt is an indicator of the adequacy of equity capital and of the cushion against loss that it provides. This relationship also reflects on the attitude of management toward risk and influences the income coverage of fixed charges.

Lenders, and bankers among them, generally look at asset values in the context of published financial statements, that is, in the context of the going-concern assumption. Clearly, the assumption of liquidation could often lead to realizable values of assets that would generally be lower than those stated on a going-concern basis. For this reason, bankers tend to attach very conservative values to fixed and other assets, and to make allowance for all possible future contingencies.

Objectives of Equity Investors

The equity interest in an enterprise is the supplier of its basic risk capital. The capital is exposed to all the risks of ownership and provides a cushion or shield for the preferred and loan capital that is senior to it. Since the equity interest is entitled to distributions only after the claims of senior securities have been met, it is referred to as the *residual* interest. In the course of normal operations as a going concern, this residual interest may receive distributions (dividends) after the prior claims of senior security holders for bond interest and/or preferred dividends have been satisfied. In liquidation, it has a claim to what remains *after* the prior claims of creditors and preferred stockholders have been met. Thus, when an enterprise prospers, the equity owners stand to reap all the gains above the fixed amount of senior capital contributors' claims and, conversely, the equity owners will be the first ones to absorb losses should the enterprise flounder.

From the above it is clear that the information needs of equity investors are among the most demanding and comprehensive of all users of financial data. Their interests in an enterprise, of which they own a share, are the broadest because their interest is affected by all aspects and phases of operations, profitability, financial condition, and capital structure.

Common Stock Valuation   The valuation of common stock is a complex procedure involving, in addition to financial statement analysis, an assessment of such factors as the general state of the economy, industry position, competitive stance, and the quality of management. Since the

most thorough and sophisticated analysis and evaluation of equity securities, for the purpose of deciding whether to buy, sell, or hold, is
performed by professional security analysts, their point of view will be
examined here.

A common stockholder, having no legal claim to a definite dividend
or to a capital distribution, looks for three principal rewards from his
or her holdings: current dividends, special distributions such as rights,
and a market value of the security at a given time in the future that will,
hopefully, result in a capital gain. The most important determinant of
both dividends and market values is earnings. Current earnings, which
are the basic source of dividends and the accumulation of undistributed
earnings, as well as the earnings record, current and prospective, are
major elements in the determination of the market price of the common
stock.

Approaches to Common Stock Valuation   The basis of most modern
stock valuation techniques and models is present value theory. This approach, first set forth in detail by John B. Williams,[2] maintains that the
present value of a share of stock is equal to the sum of all dividends
expected to be received from it, discounted to the present at an appropriate rate of interest. The difficulty here, of course, as in all other approaches based on this theory, is the estimation of such future distributions.[3] What is clear, however, is that all expected distributions, be
they of a current dividend or of a liquidation residual nature, are based
largely on earnings and the earning power of assets.

Security valuation models used by security analysts bear out the proposition that earnings, and particularly estimated future earnings, are the
most important determinant of the value of common shares.[4]

---

[2] *The Theory of Investment Value* (Cambridge, Mass.: Harvard University Press, 1938).

[3] The importance of expected distributions is largely responsible for the focus on cash
flows. However, so far, most valuation models have not concerned themselves with the
purchasing power equivalent of such cash flows, a consideration that looms large in times
of significant price-level changes. Thus, a security represents a contingent claim not only
because of the uncertain outcome of future events but also (including here a "riskless"
bond) because of an uncertain command over future goods and services.

[4] While earnings are unquestionably a most important factor they are by no means the
only factor. At times other considerations may predominate in the creation or determination
of values. For example:

a. There is value to a controlling interest in a company. While such value is not
   available to true minority investors it is available to those who through operating
   control can avail themselves of compensation arrangements and other executive
   perquisites.

b. Value can be derived by rearranging ownership interests in an entity. It can be
   rearranged in such a way that favorable tax treatments result (e.g., from write-ups of
   assets for depreciation purposes; or from the replacement of equity with debt).
   Thus the income stream going to the government is diminished and that going to
   owners and creditors is increased.

Graham, Dodd, and Cottle emphasized the importance of earnings as follows:

> The standard method of valuation of individual enterprises consists of capitalizing the expected future earnings and/or dividends at an appropriate rate of return. The average earnings will be estimated for a period running ordinarily between five and ten years.[5]

Most common stock valuation models incorporate earnings growth and earnings payout ratios as factors of prime importance.

The normal procedure in dynamic models is to state the price of a stock as the present value of a growing stream of dividends with each component of this stream discounted at the rate k. One of the best-known dynamic stock valuation models presented in recent years is that by Gordon and Shapiro. Assume that $E(t)$ are the earnings of an enterprise at time t, b is the dividend payout ratio, k is the market discount rate (the cost of capital), and g is the projected annual growth rate in earnings. The valuation formula for the company's justified market price V (intrinsic value) is:

$$V = \frac{bE(t)}{k - g}$$

The above formula reduces long and awkward statements to more manageable but nevertheless mathematically equivalent terms. It states in effect that the market value V is equal to the current dividend discounted at a rate $k - g$; that is,

$$V = \frac{\text{Current dividend rate}}{\text{Discount rate} - \text{Growth rate}}$$

The elegance and the simplicity of the above formula should not obscure the fact that the most critical element in this or similar approaches to equity valuation is the valid quantification of the variables or inputs themselves. The more conventional approach by practitioners in the field of security analysis is to value a security by multiplying its earnings, which are really a surrogate for present and future dividends, by a *price-earnings ratio*[6] that is usually an imprecise expression of their assessment of external economic factors as well as of the growth prospects, financial

---

[5] *Security Analysis* (New York: McGraw-Hill, 1962), p. 435. This volume is the successor to the seminal work in this area, Benjamin Graham and David L. Dodd, *Security Analysis* (New York: McGraw-Hill, 1934).

[6] Expressed in terms of the foregoing Gordon-Shapiro formula, the price-earnings ratio (P/E) can be stated as follows:

$$\text{P/E} = \frac{b}{k - g}$$

Thus, for example, if the dividend payout ratio *(b)* changes, so would the P/E ratio.

strengths, capital structure, and other risk factors associated with the enterprise.

The similarity of the present value models of common stock valuation to the conventional method of bond valuation is quite obvious. In the case of bonds, the value, or proper purchase price, is calculated by discounting each coupon and the ultimate principal repayment to present value at a discount rate equal to the desired yield. In the case of growth stock valuations, the expected dividend corresponds to the bond coupon and the assumed market price of the stock at the model target date corresponds to the repayment of bond principal at maturity date.

The similarity of the bond and stock valuation models under these theories has led Molodovsky and others to construct stock valuation tables that can be used in a fashion similar to the use of bond tables.[7] The formula used by them for the value *(V)* of a stock is:

$$V = D_0 + \frac{D_1}{1 + k} + \frac{D_2}{(1 + k)^2} + \ldots + \frac{D_n}{(1 + k)^n} + \ldots$$

where:

D_0 is the dividend initially.

D_n is the dividend in the nth year.

k is the discount rate, or the desired rate of return.

The model does not include a residual market value of the stock (similar to bond principal to be repaid) because it assumes dividend projections taken out to infinity. With regard to the latter, the authors assure us that because the discount factor becomes so large in the distant future, these increments to value become negligible. It is easy to bring the model closer in form to a bond model by assuming a specified sales price (realization of principal) at a specified date, but that price will itself depend on the application of the foregoing formula.

While we can readily understand why the stock valuation model builders have been attracted by the logic as well as the mathematical elegance of the bond valuation model, we must recognize the important differences that exist between the inputs required by the bond model as opposed to those required by the stock model. The focus on these differences is all the more important since the basic purpose of our discussion in this chapter is to relate the scope and the techniques of financial statement analysis to the purposes that they are designed to serve—in this instance, the valuation of equity securities.

In the case of bond valuation, the bond coupon is known and so is the amount of principal to be repaid at the maturity of the bond. Thus, as we saw in the section dealing with the objectives of credit grantors,

---

[7] N. Molodovsky, C. May, and S. Chottiner, "Common Stock Valuation—Principles, Tables, and Application," *Financial Analysts Journal,* March–April 1965.

the major questions to be considered are the *availability* of funds for the payment of interest and the repayment of principal. While the assessment of the probabilities of such availability of funds does involve the totality of enterprise prospects, the process of estimation is nevertheless less complex than the one involved in arriving at the proper parameters for the stock valuation model.

There is a basic and important difference in the certainty of results that can be expected from an analysis of debt instruments (such as bonds) and those that can be expected from the analysis of equity securities. In the case of debt instruments, the results of the analysis depend almost entirely on a valid assessment of the borrower's ability to make timely payments of interest and principal. The relationship between analysis and the results achieved are far more complex in the case of equity securities. Thus, no matter how "right" the analyst is in assumptions and forecasts, a major part of the reward of that analysis, that is, future capital values, depends on the perceptions of others. That is, on buyers agreeing with the analyst's conclusions and seeing things his or her way. No such dependence on validation by the marketplace exists in the case of results to be achieved from the analysis of debt instruments.

This difference, as well as the enormous complexities to which the analysis and evaluation of equity securities are subject, is in large part behind the skepticism with which many practicing security analysts treat those who attempt to compress the market reality into neat, streamlined, and elegant mathematical formulations.

Data Required for Stock Valuation   Let us now consider the data that are required in order to quantify the factors present in most of the stock valuation models discussed above.

The expected dividend stream in the future is dependent on earnings and dividend payout policy. The latter depends on the company's financial condition, capital structure, and its need for funds both in the present and in the future.

The projection of future earnings (see Chapter 9) is always a complex process subject to varying degrees of uncertainty. The reported earnings must be evaluated and adjusted and, in turn, form the basis for projection. Unlike the bond coupon, which remains constant, the further into the future that earnings are projected, the more conjectural the estimates become.

The size of the discount factor that may properly be used in computing the present value of a future stream of dividends and residual interests depends to a significant extent on the risk involved. The risk reflects such factors as the stability of the industry, the past variability in earnings, and the leverage inherent in its capital structure.

No stock valuation formula has yet been devised and published that has proved to be an accurate forecaster of security market values under all conditions. Perhaps the factors that bear on the determination of security values are too numerous and too complex for inclusion in a workable formula, and possibly not all such factors can be adequately measured, particularly because of the simplifying assumptions that are introduced in many such models.

Whatever method of stock valuation is used by the security analyst, be it either a simple short-term projection of earnings to be capitalized at a predetermined rate or a complex and sophisticated formula involving elegant mathematical techniques, the results can never reach a higher level of accuracy or be more reliable than the inputs used in such calculations. The reliability and the validity of these inputs, be they earnings projections, expected payout ratios, or various risk factors such as those inherent in capital structure, depend on the quality of the financial statement analysis performed.

The above view was best expressed by Douglas A. Hayes:

> Although the concept that investment results are likely to be heavily related to corporate performance in a long-term sense is generally accepted, some recent contributions to the field have alleged that the implementation methodology should be completely revolutionized. For example . . . a text of financial analysis alleges . . . that a critical investigation of the past financial statements to reveal potential problems of consistency and comparability of reported income and balance sheet data can be largely discarded because accounting and disclosure standards have improved to the point where the underlying data require no critical review. Moreover, they allege that financial risk factors no longer require appraisal because of the greatly improved stability features of the economy; in lieu thereof, they suggest elegant mathematical techniques to develop the theoretical effects of assumed patterns of various management decisions and economic data on security values.
>
> However, the empirical evidence would suggest that these allegations are seriously in error.[8]

In short, while the goal of the analyst may be to go forward *from* the figures, a thorough financial analysis requires that he also go *behind* the figures.[9] No present or prospective developments in the field of accountancy justify the assumption that this can be significantly changed in the near future (see also examples throughout the text).

---

[8] "The Dimensions of Analysis: A Critical Review," *Financial Analysts Journal,* September–October 1966.

[9] Author's note: Women have been analysts and auditors for years, and their numbers are growing. However, in this book, masculine pronouns are often being used for succinctness and are intended to refer to both males and females.

DEVELOPMENTS IN INVESTMENT THEORY

The methods and approaches of practicing security analysts have come under repeated challenge by their academic counterparts who have developed a number of theories designed to provide insight into the overall investment process.

Portfolio Theory

A pioneering contribution was that of Markowitz, who addressed the problem of portfolio construction given analysts' estimates of possible future returns from securities.[10] He demonstrated that both risk and return must be considered, provided a formal framework for quantifying both, and showed how the relationship among security risks and returns could be taken into account in portfolio construction.

He begins with the observation that the future return on a security can be estimated, and he equates risk with the variance of the distribution of returns. Markowitz demonstrated that under certain assumptions there is a linear relationship between risk and return. Using these variables, he provided a framework for deciding how much of each security to hold in constructing a portfolio. The two-dimensional risk-return approach offers the investor the ability to choose in the trade-off between risk and return. Markowitz's work is based on the assumption that rational investors will resist increases in risk without commensurate increases in expected returns. By proper diversification, one can lower risk while preserving returns.

Evaluation of Risk and Return

The relationship between the risk that must be accepted and the return that may be expected is central to all modern investing and lending decisions. It may seem obvious that the greater the perceived degree of risk of an investment or of a loan, the greater is the required rate of return to compensate for such risk.

Categories of Risk

Risk is commonly associated with the uncertainty surrounding the outcome of future events. While many investors and lenders make subjective evaluations of risk, academicians have developed statistical measures of risk that belong to the overall concept known as beta coefficient theory.

---

[10] H. Markowitz, "Portfolio Selection," *Journal of Finance,* March 1952, pp. 77–91. In 1990, Dr. Markowitz along with W. Sharpe and M. Miller shared the Nobel Prize in economics.

Under this theory, the total risk associated with an investment is composed of two elements:

1. *Systematic risk,* which is that portion of total risk attributable to the movement of the market as a whole.
2. *Unsystematic risk,* which is the residual risk that is unique to a specific security.

In the application of the theory, a quantitative expression of systematic risk (known as beta)[11] equal to one is attributed to the volatility of the market as a whole. The higher a security's beta, the greater will be its expected return. Treasury bills have a beta of zero because they are essentially riskless; that is, they do not fluctuate with the market. A stock having a beta of 1.20 could rise or fall 20 percent faster than the market, while one having a beta of 0.90 would on average register market value changes 10 percent less in amplitude than those of the market as a whole. Thus, high beta stocks can expect high returns in a "bull market" and also larger than average declines during a "bear market."

Since by definition, unsystematic risk[12] is the *residual risk* that is unexplained by market movements, no unsystematic risk exists for the market as a whole and almost none exists in a highly diversified portfolio of stocks. Consequently, as portfolios become larger and more diversified, their unsystematic risk will approach zero.

Adherents to this theory hold that the market will not reward those exposing themselves to unsystematic risk that can be removed by proper diversification. They believe that the implication of the theory for common stock investors is to diversify, and if they expect the market to rise, to increase the beta of their portfolios and vice versa. Some experimental studies have indicated that between 30 and 50 percent of an individual stock's price is due to market (systematic) risk and that such influence reaches 85 to 90 percent in a well-diversified portfolio of 30 or more stocks.[13]

It follows that the portfolio manager who does not wish to rely only on market action for returns or who cannot forecast overall market action

---

[11] Beta indexes are computed by use of regression analysis to relate the historical price movements of a stock to the movements of a general market price index such as the S&P 500 stock index. Alas, because of the ever-changing environment, capital structure, and operations of an enterprise, beta coefficients have exhibited a high degree of instability over time.

[12] A measure of unsystematic risk is alpha, which measures a stock's expected rate of return when the expected market rate of return is zero. Many academicians maintain that the expected alpha for a well-diversified portfolio is zero because the specific business circumstances that give rise to positive and negative alphas tend to cancel out in a portfolio of stocks. Practicing security analysts strive, however, to construct portfolios having positive alphas. In essence, alpha is derived from virtues in a stock that are not recognized by the market, thus resulting in returns above what beta would suggest.

[13] J. B. Cohen, E. D. Zinbarg, and A. Zeikel, *Investment Analysis and Portfolio Management,* 5th ed. (Homewoood, Ill.: Richard D. Irwin, 1987).

should seek nondiversification, that is, exposure to the amount of unsystematic risk required for achieving the desired rate of return. Such a strategy would emphasize the analysis of individual securities, as discussed in this work, as opposed to overall portfolio risk balancing. Thus, reaping the rewards of exposure to nonsystematic risk is dependent on an ability to identify undervalued securities and on the proper assessment of their risk. (See discussion of efficient market hypothesis later in this chapter.)

Components of Unsystematic Risk

Those who want to obtain their rewards from exposure to unsystematic or nonmarket risk through the rigorous analysis of individual securities must focus on the various components of such risk. While those components are undoubtedly interrelated and subject to the influence of such elements of systematic risk as overall political, economic, and social factors, they can nevertheless be usefully classified as follows:

Economic risk reflects risks of the overall economic environment in which the enterprise operates including general economic risk (fluctuations in business activity), capital market risk (including changes in interest rates), and purchasing power risk.

Business risk is concerned with the ever-present uncertainty regarding a business enterprise's ability to earn a satisfactory return on its investments as well as with the multitude of cost and revenue factors that enter into the determination of such a return. It includes the factors of competition, product mix, and management ability (see Chapters 6–9).

Financial risk is basically concerned with capital structure and with the ability of an enterprise to meet fixed and senior charges and claims. These factors of short-term liquidity and long-term solvency are discussed in detail in Chapters 3, 4, and 5.

Those who assume, as do beta theorists, that all investors are averse to risk and that they seek to diversify away the specific or unsystematic risks[14] of a security thus exposing themselves only to market risk, must also realize that the historical betas for individual securities have proven quite unstable over time and that consequently such betas seem to be poor predictors of future betas for the same security. Thus, while overall concepts and theories are easier to apply to stock aggregates than to the evaluation of individual stocks, they are at the same time far less reliable and accurate instruments for the achievement of investment results.

---

[14] What is often overlooked is that those who seek to diversify away unsystematic risk are also diversifying out a great deal of the rewards that equity investing holds for more aggressive investors.

Another, and perhaps even more troublesome, question is the assumption of beta theorists that past volatility alone is an acceptable measure of risk without reference to the current price of a security. Is a security that sells significantly *above* its value, as determined by some method of fundamental analysis, no more risky than a security of equal volatility (beta) that sells significantly *below* such fundamentally determined value? We know that paying an excessive price for a stable quality security can amount to as rank a speculation as investing in the most unseasoned of speculative securities.

While market theorists have not yet addressed the above troublesome question, they have addressed the problem of how securities are valued by the market.

The Relationship between Accounting and Market Measures of Risk

A study conducted by Professors W. Beaver, P. Kettler, and M. Scholes[15] found that accounting measures of risk, such as dividend payout ratios, capitalization ratios, coverage, and asset growth are reflected in market price risk measures such as beta. They also concluded that "a strategy of selecting and ranking portfolios according to accounting risk measures is essentially equivalent to the strategy of ranking these same portfolios according to market-determined risk measures."

Robert G. Bowman[16] illustrated a theoretical relationship between systematic risk and the firm's leverage and other accounting risk measures.

Barr Rosenberg[17] has pioneered the use of "fundamental betas" (i.e., those which are basically a function of a company's changing fundamentals such as earnings, financial structure, growth rates, etc). The important implication here is that the same economic (accounting expressed) determinants that cause a stock to be risky also cause it to have a high systematic risk (e.g., beta).

The Capital Asset Pricing Model

Sharpe[18] and Lintner[19] have extended portfolio theory to a capital asset pricing model (CAPM) that is intended to explain how prices of assets

---

[15] "The Association between Market Determined and Accounting Determined Risk Measures," *Accounting Review,* October 1970.

[16] "The Theoretical Relationship between Systematic Risk and Financial (Accounting) Variables," *Journal of Finance,* June 1979.

[17] B. Rosenberg and J. Guy, "Prediction of Beta from Investment Fundamentals," *Financial Analysts Journal,* July-August, 1976.

[18] W. F. Sharpe, "Capital Asset Prices: A Theory of Market Equilibrium under Conditions of Risk," *Journal of Finance,* September 1964, pp. 425–42.

[19] J. Lintner, "The Valuation of Risky Assets and the Selection of Risky Investments in Stock Portfolios and Capital Budgets," *Review of Economics and Statistics,* February 1965, pp. 13–37.

are determined in such a way as to provide greater return for greater risk. This model is based on the assumption that investors desire to hold securities in portfolios that are efficient in the sense that they provide a maximum return for *a given level* of risk. Moreover, the model was derived under the following simplifying assumptions:

1. That there exists a riskless security.
2. That investors are able to borrow or lend unlimited amounts at the riskless rate.
3. That all investors have identical investment horizons and act on the basis of identical expectations and predictions.

Based on these assumptions, it can be shown that when capital markets are in a state of equilibrium, the expected return on an individual security, $E(\tilde{R}_i)$, is related to its systematic risk β_i in the following linear form:

$$E(\tilde{R}_i) = E(\tilde{R}_0) + [E(\tilde{R}_M) - E(\tilde{R}_0)]\beta_i$$

The above formulation states in essence that under conditions of equilibrium, a security's expected return equals the expected return of a riskless security, $E(\tilde{R}_0)$, plus a premium for risk taking. This risk premium consists of a constant, $[E(\tilde{R}_M) - E(\tilde{R}_0)]$, which is the difference between the return expected by the market and the return on a riskless security (such as a short-term government bond) multiplied by the systematic risk of the security β_i (its beta) as discussed earlier.

The CAPM thus indicates that the expected return on any particular capital asset consists of two components: (1) the return on a riskless security and (2) a premium for the riskiness of the particular asset computed as outlined above. Thus, under the CAPM, each security has an expected return that is related to its risk. This risk is measured by the security's systematic movements with the overall market, and it cannot be eliminated by portfolio diversification. A major implication here is that only the bearing of systematic (i.e., beta) risk is rewarded by the market, whereas the holding of unsystematic risk that could be eliminated through diversification would earn no additional return.

It remains for us to consider a related hypothesis that attempts to describe a different property of security prices, that is, the efficient market hypothesis.

The Efficient Market Hypothesis

Efficient market hypothesis (EMH) deals with the reaction of market prices to financial and other data. The EMH has its origins in the random walk hypothesis that basically states that at any given point in time the size and direction of the next price change is random relative to what is known about an investment at that given time. A derivative of this hypothesis is what is known as the *weak form* of the EMH, which states that current prices reflect fully the information implied by historical price time series. In its *semistrong form,* the EMH holds that prices fully reflect all publicly available information.[20] Moreover, in its *strong form,* the theory asserts that prices reflect *all* information including that which is considered "inside information."

The EMH, in all its terms, has undergone extensive empirical testing with much of the evidence apparently supportive of the weak and semistrong forms of the theory. Lorie and Hamilton,[21] for example, present three studies in support of the semistrong form of the hypothesis indicating that:

1. Stock splits do not assure unusual profit for investors.
2. Secondary offerings depress the market price of a stock because such offerings imply that knowledgeable people are selling.
3. Unusual earnings increases are anticipated in the price of the stock before the company's earnings for the year are reported.[22]

None of these findings would, incidentally, clash with the intuition of experienced analysts or seasoned market participants.

Research supportive of the EMH by accounting scholars on the effect of accounting changes on security prices has found that changes from accelerated to straight-line depreciation for accounting purposes only had no significant effect on stock prices.[23] Another study found that the stock market ignored the effects on income of changes in accounting procedures such as those relating to inventories, depreciation, revenue recognition, and so forth.[24]

Implications for Financial Statement Analysis

The EMH is almost completely dependent on the assumption that competent and well-informed analysts, using tools of analysis such as those described in this book, will constantly strive to evaluate and act upon

---

[20] For one good discussion of this hypothesis, see E. F. Fama, "Efficient Capital Markets: A Review of Theory and Empirical Work," *Journal of Finance,* May 1970, pp. 383–417.

[21] J. H. Lorie and M. T. Hamilton, *The Stock Market: Theories and Evidence* (Homewood, Ill.: Richard D. Irwin, 1973).

[22] See, for example, R. Ball and P. Brown, "An Empirical Evaluation of Accounting Numbers," *Journal of Accounting Research,* Autumn 1968, pp. 159–78; and W. Beaver, "The Informational Content of Annual Earnings Announcements," *Empirical Research in Accounting: Selected Studies,* 1968, University of Chicago, Graduate School of Business 1969, pp. 48–53.

[23] T. R. Archibald, "Stock Market Reaction to the Depreciation Switch-Back," *The Accounting Review,* January 1972, pp. 22–30.

[24] R. Kaplan and R. Roll, "Accounting Changes and Stock Prices," *The Financial Analysts Journal,* January-February 1973, pp. 48–53; also R. Ball, "Changes in Accounting Techniques and Stock Prices," *Empirical Research in Accounting: Selected Studies,* 1972 (Chicago: Institute of Professional Accounting, Graduate School of Business, University of Chicago, 1974), pp. 1–38.

the ever-changing stream of new information entering the marketplace. And yet the theory's proponents claim that since all that is known is already instantly reflected in market prices, any attempt to gain consistently an advantage by rigorous financial statement analysis is not possible. As H. Lorie and M. T. Hamilton put it, "The most general implication of the efficient market hypothesis is that most security analysis is logically incomplete and valueless."[25]

This position presents an unexplained and unresolved paradox. The thousands of intelligent analysts are assumed to be capable enough to keep our security market efficient through their efforts, but they are not intelligent enough to realize that their efforts can yield no individual advantage. Moreover, should they suddenly realize that their efforts are unrewarded, the market would cease to be efficient.

There are a number of factors that may explain this paradox. Foremost among them is the fact that the entire EMH is built on evidence based on an evaluation of *aggregate*[26] rather than individual investor behavior. The focusing on macro or aggregate behavior results not only in the highlighting of average performance and results but also ignores and masks the results achieved by individual ability, hard work, and ingenuity, as well as by superior timing in acting on information as it becomes available.[27]

Few would doubt that important information travels fast. After all, enough is at stake to make it travel fast. Nor is it surprising that the securities markets are rapid processors of information. In fact, using the same type of deductive reasoning as used by the efficient market proponents, we could conclude that the speed and the hardworking efficiency of the market must be evidence that the market participants who make it happen are motivated by substantial rewards.

The reasoning behind the EMH's alleged implication for the usefulness of security analysis fails to recognize the essential difference between information and its proper interpretation. Even if all the information available on a security at a given point in time is impounded in its price, that price may not reflect *value*. It may be under- or overvalued depending on the degree to which an incorrect interpretation or evaluation of the

---

[25] Lorie and Hamilton, *The Stock Market*, p. 100.

[26] R. J. Chambers put it most effectively: "It is very difficult to escape the conclusion that the whole enterprise of aggregate market analysis with the object of resolving questions about the quality of accounting information is misguided. Men have never advanced their finite knowledge of any subject by attention only to what occurs in the aggregate or on average." "Stock Market Prices and Accounting Research," *Abacus,* June 1974, pp. 39–54.

[27] Evidence about superior investment performance by *individuals* is not a matter of public record and is consequently not readily available. But evidence of superior investment performance by portfolio managers is available, one example being *Forbes* magazine's annual "Honor Roll" of consistent long-term superior investment results by investment companies in both up and down markets. Such decidedly superior performance over the long term cannot be dismissed as a statistical quirk.

available information has been made by those whose actions determine the market price at a given time. Market efficiency depends not only on availability of information but also on its correct interpretation.

The work of financial statement analysis is complex and demanding. The spectrum of users of financial statements varies all the way from the institutional analyst who concentrates on only a few companies in one industry to the unsophisticated chaser of rumors. All act on financial information but surely not with the same insights and competence.[28]

The competent evaluation of "new information" entering the marketplace requires the possession of a prior fund of knowledge, of an information mosaic into which the new information can be fitted, as part of a link in a chain of analytical information, before it can be evaluated and interpreted. Only a few have the ability and are prepared to expend the efforts and resources needed to produce such information mosaics, and it is only natural that they would reap the rewards by being able to act both competently and confidently on the new information received. This advantage in timing is all-important in the marketplace. Thus the movement of new information and its correct interpretation flows from the well-informed and -prepared segments of the market to less-informed and slower-absorbing segments. That explains the *gradual* pattern rather than the immediate discounting of new information.

The vast resources that must be brought to bear on the competent analysis of equity securities have caused some segments of the securities markets to be more efficient than others. Thus, the market for shares of the largest companies is more efficient because many more analysts follow such securities and find it worthwhile to do so compared to those who follow small and lesser-known companies. Advocates of the EMH commit the common error of sweeping generalizations. In his 1988 annual report to the shareholders of Berkshire Hathaway, chairman and famed investor Warren Buffet expressed amazement that the EMH is embraced not only by academicians but also by many investment professionals. This, Buffet maintains, is because by observing correctly that the market was *frequently* efficient, they went on to conclude incorrectly that it is *always* efficient. As Buffet puts it "the difference between these propositions is night and day."

Buffet cites personal experience to refute the validity of EMH. The continuous 63-year experience of Graham Newman Corporation, Buffet Partnership, and Berkshire Hathaway resulted in unleveraged annual returns of 20 percent whereas over the same period the general market delivered returns of just under 10 percent. Recent evidence, calling into question the validity of EMH, continues to accumulate. The October

---

[28] B. Graham declared: "I deny emphatically that because the market has all the information it needs to establish a correct price, the prices it actually registers are in fact correct," in "C. D. Ellis, Ben Graham: Ideas as Momentos," *Financial Analysts Journal,* July-August 1982, p. 47.

1987 single-day sharp drop in stock prices (of 23 percent) raises the serious question of whether the opening as well as the closing prices of that day could have possibly represented efficiently priced market levels. The 1988 RJR Nabisco takeover contest offers another puzzling question to adherents of market efficiency. How can a company priced at $55 per share in the auction market be worth $75 per share to the management team and $109 per share to the winning buyout group?

The function and purpose of the analysis of equity securities is construed much too narrowly by those who judge its usefulness in an efficient market.[29] While the search for overvalued and undervalued securities is an important function of security analysis, the importance of risk assessment and loss avoidance, in the total framework of investment decision making, cannot be overemphasized. Thus, the prevention of serious investment errors is at least as important a factor in overall investment success as is the discovery of undervalued securities. Yet, our review of the CAPM and of beta theory earlier in this discussion tends to explain why this important function of analysis is neglected by adherents to these macro models of the security markets. For to some it is a basic premise of these theories that the analysis of unsystematic risk is not worthwhile because that kind of risk taking is not rewarded by the market. They maintain that such risks should be diversified away and that the portfolio manager should look only to systematic or market risk for rewards.[30]

Our basic premise here is that investment results are achieved through the careful study and analysis of *individual* enterprises rather than by an exclusive focus on market aggregates. Our approach in this area is to emphasize the value of fundamental investment analysis not only as a means of keeping our securities markets efficient and our capital markets rational and strong but also as the means by which those investors who, having obtained information, are willing and able to apply knowledge, effort, and ingenuity to its analysis.[31] For those investors, the fruits of fundamental analysis and research, long before being converted to a "public good," will provide adequate rewards. These rewards will not be discernible, however, in the performance of investors aggregated to comprise major market segments, such as mutual funds. Instead, they will remain as individual as the efforts needed to bring them about.

---

[29] For a more comprehensive discussion of these issues, see the author's article "In Defense of Fundamental Investment Analysis," *Financial Analysts Journal,* January-February 1975, pp. 57–61.

[30] An investment practice, based on the efficient market adherents' disenchantment with investment results, is the index fund. An index portfolio is merely designed to copy the composition of a market index to such an extent that it will replicate its market performance. This approach represents a mechanical substitute for analysis and judgment, and may not satisfy its adherents over the longer term.

[31] The value of such analysis for other purposes, such as credit evaluation, is not even at issue here.

The role of financial statement analysis in the professional decision-making process leading to the buying, selling, or holding of equity securities has always been the subject of controversy and debate. In times of high speculative market activity, fundamental factors inevitably give way in relative importance to the psychological or technical ones in the overall security appraisal and "valuation" process. The fact that these fundamental factors, based as they are on a concrete analysis of measurable elements, can lead to sounder decisions and to the avoidance of serious judgmental errors will not always prevent their abandonment in favor of the snap decisions that occur in times of speculative frenzy. Nevertheless, the ultimate return of more sober times after periods of speculation and the inevitable corrections of speculative excesses recurringly bring along with them a rediscovery of the virtues of thorough financial analysis as a sound and necessary procedure. In the aftermath of the 1969–70 bear market, David L. Babson urged such a return by stating:

> What we all should do now is to roll up our sleeves and go back to doing what we are paid for—to follow company and industry trends closely, to really dissect balance sheets and to dig into accounting practices—and maybe some future Jim Lings, Delbert Colemans and Cortes Randells won't make monkeys out of many of the prestigious firms in our industry again.[32]

The collapse in security values in the early 1970s was, of course, not the first such occurrence that was preceded by a widespread and reckless disregard for fundamentals. It is noteworthy that each generation of analysts has to relearn the lessons so heavily paid for by its predecessors. A. P. Richardson, in an editorial on "The 1929 Stock Market Collapse" published in the *Journal of Accountancy* of December 1929, emphasized this recurring phenomenon of the flight from facts and reason into the world of fancy and wishful thinking:

> The astounding feature of the decline and fall of the stock market in late October and early November was not the fact of descent itself, but the altogether unreasoning consternation which the public in and out of Wall Street displayed. There was nothing at all in the course of events which distinguished the break from its many predecessors. Month after month, even year after year, market prices of securities had climbed to even dizzier heights. Now and then a Jeremiah uttered warning and lament, but the people gave no heed. They thought and consequently dealt in far futures. What a company might earn when the next generation would come to maturity was made the measure of the current value of its stock. In many cases companies whose operations had never yet produced a penny of profit were selected, fortuitously or under artificial stimulation,

---

[32] "The Stock Market's Collapse and Constructive Aftermath," *The Commercial and Financial Chronicle,* June 4, 1970.

as a sort of Golconda of the next voyage; and otherwise sane men and women eagerly bought rights of ownership in adventures whose safe return was on the knees of the sea gods. It was not considered enough to look ahead to what was visible. The unseen was the chief commodity. Good stocks, bad stocks and stocks neither good nor bad but wholly of the future rose with almost equal facility, until at last they were sold at prices which seemed to be entirely uninfluenced by the rates of dividend or even by the earnings of the issuing companies. Government bonds and other "gilt-edged" securities were sold at prices nearer the actual interest yield than were the prices of highly speculative stocks to the dividend return or even to the net earnings, past or soon expected, of the companies concerned. Anything was possible when vision was so blurred by success.

The bull market that started in the early 1980s proved again that financial history repeats itself because we ignore the lessons of the past. Or, as Professor J. K. Galbraith put it, all that is required for genius on Wall Street is a rising market and a short memory. Thus, as long as the motivating forces behind the buying and selling of securities are measurable fundamental factors affecting the security-issuing enterprises, financial statement analysis has an important part in the investment decision process. However, once the dynamics of speculation take over, rational considerations begin to be relegated to a minor role. As the euphoria of rising prices takes hold, the speculative component in the price structure grows larger and larger. It is no longer a question of whether this speculative component, which has no basis in rational analysis, will be deflated but only when. The October 1987 stock market crash proved again that when equity yields reach historic lows and price-earnings ratios climb to unreasonable heights, the deflation of the speculative component can occur suddenly and with dramatic speed. Since it is created by nothing measurable or subject to value analysis, it can be deflated by a mere change in sentiment. Thus the speculative component is not subject to analysis by means of the approaches described in this work.

Financial statement analysis, while certainly not providing answers to all the problems of security analysis, at least keeps the decision maker in touch with the underlying realities of the enterprise that is investigated. It imposes the discipline of comparing the results already attained with the wide-ranging promises made for the future. As a very minimum, it represents a safeguard against the repetition of the grievous mistakes of judgment recurringly made by investors in time of speculative euphoria.

We have, in this section, examined the needs for information by equity investors. Not all such information can be obtained by means of financial statement analysis nor is the information so obtainable always the most critical in the determination of security values. However, it should by now be clear to the reader that any rational and systematic approach to the valuation of common stocks must involve the use of quantified data that are mostly the end product of financial statement analysis, evaluation, and interpretation.

Objectives of Management

Management's interest in an enterprise's financial condition, profitability, and progress is pervasive and all-encompassing. Management has a number of methods, tools, and techniques available to it in monitoring and keeping up with the ever-changing condition of the enterprise. Financial data analysis is one important type of such methods.

Financial data analysis can be undertaken by management on a continuous basis because it has unlimited access to internal accounting and other records. Such analysis encompasses changes in ratios, trends, and other significant relationships. Ratio, change, and trend analysis is based on an intelligent, alert, and systematic surveillance of significant relationships in a business situation and the timely detection and interpretation of problem areas by an analysis of changes taking place.

Management's primary objective in utilizing the tools of analysis described in this book is to exercise control over and to view the enterprise in the way important outsiders, such as creditors and investors, view it.

Ratio change and trend analysis make use of the numerous and inevitable relationships and interrelationships among the variables occurring in any business situation. Constant surveillance over the size and amplitude of change in these interrelationships provides valuable clues to important changes in underlying financial and operating conditions. Recognition of such changes and timely action to check adverse trends is the essence of control.

Management derives a number of important advantages from a systematic monitoring of financial data and the basic relationships that they display:

1. There is recognition that no event in a business situation is isolated and that it represents a cause or the effect of a chain of which it is but a link. This approach aims at discovering whether a given event or relationship is the cause or the effect of an underlying situation.

2. There is a recognition that one should not act on an isolated event, but rather by an examination of related changes, one should determine the basic causes of the event. Thus, an event cannot be judged as positive or negative until it has been properly related to other factors that have a bearing on it.

3. Such monitoring prevents management from getting submerged in a maze of facts and figures that in the typical business situation consist of a great variety of factors of varying sizes, velocities of change, and degrees of impact. Instead, it organizes the data and relates them to a pattern of prior experience and external standards.

4. Such monitoring calls for prompt and effective action as the situation unfolds, rather than for "*post mortem*" analyses of causes and effects.

Objectives of Acquisition and Merger Analysts

The valuation of an enterprise in its entirety, for the purpose of purchasing a going concern or for the purpose of assessing the merger of two or more enterprises, represents an attempt to determine economic values, the relative worth of the merging entities, and the relative bargaining strengths and weaknesses of the parties involved. Financial statement analysis is a valuable technique in the determination of economic value and in an assessment of the financial and operating compatibility of potential merger candidates.

The objectives of the acquisition and merger analyst are in many respects similar to those of the equity investor except that the analysis of the acquisition of an entire enterprise must go further and stress the valuation of assets, including intangible assets such as goodwill, and liabilities included in the acquisition or merger plan.

Objectives of Auditors

The end product of the financial audit is an expression of opinion on the fairness of presentation of financial statements setting forth the financial conditions and the results of operations of an enterprise. One of the basic objectives of the audit process is to obtain the greatest possible degree of assurance about the absence of errors and irregularities, intentional or otherwise, that if undetected could materially affect the fairness of presentation of financial summarizations or their conformity with generally accepted accounting principles (GAAP).

Financial statement analysis and ratio change and trend analysis represent an important group of audit tools that can significantly supplement other audit techniques such as procedural and validation tests.[33] This is so because errors and irregularities, whatever their source, can, if significant, affect the various financial operating and structural relationships; and the detection and analysis of such changes can lead to the detection of errors and irregularities. Moreover, the process of financial analysis requires of the auditor, and imparts to him, the kind of understanding and grasp of the audited enterprise that indicates the most relevant type of supportive evidence required in his audit work.

The application of financial statement analysis as part of the audit program is best undertaken at the very beginning of the audit because such analysis will often reveal the areas of greatest change and vulnerability, areas to which the auditor will want to direct a major part of his attention. At the end of the audit, these tools represent an overall check on the reasonableness of the financial statements taken as a whole.[34]

---

[33] In 1978, the accounting profession formally recognized the importance of analytical audit approaches through issuance of *Statement of Auditing Standards No. 23,* "Analytical Review Procedures."

[34] For a more detailed discussion of this subject, see Leopold A. Bernstein, "Analytical Auditing," in *Handbook for Auditors,* ed. James A. Cashin (New York: McGraw-Hill, 1986).

Objectives of Other Interested Groups

Financial statement analysis can serve the needs of many other user groups. Thus, the Internal Revenue Service can apply tools and techniques of financial statement analysis to the audit of tax returns and the checking of the reasonableness of reported amounts.[35] Various governmental regulatory agencies can use such techniques in the exercise of their supervisory and rate-determination functions.

Labor unions can use the techniques of financial statement analysis to evaluate the financial statements of enterprises with which they engage in collective bargaining. Lawyers can employ these techniques in the furtherance of their investigative and legal work, while economic researchers will find them of great usefulness in their work.

Similarly, customers can use such approaches to determine the profitability (staying power) of their suppliers, the returns they earn on capital, and other factors of consequence to them.

CONCLUSION

This chapter has examined the points of view and the objectives of a variety of important users of financial statements. These various objectives determine what aspects of financial statement analysis are relevant to the decision-making process of a particular user. In the chapters that follow, we shall first examine the relationship between financial statement analysis and the accounting framework as well as the tools and techniques of financial statement analysis in general. This will be followed by an examination of the major missions or objectives of financial analysis and the means by which they can be realized.

QUESTIONS

1. Describe some of the analytical uses to which financial statement analysis can be put.
2. Why are the information needs of equity investors among the most demanding of all users of financial statements?
3. Why is the measurement and evaluation of earning power the key element in the valuation of equity securities?
4. What is the essential difference between a bond valuation model based on the present value of future inflows and a stock valuation model based on the same principles?

---

[35] Among the areas that can be analyzed are questions such as whether (1) the income reported is enough to support exemptions or expenses claimed, (2) the profit margin reported is out of line with that normal for that type of business, (3) the return reported is less than that which can be earned by banking the money, and (4) the changes in net worth support the amounts of reported income.

5. Differentiate between systematic risk and unsystematic risk and discuss the various components of the latter.

6. Discuss the capital asset pricing model (CAPM) and explain how it deals with the problem of securities valuation by the market.

7. Explain how the efficient market hypothesis (EMH) deals with the reaction of market prices to financial and other data.

8. Explain the concept of the trade-off between risk and return as well as its significance to portfolio construction.

9. Discuss the implications that the CAPM and the EMH present for financial statement analysis.

10. Why is the reliability and the validity of any method of stock valuation, no matter how complete and sophisticated, dependent on the prior performance of a quality analysis of financial statements?

11. Identify clearly three separate factors which have a significant influence on a stock's price-earnings ratio. (CFA)

12. What are the differences in point of view between lenders and equity investors? How do these differences express themselves in the way these two groups analyze financial statements and in the objectives that they seek?

13. *a.* Outline the principal risks inherent in a preferred stock as an investment instrument, relative to a bond or other credit obligation of the same company.

    b. Discuss the various influences of U.S. (or Canadian) income taxation trends on the inherent risks and yields of preferred stocks.

    c. What terms can be included in a preferred stock issue to compensate for its subordination to debt and its relationship to common stock? (CFA)

14. What uses can the management of an enterprise make of financial statement analysis?

15. Of what use can financial statement analysis be to the audit of an enterprise?

Chapter 2

Tools and Techniques of Financial Statement Analysis–An Overview

Basic Approaches to Financial Statement Analysis

In the first chapter, we examined the various objectives of financial statement analysis as viewed from the point of view of specific user groups. In the performance of an analysis, such objectives can, in turn, be translated into a number of specific questions to which the decision maker needs an answer. Thus, for example, the equity investor may want to know:

1. What has the company's operating performance been over the longer term and over the recent past? What does this record hold for future earnings prospects?
2. Has the company's earnings record been one of growth, stability, or decline? Does it display significant variability?
3. What is the company's current financial condition? What factors are likely to affect it in the near future?
4. What is the company's capital structure? What risks and rewards does it hold for the investor?
5. How does this company compare on the above counts with other companies in its industry?

The banker who is approached with a short-term loan request may look to the financial statements for answers to questions such as the following:

1. What are the underlying reasons for the company's needs for funds? Are these needs truly short term, and if so, will they be self-liquidating?
2. From what sources is the company likely to get funds for the payment of interest and the repayment of principal?
3. How has management handled its needs for short-term and long-term funds in the past? What does this portend for the future?

An important first step in any decision-making process is to identify the most significant, pertinent, and critical questions that have a bearing on the decision. Financial statement analysis does not, of course, provide answers to all such questions. However, each of the questions exemplified above can, to a significant extent, be answered by such analysis.

RECONSTRUCTION OF BUSINESS ACTIVITIES AND TRANSACTIONS

Basic to the analyst's work is the ability to reconstruct the business transactions that are summarized in the financial statements. One can visualize this important skill as the ability to replicate the accountant's work but in reverse order. The flow of the accountant's work is as follows:

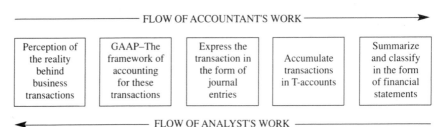

The accountant's effort and skill is first directed to understanding the reality of the transactions or events to be recorded. Next, there must be brought to bear the knowledge of the accounting framework—the generally accepted accounting principles (GAAP) that govern the recording of the transaction, its expression in the form of a journal entry, and its accumulation in accounts. No matter what form data recording and accumulation takes in this electronic age, the basic concepts of the journal entry and the T-account prevail. These, as we shall see, are particularly useful in analytical work. Finally, continuing to be guided by accepted standards of the accounting framework, the accountant summarizes all accounts of a period in the format of financial statements.

The flow of the analyst's work is basically in reverse order. Moreover, while the accountant's work is basically oriented to events of the past, that of the analyst is focused on future developments. The analyst starts with the financial statements made available by the enterprise. The basic task is to recapture, as far as possible, the reality that is imbedded and summarized in these financial statements—the degree to which this is done being dependent on the particular analytical objectives at hand. This analytical process requires that the analyst visualize the journal entries made and that he or she reconstruct, in summary fashion, all or selected accounts in the financial statements. It also requires an understanding of the reality underlying such business transactions as well as a knowledge of the *accounting standards* employed in recording it properly within the accounting framework.

By these means, the analyst will be able to understand the changes in specific balance sheet items, trace the effect of a given transaction or specific accounts, and answer questions such as the following:

- What was the reason for the increase or the decrease in the investment in X Company?
- What effect did the debt refunding have on working capital or on cash?
- How much long-term debt was repaid this year?
- What was the effect of income taxes on the financial statements and how much tax was actually paid this year?

The reconstruction of business transactions (i.e., significant economic events) requires a knowledge of accounting, that is, the ability to visualize how a particular transaction is recorded and what kind of activities or events will increase or decrease a specific account. It also requires the ability to read carefully, understand, and interpret financial statements and related footnotes. Thus, the knowledge of what information can be found in financial statements, where it is to be found, and how to reconstruct transactions, including the making of reasonable assumptions, are important skills in the analysis of financial statements.

Financial statement analysis depends on a knowledge of related disciplines, such as accounting, economics, and finance, as well as on skills of analysis such as derivation and inference. It involves a degree of detective work based on marshaling all known facts while using the limited and incomplete data that are available. As the creator of Sherlock Holmes put it: "After you have eliminated the impossible, whatever remains, however improbable, must be the truth." Thus, in reconstructing transactions, the analyst will work with known information before attempting to deduce unknown facts. The degree of accuracy that can be expected in such reconstructions and the resulting analysis cannot be expected to be nor need it approach the degree of accuracy required in the accounting and recording function.

Throughout this book the T-account will be used as an important analytical tool. The emphasis is not on bookkeeping mechanics but rather on the use of T-account analysis in the reconstruction and understanding of transactions. Thus, while the emphasis is on analysis rather than on accounting or bookkeeping technique, the analyst must recognize that we use the accounting function as a most useful analytical technique. The use of T-account analysis depends on the analyst's ability to visualize transactions in the form of journal entries which are in turn summarized in T-accounts.

ILLUSTRATION 1.   The analyst of the financial statements of the Campbell Soup Company
(also referred to as Campbell, see Appendix 2B) needs to determine the amount
of cash collected from customers during the fiscal year 1991 (also referred to as
1991). In this simple example the analyst will reconstruct the accounts receivable
account. For ease of reference, boldface numbers in squares refer to those found
in the financial statements of Campbell.

The analyst finds the Accounts Receivable account on the balance sheet (item
33) and knows that the reconstruction of this account is the key to a determination
of the cash collected from customers in fiscal 1991. Also needed is a knowledge
of the typical entries that can be expected in the Accounts Receivable account.

The first step is to set up the accounts receivable T-account with opening and
closing balances (details are in Note 13):

Accounts Receivable (Net)

148A Bal	534.1	
Net sales **13**	6204.1	6276.5—collections-to balance
148A Bal	461.7	

The second step is to determine the aggregate debits to this account. Note that
the analyst, working with financial statements which represent summarizations, can
only work with aggregates rather than the multitude of detailed entries which comprise them. Knowing that the debits represent the counterpart of sales **13** we debit
accounts receivable with total sales of $6,204.1 (all in millions). We know that not
all sales are for cash, but to arrive at cash collections from customers it does not
matter whether the charges are cash sales or credit sales. The amount needed to
balance the accounts receivable account, that is, $6276.5, represents the best
estimate of approximate cash collections from customers. In fact, we know that this
amount is overstated because it includes credits to customers for cash discounts
and bad debts. However, in order to reconstruct the Allowance for Bad Debts account we would need at least the amount of the bad debt expense charged to
income during the year—a detail not provided in the financial statements. These
amounts are, however, small in relation to total collections so that the estimated
collections are not off by much.

When there is inadequate information, the analyst may have to combine accounts and transactions and consider them together. Having pinpointed what type of information is lacking, the analyst can develop
informed questions for management in order to obtain the desired information that was not disclosed in the financial statements.

The analyst must also know what information is not generally available
in financial statements so that he or she may attempt to secure it. In
addition to information such as commitments, lines of credit, and order
backlogs, the analyst will also generally not find the details of changes in
many important accounts. Thus, for example, a Notes Payable account
or a Loan to Officers account may show little or no change in year-end

balances but may, in fact, have had significant interim balances that were liquidated during the year.

The analysis and reconstruction of business transactions is an important analytical procedure and will be illustrated throughout this book. Some illustrations will be based on the financial statements of Campbell Soup Company, (Appendix 2B), and others on the financial statements of Quaker Oats Company (Appendix to Chapter 10, referred to as Appendix 10).

IMPORTANCE OF THE STATEMENT OF CASH FLOWS

The analytical steps involved in the reconstruction of business transactions often involve use of the statement of cash flows (SCF). For this and other reasons, this statement is of key importance to the analyst. Consequently, the placement of a chapter dealing with this statement in this book involves difficult choices. It would be advantageous to consider this subject as early as possible. On the other hand, a thorough and detailed consideration of the statement can be undertaken only *after* a consideration of all elements of the financial statements.

ADDITIONAL ANALYTICAL FUNCTIONS

The following are some additional analytical processes in widespread use:

Direct Measurements   Some factors and relationships can be measured directly. For example, the relationship between the debt and the equity of an entity is a direct measurement. Both the amount of debt and that of equity can be measured in absolute terms (i.e., in dollars) and their relationship computed therefrom.

Indirect Evidence   Financial statement analysis can provide indirect evidence bearing on important questions. Thus, the analysis of past statements of cash flows can offer evidence as to the financial habits of a management team. Moreover, the analysis of operating statements will yield evidence regarding management's ability to cope with fluctuations in the level of the firm's business activity. While such indirect evidence and evaluation are often not precise or quantifiable, the data derived therefrom nevertheless possess importance because the effects of almost all managerial decisions, or the lack of them, are reflected in the entity's financial statements.

Predictive Functions   Almost all decision questions are oriented toward the future. Thus, an important measure of the usefulness of financial statement analysis tools and techniques is their ability to assist in the prediction of expected future conditions and results.

Comparison   This is a very important analytical process. It is based on the elementary proposition that in financial analysis no number standing by itself can be meaningful, and that it gains meaning only when related to some other comparable quantity. By means of comparison, financial analysis is useful in performing important evaluative, as well as attention-directing and control, functions. Thus, it focuses on exceptions and variations, and saves the analyst the need to evaluate the normal and the expected. Moreover, by means of comparison, selection among alternative choices is accomplished.

Comparison may be performed by using:

1. A company's own experience over the years (i.e., internally derived data);
2. External data, such as comparisons with individual companies or industry composites; or
3. Compiled yardsticks, including standards, budgets, and forecasts.

Historical company data can usually be readily obtained and most readily adjusted for inconsistencies.

Uses of External Data   Useful comparison may also be made with external data. The advantages of external data are: (1) they are normally objective and independent; (2) they are derived from similar operations, thus performing the function of a standard of comparison; and (3) if current, they reflect events occurring during an identical period having as a consequence similar business and economic conditions in common.

External information must, however, be used with great care and discrimination. Knowledge of the basis and method of compilation, the period covered, and the source of the information will facilitate a decision of whether the information is at all comparable. At times, sufficient detail may be available to adjust data so as to render them comparable. In any event, a decision on a proper standard of comparison must be made by choosing from those available. Differences between situations compared must be noted. Such differences may be in accounting practices or specific company policies. It must also be borne in mind that the past is seldom an unqualified guide to the future.

SOURCES OF INFORMATION

For basic data on an enterprise and for comparative data of comparable entities in its industry, published financial statements provide the best and most readily available source.

Appendix 2A to this chapter presents a listing of sources of information on financial and operating ratios of various industries as well as sample presentations from these sources. These data, while representing valuable sources for comparison, must be used with care and with as complete a knowledge of the basis of their compilation as is possible to obtain. A realistic and sometimes superior alternative for the analyst is to use as a basis of comparison the financial statements of one or more comparable companies in the same industry. In this way, one can usually have a better command over, and comprehension of, the data entering into the comparison base.

Annual reports to shareholders contain an ever-expanding amount of information required by either GAAP or by specific SEC requirements.[1]

In addition, company filings with the SEC, such as Registration Statements[2] pursuant to the Securities Act of 1933, supplemental and periodic reports which are required to be filed (such as Forms 8-K, 10-K, 10-Q, 14-K, and 16-K), or proxy statements contain a wealth of information of interest to the analyst.

Additional information may be available and may require an extra effort to obtain. Some companies offer financial analysts and others additional financial and operating data which can be obtained on request (e.g., by postcard included in the annual report). Information required to be filed with federal or state regulatory agencies (e.g., insurance, banking) is usually publicly available. Such differential disclosure is made available to those who seek it out.

Some information is not generally available but can be obtained by those able to exert a degree of influence. Thus, bond rating agencies are generally provided with financial and operating details that go beyond those found in published financial statements. Major lenders and investors may also have access to more detailed information. This is also true of potential lenders and investors.

THE TOTAL INFORMATION SET

The total information set on which the decision maker draws includes financial as well as other types of information, and the relative importance of each varies from decision to decision. Exhibit 2–1 presents the composition of this information set (or spectrum).

---

[1] For example, Rule 14c-3 of the Securities Exchange Act of 1934 specifies that annual reports furnished to stockholders in connection with the annual meeting of stockholders include, among others, the following financial information: (1) audited financial statements—balance sheets as of the two most recent fiscal years, and statements of income and changes in financial position (now cash flows) for each of the three most recent fiscal years; (2) selected quarterly financial data for each quarterly period within the two most recent fiscal years; (3) summary of selected financial data for last five years; (4) management's discussion and analysis of financial condition and results of operations; (5) market price of company's common stock for each quarterly period within the two most recent fiscal years; and (6) segment information.

[2] SEC Regulation S-X, which specifies the form and content of financial statements filed with the Commission, contains numerous requirements for specific disclosures.

Exhibit 2-1 Information set (or spectrum)

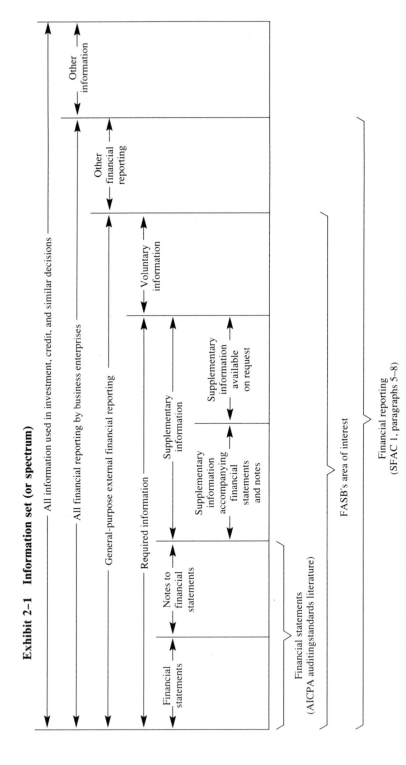

All information used in investment, credit, and similar decisions

All financial reporting by business enterprises

General-purpose external financial reporting

Other information

Other financial reporting

Required information

Voluntary information

Supplementary information

Financial statements

Notes to financial statements

Supplementary information accompanying financial statements and notes

Supplementary information available on request

Financial statements (AICPA auditingstandards literature)

FASB's area of interest

Financial reporting (SFAC 1, paragraphs 5–8)

Source: FASB, *Invitation to Comment on Financial Statements and Other Means of Financial Reporting* (Stamford, Conn., 1980), p.2.

THE PRINCIPAL TOOLS OF ANALYSIS

In the analysis of financial statements, the analyst has available a variety of tools from which he can choose those best suited to his specific purpose. The following principal tools of analysis will be discussed in this chapter:

1. Comparative financial statements.
   a. Year-to-year changes.
2. Index-number trend series.
3. Common-size financial statements.
   a. Structural analysis.
4. Ratio analysis.
5. Specialized analyses.
   a. Cash forecasts.
   b. Analysis of changes in cash flows.
   c. Statement of variation in gross margin.
   d. Break-even analysis.

The application of these tools as well as other aspects of analysis will be illustrated throughout by means of the financial statements of Campbell Soup Company presented in Appendix 2B and those of Quaker Oats Co. in the Appendix to Chapter 10. Further examples of tabulations of analytical measures can be found in Chapter 10 and throughout the text.

Comparative Financial Statements

The comparison of financial statements is accomplished by setting up balance sheets, income statements, or statements of cash flows (SCF), side by side, and reviewing the changes that have occurred in individual categories therein from year to year and over the years.

The most important factor revealed by comparative financial statements is *trend.* The comparison of financial statements over a number of years will also reveal the direction, velocity, and the amplitude of trend. Further analysis can be undertaken to compare the trends in related items. For example, a year-to-year increase in sales of 10 percent accompanied by an increase in freight-out costs of 20 percent requires an investigation and explanation of the reasons for the difference. Similarly, an increase of accounts receivable of 15 percent during the same period would also warrant an investigation into the reasons for the difference in the rate of increase of sales as against that of receivables.

Year-to-Year Change   A comparison of financial statements over two to three years can be undertaken by computing the *year-to-year change* in absolute amounts and in terms of percentage changes. Longer-term comparisons are best undertaken by means of *index-number trend series.*

Year-to-year comparisons of financial statements are illustrated in Appendix 2B. When a two- or three-year comparison is attempted, such presentations are manageable and can be understood by the reader. They have the advantage of presenting changes in terms of absolute dollar amounts as well as in percentages. Both have to be considered because the dollar size of the different bases on which percentage changes are computed may yield large percentage changes that are out of proportion to their real significance. For example, in the same financial statements, a 50 percent change from a base figure of $1,000 is far less significant than the same percentage change from a base of $100,000. Thus, reference to the dollar amounts involved is always necessary in order to retain the proper perspective and to reach valid conclusions regarding the relative significance of the changes disclosed by this type of analysis.

The computation of year-to-year changes is a simple matter. However, a few clarifying rules should be borne in mind. When a negative amount appears in the base year and a positive amount in the following year, or vice versa, no percentage change can be meaningfully computed. When an item has a value in a base year and none in the following period, the decrease is 100 percent. Where there is no figure for the base year, no percentage change can be computed. The following summary will illustrate this:

| | | | Change increase (decrease) | |
Item	Year 1	Year 2	Amount	Percent
Net income (loss)	$(4,500)	$ 1,500	$ 6,000	—
Tax expense	2,000	(1,000)	(3,000)	—
Notes payable	—	8,000	8,000	—
Notes receivable	10,000	—	(10,000)	(100)

Comparative financial statements can also be presented in such a way that the cumulative total for the period for each item under study and the average for that period are shown.

The value of comparing yearly amounts with an average covering a number of years is that unusual factors in any one year are highlighted. Averages smooth out erratic or unusual fluctuations in data.

Index-Number Trend Series

When a comparison of financial statements covering more than three years is undertaken, the year-to-year method of comparison may become too cumbersome. The best way to effect such longer-term trend comparisons is by means of index numbers. Such a comparative statement for Campbell Soup Company is illustrated in Chapter 10.

The computation of a series of index numbers requires the choice of a base year that will, for all items, have an index amount of 100. Since such a base year represents a frame of reference for all comparisons, it is best to choose a year that, in a business conditions sense, is as typical or normal as possible. If the earliest year in the series compared cannot fulfill this function, another year is chosen. In our example of the Campbell comparative statements, the year 1986 was chosen.

As is the case with the computation of year-to-year percentage changes, certain changes, such as those from negative to positive amounts, cannot be expressed by means of index numbers. All index numbers are computed by reference to the base year.

ILLUSTRATION 2.   Assume that in the base year at 12/31/20xA, there is a cash balance of $12,000. Based on an index number of 100 for 20xA, if the cash balance in the following year (at 12/31/20xB) is $18,000, then the index number will be

$$\frac{\$18,000}{\$12,000} \times 100 = 150$$

On 12/31/20xC the cash balance is $9,000, the index will stand at 75 arrived at as follows:

$$\frac{\$9,000}{\$12,000} \times 100 = \left(\frac{\text{Balance in current year}}{\text{Balance in base year}} \times 100\right)$$

It should be noted that when using index numbers, percentage changes cannot be read off directly except by reference to the base year. Thus, the change of the cash balance between 20xA and 20xB is 50 percent (index 150 − index 100), and this can be read off directly from the index numbers. The change from 20xB to 20xC, however, is not 75 percent (150 − 75), as a direct comparison may suggest, but rather 50 percent (i.e., $9,000/$18,000), which involves computing the 20xB to 20xC change by reference to the amount at 20xB. The percentage change can, however, be computed by use of the index numbers only, for example, 75/150 = 0.5, or a change of 50 percent.

In planning an index-number trend comparison, it is not necessary to include in it all the items in the financial statements. Only the most significant items need be included in such a comparison.

Care should be exercised in the use of index-number trend comparisons because such comparisons have weaknesses as well as strengths. Thus, in trying to assess changes in the current financial condition, the analyst may use to advantage comparative statements of cash flows. On the other hand, the index-number trend comparison is very well suited to a comparison of the changes in the *composition* of working capital items over the years.

The interpretation of percentage changes as well as those of index-number trend series must be made with a full awareness of the effect that the inconsistent application of accounting principles over the years can have on such comparisons. Thus, where possible, such inconsistencies must be adjusted. In addition, the longer the period covered by the comparison, the more distortive are the effects of price-level changes on such comparisons likely to be, and the analyst must be aware of such effects.

One important value of trend analysis is that it can convey to the analyst a better understanding of management's philosophies, policies, and motivations, conscious or otherwise, that have brought about the changes revealed over the years. The more diverse the economic environments covering the periods compared are, the better a picture can be obtained by the analyst of the ways in which the enterprise has weathered its adversities and taken advantage of its opportunities.

Common-Size Financial Statements

In the analysis of financial statements, it is often instructive to find out the proportion that a single item represents of a total group or subgroup. In a balance sheet, the assets as well as the liabilities and capital are each expressed as 100 percent, and each item in these categories is expressed as a percentage of the respective totals. Similarly, in the income statement, net sales are set at 100 percent and every other item in the statement is expressed as a percent of net sales. Since the totals always add up to 100 percent, this community of size has resulted in these statements being referred to as "common size." Similarly, following the eye as it reviews the common-size statement, this analysis is referred to as "vertical" for the same reason that the trend analysis is often referred to as "horizontal" analysis.

Selected common-size statements of Campbell are presented in Chapter 10.

Structural Analysis   The analysis of common-size financial statements may best be described as an analysis of the internal structure of the financial statements. In the analysis of a balance sheet, this structural analysis focuses on two major aspects:

1. What are the sources of capital of the enterprise, that is, what is the distribution of equities as between current liabilities, long-term liabilities, and equity capital?
2. Given the amount of capital from all sources, what is the distribution of assets (current, fixed, and other) in which it is invested? Stated differently, what is the mix of assets with which the enterprise has chosen to conduct its operations?

The common-size balance sheet analysis can, of course, be carried further and extended to an examination of what proportion of a subgroup, rather than the total, an item is. Thus, in assessing the liquidity of current assets, it may be of interest to know not only what proportion of total assets is invested in inventories but also what proportion of current assets is represented by this asset.

In the case of the income statement, common-size statement analysis is a very useful tool transcending perhaps in importance the analysis of the balance sheet by such means. This is so because the income statement lends itself very well to an analysis whereby each item in it is related to a central quantum, that is, sales. With some exceptions, the level of each expense item is affected to some extent by the level of sales, and thus it is instructive to know what proportion of the sales dollar is absorbed by the various costs and expenses incurred by the enterprise. There are exceptions, of course. For example, income taxes are not related to sales but rather to pretax income.

Comparisons of common-size statements of a single enterprise over the years are valuable in that they show the changing proportions of components within groups of assets, liabilities, costs, and other financial statement categories. However, care must be exercised in interpreting such changes and the trend that they disclose. For example, the table below shows the amount of patents and total assets of an enterprise over three years:

	Year 3	Year 2	Year 1
Patents	$ 50,000	$ 50,000	$ 50,000
Total assets	$1,000,000	$750,000	$500,000
Patents as a percentage of total assets	5%	6.67%	10%

While the amount of patents remained unchanged, the increase in total assets made this item a progressively smaller proportion of total assets. Since this proportion can change with either a change in the absolute amount of the item or a change in the total of the group of which it is a part, the interpretation of a common-size statement comparison requires an examination of the actual figures and the basis on which they are computed.

Common-size statements are very well suited to intercompany comparison because the financial statements of a variety of companies can be recast into the uniform common-size format regardless of the size of individual accounts. While common-size statements do not reflect the relative sizes of the individual companies that are compared, the problem of actual comparability between them is a matter to be resolved by the analyst's judgment.

Comparison of the common-size statements of companies within an industry or with common-size composite statistics of that industry can alert the analyst's attention to variations in account structure or distribution, the reasons for which should be explored and understood. A comparison of selected common-size statement items of the Campbell Soup Company with similar industry statistics will be found in Chapter 10.

Ratio Analysis

Ratios are among the best known and most widely used tools of financial analysis. At the same time, their function is often misunderstood, and consequently their significance may easily be overrated.

A ratio expresses the mathematical relationship between one quantity and another. The ratio of 200 to 100 is expressed as 2:1, or as 2. While the computation of a ratio involves a simple arithmetical operation, its interpretation is a far more complex matter.

To begin with, to be significant, the ratio must express a relationship that has significance. Thus, there is a clear, direct, and understandable relationship between the sales price of an item, on one hand, and its cost, on the other. As a result, the ratio of cost of goods sold to sales is a significant one. On the other hand, there is no a priori or understandable relationship between freight costs incurred and the marketable securities held by an enterprise; and hence, a ratio of one to the other must be deemed to be of no significance.

Ratios are tools of analysis that in most cases provide the analyst with clues and symptoms of underlying conditions. Ratios, properly interpreted, can also point the way to areas requiring further investigation and inquiry. The analysis of a ratio can disclose relationships as well as bases of comparison that reveal conditions and trends that cannot be detected by an inspection of the individual components of the ratio.

Since ratios, like other tools of analysis, are future oriented, the analyst must be able to adjust the factors present in a relationship to their probable shape and size in the future. He must also understand the factors that will influence such ratios in the future. Thus, in the final analysis, the usefulness of ratios is wholly dependent on their intelligent and skillful interpretation. This is, by far, the most difficult aspect of ratio analysis. Let us, by way of example, consider the interpretation of a ratio derived from an area outside that of the business world: In comparing the ratio of gas consumption to mileage driven, A claims to have a superior performance, that is, 28 mpg compared to B's 20 mpg. Assuming that they drove identical cars, the following are factors that affect gas consumption and that will have to be considered before one can properly interpret the ratios and judge whose performance is better:

1. Weight of load driven.
2. Type of terrain (flat versus hilly).
3. City or country driving.
4. Kind of gasoline used.
5. Speed at which cars were driven.

Numerous as the factors that influence gas consumption are, the evaluation of the gas consumption ratio is, nevertheless, a simpler process than the evaluation of most ratios derived from business variables. The reason for this is that the interrelationships of business variables and the factors that affect them are multifaceted and very complex.

Factors Affecting Ratios

In addition to the internal operating conditions that affect the ratios of an enterprise, the analyst must be aware of the factors, such as general business conditions, industry position, management policies, as well as accounting principles, that can affect them. As far as the latter are concerned, the discussion of accounting principles in this book points up their influence on the measurements on which ratios are based. Weaknesses in the accounting model impact the validity of ratios as well. Thus, historical costs are often far less relevant than current market values.

Before ratios, or similar measures such as trend indexes or percentage relationships, are computed, the analyst must make sure that the figures entering into their computation are valid and consistent. For example, when inventories are valued on the LIFO basis, under conditions of increasing prices, the current ratio may be understated because LIFO basis inventories may be significantly understated in terms of current value. Similarly, some pension liabilities may be unrecorded and disclosed in footnotes only. Some analysts may wish to recognize these liabilities when computing the debt-to-equity ratio of an enterprise. Care must also be taken to recognize that when such adjustments are made in one ratio, consistency may also require that they be made in other ratios as well. Thus, the omission of the pension liability also means that pension expenses have been understated. As a result, the net income amount used in the computation of certain ratios may require adjustment.

The validity of ratios depends also on the validity of the numbers entering into their computation. Thus, when a company's internal controls are such that the accounting system cannot be relied upon to produce reliable figures, the ratios based on such figures are, of course, also unreliable. It is widely believed that such was the situation in the case of W. T. Grant Company in the years immediately preceding the giant retailer's bankruptcy.

Interpretation of Ratios

Ratios should always be interpreted with great care since factors affecting the numerator may correlate with those affecting the denominator. Thus, for example, it is possible to improve the ratio of operating expenses to sales by reducing costs that act to stimulate sales. If the cost reduction consequently results in a loss of sales or share of market, such a seeming improvement in profitability may, in fact, have an overall detrimental effect on the future prospects of the enterprise and must be interpreted accordingly.

It should also be recognized that many ratios have important variables in common with other ratios, thus tending to make them vary and be influenced by the same factors. Consequently, there is no need to use all available ratios in order to diagnose a given condition.

Ratios, like most other relationships in financial analysis, are not significant in themselves and can be interpreted only by comparison with (1) past ratios of the same enterprise, or (2) some predetermined standard, or (3) ratios of other companies in the industry. The range of a ratio over time is also significant as is the trend of a given ratio over time.

MARKET MEASURES

Analysts and investors use a variety of measures to evaluate the price and yield behavior of securities. The *price-earnings ratio* measures the multiple at which the market is capitalizing the earnings per share of a company at any given time. The *earnings yield* is the inverse of the price-earnings ratio and represents the income-producing power of a share of common stock at the current price. The *dividend yield* is the cash return accruing to an investor on a share of stock based on the current dividend rate and current price. Thus, part of the earned yield may be distributed as dividends and the balance retained in the business. The *dividend payout ratio* measures the proportion of earnings that is currently paid out as common stock dividends.

COMPARABILITY OF FINANCIAL DATA

The task of comparing data of enterprises in a given industry presents the analyst with a number of challenges.

Data of companies in a given industry may be limited or unavailable. This may be due to reasons such as lack of disclosure of segmental data (see also Chapter 7), or to companies being privately held and thus not providing public disclosure. Other obstacles to comparability are discussed below.

Differing Reporting Periods   While many companies use the calendar year-end, others use a variety of different year-ends for reporting purposes.

The adjustments required in order to allow for different year-ends among companies included in comparisons depend on the size of the year-end time gap and on other factors.

If the year-end time difference does not exceed three months, adjustments will generally not be required. If the year-end time difference exceeds three months, then quarterly reports (see also Chapter 8) may be used to make data comparable so that a valid financial statement analysis can be performed. By adding up four quarters, year-ends can be adjusted to end, for example, in March, June, September, or December. The need to adjust for year-end time differences and the degree of such adjustments also depends on whether extraordinary events, such as strikes or severe property damage, will distort the results of a given quarter. In addition, the effects of seasonal and cyclical influences on the comparability of time periods will need to be carefully evaluated.

Differences on the Application of Accounting Principles   As will be seen in discussion throughout this book, the use of alternative accounting principles or methods can render the data of companies noncomparable. Such lack of comparability must be corrected by the analyst by means of data adjustments before a valid financial statement analysis can be performed.

SEC *Staff Accounting Bulletin No. 74* requires disclosure about the potential impact of accounting standards that have been promulgated but not yet adopted by the company.

Restatement and Reclassification of Financial Statements

A number of circumstances require that financial statements be restated:

1. The merger of entities under the pooling method of accounting requires that prior years be restated as if the entities had been merged from inception. As a practical matter only the financial statements presented at the time the merger is reported will be presented in restated form.
2. Discontinuances or disposals of a segment of a business require that revenues and expenses of the disposed units as well as losses expected on disposal be classified in the income statement under "discontinued operations." Similarly, the net assets of business expected to be discontinued are shown as a single category on the balance sheet. Financial statements presented at the time the discontinuances are reported must be restated accordingly.

3. Certain accounting principles changes (e.g., changes in inventory cost flow assumptions or changes in income recognition on long-term contracts) require that the prior years of financial statements presented at the time the change is reported be restated to reflect the newly adopted accounting method.

Since analysis is forward-looking, financial analysts will want to use the restated data in most cases. Inevitably difficulties will arise because the restated period may be shorter than the time period under analysis. Generally, companies present balance sheets for two years and income statements and statements of cash flow for three years. These are the periods for which restated financial statements are likely to be available although restatements for longer periods may be found in SEC filings such as registration statements. Financial analysts will have to utilize restated as well as originally reported financial statements in the most creative manner possible.

Finally, we must recognize that there can exist account classification differences between financial statements used in comparisons. Some classification differences are easier to adjust for than are others. If, for example, one company includes depreciation expense in cost of goods sold while another shows this expense as a separate item, adjustments to put analytical measures (such as ratios) on a comparable basis can be readily made.

ILLUSTRATION OF RATIO COMPUTATIONS

A great many ratios can be developed from the multitude of items included in an enterprise's financial statements. Some ratios have general application in financial analysis, while others have specific uses in certain circumstances or in specific industries. Listed below in Exhibit 2–2 are some of the more significant ratios that have general applicability to most business situations. They are grouped by major objectives of financial analysis, and the data used to illustrate their computation are taken from the financial statements of Campbell Soup Company (see Appendix 2B).

Each of the above five major areas of objectives of financial statement analysis will be examined in this book; and therein the computation, use, and interpretation of the ratios listed under each category as well as other ratios will be examined in detail and thoroughly discussed.

TESTING THE UNDERSTANDING OF RELATIONSHIPS

The following is an example of an exercise designed to test the reader's understanding of various intra- and interstatement ratios and relationships.   *(text continues on page 47)*

Exhibit 2–2 Illustration of major categories of ratios

Major categories of ratios	Method of computation (dollars in millions)	Campbell Soup ratio for 1991
Short-term liquidity ratios:		
Current ratio	$\dfrac{\text{Current assets}}{\text{Current liabilities}} = \dfrac{1518.5\ \boxed{36}^{(a)}}{1278.\ \boxed{45}} =$	1.19
Acid test ratio	$\dfrac{\text{Cash + Cash equivalents + Receivables}}{\text{Current liabilities}} = \dfrac{178.9\ \boxed{31} + 12.8\ \boxed{32} + 527.4\ \boxed{33}}{1278.0\ \boxed{45}} =$	0.56
Days' sales in receivables (collection period) .... *Year-end in this case	$\dfrac{\text{Accounts receivable*}}{\text{Credit sales} \div 360} = \dfrac{527.4\ \boxed{33}}{6204.1\ \boxed{13} \div 360} =$	31 days
Inventory turnover	$\dfrac{\text{Cost of goods sold}}{\text{Average inventory during period}} = \dfrac{4095.4\ \boxed{14}}{706.7 + 819.8\ \boxed{34} \div 2} =$	5.37
Capital structure and long-term solvency ratios:		
Total debt to total capital$^{(b)}$	$\dfrac{\text{Current liabilities + Long-term liabilities}}{\text{Equity capital* + Total liabilities}}$ $= \dfrac{2355.6\ \boxed{45} + \boxed{46} + \boxed{47} - 23.5\ \boxed{178}}{1793.4\ \boxed{54} + 2355.6\ \boxed{45} + \boxed{46} + \boxed{47}} =$	0.56
Long-term debt to equity capital	$\dfrac{\text{Long-term liabilities}}{\text{Equity capital*}} = \dfrac{1077.6\ \boxed{46} + \boxed{47} - 23.5\ \boxed{178}}{1793.4\ \boxed{54} + 23.5\ \boxed{178}} =$	0.58
Times interest earned$^{(b)}$	$\dfrac{\text{Income before interest and taxes}}{\text{Interest}} = \dfrac{667.4\ \boxed{26} + 116.2\ \boxed{100}}{136.9\ \boxed{98}} =$	5.72

*Including minority interest.

Exhibit 2-2 Continued

Major categories of ratios	Method of computation (dollars in millions)	Campbell Soup ratio for 1991

Return-on-investment ratios:

Return on total assets 11.75%

$$\frac{\text{Net income} + \text{Interest expense }(1-\text{Tax rate})^c + \text{Minority interest income}}{\text{Average total assets}}$$

$$= \frac{401.5 \;\boxed{28} + 116.2 \;\boxed{100}\,(1-0.34) + 7.2 \;\boxed{25}}{(4149.0 + 4115.6)\;\boxed{39A} \div 2} =$$

Return on equity capital 23.04%

$$= \frac{\text{Net income}}{\text{Average equity capital}} = \frac{401.5 \;\boxed{28}}{(1793.4 + 1691.8)\;\boxed{54} \div 2} =$$

Operating performance ratios:

Gross margin ratio 33.99%

$$= \frac{\text{Gross profit (margin)}}{\text{Sales}} = \frac{6204.1 \;\boxed{13} - 4095.5 \;\boxed{14}}{6204.1 \;\boxed{13}} =$$

Operating profits to sales 12.71%

$$= \frac{\text{Operating profit}}{\text{Sales}}$$

$$= \frac{6204.1 \;\boxed{13} - 5415.6 \;\boxed{14} - \boxed{15} - \boxed{16} - \boxed{17} + \boxed{19} - \boxed{20} - \boxed{21}}{6204.1 \;\boxed{13}} =$$

Pretax income to sales 10.76%

$$= \frac{\text{Pretax income}}{\text{Sales}} = \frac{667.4 \;\boxed{26}}{6204.1 \;\boxed{13}} =$$

Net income to sales 6.47%

$$= \frac{\text{Net income}}{\text{Sales}} = \frac{401.5 \;\boxed{28}}{6204.1 \;\boxed{13}} =$$

Asset-utilization ratios:

Sales to cash . . . . $\dfrac{\text{Sales}}{\text{Cash}} = \dfrac{6204.1 \;\boxed{13}}{178.9 \;\boxed{31} + 12.8 \;\boxed{32}} =$ 32.36

Sales to accounts receivable . . . $\dfrac{\text{Sales}}{\text{Accounts receivable}} = \dfrac{6204.1 \;\boxed{13}}{527.4 \;\boxed{33}} =$ 11.76

Sales to inventories . . . . $\dfrac{\text{Sales}}{\text{Inventories}} = \dfrac{6204.1 \;\boxed{13}}{706.7 \;\boxed{34}} =$ 8.78

Sales to working capital . . . . $\dfrac{\text{Sales}}{\text{Working capital}} = \dfrac{6204.1 \;\boxed{13}}{1518.5 \;\boxed{36} - 1278.0 \;\boxed{45}} =$ 25.80

Sales to fixed assets . . . . $\dfrac{\text{Sales}}{\text{Fixed assets}} = \dfrac{6204.1 \;\boxed{13}}{1790.4 \;\boxed{37}} =$ 3.47

Sales to total assets . . . . $\dfrac{\text{Sales}}{\text{Total assets}} = \dfrac{6204.1 \;\boxed{13}}{4149 \;\boxed{39A}} =$ 1.50

*Interest income

Exhibit 2–2 (concluded)

Major categories of ratios	Method of computation (dollars in millions)	Campbell Soup ratio for 1991
Market measures:		
Price-earnings ratio	$\dfrac{\text{Market price}}{\text{Earnings per share}} = \dfrac{(84.88 + 72.38) \div 2^{(d)}}{3.16\ \boxed{29}} =$	24.88
Earnings yield	$\dfrac{\text{Earnings per share}}{\text{Market price}} = \dfrac{3.16\ \boxed{29}}{(84.88 + 72.38)\ \boxed{184} \div 2} =$	4.02%
Dividend yield	$\dfrac{\text{Dividends per share}}{\text{Market price per share}} = \dfrac{1.12\ \boxed{89}}{(84.88 + 72.38)\ \boxed{184} \div 2} =$	1.42%
Dividend payout ratio	$\dfrac{\text{Dividends per share}}{\text{Earnings per share}} = \dfrac{1.12\ \boxed{89}}{3.16\ \boxed{29}} =$	35.44%

(a) Key references are to financial statements of Campbell Soup Company.
(b) These are simpler versions of more elaborate ratios discussed in Chapter 5.
(c) Using the marginal (corporate) tax rate.
(d) Average of high and low price for last quarter $\boxed{184}$.

ILLUSTRATION 3. Given the following information, we are to complete the balance sheet below:

Cash
Accounts receivable
Inventory .... $ 50
Building
Land
Current liabilities
Common stock
Retained earnings 100

Assets − Liabilities = $600.
Stockholders' equity = 3 × debt.
The carrying amount of land is two thirds of that of the building.
Acid-test ratio = 1.25.
Ending inventory turnover is 15.
Gross profit is 44 percent of the cost of goods sold.
There are 20 days' sales in accounts receivable.

The determination of the balance sheet that follows is based on the steps described below:

Cash	$190	Current liabilities	$200
Accounts receivable	60	Common stock	500
Inventory	50	Retained earnings	100
Buildings.............	300		$800
Land	200		
	$800		

STEP 1:

Assets—Liabilities	= $600
Stockholders' equity	= 600
Retained earnings	= 100 (as given)
Common stock	= 500

STEP 2:

Equity = 3 × debt

3 × current liabilities (which are the total debt) = $600
Add current liabilities 200
So total assets equal $800

STEP 3:

Acid test = 1.25

$$\frac{\text{Cash} + \text{Accounts receivable}}{\$200} = 1.25$$

Hence,

Cash + Accounts receivable = $250

STEP 4:

Inventory + Buildings + Land = $550 [i.e., Total assets − (Cash + A/R)]
                Buildings + Land = $500 (since inventory is given at $50)
Land = ⅔ of building; thus, if x = carrying amount of building
    $x + ⅔ x = \$500$ $x = \underline{\$300}$ (building)

        Land = $500 − $300 = $200

STEP 5:

$$\frac{\text{Cost of goods sold (CGS)}}{\text{Inventory}} = \text{Inventory turnover;} \quad \frac{\text{CGS}}{\$50} = 15$$

Cost of goods sold = $750   Gross profit, 44% of $750 = $330

STEP 6:

Cost of goods sold + Gross profit ($750 + $330) = Sales = $1,080

Amount of sales per day $\dfrac{\$1,080}{360} = \$3$

Accounts receivable = 20 days sales = 20 × $3 = $60
Cash = $250 − Accounts receivable ($60) = $190

Specialized Tools of Analysis

In addition to the multipurpose tools of financial statement analysis that we discussed above, such as trend indexes, common-size statements, and ratios, the analyst has at his or her disposal a variety of special-purpose tools. These tools focus on specific financial statements or segments of such statements, or they can address themselves specifically to the operating conditions of a particular industry, for example, occupancy-capacity analysis in the hotel, hospital, or airline industries. These special-purpose tools of analysis include cash forecasts, analyses of cash flows, statements of variation in gross margin, and break-even analyses.

BUILDING BLOCKS OF FINANCIAL STATEMENT ANALYSIS

Whatever approach to financial statement analysis the analyst takes and whatever methods are used, he or she will always have to examine one or more of the important aspects of an enterprise's financial condition and results of its operations. All such aspects, with perhaps the exception of the most specialized ones, can be found in one of the following six categories:

1. Short-term liquidity.
2. Funds flow.
3. Capital structure and long-term solvency.

4. Return on investment.
5. Operating performance.
6. Assets utilization.

Each of the above categories and the tools used in measuring them will be discussed in greater depth later in this book. In this way, the financial analysis required by any conceivable set of objectives may be structured by examining any or all of the above areas in any sequence and with any degree of relative emphasis called for by circumstances. Thus, these six areas of inquiry and investigation can be considered as building blocks of financial statement analysis.

COMPUTER-ASSISTED FINANCIAL ANALYSIS

The major emphasis throughout this book is on the application of thoughtful and logical analysis upon carefully evaluated and verified data. Financial statement analysis does, however, involve a significant amount of work of a computational nature as well as numerous logical steps that can be preplanned and programmed. It is in these areas that the financial analyst can utilize computers to great advantage.

The modern electronic computer has a remarkable facility for performing complex computations with great speed. Moreover, it can perform these computations, comparisons, and other logical steps for long periods of time without exhaustion and once properly programmed will do them without error. In today's environment, when business complexity has outstripped our ability to grasp it and when our ability to generate information has outrun our ability to utilize it, the computer can render vital assistance.

The intelligent use of the computer's formidable capabilities in financial analysis depends, however, on thorough understanding of the limitations to which this powerful tool is subject. Thus, the computer lacks the ability to make intuitive judgments or to gain insights, capabilities that are essential to a competent and imaginative financial analysis.[3]

There is nothing that the computer can do that a competent analyst armed with a calculator cannot do. On the other hand, the speed and the capabilities of modern computers are such that to accomplish what they can do would require so many hours of work as to render most such efforts uneconomical or infeasible. Computers have thus effectively automated some of the statistical and analytical steps that were previously done manually.

With the exception of databases which provide a full on-line presentation of financial reports, the stored databases on which computer-assisted security analysis often relies do not include all the information

---

[3] To date, developments in the area of artificial intelligence do not require us to qualify this statement significantly.

that is needed to adjust accounting data in order to render it comparable or in order to make it conform to the analyst's specific needs. This is particularly true for the following reasons:

1. The data banks generally lack information on accounting policies and principles employed by a given enterprise. This information is essential to an interpretation of the data and to its comparison to other data.
2. Footnotes and other explanatory or restrictive information usually found in individual enterprise reports containing the financial statements are also generally not available in any meaningful detail.
3. Lack of retroactive adjustments because the necessary data are often not available. Such adjustments are not made even if audited data are subsequently found to be wrong or misleading.
4. Errors and omissions may occur when large masses of financial data are processed on a uniform basis for purposes of inclusion in the database. In addition, data may be classified inconsistently across firms.
5. The aggregation of dissimilar or noncomparable data results in a loss of vital distinctions and thus reduces its meaning and its value for analysis.

Given an understanding of the capabilities as well as the limitations to which the computer is subject, the following are the more significant uses that can be made of this important tool in the broad area of financial analysis.

1. Data Storage, Retrieval, and Computational Ability

A machine-accessible comprehensive database is essential to the use of the computer in most phases of security and credit analysis. The ability of the computer to store vast amounts of data and to afford access to them is one of its important capabilities. Another is the ability to sift these data, to manipulate them mathematically, and to select from among them in accordance with set criteria, as well as to constantly update and modify them. Moreover, the ability of computers to perform computations (of ratios, etc.) is almost unlimited.

A large commercially available database comprising financial information on thousands of corporations covering 20 or more years is available from COMPUSTAT, a service of Standard & Poor's Corporation. Another important database is that provided by Value Line. Many other specialized databases and time-sharing services are available from various sources and those include the AICPA time-sharing program library. See, however, comments in the preceding section on the limitations on the use of such databases in financial statement analysis.

2. Screening Large Masses of Data

The computer can be used to screen for specified criteria as a means of selecting investment opportunities and for other purposes. A variation of these techniques consists of "filtering" data in accordance with a set of preselected criteria (e.g., certain sales levels, returns, growth rates, financial characteristics, etc.)

3. A Research Tool

The computer can be used as a research tool for uncovering characteristics of and relationships between data on companies, industries, market behavior, and the economy.

4. Specialized Financial Analyses

The computer can be an input tool for financial analysis in credit extension and security analysis.

A. Financial analysis in credit extension.[4]
1. Storage of facts for comparison and decision making.
2. Projection of enterprise cash requirements under a variety of assumptions.
3. Projection of financial statements under a variety of assumptions showing the impact of changes on key variables. Known as *sensitivity analysis,* this technique allows the user to explore the effect of systematically changing a given variable repeatedly by a predetermined amount.
4. The introduction of probabilistic inputs. The data can be inserted as probability distributions, either normally shaped or skewed, or random probability distributions, otherwise known as Monte Carlo trials.

B. Security analysis.
1. Calculations based on past data.
2. Trend computations.
   a. Simple
   b. Regression analysis.
3. Predictive models.
4. Projections and forecasts.

---

[4] Software for so-called expert systems has been developed through interviews with senior loan officers and is designed to capture both objective and subjective factors they use in lending decisions. Beyond number crunching they are programmed to make judgments about many important factors entering the lending decision.

5. Sensitivity analysis.
6. Complex probabilistic analysis.

Given an understanding of the capabilities of the modern electronic computer, both mainframe and PC, as well as the limitations to which it is subject, the financial analyst will find in it an important tool that promises to grow in importance as new applications to which it can be put are perfected.

ANALYTICAL REVIEW OF ACCOUNTING PRINCIPLES—PURPOSES AND FOCUS

In the chapters that follow, we shall present a review of accounting standards used in the preparation of financial statements. The purpose of this review is to examine the variety of standards that can be applied to similar transactions and circumstances, as well as the latitude that is possible in the interpretation and application of these standards in practice. Thus, the focus is on an understanding of accounting standards as well as on an appreciation of the impact that the application of these standards can have on the reported financial condition and results of operations of an enterprise. Such possible impact must be appreciated and understood before any intelligent analysis can be undertaken or any useful and meaningful comparison is made.

Example of Importance of Accounting Assumptions, Standards, and Determinations: Illustration of a Simple Investment Decision

The importance of standards and assumptions in accounting determinations can perhaps be best illustrated and understood within the framework of a very simple example of a business situation. Let us assume that the owner of an apartment building has found an interested buyer. How should the price be set? How should the buyer gain confidence in the soundness and profitability of such investment at a given price?

The first question is the method to be followed in arriving at a fair value of the building. While many approaches are possible, such as comparable current values, reproduction costs, and so forth, let us settle here on the most widely accepted method for the valuation of income-producing properties as well as other investments: the capitalization of earnings. If earning power is the major consideration, then the focus must be on the income statement. The prospective buyer is given the following income statement:

184 EAGLE STREET APARTMENT HOUSE
Income Statement
For the Year Ending December 31, Year 9

Revenue:		
Rental revenue		$46,000
Garage rentals		2,440
Other income from washer and dryer concession ..		300
Total revenue		48,740
Expenses:		
Real estate taxes	$4,900	
Mortgage interest	2,100	
Electricity and gas	840	
Water	720	
Superintendent's salary	1,600	
Insurance	680	
Repairs and maintenance	2,400	13,240
Income before depreciation		35,500
Depreciation		9,000
Net income*		$26,500

*Income taxes are excluded from consideration here because they depend on the owner's tax status.

The first questions the prospective buyer will want to ask about the foregoing income statement are these:

1. Can I rely on the fairness of presentation of the income statement?
2. What adjustments have to be made so as to obtain a net income figure that can be used with confidence in arriving at a proper purchase price?

In our society, the most common way of gaining assurance about the fairness of presentation of financial statements is to rely on the opinion of an independent certified public accountant. This professional is assumed to perform a skillful audit and to satisfy himself that the financial statements do accurately portray the results of operations and the financial position, in accordance with principles that are generally accepted as proper and useful in the particular context in which they are applied. Such an auditor is also presumed to understand that someone like our prospective buyer will rely on his or her opinion in reaching a decision on whether to buy and at what price. In the Appendix, we will explore in more detail the function of the auditor and what his opinion means to the use of financial statements.

Our prospective buyer's second question is far more complex. The auditor's opinion relates to the income statement as representing fairly the net income for the year ended December 31, year 9. That in no way means that this is *the* relevant figure to use in arriving at a valuation of the apartment building. Nor would an auditor ever claim that his opinion is directed at the relevance of financial statement figures to any particular decision. Let us then examine what information our buyer will need and what assumptions will have to be made in order to arrive at a figure of net income that can be used in setting the value of the apartment building.

Rental Income   Does the $46,000 figure represent 100 percent occupancy during the year? If so, should an allowance be made for possible vacancies? What are rental trends in the area? What would rents be in five years? In 10 years? Are demand factors for apartments in the area going to stay stable, improve, or deteriorate? The aim, of course, is to come nearest to that figure of yearly rental income that approximates a level that, on the average, can be expected to prevail over the foreseeable future. Prior years' data will be useful in judging this.

Real Estate Taxes   Here the trend of taxes over the years is an important factor. That in turn depends on the character of the taxing community and revenue and expense trends within it.

Mortgage Interest   This expense is relevant to the buyer only if he or she assumes the existing mortgage. Otherwise the interest cost that will be incurred as a result of new financing will have to substituted.

Utilities   These expenses must be scrutinized with a view to ascertaining whether they are at a representative level of what can be expected to prevail.

Superintendent's Salary   Is the pay adequate to secure acceptable services? Can the services of superintendent be retained?

Insurance   Are all foreseeable risks insured for? Is the coverage adequate?

Repairs and Maintenance   These expenses must be examined over a number of years in order to determine an average or representative level. Is the level of expenses such that it affords proper maintenance of the property or is the expense account "starved" so as to show a higher net income?

Depreciation   This figure is not likely to be relevant to the buyer's decision unless his cost approximates that of the seller. If the cost to the buyer differs, then depreciation will have to be computed on that cost using a proper method of depreciation over the useful life of the building, so as to recover the buyer's original cost.

The buyer must also ascertain whether any expenses that he will be properly expected to incur are omitted from the above income statement. Additional considerations concern the method of financing this acquisition and other costs related thereto.

It should be understood that most of the above questions will have to be asked and properly answered even if the auditor issues an unqualified opinion on the financial statements. Thus, for example, while generally accepted accounting principles (GAAP) require that insurance expense include accruals for the full year, they are not concerned with the adequacy of insurance coverage or of the maintenance policy, or the superintendent's pay, or with expected, as opposed to actual, revenues or expense levels.

If one views the many complex questions and problems that arise in the attempt to analyze this very simple income statement for decision-making purposes, one can begin to grasp the complexities involved in the analysis of the financial statements of a sizable, modern business enterprise.

It is clear that essential to an intelligent analysis of such statements is an appreciation of what financial statements do portray as well as what they do not or cannot portray. As we have seen, there are items that properly belong in such statements and there are items that, because of an inability to quantify them or to determine them objectively, cannot be included.

Those items that properly belong in the financial statements should be presented therein in accordance with principles of accounting that enjoy general acceptance. The wide variety of standards that are "acceptable" as well as the even greater variety in the ways in which they can be applied in practice make it imperative that the user of financial statements be fully aware of these possibilities and their implications. The following chapters will explore this important area.

The example of the apartment house buyer illustrates the obvious fact that despite their limitations, financial statements and presentations are indispensable to the decision-making process. While the potential buyer could not use the income statement without obtaining more information and making further assumptions and adjustments, he or she would not have had any basis for his decision without it. Had he not received one, he would have had to make one up without utilization of the objectivity and the benefit of the experience of actual transactions over a period of time. Thus, in most cases, the interpretation of historical financial statements represents the essential first step in the decision-making process.

APPENDIX 2A

SOURCES OF INFORMATION ON FINANCIAL AND OPERATING RATIOS

A good way to achieve familiarity with the wide variety of published financial and operating ratios available is to classify them by the type of source that collects or compiles them. The specific sources given under each category are intended to exemplify the type of material available. These are by no means complete lists:

Professional and Commercial Organizations

Dun & Bradstreet, Inc., Business Economics Division, New York, N.Y.
  Industry Norms and Key Business Ratios.
  Key Business Ratios. Important operating and financial ratios in 190 lines.
  Selected operating expense figures for many retailing, wholesaling, manufacturing lines, as well as for contract construction; service/transportation/ communication; finance/insurance/real estate; agriculture/forestry/fishing; mining.
  Cost-of-Doing Business Series. Typical operating ratios for 185 lines of business, showing national averages. They represent a percentage of business receipts reported by a representative sample of the total of all federal tax returns. (Published irregularly.)
Moody's Investor Service, New York, N.Y.
  Moody's Manuals contain financial and operating ratios on individual companies covered.
Nelson's Directory of Investment Research, Port Chester, N.Y.: W.R. Nelson & Co./Nelson Publications, annual.
Robert Morris Associates. *Annual Statement Studies.*
  Financial and operating ratios for about 300 lines of business—manufacturers, wholesalers, retailers, services, and contractors—based on information obtained from member banks of RMA. Data is broken down by company size.
Standard & Poor's Corporation
  Industry Surveys in two parts: (1) Basic Analysis and (2) Current Analysis contains many industry and individual company ratios.
  Analysts Handbook. "Composite corporate per share data—by industries," for over 90 industries. Statistics and percentages cover 13 components, including sales, operating profits, depreciation, earnings dividends, and the like.
  Industry Surveys. Basic data on 36 important industries, with financial comparisons of the leading companies in each industry. Includes a "Basic Analysis" for each, revised annually. A "Current Analysis" is published quarterly for each industry. A monthly "Trends and Projections" includes tables of economic and industry indicators.
Almanac of Business and Industrial Financial Ratios by Leo Troy. Prentice Hall, Englewood Cliffs, N.J.
  A compilation of corporate performance ratios (operating and financial). The significance of these ratios is explained. All industries are covered in the study, each industry is subdivided by asset size.
Value Line Investment Survey, New York: Value Line Publishing, Inc. weekly updating

The Federal Government

Small Business Administration
Publications containing industry statistics (published sporadically—may not be up to date):
Small Marketers Aid.
Small Business Management Series.
Business Service Bulletins.
U.S. Department of Commerce
Census of Business—Wholesale Trade—Summary Statistics. Monthly Wholesale Trade Report. Ratio of operating expenses to sales.
Department of the Treasury
Statistics of Income, Corporation Income Tax Returns. Operating statistics based on income tax returns.
Federal Trade Commission—Securities and Exchange Commission.
Quarterly Financial Report for Manufacturing, Mining and Trade Corporations. Contains operating ratios and balance sheet ratios as well as the balance sheet in ratio format.
U.S. Internal Revenue Service
Source Book: Statistics of Income: Corporation Income Tax Returns. Washington, D.C. Annual. "Balance sheet, income statement, tax and investment credit items by major and minor industries, broken down by size of total assets."
Statistics of Income: Corporation Income Tax Returns. Washington, D.C.: U.S. Government Printing Office. Annual. Balance sheet and income statement statistics from a sample of corporate returns. Includes tables by major industry, by asset size, and so on. Includes historical summaries.

Sources of Specific Industry Ratios

Many retail and wholesale trade associations compile and publish periodic ratio statistics. Very few manufacturing associations compile ratios they make available to the public; and so for most manufacturing industries one must rely on general sources or on annual reports of specific entities.

American Meat Institute. *Annual Financial Review of the Meat Packing Industry.* Washington, D.C. Includes operating ratios.
Bank Operating Statistics. Federal Deposit Insurance Corporation. Annual.
Institute of Real Estate Management. Experience Exchange Committee. *A Statistical Compilation and Analysis of Actual (year) Income and Expenses Experienced in Apartment, Condominium and Cooperative Building Operation.* Annual.
Discount Merchandiser. *The True Look of the Discount Industry.* June issue each year. Includes operating ratios.
National Electrical Contractors Association. *Operation Overhead.* Annual.
National Farm & Power Equipment Dealers Association. *Cost of Doing Business Study.* Annual.
National Retail Hardware Association. *Lumber/Building Material Financial Report.* Indianapolis. Annual.
Journal of Commercial Bank Lending. "Analysis of Year End Composite Ratios of Installment Sales Finance and Small Loan Companies."

National Association of Music Merchants. *Merchandising and Operating Statistics.* New York. Annual.

National Decorating Products Association. *NDPA'S Annual Cost of Doing Business Survey.* St. Louis. Taken from *Decorating Retailer,* e.g., September 1980 issue.

National Office Products Association. *NOPA Dealers Operating Results.* Alexandria, Va. Annual.

Restaurant Industry Operations Report for the United States. Washington, D.C.: National Restaurant Association. Annual.

Computerized Databases

ABI/Inform. [On-line database and CD-ROM.] Ann Arbor, MI: University Microfilms International. Weekly [on-line], monthly [CD-ROM].

Corporate Information Research Reports (CIRR). [Microfiche collection, on-line database, and CD-ROM database.] East Chester, NY: J.A. Micropublishing, monthly.

Compact Disclosure. [CD-ROM database.] Bethesda, MD: Disclosure Incorporated, monthly.

Compustat. [Computer tape files and CD-ROM database.] New York: Standard & Poor's Compustat Services, Inc., weekly.

Lotus OneSource. [CD-ROM database.] Cambridge, MA: Lotus Development Corporation, monthly.

APPENDIX 2B

This appendix contains the financial statements of Campbell Soup Company contained in its 1991 annual report. These financial statements, along with financial summaries contained in Appendix 10, form the basis for illustrations[5] throughout the text as well as the basis of a comprehensive analysis of the financial statements of the company contained in Chapter 10.

Chapter 10 contains a description of the company's business. For ease of reference the most important captions in Campbell Soup's financial statements, and selected Form 10-K schedules, have been identified by key numbers.

---

[5] In order to draw on a richer database, the text also contains illustrations based on similarly keyed-in captions contained in the 1991 financial statements of Quaker Oats Co. found in Appendix 10.

SUPPLEMENTAL SCHEDULE OF SALES AND EARNINGS **Campbell Soup Company**
Annual Report 1991

(million dollars)

	1991 Sales	1991 Earnings	1990 Sales	1990 Earnings	1989 Sales	1989 Earnings
1 **CONTRIBUTIONS BY DIVISION:**						
Campbell North America						
Campbell U.S.A.	$3,911.8	$632.7	$3,932.7	$370.8	$3,666.9	$242.3
Campbell Canada	352.0	35.3	384.0	25.6	313.4	23.8
	4,263.8	668.0	4,316.7	396.4	3,980.3	266.1
Campbell Biscuit and Bakery						
Pepperidge Farm	569.0	73.6	582.0	57.0	548.4	53.6
International Biscuit	219.4	17.6	195.3	8.9	178.0	11.7
	788.4	91.2	777.3	65.9	726.4	65.3
Campbell International	1,222.9	39.4	1,189.8	(168.6)	1,030.3	(117.8)
Interdivision	(71.0)		(78.0)		(64.9)	
TOTAL SALES	$6,204.1		$6,205.8		$5,672.1	
TOTAL OPERATING EARNINGS		798.6		293.7		213.6
Unallocated corporate expenses		(41.1)		(16.5)		(31.3)
Interest, net		(90.2)		(94.0)		(55.8)
Foreign currency translation adjustments		.1		(3.8)		(20.0)
Taxes on earnings		(265.9)		(175.0)		(93.4)
NET EARNINGS		$401.5		$4.4		$13.1
NET EARNINGS PER SHARE		$3.16		$.03		$.10

Contributions by division in 1990 include the effects of divestitures, restructuring and unusual charges of $339.1 million as follows: Campbell U.S.A. $121.8 million, Campbell Canada $6.6 million, Pepperidge Farm $11.0 million, International Biscuit $14.3 million, and Campbell International $185.4 million. Contributions by division in 1989 include the effects of restructuring and unusual charges of $343.0 million as follows: Campbell U.S.A. $183.1 million, Campbell Canada $6.0 million, Pepperidge Farm $7.1 million, International Biscuit $9.5 million, and Campbell International $137.3 million.

MANAGEMENT'S DISCUSSION AND ANALYSIS OF RESULTS OF OPERATIONS AND FINANCIAL CONDITION

 RESULTS OF OPERATIONS

Overview

Campbell had record net earnings in 1991 of $401.5 million, or $3.16 per share, compared to net earnings of $4.4 million, or 3 cents per share, in 1990. Excluding 1990's divestiture and restructuring charges, earnings per share increased 34% in 1991. In 1991, the Company sold five non-strategic businesses, sold or closed several manufacturing plants, and discontinued certain unprofitable product lines. Net sales of $6.2 billion in 1991 were even with 1990. Sales were up 4% excluding businesses that were divested and product lines that were discontinued in 1991.

In 1990, the Company incurred charges for divestitures and restructuring of $2.33 per share, reducing net earnings to 3 cents per share. In 1989, restructuring charges of $2.02 per share reduced earnings to 10 cents per share. Excluding these charges from both years, earnings per share rose 11% in 1990. Sales increased 9%. In 1990, the Company's domestic divisions had strong earnings performances, excluding the divestiture and restructuring charges, but the International Division's performance was disappointing principally due to the poor performance of United Kingdom frozen food and Italian biscuit operations. The Italian biscuit operations were divested in 1991.

The divestiture and restructuring programs were designed to strengthen the Company's core businesses and improve long-term profitability. The 1990 divestiture program involved the sale of several low-return or non-strategic businesses. The 1990 restructuring charges provided for the elimination of underperforming assets and unnecessary facilities and included a write-off of goodwill. The restructuring charges in 1989 involved plant consolidations, work force reductions, and goodwill write-offs.

1991 Compared to 1990

3 **RESULTS BY DIVISION**

CAMPBELL NORTH AMERICA—Operating earnings of Campbell North America, the Company's largest division, were $668.0 million in 1991 compared to $396.4 million in 1990 after restructuring charges of $128.4 million. Operating earnings increased 27% in 1991 over 1990, excluding the restructuring charges from 1990. All of the division's core businesses had very strong

earnings growth. Continued benefits of restructuring drove significant improvements in operating margins.

Sales were $4.26 billion in 1991. Excluding divested businesses and discontinued product lines, sales increased 2% with overall volume down 2%. Soup volume was off 1.5% as a result of reduced year-end trade promotional activities. Significant volume increases were achieved in the cooking soup, ramen noodle and family-size soup categories and "Healthy Request" soup. Exceptionally strong volume performances were turned in by "Swanson" frozen dinners, "Franco-American" gravies and "Prego" spaghetti sauces with positive volume results for "LeMenu Healthy" entrees, Food Service frozen soups and entrees, and Casera Foods in Puerto Rico.

CAMPBELL BISCUIT AND BAKERY—Operating earnings of the Biscuit and Bakery division, which includes Pepperidge Farm in the United States, Delacre in Europe and an equity interest in Arnotts Limited in Australia, were $91.2 million in 1991 compared with $65.9 million in 1990 after restructuring charges of $25.3 million. Operating earnings were flat in 1991, excluding the restructuring charges from 1990. Sales increased 1%, however, volume declined 3%.

Pepperidge Farm operating earnings in 1991 increased despite a drop in sales, which reflects the adverse effect of the recession on premium cookies. Several new varieties of "Hearty Slices" bread performed well. Delacre, benefitting from new management and integration into the worldwide biscuit and bakery organization, turned in significant improvements in 1991 sales and operating earnings. Arnotts' performance in 1991 was disappointing and included restructuring charges. Its restructuring program should have a positive impact on fiscal 1992 results. The 1991 comparison with 1990 was also adversely impacted by gains of $4.0 million realized in 1990 on the sales of businesses by Arnotts.

CAMPBELL INTERNATIONAL—Operating earnings of the International division were $39.4 million in 1991 compared to an operating loss of $168.6 million in 1990 after restructuring charges of $185.4 million.

In 1991, Campbell International achieved a significant turnaround. Operating earnings for the year more than doubled above the pre-restructuring results of the prior year. There were margin improvements throughout the system. Europe led the division's positive results. A key component was the United Kingdom's move from a loss position to profitability, driven by the benefits of restructuring and product line reconfiguration. European Food and Confectionery units turned in another year of solid earnings growth. Mexican operations, strengthened by a new management team, also turned around from a loss to a profit position. Sales were $1.22 billion in 1991, an increase of 6%, excluding divested businesses and discontinued product lines, and the effects of foreign currency rates. Volume was approximately the same as in 1990.

4 STATEMENTS OF EARNINGS

Sales in 1991 were even with 1990. Excluding divested businesses and unprofitable product lines discontinued during 1991, sales increased 4% while volume declined approximately 2%. The decline in volume was caused by reduced year-end trade promotional activities and the adverse effect of the recession on certain premium products.

Gross margins improved 2.6 percentage points to 34.0% in 1991 from 31.4% in 1990. All divisions improved due to the significant benefits from restructuring and the divestitures and product-pruning activities. Productivity improvements worldwide and declining commodity prices also contributed to the higher margins.

Marketing and selling expenses, as a percentage of net sales, were 15.4% in 1991 compared to 15.8% in 1990. The decrease in 1991 is due to more focused marketing efforts and controlled new product introductions. For each of the prior 10 fiscal years, these expenses had increased significantly. Advertising was down 11% in 1991. Management expects advertising expenditures to increase in 1992 in order to drive volume growth of core products and to support the introduction of new products.

Administrative expenses, as a percentage of net sales, were 4.9% in 1991 compared to 4.7% in 1990. The increase in 1991 results principally from annual executive incentive plan accruals due to outstanding financial performance and foreign currency rates.

Interest expense increased in 1991 due to timing of fourth quarter borrowings in order to obtain favorable long-term interest rates. Interest income was also higher in 1991 as the proceeds from these borrowings were invested temporarily until needed. Interest expense, net of interest income, decreased from $94.0 million in 1990 to $90.2 million in 1991 as the increased cash flow from operations exceeded cash used for share repurchases and acquisitions.

Foreign exchange losses declined principally due to reduced effects of currency devaluations in Argentina.

Other expense was $26.2 million in 1991 compared to $14.7 million in 1990. The increase results principally from accruals for long-term incentive compensation plans reflecting changes in Campbell's stock price.

As discussed in the "Overview" section above, 1990 results include divestiture, restructuring, and unusual charges of $339.1 million ($301.6 million or $2.33 per share after taxes).

Equity in earnings of affiliates declined in 1991 principally due to the disappointing performance at Arnotts and to a $4.0 million gain on sales of businesses realized by Arnotts in 1990.

1990 Compared to 1989

5 RESULTS BY DIVISION

CAMPBELL NORTH AMERICA—In 1990, Campbell North America had operating earnings of $396.4 million after restructuring charges of $128.4 million. In 1989, the division had operating earnings of $266.1 million, after restructuring charges of $189.1 million. Excluding restructuring charges from both 1990 and 1989, operating earnings increased 15% in 1990, led by strong performances by the soup, grocery, "Mrs. Paul's" frozen seafood, and Canadian sectors. The olives business performed poorly in 1990.

Sales increased 8% in 1990 to $4.32 billion on a 3% increase in volume. There were solid volume increases in ready-to-serve soups, "Great Starts" frozen breakfasts, and "Prego" spaghetti sauces. Overall soup volume was up 1%. "Mrs. Paul's" regained the number one share position in frozen prepared seafood.

CAMPBELL BISCUIT AND BAKERY—In 1990, Campbell Biscuit and Bakery had operating earnings of $65.9 million after restructuring charges of $25.3 million. In 1989, the division's operating earnings were $65.3 million after restructuring charges of $16.6 million. Excluding restructuring charges from both 1990 and 1989, operating earnings of the division increased 11% in 1990. The increase in operating earnings was driven by Pepperidge Farm's biscuit and bakery units along with Arnotts' gain on sales of businesses. Pepperidge Farm's frozen unit and Delacre performed poorly. Sales increased 7% to $777.3 million. Volume increased 1%, with Pepperidge Farm's biscuit, bakery and food service units and Delacre the main contributors to the growth.

CAMPBELL INTERNATIONAL — In 1990, Campbell International had an operating loss of $168.6 million after restructuring charges of $185.4 million. In 1989, the division sustained an operating loss of $117.8 million after restructuring charges of $137.3 million. Excluding restructuring charges from both 1990 and 1989, operating earnings declined 14% in 1990, as strong performances in the European Food and Confectionery and Argentine operations were more than offset by poor performances in the United Kingdom frozen food and Italian biscuit operations. Sales in 1990 were $1.19 billion, an increase of 15%. Volume was up 14% of which 11% came from acquisitions.

6 STATEMENTS OF EARNINGS

'In 1990 sales increased 9% on a 5% increase in volume, about half of which came from established businesses.

Gross margins improved by 1.9 percentage points to 31.4% in 1990 from 29.5% in 1989. All divisions had improved margins in 1990, with Campbell North America operations posting substantial improvements.

Marketing and selling expenses, as a percentage of net sales, were 15.8% in 1990 compared to 14.4% in 1989. The 1990 increase was due to heavy marketing expenditures by Campbell U.S.A. at both the national and regional levels.

Administrative expenses, as a percentage of net sales, were 4.7% in 1990 compared to 4.4% in 1989. The increase in 1990 was driven by some unusual one-time expenditures, employee benefits, the weakening dollar and acquisitions.

Interest expense increased in 1990 due to higher debt levels resulting from funding of acquisitions, higher inventory levels during the year, purchases of Campbell's stock for the treasury and restructuring program expenditures. Interest income declined in 1990 because of a shift from local currency to lower-yielding dollar denominated temporary investments in Latin America to minimize foreign exchange losses.

Foreign exchange losses resulted principally from currency devaluations in Argentina. There was a large devaluation in Argentina in 1989. Also, 1990 losses were lower due to the shift in temporary investments described in the previous paragraph.

Other expense was $14.7 million in 1990 compared to $32.4 million in 1989. This decline results principally from reduced accruals for long-term incentive compensation plans reflecting changes in Campbell's stock price.

As discussed in the "Overview" section above, results include divestiture, restructuring and unusual charges of $339.1 million ($301.6 million or $2.33 per share after taxes) in 1990 and $343.0 million ($260.8 million or $2.02 per share after taxes) in 1989.

Equity in earnings of affiliates increased in 1990 principally due to a $4.0 million gain on sales of businesses realized by Arnotts in 1990.

7

Income Taxes

The effective income tax rate was 39.8% in 1991, 97.5% in 1990 and 87.7% in 1989. The principal reason for the high tax rates in 1990 and 1989 is that certain of the divestiture, restructuring and unusual charges are not tax deductible. Excluding the effect of these charges, the rate would be 41.0% in 1990 and 38.9% in 1989. The variances in all years are principally due to the level of certain foreign losses for which no tax benefit is currently available.

8

Inflation

The Company attempts to mitigate the effects of inflation on sales and earnings by appropriately increasing selling prices and aggressively pursuing an ongoing cost improvement effort which includes capital investments in more efficient plants and equipment. Also, the divestiture and restructuring programs enacted in 1989 and 1990 have made the Company a more cost-effective producer, as previously discussed with reference to cost of products sold.

9

Recent Developments

In December 1990, the Financial Accounting Standards Board issued Statement of Financial Accounting Standards No. 106, "Employer's Accounting for Post-retirement Benefits Other Than Pensions," which requires employers to account for retiree health obligations on an accrual basis beginning with the Company's 1994 fiscal year. For a discussion of its impact on the Company, see Note 8 to the Consolidated Financial Statements.

10

LIQUIDITY AND CAPITAL RESOURCES

The Consolidated Statements of Cash Flows and Balance Sheets demonstrate the Company's continued superior financial strength.

[11] **Statements of Cash Flows**

OPERATING ACTIVITIES—Cash provided by operations was $805.2 million in 1991, an 80% increase from $448.4 million in 1990. This increased cash flow was driven by the Company's record earnings level and reduced working capital resulting from improved asset management and the restructuring program.

INVESTING ACTIVITIES—The majority of the Company's investing activities involve the purchase of new plant assets to maintain modern manufacturing processes and increase productivity. Capital expenditures for plant assets amounted to $371.1 million in 1991, including $10.0 million of capital lease activity, down slightly from 1990. The Company expects capital expenditures in 1992 to be about $400 million.

Another key investing activity of the Company is acquisitions. The total cost of acquisitions in 1991 was $180.1 million, most of which was spent to acquire the publicly-held shares of the Company's 71% owned subsidiary, Campbell Soup Company Ltd in Canada. This will allow Campbell North America to more efficiently integrate its U.S. and Canadian operations to provide Campbell with competitive advantage in North America.

One of the Company's strategies has been to prune low-return assets and businesses from its portfolio. In 1991 the Company realized over $110 million in cash from these activities, with $67.4 million coming from sales of businesses and $43.2 million realized from asset sales.

Also, during 1991 the Company made contributions to its pension plans substantially in excess of the amounts expensed. This was the principal reason for the increase in other assets.

FINANCING ACTIVITIES—During 1991, the Company issued debt in the public markets for a total of $400 million: $100 million of 9% Notes due 1998, $100 million of Medium-Term Notes due 2001 at interest rates from 8.58% to 8.75%, and $200 million of 8.875% Debentures due 2021. The proceeds were used to reduce short-term debt by $227 million, pay off long-term debt maturing in 1991 of $129.9 million, and to fund the purchase of the minority interest of Campbell Canada.

During 1991, the Company repurchased approximately 3.4 million shares of its capital stock at a cost of $175.6 million. Cash received from the issuance of approximately 1.1 million treasury shares pursuant to the stock option and long-term incentive plans amounted to $47.7 million in 1991.

Dividends of $137.5 million represent the dividends paid in 1991. Dividends declared in 1991 were $142.2 million or $1.12 per share, an increase of 14% over 1990.

[12] **Balance Sheets**

Total borrowings at the end of fiscal 1991 were $1.055 billion compared to $1.008 billion at the end of 1990. Even after the effects of the borrowing and treasury stock activity previously discussed, total debt as a percentage of total capitalization was 33.7%—the same as a year ago. The Company has ample sources of funds. It has access to the commercial paper markets with the highest rating. The Company's long-term debt is rated double A by the major rating agencies. It has filed a shelf registration with the Securities and Exchange Commission for the issuance from time to time of up to $100 million of debt securities. Also, the Company has unused lines of credit of approximately $635 million.

Debt-related activity is discussed in the Statements of Cash Flows section above. In addition to that, the debt balances on the Balance Sheets were affected by current maturities of long-term debt and by the classification of commercial paper to be refinanced as long-term debt in 1990.

Aggressive management of working capital and the effect of divested businesses are evidenced by a $235.5 million decrease in current assets exclusive of changes in cash and temporary investments. Receivables are down $97.1 million and inventories declined $113.1 million from 1990. Accounts payable are down $42.8 million because of the reduced inventory levels and divestitures. Accrued liabilities and accrued income taxes declined $61.9 million as increases due to higher earnings levels and the timing of certain payments were offset by payments and charges resulting from the divestitures and restructuring programs.

Plant assets increased $72.7 million due to capital expenditures of $371.1 million offset by the annual provision for depreciation of $194.5 million, asset sales and divestitures. Intangible assets increased $52.1 million as the acquisitions resulted in $132.3 million of additional goodwill. Amortization and divestitures accounted for the remainder of the change. Other assets increased principally as the result of the pension contribution.

Other liabilities decreased $14.9 million as the reduction of minority interest resulting from the purchase of the publicly-held shares of Campbell Canada and changes in foreign currency rates on other liabilities offset the annual deferred tax provision.

CONSOLIDATED STATEMENTS OF EARNINGS   Campbell Soup Company

(millions)

		1991	1990	1989
[13]	**NET SALES**	**$6,204.1**	$6,205.8	$5,672.1
	Costs and expenses			
[14]	Cost of products sold	**4,095.5**	4,258.2	4,001.6
[15]	Marketing and selling expenses	**956.2**	980.5	818.8
[16]	Administrative expenses	**306.7**	290.7	252.1
[17]	Research and development expenses	**56.3**	53.7	47.7
[18]	Interest expense (Note 3)	**116.2**	111.6	94.1
[19]	Interest income	**(26.0)**	(17.6)	(38.3)
[20]	Foreign exchange losses, net (Note 4)	**.8**	3.3	19.3
[21]	Other expense (Note 5)	**26.2**	14.7	32.4
[22]	Divestitures, restructuring and unusual charges (Note 6)	**—**	339.1	343.0
[22A]	Total costs and expenses	**5,531.9**	6,034.2	5,570.7
[23]	Earnings before equity in earnings of affiliates and minority interests	**672.2**	171.6	101.4
[24]	Equity in earnings of affiliates	**2.4**	13.5	10.4
[25]	Minority interests	**(7.2)**	(5.7)	(5.3)
[26]	Earnings before taxes	**667.4**	179.4	106.5
[27]	Taxes on earnings (Note 9)	**265.9**	175.0	93.4
[28]	**NET EARNINGS**	**$ 401.5**	$ 4.4	$ 13.1
[29]	**NET EARNINGS PER SHARE (NOTE 22)**	**$3.16**	$.03	$.10
[30]	Weighted average shares outstanding	**127.0**	129.6	129.3

The accompanying Summary of Significant Accounting Policies and Notes on pages 26 to 33 are an integral part of the financial statements.

CONSOLIDATED BALANCE SHEETS   Campbell Soup Company

(million dollars)

		July 28, 1991	July 29, 1990
	CURRENT ASSETS		
31	Cash and cash equivalents (Note 12)	$ 178.9	$ 80.7
32	Other temporary investments, at cost which approximates market	12.8	22.5
33	Accounts receivable (Note 13)	527.4	624.5
34	Inventories (Note 14)	706.7	819.8
35	Prepaid expenses (Note 15)	92.7	118.0
36	Total current assets	1,518.5	1,665.5
37	**PLANT ASSETS, NET OF DEPRECIATION (NOTE 16)**	1,790.4	1,717.7
38	**INTANGIBLE ASSETS, NET OF AMORTIZATION (NOTE 17)**	435.5	383.4
39	**OTHER ASSETS (NOTE 18)**	404.6	349.0
	Total assets	$4,149.0	$4,115.6
	CURRENT LIABILITIES		
40	Notes payable (Note 19)	$ 282.2	$ 202.3
41	Payable to suppliers and others	482.4	525.2
42	Accrued liabilities (Note 20)	408.7	491.9
43	Dividend payable	37.0	32.3
44	Accrued income taxes	67.7	46.4
45	Total current liabilities	1,278.0	1,298.1
46	**LONG-TERM DEBT (NOTE 19)**	772.6	805.8
47	**OTHER LIABILITIES, PRINCIPALLY DEFERRED INCOME TAXES (NOTE 21)**	305.0	319.9
	SHAREOWNERS' EQUITY (NOTE 22)		
48	Preferred stock; authorized 40,000,000 shares; none issued	—	—
49	Capital stock, $.15 par value; authorized 140,000,000 shares; issued 135,622,676 shares	20.3	20.3
50	Capital surplus	107.3	61.9
51	Earnings retained in the business	1,912.6	1,653.3
52	Capital stock in treasury, 8,618,911 shares in 1991 and 6,353,697 shares in 1990, at cost	(270.4)	(107.2)
53	Cumulative translation adjustments (Note 4)	23.6	63.5
54	Total shareowners' equity	1,793.4	1,691.8
55	Total liabilities and shareowners' equity	$4,149.0	$4,115.6

The accompanying Summary of Significant Accounting Policies and Notes on pages 26 to 33 are an integral part of the financial statements.

CONSOLIDATED STATEMENTS OF CASH FLOWS   Campbell Soup Company

(million dollars)

	1991	1990	1989
CASH FLOWS FROM OPERATING ACTIVITIES:			
[56] Net earnings	$401.5	$ 4.4	$ 13.1
To reconcile net earnings to net cash provided by operating activities:			
[57] Depreciation and amortization	208.6	200.9	192.3
[58] Divestitures and restructuring provisions		339.1	343.0
[59] Deferred taxes	35.5	3.9	(67.8)
[60] Other, net	63.2	18.6	37.3
[61] (Increase) decrease in accounts receivable	17.1	(60.4)	(46.8)
[62] (Increase) decrease in inventories	48.7	10.7	(113.2)
[63] Net change in other current assets and liabilities	30.6	(68.8)	(.6)
[64] Net cash provided by operating activities	805.2	448.4	357.3
CASH FLOWS FROM INVESTING ACTIVITIES:			
[65] Purchases of plant assets	(361.1)	(387.6)	(284.1)
[66] Sales of plant assets	43.2	34.9	39.8
[67] Businesses acquired	(180.1)	(41.6)	(135.8)
[68] Sales of businesses	67.4	21.7	4.9
[69] Increase in other assets	(57.8)	(18.6)	(107.0)
[70] Net change in other temporary investments	9.7	3.7	9.0
[71] Net cash used in investing activities	(478.7)	(387.5)	(473.2)
CASH FLOWS FROM FINANCING ACTIVITIES:			
[72] Long-term borrowings	402.8	12.6	126.5
[73] Repayments of long-term borrowings	(129.9)	(22.5)	(53.6)
[74] Increase (decrease) in borrowings with less than three month maturities	(137.9)	(2.7)	108.2
[75] Other short-term borrowings	117.3	153.7	227.1
[76] Repayments of other short-term borrowings	(206.4)	(89.8)	(192.3)
[77] Dividends paid	(137.5)	(124.3)	(86.7)
[78] Treasury stock purchases	(175.6)	(41.1)	(8.1)
[79] Treasury stock issued	47.7	12.4	18.5
[80] Other, net	(.1)	(.1)	23.5
[81] Net cash provided by (used in) financing activities	(219.6)	(101.8)	163.1
[82] Effect of exchange rate changes on cash	(8.7)	.7	(12.1)
[83] **NET INCREASE (DECREASE) IN CASH AND CASH EQUIVALENTS**	98.2	(40.2)	35.1
[84] Cash and cash equivalents at beginning of year	80.7	120.9	85.8
[85] **CASH AND CASH EQUIVALENTS AT END OF YEAR**	$178.9	$ 80.7	$120.9

The accompanying Summary of Significant Accounting Policies and Notes on pages 26 to 33 are an integral part of the financial statements.
Prior years have been reclassified to conform to the 1991 presentation.

CONSOLIDATED STATEMENTS OF SHAREOWNERS' EQUITY   Campbell Soup Company

(million dollars)

	Preferred stock	Capital stock	Capital surplus	Earnings retained in the business	Capital stock in treasury	Cumulative translation adjustments	Total Shareowners' Equity
86 Balance at July 31, 1988	—	$20.3	$ 42.3	$1,879.1	$ (75.2)	$28.5	$1,895.0
Net earnings				13.1			13.1
Cash dividends ($.90 per share)				(116.4)			(116.4)
Treasury stock purchased					(8.1)		(8.1)
Treasury stock issued under Management incentive and Stock option plans			8.5		12.6		21.1
Translation adjustments						(26.4)	(26.4)
87 Balance at July 30, 1989	—	20.3	50.8	1,775.8	(70.7)	2.1	1,778.3
Net earnings				4.4			4.4
Cash dividends ($.98 per share)				(126.9)			(126.9)
Treasury stock purchased					(41.1)		(41.1)
Treasury stock issued under Management incentive and Stock option plans			11.1		4.6		15.7
Translation adjustments						61.4	61.4
Balance at July 29, 1990	—	20.3	61.9	1,653.3	(107.2)	63.5	1,691.8
88 *Net earnings*				*401.5*			*401.5*
89 *Cash dividends ($1.12 per share)*				*(142.2)*			*(142.2)*
90 *Treasury stock purchased*					*(175.6)*		*(175.6)*
91 *Treasury stock issued under Management incentive and Stock option plans*			*45.4*		*12.4*		*57.8*
92 *Translation adjustments*						*(29.9)*	*(29.9)*
93 *Sale of foreign operations*						*(10.0)*	*(10.0)*
94 **Balance at July 28, 1991**	—	**$20.3**	**$107.3**	**$1,912.6**	**$(270.4)**	**$23.6**	**$1,793.4**

95 **CHANGES IN NUMBER OF SHARES**

(thousands of shares)

	Issued	Outstanding	In Treasury
Balance at July 31, 1988	135,622.7	129,038.6	6,584.1
Treasury stock purchased		(250.6)	250.6
Treasury stock issued under Management incentive and Stock option plans		790.6	(790.6)
Balance at July 30, 1989	135,622.7	129,578.6	6,044.1
Treasury stock purchased		(833.0)	833.0
Treasury stock issued under Management incentive and Stock option plans		523.4	(523.4)
Balance at July 29,1990	135,622.7	129,269.0	6,353.7
Treasury stock purchased		*(3,395.4)*	*3,395.4*
Treasury stock issued under Management incentive and Stock option plans		*1,130.2*	*(1,130.2)*
Balance at July 28, 1991	**135,622.7**	**127,003.8**	**8,618.9**

The accompanying Summary of Significant Accounting Policies and Notes on pages 26 to 33 are an integral part of the financial statements.

NOTES TO CONSOLIDATED FINANCIAL STATEMENTS

(million dollars)

96 **❶ SUMMARY OF SIGNIFICANT ACCOUNTING POLICIES**

CONSOLIDATION—The consolidated financial statements include the accounts of the Company and its majority-owned subsidiaries. Significant intercompany transactions are eliminated in consolidation. Investments in affiliates owned 20% or more are accounted for by the equity method.

INVENTORIES—Substantially all domestic inventories are priced at the lower of cost or market, with cost determined by the last-in, first-out (LIFO) method. Other inventories are priced at the lower of average cost or market.

INTANGIBLES—The excess of cost of investments over net assets of purchased companies is amortized on a straight-line basis over periods not exceeding forty years.

PLANT ASSETS—Alterations and major overhauls which substantially extend the lives of properties or materially increase their capacity are capitalized. The amounts for property disposals are removed from plant asset and accumulated depreciation accounts and any resultant gain or loss is included in earnings. Ordinary repairs and maintenance are charged to operating costs.

DEPRECIATION—Depreciation provided in costs and expenses is on the straight-line method. The United States, Canadian and certain other foreign companies use accelerated methods of depreciation for income tax purposes.

PENSION PLANS—Pension costs are accrued over employees' careers based on plan benefit formulas.

CASH AND CASH EQUIVALENTS—All highly liquid debt instruments purchased with a maturity of three months or less are classified as Cash Equivalents.

FINANCIAL INSTRUMENTS—In managing interest rate exposure, the Company at times enters into interest rate swap agreements. When interest rates change, the difference to be paid or received is accrued and recognized as interest expense over the life of the agreement. In order to hedge foreign currency exposures on firm commitments, the Company at times enters into forward foreign exchange contracts. Gains and losses resulting from these instruments are recognized in the same period as the underlying hedged transaction. The Company also at times enters into foreign currency swap agreements which are effective as hedges of net investments in foreign subsidiaries. Realized and unrealized gains and losses on these currency swaps are recognized in the Cumulative Translation Adjustments account in Shareowners' Equity.

97 **❷ GEOGRAPHIC AREA INFORMATION**

The Company is predominantly engaged in the prepared convenience foods industry. The following presents information about operations in different geographic areas:

	1991	1990	1989
Net sales			
United States	$4,495.6	$4,527.2	$4,233.4
Europe	1,149.1	1,101.4	983.7
Other foreign countries	656.0	673.6	542.9
Adjustments and eliminations	(96.6)	(96.4)	(87.9)
Consolidated	$6,204.1	$6,205.8	$5,672.1
Earnings (loss) before taxes			
United States	$ 694.8	$ 427.8	$ 294.5
Europe	48.8	(178.7)	(21.3)
Other foreign countries	55.0	44.6	(59.6)
	798.6	293.7	213.6
Unallocated corporate expenses	(41.1)	(16.5)	(31.3)
Interest, net	(90.2)	(94.0)	(55.8)
Foreign currency translation adjustments	.1	(3.8)	(20.0)
Consolidated	$ 667.4	$ 179.4	$ 106.5
Identifiable assets			
United States	$2,693.4	$2,535.0	$2,460.5
Europe	711.3	942.2	886.9
Other foreign countries	744.3	638.4	584.7
Consolidated	$4,149.0	$4,115.6	$3,932.1

Transfers between geographic areas are recorded at cost plus markup or at market. Identifiable assets are all assets identified with operations in each geographic area.

❸ INTEREST EXPENSE

	1991	1990	1989
98 Interest expense	$136.9	$121.9	$97.6
99 Less interest expense capitalized	20.7	10.3	3.5
100	$116.2	$111.6	$94.1

(million dollars)

101 ④ FOREIGN CURRENCY TRANSLATION

Fluctuations in foreign exchange rates resulted in decreases in net earnings of $.3 in 1991, $3.2 in 1990 and $19.1 in 1989.

The balances in the Cumulative translation adjustments account are the following:

	1991	1990	1989
Europe	$ 5.6	$43.2	$(3.5)
Canada	3.8	3.6	(2.5)
Australia	13.4	16.1	7.3
Other	.8	.6	.8
	$23.6	$63.5	$ 2.1

⑤ OTHER EXPENSE

Included in other expense are the following:

	1991	1990	1989
102 Stock price related incentive programs	$15.4	$ (.1)	$17.4
103 Amortization of intangible and other assets	14.1	16.8	16.4
104 Other, net	(3.3)	(2.0)	(1.4)
	$26.2	$14.7	$32.4

105 ⑥ DIVESTITURES, RESTRUCTURING AND UNUSUAL CHARGES

In 1990, charges for divestiture and restructuring programs, designed to strengthen the Company's core businesses and improve long-term profitability, reduced operating earnings by $339.1; $301.6 after taxes, or $2.33 per share. The divestiture program involves the sale of several low-return or non-strategic businesses. The restructuring charges provide for the elimination of underperforming assets and unnecessary facilities and include a charge of $113 to write off goodwill in the United Kingdom.

In 1989, charges for a worldwide restructuring program reduced operating earnings by $343.0; $260.8 after taxes, or $2.02 per share. The restructuring program involved plant consolidations, work force reductions, and goodwill write-offs.

106 ⑦ ACQUISITIONS

Prior to July 1991, the Company owned approximately 71% of the capital stock of Campbell Soup Company Ltd ("Campbell Canada"), which processes, packages and distributes a wide range of prepared foods exclusively in Canada under many of the Company's brand names. The financial position and results of operations of Campbell Canada are consolidated with those of the Company. In July 1991, the Company acquired the remaining shares (29%) of Campbell Canada which it did not already own at a cost of $159.7. In addition, the Company made one other acquisition at a cost of $20.4. The total cost of 1991 acquisitions of $180.1 was allocated as follows:

107

Working capital	$ 5.1
Fixed assets	4.7
Intangibles, principally goodwill	132.3
Other assets	1.5
Elimination of minority interest	36.5
	$180.1

During 1990, the Company made several small acquisitions at a cost of $43.1 which was allocated as follows:

108

Working capital	$ 7.8
Fixed assets	24.7
Intangibles, principally goodwill	18.5
Long-term liabilities and other	(7.9)
	$43.1

During 1989, the Company made several acquisitions at a cost of $137.9, including a soup and pickle manufacturing business in Canada. The cost of the acquisitions was allocated as follows:

109

Working capital	$ 39.9
Fixed assets	34.6
Intangibles, principally goodwill	65.5
Long-term liabilities and other	(2.1)
	$137.9

These acquisitions were accounted for as purchase transactions, and operations of the acquired companies are included in the financial statements from the dates the acquisitions were recorded. Proforma results of

NOTES TO CONSOLIDATED FINANCIAL STATEMENTS

(million dollars)

operations have not been presented as they would not vary materially from the reported amounts and would not be indicative of results anticipated following acquisition due to significant changes made to acquired companies' operations.

[110] ⊙ PENSION PLANS AND RETIREMENT BENEFITS

PENSION PLANS—Substantially all of the employees of the Company and its domestic and Canadian subsidiaries are covered by noncontributory defined benefit pension plans. Plan benefits are generally based on years of service and employees' compensation during the last years of employment. Benefits are paid from funds previously provided to trustees and insurance companies or are paid directly by the Company or its subsidiaries. Actuarial assumptions and plan provisions are reviewed regularly by the Company and its independent actuaries to ensure that plan assets will be adequate to provide pension and survivor benefits. Plan assets consist primarily of shares of or units in common stock, fixed income, real estate and money market funds.

Pension expense included the following:

	1991	1990	1989
For Domestic and Canadian trusteed plans:			
[111] Service cost-benefits earned during the year	$ 22.1	$ 19.3	$17.2
[112] Interest cost on projected benefit obligation	69.0	63.3	58.8
[113] Actual return on plan assets	(73.4)	(27.1)	(113.8)
[114] Net amortization and deferral	6.3	(38.2)	57.8
	24.0	17.3	20.0
[115] Other pension expense	7.4	6.4	6.8
[116] Consolidated pension expense	$ 31.4	$ 23.7	$26.8

Principal actuarial assumptions used in the United States were:

Measurement of projected benefit obligation—			
[117] Discount rate	8.75%	9.00%	9.00%
[118] Long-term rate of compensation increase	5.75%	5.50%	5.00%
[119] Long-term rate of return on plan assets	9.00%	9.00%	9.00%

The funded status of the plans was as follows:

[120]	July 28, 1991	July 29, 1990
Actuarial present value of benefit obligations:		
Vested	$(679.6)	$(624.4)
Non-vested	(34.8)	(35.0)
Accumulated benefit obligation	(714.4)	(659.4)
Effect of projected future salary increases	(113.3)	(101.0)
Projected benefit obligation	(827.7)	(760.4)
Plan assets at market value	857.7	773.9
Plan assets in excess of projected benefit obligation	30.0	13.5
Unrecognized net loss	122.9	86.3
Unrecognized prior service cost	54.9	55.9
Unrecognized net assets at transition	(35.3)	(39.5)
Prepaid pension expense	$ 172.5	$ 116.2

Pension coverage for employees of the Company's foreign subsidiaries, other than Canada, and other supplemental pension benefits of the Company are provided to the extent determined appropriate through their respective plans. Obligations under such plans are systematically provided for by depositing funds with trusts or under insurance contracts. The assets and obligations of these plans are not material.

SAVINGS PLANS—The Company sponsors employee savings plans which cover substantially all domestic employees. After one year of continuous service the Company matches 50% of employee contributions up to five percent of compensation within certain limits. In fiscal 1992 the Company will increase its contribution by up to 20% if certain earnings' goals are achieved. Amounts charged to costs and expenses were $10.0 in 1991, $10.6 in 1990, and $10.7 in 1989.

Campbell Soup Company

(million dollars)

RETIREE BENEFITS—The Company and its domestic subsidiaries provide certain health care and life insurance benefits to substantially all retired employees and their dependents. The cost of these retiree health and life insurance benefits are expensed as claims are paid and amounted to $15.3 in 1991, $12.6 in 1990 and $11.0 in 1989. Substantially all retirees of foreign subsidiaries are provided health care benefits by government sponsored plans. The cost of life insurance provided to retirees of certain foreign subsidiaries is not significant.

In December 1990, the Financial Accounting Standards Board issued Statement of Financial Accounting Standards No. 106, "Employer's Accounting for Postretirement Benefits Other Than Pensions," which will require the Company to account for retiree health obligations on an accrual basis beginning with the 1994 fiscal year. The Company is in the process of studying the effects of this complex new accounting standard. The standard permits an employer to recognize the effect of the initial liability either immediately or to amortize it over a period of up to 20 years. The Company has not yet decided which option to select. Management expects that the adoption of this standard will increase annual expense, but the amount has not yet been determined.

....

[121] ● **TAXES ON EARNINGS**

The provision for income taxes consists of the following:

	1991	1990	1989
Currently payable			
[122] Federal	$185.8	$132.4	$118.8
[123] State	23.4	20.8	20.9
[124] Foreign	21.2	17.9	21.5
[124A]	230.4	171.1	161.2
Deferred			
[125] Federal	21.9	1.2	(49.3)
[126] State	7.5	2.6	(8.0)
[127] Foreign	6.1	.1	(10.5)
[127A]	35.5	3.9	(67.8)
[127B]	$265.9	$175.0	$ 93.4

The deferred income taxes result from temporary differences between financial statement earnings and taxable earnings as follows:

	1991	1990	1989
[128] Depreciation	$ 5.9	$ 18.6	$ 11.9
[129] Pensions	13.6	11.7	8.3
[130] Prefunded employee benefits	(3.3)	(4.8)	(3.4)
[131] Accruals not currently deductible for tax purposes	(11.4)	(5.8)	(5.3)
[132] Divestitures, restructuring and unusual charges	29.3	(11.1)	(78.2)
[133] Other	1.4	(4.7)	(1.1)
	$35.5	$ 3.9	$(67.8)

The following is a reconciliation of effective income tax rates with the statutory Federal income tax rate:

	1991	1990	1989
[134] Statutory Federal income tax rate	34.0%	34.0%	34.0%
[135] State income taxes (net of Federal tax benefit)	3.0	3.7	3.6
[136] Nondeductible divestitures, restructuring and unusual charges		56.5	48.7
[137] Nondeductible amortization of intangibles	.6	.9	1.1
[138] Foreign earnings not taxed or taxed at other than statutory Federal rate	(.3)	1.2	.2
[139] Other	2.5	1.2	.1
[140] Effective income tax rate	39.8%	97.5%	87.7%

The provision for income taxes was reduced by $3.2 in 1991, $5.2 in 1990 and $3.5 in 1989 due to the utilization of loss carryforwards by certain foreign subsidiaries.

Certain foreign subsidiaries of the Company have tax loss carryforwards of approximately $103.4 ($77.4 for financial purposes), of which $10.5 relate to periods prior to acquisition of the subsidiaries by the Company. Of these carryforwards, $54.8 expire through 1996 and $48.6 may be carried forward indefinitely. The current statutory tax rates in these foreign countries range from 20% to 51%.

NOTES TO CONSOLIDATED FINANCIAL STATEMENTS

(million dollars)

Income taxes have not been accrued on undistributed earnings of foreign subsidiaries of $219.7 which are invested in operating assets and are not expected to be remitted. If remitted, tax credits are available to substantially reduce any resultant additional taxes.

The following are earnings before taxes of United States and foreign companies.

		1991	1990	1989
[141]	United States	$570.9	$277.0	$201.5
[142]	Foreign	96.5	(97.6)	(95.0)
		$667.4	$179.4	$106.5

[143] **⑩ LEASES**

Rent expense was $59.7 in 1991, $62.4 in 1990 and $60.2 in 1989 and generally relates to leases of machinery and equipment. Future minimum lease payments under operating leases are $71.9.

[**⑪ SUPPLEMENTARY STATEMENTS OF EARNINGS INFORMATION**]

		1991	1990	1989
[144]	Maintenance and repairs	$173.9	$180.6	$173.9
[145]	Advertising	$195.4	$220.4	$212.9

[146] **⑫ CASH AND CASH EQUIVALENTS**

Cash and Cash Equivalents includes cash equivalents of $140.7 at July 28, 1991 and $44.1 at July 29, 1990.

⑬ ACCOUNTS RECEIVABLE

		1991	1990
[147]	Customers	$478.0	$554.0
[148]	Allowances for cash discounts and bad debts	(16.3)	(19.9)
		461.7	534.1
[148A]	Other	65.7	90.4
[150]		$527.4	$624.5

⑭ INVENTORIES

		1991	1990
[151]	Raw materials, containers and supplies	$342.3	$384.4
[152]	Finished products	454.0	520.0
		796.3	904.4
[153]	Less-Adjustments of inventories to LIFO basis	89.6	84.6
		$706.7	$819.8

Liquidation of LIFO inventory quantities had no significant effect on net earnings in 1991, 1990 or 1989. Inventories for which the LIFO method of determining cost is used represented approximately 70% of consolidated inventories in 1991 and 64% in 1990.

⑮ PREPAID EXPENSES

		1991	1990
[154]	Pensions	$19.8	$ 22.3
[155]	Deferred taxes	36.6	37.7
[156]	Prefunded employee benefits	1.2	13.9
[157]	Other	35.1	44.1
		$92.7	$118.0

⑯ PLANT ASSETS

		1991	1990
[158]	Land	$ 56.3	$ 63.8
[159]	Buildings	758.7	746.5
[160]	Machinery and equipment	1,779.3	1,657.6
[161]	Projects in progress	327.6	267.0
[161A]		2,921.9	2,734.9
[162]	Accumulated depreciation	(1,131.5)	(1,017.2)
		$1,790.4	$1,717.7

Depreciation provided in costs and expenses was $194.5 in 1991, $184.1 in 1990 and $175.9 in 1989. Approximately $158.2 of capital expenditures is required to complete projects in progress at July 28, 1991.

Campbell Soup Company

(million dollars)

17 INTANGIBLE ASSETS

	1991	1990
163 Cost of investments in excess of net assets of purchased companies (goodwill)	$347.8	$281.1
164 Other intangibles	129.8	134.0
	477.6	415.1
165 Accumulated amortization	(42.1)	(31.7)
	$435.5	$383.4

18 OTHER ASSETS

	1991	1990
166 Investment in affiliates	$155.8	$169.4
167 Noncurrent prepaid pension expense	152.7	93.9
168 Other noncurrent investments	44.2	52.0
169 Other	51.9	33.7
169A	$404.6	$349.0

Investment in affiliates consists principally of the Company's ownership of 33% of the outstanding capital stock of Arnotts Limited, an Australian biscuit manufacturer. This investment is being accounted for by the equity method. Included in this investment is goodwill of $28.3 which is being amortized over 40 years. At July 28, 1991, the market value of the investment based on quoted market prices was $213.8. The Company's equity in the earnings of Arnotts Limited was $1.5 in 1991, $13.0 in 1990 and $8.7 in 1989. The 1990 amount includes a $4.0 gain realized by Arnotts on the sales of businesses. Dividends received were $8.2 in 1991, $7.4 in 1990 and $6.6 in 1989. The Company's equity in the undistributed earnings of Arnotts was $15.4 at July 28, 1991 and $22.1 at July 29, 1990.

170 19 NOTES PAYABLE AND LONG-TERM DEBT

Notes payable consists of the following:

	1991	1990
Commercial paper	$ 24.7	$191.8
8.25% Notes due 1991		100.3
13.99% Notes due 1992	182.0*	
Banks	23.6	91.1
Other	51.9	69.4
Amounts reclassified to long-term debt		(250.3)
	$282.2	$202.3

Present value of $200.0 zero coupon notes, net of unamortized discount of $18.0.

At July 29, 1990, $150 of outstanding commercial paper and $100.3 of currently maturing notes were reclassified to long-term debt and were refinanced in 1991.

Information on notes payable follows:

171

	1991	1990	1989
Maximum amount payable at end of any monthly accounting period during the year	$603.3	$518.7	$347.1
Approximate average amount outstanding during the year	$332.5	$429.7	$273.5
Weighted average interest rate at year-end	10.1%	10.7%	12.1%
Approximate weighted average interest rate during the year	9.8%	10.8%	10.6%

The amount of unused lines of credit at July 28, 1991 approximates $635. The lines of credit are unconditional and generally cover loans for a period of a year at prime commercial interest rates.

NOTES TO CONSOLIDATED FINANCIAL STATEMENTS

(million dollars)

Long-term debt consists of the following:

[172]

Fiscal year maturities	1991	1990
13.99% Notes due 1992	$	$159.7***
9.125% Notes due 1994	100.6	100.9
10.5% Notes due 1996*	100.0	100.0
7.5% Notes due 1998*	99.6	99.5
9.0% Notes due 1998	99.8	
8.58%-8.75% Medium-Term Notes due 2001**	100.0	
8.875% Debentures due 2021	199.6	
Other Notes due 1992-2004 (interest 4.7%-14.4%)	58.2	82.5
Notes payable, reclassified		250.3
Capital lease obligations	14.8	12.9
	$772.6	$805.8

*Redeemable in 1993.
**$50 redeemable in 1998.
***Present value of $200.0 zero coupon notes, net of unamortized discount of $40.3.

[173] Future minimum lease payments under capital leases are $28.0 and the present value of such payments, after deducting implicit interest of $6.5, is $21.5 of which $6.7 is included in current liabilities.

Principal amounts of long-term debt mature as follows 1992-$227.7 (in current liabilities); 1993-$118.9; 1994 $17.8; 1995-$15.9; 1996-$108.3 and beyond-$511.7.

The Company has filed a shelf registration statement with the Securities and Exchange Commission for the issuance from time to time of up to $300 of debt securities, of which $100 remains unissued.

Information on financial instruments follows:

At July 28, 1991, the Company had an interest rate swap agreement with financial institutions having a notional principal amount of $100, which is intended to reduce the impact of changes in interest rates on floating rate commercial paper. In addition, at July 28, 1991, the Company had two swap agreements with financial institutions which covered both interest rates and foreign currencies. These agreements have a total notional principal amount of $103, and are intended to reduce exposure to higher foreign interest rates and to hedge the Company's net investments in the United Kingdom and Australia. The Company is exposed to credit loss in the event of nonperformance by the other parties to the interest rate swap agreements; however, the Company does not anticipate nonperformance by the counterparties.

At July 28, 1991, the Company had contracts to purchase approximately $109 in foreign currency. The contracts are mostly for European currencies and have maturities through 1992.

20 ACCRUED LIABILITIES

	1991	1990
[174] Divestiture and restructuring charges	$ 88.4	$238.8
[175] Other	320.3	253.1
	$408.7	$491.9

21 OTHER LIABILITIES

	1991	1990
[176] Deferred income taxes	$258.5	$235.1
[177] Other liabilities	23.0	28.5
[178] Minority interests	23.5	56.3
	$305.0	$319.9

Campbell Soup Company

(million dollars)

179 22 SHAREOWNERS' EQUITY

The Company has authorized 140 million shares of Capital Stock of $.15 par value and 40 million shares of Preferred Stock, issuable in one or more classes, with or without par as may be authorized by the Board of Directors. No Preferred Stock has been issued.

The following summarizes the activity in option shares under the Company's employee stock option plans:

(thousands of shares)	1991	1990	1989
Beginning of year	4,301.1	3,767.9	3,257.0
Granted under the 1984 long-term incentive plan at average price of $63.64 in 1991; $47.27 in 1990; $30.37 in 1989	2,136.3	1,196.0	1,495.5
Exercised at average price of $29.82 in 1991; $24.78 in 1990; $20.65 in 1989 in form of:			
Stock appreciation rights	(14.9)	(110.2)	(137.3)
Shares	(1,063.7)	(367.2)	(615.1)
Terminated	(216.9)	(185.4)	(232.2)
End of year	5,141.9	4,301.1	3,767.9
Exercisable at end of year	2,897.0	2,654.4	2,104.1
Shares under option-price per share:			
Range of prices: Low	$14.68	$ 6.98	$ 6.98
High	$83.31	$57.61	$34.31
Average	$46.73	$33.63	$28.21

In addition to options granted under the 1984 long-term incentive plan, 233,200 restricted shares of capital stock were granted to certain key management employees in 1991; 168,850 in 1990; and 162,000 in 1989.

There are 4,229,111 shares available for grant under the long-term incentive plan.

Net earnings per share are based on the weighted average shares outstanding during the applicable periods. The potential dilution from the exercise of stock options is not material.

23 STATEMENTS OF CASH FLOWS

	1991	1990	1989
180 Interest paid, net of amounts capitalized	$101.3	$116.3	$ 88.9
181 Interest received	$ 27.9	$ 17.1	$ 35.5
182 Income taxes paid	$199.3	$152.8	$168.6
183 Capital lease obligations incurred	$ 10.0	$ 9.7	$ 18.0

184 24 QUARTERLY DATA (unaudited)

	1991			
	First	Second	Third	Fourth
Net sales	$1,594.3	$1,770.9	$1,490.8	$1,348.1
Cost of products sold	1,082.7	1,152.6	981.6	878.6
Net earnings	105.1	135.3	76.4	84.7
Per share				
Net earnings	.82	1.07	.60	.67
Dividends	.25	.29	.29	.29
Market price				
High	54.00	60.38	87.13	84.88
Low	43.75	48.50	58.75	72.38

	1990			
	First	Second	Third	Fourth
Net sales	$1,523.5	$1,722.5	$1,519.6	$1,440.2
Cost of products sold	1,057.2	1,173.0	1,049.3	978.7
Net earnings (loss)	83.0	105.2	54.6	(238.4)
Per share				
Net earnings (loss)	.64	.81	.42	(1.84)
Dividends	.23	.25	.25	.25
Market price				
High	58.50	59.63	54.13	62.00
Low	42.13	42.50	45.00	50.13

The fourth quarter of 1990 includes divestitures, restructuring and unusual charges of $301.6 after taxes, or $2.33 per share.

ELEVEN YEAR REVIEW—CONSOLIDATED

(millions except per share amounts)

Fiscal Year	1991	1990 (a)	1989 (b)
[185] **SUMMARY OF OPERATIONS**			
Net sales	$6,204.1	$6,205.8	$5,672.1
Earnings before taxes	667.4	179.4	106.5
Earnings before cumulative effect of accounting change	401.5	4.4	13.1
Net earnings	401.5	4.4	13.1
Percent of sales	6.5%	.1%	.2%
Return on average shareowners' equity	23.0%	.3%	.7%
FINANCIAL POSITION			
Working capital	$ 240.5	$ 367.4	$ 369.4
Plant assets—net	1,790.4	1,717.7	1,540.6
Total assets	4,149.0	4,115.6	3,932.1
Long-term debt	772.6	805.8	629.2
Shareowners' equity	1,793.4	1,691.8	1,778.3
PER SHARE DATA			
Earnings before cumulative effect of accounting change	$ 3.16	$ .03	$ .10
Net earnings	3.16	.03	.10
Dividends declared	1.12	.98	.90
Shareowners' equity	14.12	13.09	13.76
OTHER STATISTICS			
Salaries, wages, pensions, etc.	$1,401.0	$1,422.5	$1,333.9
Capital expenditures	371.1	397.3	302.0
Number of shareowners (in thousands)	37.7	43.0	43.7
Weighted average shares outstanding	127.0	129.6	129.3

(a) 1990 includes pre-tax divestiture and restructuring charges of $339.1 million; $301.6 million or $2.33 per share after taxes.
(b) 1989 includes pre-tax restructuring charges of $343.0 million; $260.8 million or $2.02 per share after taxes.
(c) 1988 includes pre-tax restructuring charges of $49.3 million; $29.4 million or 23 cents per share after taxes. 1988 also includes cumulative effect of change in accounting for income taxes of $32.5 million or 25 cents per share.
(d) Includes employees under the Employee Stock Ownership Plan terminated in 1987.

Campbell Soup Company

1988 (c)	1987	1986	1985	1984	1983	1982	1981
$4,868.9	$4,490.4	$4,286.8	$3,916.6	$3,636.9	$3,292.4	$2,955.6	$2,797.7
388.6	417.9	387.2	333.7	332.4	306.0	276.9	244.4
241.6	247.3	223.2	197.8	191.2	165.0	149.6	129.7
274.1	247.3	223.2	197.8	191.2	165.0	149.6	129.7
5.6%	5.5%	5.2%	5.1%	5.3%	5.0%	5.1%	4.6%
15.1%	15.1%	15.3%	15.0%	15.9%	15.0%	14.6%	13.2%
$ 499.6	$ 744.1	$ 708.7	$ 579.4	$ 541.5	$ 478.9	$ 434.6	$ 368.2
1,508.9	1,349.0	1,168.1	1,027.5	970.9	889.1	815.4	755.1
3,609.6	3,097.4	2,762.8	2,437.5	2,210.1	1,991.5	1,865.5	1,722.9
525.8	380.2	362.3	297.1	283.0	267.5	236.2	150.6
1,895.0	1,736.1	1,538.9	1,382.5	1,259.9	1,149.4	1,055.8	1,000.5
$ 1.87	$ 1.90	$ 1.72	$ 1.53	$ 1.48	$ 1.28	$ 1.16	$ 1.00
2.12	1.90	1.72	1.53	1.48	1.28	1.16	1.00
.81	.71	.65	.61	.57	.54	.53	.51
14.69	13.35	11.86	10.69	9.76	8.92	8.19	7.72
$1,222.9	$1,137.3	$1,061.0	$ 950.1	$ 889.5	$ 755.1	$ 700.9	$ 680.9
261.9	328.0	251.3	212.9	183.1	154.1	147.6	135.4
43.0	41.0	50.9(d)	49.5(d)	49.4(d)	40.1	39.7	41.6
129.4	129.9	129.5	129.1	129.0	129.0	129.0	129.6

186   **Form 10K**

Schedule V
CAMPBELL SOUP COMPANY AND CONSOLIDATED SUBSIDIARIES
Property, Plant, and Equipment at Cost
(million dollars)

	Land	Buildings	Machinery and equipment	Projects in progress	Total
Balance at July 31, 1988 ..	$53.2	$735.5	$1,624.4	$126.6	$2,539.7
Additions	2.8	47.6	216.4	35.2	302.0
Acquired assets*	4.8	13.6	22.6	—	41.0
Retirements and sales	(4.5)	(88.4)	(238.3)	—	(331.2)
Translation adjustments . .	(.5)	(2.5)	(5.9)	.4	(8.5)
Balance at July 30, 1989 ..	55.8	705.8	1,619.2	162.2	2,543.0
Additions	3.2	69.2	219.6	105.3	397.3
Acquired assets*	3.8	14.1	6.8	—	24.7
Retirements and sales	(2.8)	(64.0)	(222.9)	(1.1)	(290.8)
Translation adjustments . .	3.8	21.4	34.9	.6	60.7
Balance at July 29, 1990 ..	63.8	746.5	1,657.6	267.0	2,734.9
Additions	1.5	70.2	239.5	59.9	371.1
Acquired assets*	.5	3.3	.9	—	4.7
Retirements and sales	(7.5)	(49.3)	(99.9)	—	(156.7)
Rate variance	(2.0)	(12.0)	(18.8)	.7	(32.1)
Balance at July 28, 1991 ..	$56.3	$758.7	$1,779.3	$327.6	$2,921.9

*See "Acquisitions" in Notes to Consolidated Financial Statements.

187

Form 10K

Schedule VI
CAMPBELL SOUP COMPANY AND CONSOLIDATED SUBSIDIARIES
Accumulated Depreciation and Amortization of Property, Plant, and Equipment
(million dollars)

	Buildings	Machinery and Equipment	Total
Balance at July 31, 1988	$285.4	$745.4	$1,030.8
Additions charged to income	31.5	144.4	175.9
Retirements and sales	(57.8)	(143.5)	(201.3)
Translation adjustments	(.8)	(2.2)	(3.0)
Balance at July 30, 1989	258.3	744.1	1,002.4
Additions charged to income	34.2	149.9	184.1
Retirements and sales	(32.5)	(154.7)	(187.2)
Translation adjustments	5.2	12.7	17.9
Balance at July 29, 1990	265.2	752.0	1,017.2
Additions charged to income	35.3	159.2	194.5
Retirements and sales	(17.4)	(52.1)	(69.5)
Translation adjustments	(2.8)	(7.9)	(10.7)
Balance at July 28, 1991	$280.3	$851.2	$1,131.5

QUESTIONS

1. Compare the flow of the analyst's work in reconstructing business transactions to that of the accountant's work. How does such reconstruction of accounts contribute to the analysis of financial statements?
2. As a potential investor in a common stock, what information would you seek? How do you get such information?
3. The president of your client company approached you, the financial officer of a local bank, for a substantial loan. What could you do?
4. What, in broad categories, are some of the approaches utilized by the financial analyst in diagnosing the financial health of a business?
5. How useful is a comparative financial analysis? How do you make useful comparison?
6. What are some of the precautions required of a financial analyst in his comparative analytical work?
7. Give four broad categories of analysis tools.
8. Is the trend of the past a good predictor of the future? Give reasons for your argument.
9. Which is the better indicator of significant change—the absolute amount of change or the change in percentage? Why?

10. What conditions would prevent the computation of a valid percentage change? Give an example.
11. What are some of the criteria to be used in picking out a base year in an index number comparative analysis?
12. What information can be obtained from trend analysis?
13. What is a common-size financial statement? How do you prepare one?
14. What does a common-size financial statement tell about an enterprise?
15. Do all ratios have significance? Explain.
16. What are some of the limitations of ratio analysis?
17. Give five ratios that can be prepared by use of balance sheet figures only.
18. Give five ratios that can be prepared by use of income statement data only.
19. Give seven ratios that require data from both the balance sheet and the income statement.
20. Give four examples of special-purpose analytical tools commonly utilized by the financial analyst.
21. What are the steps generally taken by the financial analyst in his work? What do these steps achieve?
22. Identify and explain two significant limitations associated with ratio analysis of financial statements. (CFA)
23. A number of circumstances require the restatement of financial statements. Which are they?
24. What are some of the principal uses of computers in investment analysis? (CFA)
25. What are the most important limitations or disadvantages to the application of computers to security analysis? (CFA)

Chapter 3

ANALYSIS OF SHORT-TERM LIQUIDITY

SIGNIFICANCE OF SHORT-TERM LIQUIDITY

The short-term liquidity of an enterprise is measured by the degree to which it can meet its short-term obligations. Liquidity implies the ready ability to convert assets into cash or to obtain cash. The short term is conventionally viewed as a time span up to a year, although it is sometimes also identified with the normal operating cycle of a business, that is, the time span encompassing the buying-producing-selling and collecting cycle of an enterprise.

The importance of short-term liquidity can best be gauged by examining the repercussions that stem from a lack of ability to meet short-term obligations.

Liquidity is a matter of degree. A lack of liquidity may mean that the enterprise is unable to avail itself of favorable discounts and is unable to take advantage of profitable business opportunities as they arise. At this stage, a lack of liquidity implies a lack of freedom of choice as well as constraints on management's freedom of action.

A more serious lack of liquidity means that the enterprise is unable to pay its current debts and obligations. This can lead to the forced sale of long-term investments and assets and, in its most severe form, to insolvency and bankruptcy.

To the owners of an enterprise, a lack of liquidity can mean reduced profitability and opportunity or it may mean loss of control and partial or total loss of the capital investment. In the case of owners with unlimited liability, the loss can extend beyond the original investment.

To creditors of the enterprise, a lack of liquidity can mean delay in collection of interest and principal due them or it can mean the partial or total loss of the amounts due them.

Customers as well as suppliers of goods and services to an enterprise can also be affected by its short-term financial condition. Such effects may take the form of inability of the enterprise to perform under contracts and the loss of supplier relationships.

From the above description of the significance of short-term liquidity it can be readily appreciated why the measures of such liquidity have been accorded great importance. For, if an enterprise cannot meet its current obligations as they become due, its continued existence becomes doubtful and that relegates all other measures of performance to secondary importance if not to irrelevance. In terms of the framework of objectives discussed in Chapter 1, the evaluation of short-term liquidity is concerned with the assessment of the unsystematic risk of the enterprise.

While accounting determinations are made on the assumption of indefinite continuity of the enterprise, the financial analyst must always submit the validity of such assumption to the test of the enterprise's liquidity and solvency.

One widely used measure of liquidity is working capital. In addition to its importance as a pool of liquid assets that provides a safety cushion to creditors, net working capital is also important because it provides a liquid reserve with which to meet contingencies and the ever-present uncertainty regarding an enterprise's ability to balance the outflow of cash with an adequate inflow of cash.

WORKING CAPITAL

The basic concept of working capital is relatively simple. It is the excess of current assets over current liabilities. That excess is sometimes referred to as *net working capital* because some businessmen consider current assets as working capital. A working capital deficiency exists when current liabilities exceed current assets.

The importance attached by credit grantors, investors, and others to working capital as a measure of liquidity and solvency has caused some enterprises, desiring to present their current condition in the most favorable light, to stretch to the limit the definition of what constitutes a current asset and a current liability. For this reason, the analyst must use his or her own judgment in evaluating the proper classification of items included in working capital.

Current Assets

Current assets include cash and other assets that are reasonably expected to be realized in cash or sold or consumed during the normal operating cycle of the business or within one year if the operating cycle is shorter than one year. Current liabilities include those expected to be satisfied by either the use of assets classified as current in the same balance sheet or the creation of other current liabilities, or those expected to be satisfied within a relatively short period of time, usually one year. [APB *Statement 4*, par. 198.]

The general rule about the ability to convert current assets into cash within a year is subject to important qualifications. The most important qualification relates to the operating cycle. The operating cycle comprises the average time span intervening between the acquisition of materials and services entering the production or trading process to the final realization in cash of the proceeds from the sale of the enterprise's products. This time span can be quite extended in industries that require a long inventory holding period (e.g., tobacco, distillery, and lumber) or those that sell on the installment plan. Whenever no clearly defined operating cycle is evident, the arbitrary one-year rule prevails.

The most common categories of current assets are:

1. Cash.
2. Cash equivalents (i.e., temporary investments).
3. Accounts and notes receivable.
4. Inventories.
5. Prepaid expenses.

Cash is, of course, the ultimate measure of a current asset since current liabilities are paid off in cash. However, earmarked cash held for specific purposes, such as plant expansion, should not be considered as current. Compensating balances under bank loan agreements cannot, in most cases, be regarded as "free" cash, SEC *FRR* No. 1 Section 203 requires the disclosure of compensating balance arrangements with the lending banks as well as the segregation of such balances.

Cash equivalents represent temporary investments of cash in excess of current requirements made for the purpose of earning a return on these funds. These investments must be short-term and of the highest quality, thus ensuring that they can be sold without loss.

The analyst must be alert to the valuation of such investments. Equity investments are now accounted for in accordance with *SFAS 12*. Debt securities may still be carried above market if management views a decline as merely "temporary" in nature. Similarly, the "cash equivalent" nature of securities investments may sometimes be stretched quite far.

The mere ability to convert an asset to cash is not the sole determinant of its current nature. It is the intention and normal practice that governs. Intention is, however, not always enough. Thus, the cost of fixed assets that are intended for sale should be included in current assets only if the enterprise has a contractual commitment from a buyer to purchase the asset at a given price within the following year or the following operating cycle.

ILLUSTRATION 1. Champion International Corporation classified "Operations held for disposition" as current assets and explained as follows:

The company has entered into an agreement to sell three paperboard mills, its corrugated box manufacturing operations and all but one of its bag manufacturing operations to Stone Container Corporation ("Stone") for cash and Stone common stock. Upon consummation of the sale to Stone, the company expects to receive $372,900,000 in cash, subject to adjustment in certain circumstances. . . .

Attempts by managements to bend the rules of what constitutes a current asset reinforces the ever-recurring message in this text that the analyst cannot rely on adherence to rules or accepted principles of preparation of financial statements, but instead must exercise eternal vigilance in his or her use of ratios and all other analytical measures that are based on such statements. If anything, attempts by managements to stretch the rules in order to present a situation as better than it really is should serve as an added warning of potential trouble and risk.

Accounts receivable, net of provisions for uncollectible accounts, are current unless they represent receivables for sales, not in the ordinary course of business, which are due after one year. Installment receivables from customary sales usually fall within the operating cycle of the enterprise.

The analyst must be alert to the valuation as well as validity of receivables particularly in cases such as those where "sales" are made on consignment or subject to the right of return.

Receivables from affiliated companies or from officers and employees can be considered current only if they are collectible in the ordinary course of business within a year or, in the case of installment sales, within the operating cycle.

Inventories are considered current assets except in cases where they are in excess of current requirements. Such excess inventories, which should be shown as noncurrent, must be distinguished from inventories, such as tobacco, which require a long aging cycle. The variations in practice in this area are considerable and should be carefully scrutinized by the analyst.

ILLUSTRATION 2.   Some trucking concerns include the tires on their trucks as current assets, presumably on the theory that they will be used up during the normal operating cycle.

The analyst must pay particular attention to inventory valuation. Thus, for example, the inclusion of inventories at LIFO can result in a significant understatement of working capital.

Prepaid expenses are considered current, not because they can be converted into cash but rather because they represent advance payments for services and supplies that would otherwise require the current outlay of cash.

Current Liabilities

Current liabilities are obligations that would, generally, require the use of current assets for their discharge or, alternatively, the creation of other current liabilities. The following are current liabilities most commonly found in practice:

1. Accounts payable.
2. Notes payable.
3. Short-term bank and other loans.
4. Tax and other expense accruals.
5. Current portion of long-term debt.

The foregoing current liability categories are usually clear and do not require further elaboration. However, as is the case with current assets, the analyst cannot assume that they will always be properly classified. Thus, for example, current practice sanctions the presentation as non-current of current obligations that are expected to be refunded. The degree of assurance of the subsequent refunding is mostly an open question that in the case of adverse developments may well be resolved negatively as far as the enterprise is concerned.

SEC *FRR* No. 1 Section 203 has expanded significantly the disclosure requirements regarding short-term bank and commercial paper borrowing. *SFAS* 6 established criteria for the balance sheet classification of short-term obligations that are expected to be refinanced.

The analyst must also be alert to the possibility of presentations designed to present the working capital in a better light than warranted by circumstances.

ILLUSTRATION 3.   Penn Central Company excluded the current maturities of long-term debt from the current liability category and included it in the "long-term debt" section of the balance sheet. This treatment resulted in an excess of current assets over current liabilities of $21 million, whereas the inclusion of current debt maturities among current liabilities would have resulted in a working capital *deficit* of $207 million. (The subsequent financial collapse of this enterprise is a well-known event.)

The analyst must also ascertain whether all obligations, regarding which there is a reasonably high probability that they will have to be met, have been included as current liabilities in computing an effective working capital figure. Two examples of such obligations follow:

1. The obligation of an enterprise for notes discounted with a bank where the bank has full recourse in the event the note is not paid when due is generally considered a contingent liability. However, the likelihood of the contingency materializing must be considered in the computation of working capital. The same principle applies in case of loan guarantees.

2. A contract for the construction or acquisition of long-term assets may call for substantial progress payments. Such obligations for payments are, for accounting purposes, considered as commitments rather than liabilities, and hence are not found among the latter. Nevertheless, when computing the excess of liquid assets over short-term obligations such commitments may have to be recognized.

Other Problem Areas in the Definition of Current Assets and Liabilities

Current deferred tax debits are no more true current assets than current deferred tax credits are real current liabilities. While these are the result of present generally accepted methods of accounting for taxes, the resulting debits do not represent expected means of payment nor do the resulting credits necessarily represent obligations currently due.

Many concerns that have fixed assets as the main "working assets," such as, for example, trucking concerns and some leasing companies, carry as current prospective receipts from billings out of which their current equipment purchase obligations must be met. Such treatments, or the absence of any distinction between current and noncurrent on the balance sheet, as is the case with real estate companies, some contractors, banks, and insurance companies, are attempts by such concerns to convey to the reader their "special" financing and operating conditions that, they claim, make the current versus noncurrent distinction inapplicable and that have no parallel in the regular trading or industrial concern.

Some of these "special" circumstances may indeed be present, but they do not necessarily change the relationship existing between current obligations and the liquid funds available, or reasonably expected to become available, to meet them. It is to this relationship that the analyst, faced with the task of evaluating liquidity, must train his attention.

Working Capital as a Measure of Liquidity

The popularity of working capital as a measure of liquidity and of short-term financial health is so widespread that it hardly needs documentation. Credit grantors compute the relationship between current assets and current liabilities; financial analysts measure the size of the working capital of enterprises they analyze; government agencies compute aggregates of working capital of corporations; and most published balance sheets distinguish between current and noncurrent assets and liabilities. Moreover, loan agreements and bond indentures often contain stipulations regarding the maintenance of minimum working capital levels.

The absolute amount of working capital has significance only when related to other variables such as sales, total assets, and so forth. It is at best of limited value for comparison purposes and for judging the adequacy of working capital. This can be illustrated as follows:

	Company A	Company B
Current assets	$300,000	$1,200,000
Current liabilities ...	100,000	1,000,000
Working capital	$200,000	$ 200,000

While both companies have an equal amount of working capital, a cursory comparison of the relationship of current assets to current liabilities suggests that Company A's current condition is superior to that of Company B.

CURRENT RATIO

The above conclusion is based on the ratio of current assets to current liabilities. It is $3:1$ ($300,000/$100,000) for Company A and $1.2:1$ ($1,200,000/$1,000,000) for Company B. It is this ratio that is accorded substantial importance in the assessment of an enterprise's current liquidity.

Some of the basic reasons for the widespread use of the current ratio as a measure of liquidity are obvious:

1. It measures the degree to which current assets cover current liabilities. The higher the amount of current assets in relation to current liabilities, the greater the assurance that these liabilities can be paid out of such assets.
2. The excess of current assets over current liabilities provides a buffer against losses that may be incurred in the disposition or liquidation of the current assets other than cash. The more substantial such a buffer is, the better for creditors. Thus, the current ratio measures the margin of safety available to cover any possible shrinkage in the value of current assets.
3. It measures the reserve of liquid funds in excess of current obligations that is available as a margin of safety against uncertainty and the random shocks to which the flows of funds in an enterprise are subject. Random shocks, such as strikes, extraordinary losses, and other uncertainties, can temporarily and unexpectedly stop or reduce the inflow of funds.

What is not so obvious, however, is the fact that the current ratio, as a measure of liquidity and short-term solvency, is subject to serious theoretical as well as practical shortcomings and limitations. Consequently, before we embark on a discussion of the uses of the current ratio and related measures of liquidity, these limitations must be thoroughly understood.

Limitations of the Current Ratio

The first step in our examination of the current ratio as a tool of liquidity and short-term solvency analysis is to examine the components that are normally included in the ratio shown in Exhibit 3–1.

Disregarding, for purposes of this evaluation, prepaid expenses and similar unsubstantial items entering the computation of the current ratio, we are left with the above four major elements that comprise this ratio.

Now, if we define liquidity as the ability to balance required cash outflows with adequate inflows, including an allowance for unexpected interruptions of inflows or increases in outflows, we must ask: Does the relationship of these four elements at a given point in time—

1. Measure and predict the pattern of future cash flows?
2. Measure the adequacy of future cash inflows in relation to outflows?

Unfortunately, the answer to these questions is mostly negative. The current ratio is a static or "stock" concept of what cash resources are available at a given moment in time to meet the obligations at that moment. The existing reservoir of cash resources does not have a logical or causative relationship to the future cash that will flow through it. And yet it is the future flows that are the subject of our greatest interest in the assessment of liquidity. These flows depend importantly on elements *not* included in the ratio itself, such as sales, cash costs and expenses, profits, and changes in business conditions. To elaborate, let us examine more closely the four elements comprising the ratio.

Cash and cash equivalents   The amount of cash held by a well-managed enterprise is in the nature of a precautionary reserve, intended to take care of short-term imbalances in cash flows. For example, in cases of a business downturn, sales may fall more rapidly than outlays for purchases and expenses. Since cash is a nonearning asset and cash equivalents are usually low-yielding securities, the investment in such assets

Exhibit 3–1

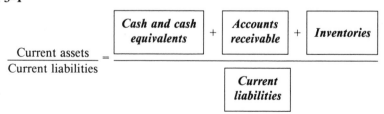

is kept at a safe minimum. To conceive of this minimum balance as available for payment of current debts would require the dropping of the going-concern assumption underlying accounting statements. While the balance of cash has some relation to the existing level of activity, such a relationship is not very strong nor does it contain predictive implications regarding the future. In fact, some enterprises may use cash substitutes in the form of open lines of credit that, of course, do not enter at all into the computation of the current ratio.

The important link between cash and solvency in the minds of many is due to the well-known fact that a shortage of cash, more than any other factor, is the element that can clinch the insolvency of an enterprise.

| *Accounts receivable* | The major determinant of the level of accounts receivable is sales. The size of accounts receivable in relation to sales |

is governed by terms of trade credit policy, and collection experience. Changes in receivables will correspond to changes in sales though not necessarily on a directly proportional basis.

When we look at accounts receivable as a source of cash, we must, except in the case of liquidation, recognize the revolving nature of the asset with the collection of one account replaced by the extension of fresh credit. Thus, the level of receivables per se is not an index to future net inflows of cash.

| *Inventories* | As is the case with accounts receivable, the main determinant of the size of inventories is the level of sales, or |

expected sales, rather than the level of current liabilities. Given that the level of sales is a measure of the level of demand then, scientific methods of inventory management (economic order quantities, safe stock levels, and reorder points) generally establish that inventory increments vary not in proportion to demand but vary rather with the *square root* of demand.

The relationship of inventories to sales is further accented by the fact that it is sales that is the one essential element that starts the conversion of inventories to cash. Moreover, the determination of future cash inflows through the sale of inventories is dependent on the profit margin that can be realized because inventories are generally stated at the lower of *cost* or market. The current ratio, while including inventories, gives no recognition to the sales level or to profit margin, both of which are important elements entering into the determination of future cash inflows.

| *Current liabilities* | The level of current liabilities, the probability of satisfaction of which the current ratio is intended to measure, is also |

largely determined by the level of sales.

Current liabilities are a source of cash in the same sense that receivables and inventories tie up cash. Since purchases, which give rise to accounts payable, are a function of the level of activity (i.e., sales), these payables vary with sales. As long as sales remain constant or are rising, the payment of current liabilities is essentially a refunding operation. Here again the components of the current ratio give little, if any, recognition to these elements and their effects on the future flow of cash. Nor do the current liabilities that enter into the computation of the current ratio include prospective outlays, such as commitments under construction contracts, loans, leases, or pensions, all of which affect the future outflow of funds.

Implications of Current Ratio Limitations

There are a number of conclusions that can be reached on the basis of the foregoing discussion:

1. Liquidity depends to some extent on cash or cash equivalents balances and to a much more significant extent on prospective cash flows.
2. There is no direct or established relationship between balances of working capital items and the pattern that future cash flows are likely to assume.
3. Managerial policies directed at optimizing the levels of receivables and inventories are oriented primarily toward efficient and profitable assets utilization and only secondarily at liquidity.[1]

Given these conclusions, which obviously limit the value of the current ratio as an index of liquidity, and given the static nature of this ratio and the fact that it is composed of items that affect liquidity in different ways, we may ask why this ratio enjoys such widespread use and in what way, if any, it can be used intelligently by the analyst.

The most probable reasons for the popularity of the current ratio are evidently the simplicity of its basic concept, the ease with which it can be computed, and the readiness with which data for it can be obtained. It may also derive its popularity from the credit grantor's, and especially the banker's, propensity to view credit situations as conditions of last resort. They may ask themselves: "What if there were a complete cessation of funds inflow? Would the current assets then be adequate to pay off the current liabilities?" The assumption of such extreme conditions is, of course, not always a useful way of measuring liquidity.

To what use can the intelligent analyst put the current ratio?

---

[1] The nature of the business is also a factor. In the case of many electric utilities, current liabilities exceed current assets because the prompt payment by utility customers enables the utilities to pay off their obligations on time. In other words, utility current assets get converted into cash faster than current obligations must be met. As an added example from another field, Fair Lanes, a bowling lanes operator, obviously does not sell on credit and thus has no receivables. It also carries no inventories of any consequence. As a result, it has during most of its 50-year existence operated with a working capital deficiency. With almost all of its current assets in cash, it has no problem meeting current obligations.

Let it first be said that the analyst who wishes to measure short-term liquidity and solvency will find cash flow projections and pro forma financial statements to be the more relevant and reliable tools to use. This involves obtaining information that is not readily available in published financial statements and it also involves the need for a great deal of estimation. This area of analysis will be discussed in the next chapter.

The Current Ratio as a Valid Tool of Analysis

Should the analyst want to use the current ratio as a static measure of the ability of current assets to satisfy the current liabilities, he or she will be employing a different concept of liquidity from the one discussed above. In this context, liquidity means the readiness and speed with which current assets can be converted to cash and the degree to which such conversion will result in shrinkage in the stated value of current assets.

It is not our purpose here to discredit the current ratio as a valid tool of analysis but rather to suggest that its legitimate area of application is far less wide than popularly believed.

Defenders of this, the oldest and best known of financial ratios, may say that they are aware of the multitude of limitations and inconsistencies of concept outlined above but that they will "allow" for them in the evaluation of the ratio. A careful examination of these limitations suggests that such process of "allowing" for such limitations is well nigh impossible.

The best and most valid way to use this ratio is to recognize its limitations and to restrict its use to the analytical job it can do, that is, measuring the ability of *present* current assets to discharge *existing* current liabilities and considering the excess, if any, as a liquid surplus available to meet imbalances in the flow of funds and other contingencies. This should be done with an awareness of the fact that the test envisages a situation of enterprise liquidation,[2] whereas in the normal, going-concern situation current assets are of a revolving nature (for example, the collected receivable is replaced with a newly created one) while the current liabilities are essentially of a refunding nature (the repayment of one is followed by the creation of another).

Given the analytical function of the current ratio, as outlined above, there are two basic elements that must be measured before the current ratio can form the basis for valid conclusions:

1. The quality of the current assets and the nature of the current liabilities that enter the determination of the ratio.

---

[2] The circumstances leading to bankruptcy or liquidation will have an effect on how much the amounts realized on asset dispositions will shrink. They will, for example, be likely to shrink more severely if the liquidation is caused by overall adverse industry conditions than if caused by specific difficulties such as poor management or inadequate capitalization.

2. The rate of turnover of these assets and liabilities, that is, the average time span needed to convert receivables and inventories into cash and the amount of time that can be taken for the payment of current liabilities.

To measure the above, a number of ratios and other tools have been devised, and these can enhance the use of the current ratio as an analytic tool.

Measures That Supplement the Current Ratio

The most liquid of current assets is, of course, cash, which is the standard of liquidity itself. A close second to cash is "temporary investments" that are usually highly marketable and relatively safe temporary repositories of cash. These are, in effect, considered as "cash equivalents" and usually earn a modest return.

Cash Ratios   The proportion that cash and cash equivalents constitute of the total current assets group is a measure of the degree of liquidity of this group of assets. It is measured by the cash ratio that is computed as follows:

$$\frac{\text{Cash} + \text{Cash equivalents}}{\text{Total current assets}}$$

Evaluation   The higher the ratio, the more liquid is the current asset group. This, in turn, means that with respect to this cash and cash equivalents component there is a minimal danger of loss in value in case of liquidation and that there is practically no waiting period for conversion of these assets into usable cash.

APB Opinion 18 generally requires the carrying of investments, representing an interest of 20 percent or higher, at underlying equity. This is, of course, neither cost nor, necessarily, market value. While such substantial positions in the securities of another company are not usually considered cash equivalents, *should* they nevertheless be so considered, their market value would be the most appropriate figure to use in the computation of liquidity ratios.

As to the availability of cash, the analyst should bear in mind possible restrictions that may exist with respect to the use of cash balances. An example is compensating balances that banks extending credit expect their customers to keep. While such balances can be used, the analyst must nevertheless assess the effect on a company's credit standing and credit availability, as well as on its banking connection, of a breach of the tacit agreement not to draw on the compensating cash balance.

Two additional factors bearing on the evaluation of cash ratios should be mentioned. One is that modern computerized cash management methods have led to more efficient uses of cash by corporations and this has led to lower need for cash for ordinary operations. The other is that open lines of credit and other standby credit arrangements are effective substitutes for cash balances and should be so considered.

An additional ratio that measures cash adequacy should be mentioned. The cash to current liabilities ratio is computed as follows:

$$\frac{\text{Cash + Cash equivalents}}{\text{Current liabilities}}$$

It measures how much cash is available to pay current obligations. This is a severe test that ignores the refunding nature of current assets and liabilities. It supplements the cash ratio discussed above in that it measures cash availability from a somewhat different point of view.

To view the cash ratio as a further extension of the acid-test ratio (see page 110) would, except in extreme cases, constitute a test of short-term liquidity too severe to be meaningful. Nevertheless, the importance of cash as the ultimate form of liquidity should never be underestimated. The record of business failures provides many examples of insolvent companies, possessing sizable noncash assets, current and noncurrent, and no cash to pay debts or to operate with.

Measures of Accounts Receivable Liquidity

In most enterprises that sell on credit, accounts and notes receivable are a significant part of working capital. In assessing the quality of working capital and of the current ratio, it is important to get some measure of the quality and the liquidity of the receivables.

Both the quality[3] and liquidity of accounts receivable are affected by their rate of turnover. By quality is meant the likelihood of collection without loss. An indicator of this likelihood is the degree to which receivables are within the terms of payment set by the enterprise. Experience has shown that the longer receivables remain outstanding beyond the date on which they are due, the lower is the probability of their collection in full. Turnover is an indicator of the age of the receivables, particularly when it is compared with an expected turnover rate that is determined by credit terms granted.

The measure of liquidity is concerned with the speed with which accounts receivable will, on average, be converted into cash. Here again turnover is among the best measures to use.

---

[3] The validity of the collection claim is also one aspect of quality. Thus, the analyst must be alert to problems that can arise from "sales" on consignment or those with right of return.

AVERAGE ACCOUNTS RECEIVABLE TURNOVER RATIO

The receivable turnover ratio is computed as follows:

$$\frac{\text{Net sales on credit}}{\text{Average accounts receivable}}$$

The quickest way for an external analyst to determine the average accounts receivable is to take the beginning receivables of the period, add the ending receivables, and divide the sum by two. The use of monthly or quarterly sales figures can lead to an even more accurate result. The more widely sales fluctuate, the more subject to distortion this ratio is, unless the receivables are properly averaged.

Notes receivable arising from normal sales should be included in the accounts receivable figure in computing the turnover ratio. Discounted notes receivable that are still outstanding should also be included in the accounts receivable total.

The sales figure used in computing the ratio should be that of credit sales only, because cash sales obviously do not generate receivables. Since published financial statements rarely disclose the division between cash and credit sales, the external analyst may have to compute the ratio under the assumption that cash sales are relatively insignificant. If they are not insignificant, then a degree of distortion may occur in the ratio. However, if the proportion of cash sales to total sales remains relatively constant, the year-to-year comparison of changes in the receivables turnover ratio may nevertheless be validly based.

The average receivables turnover figure indicates how many *times,* on average, the receivables revolve, that is, are generated and collected during the year.

For example, if sales are $1,200,000 and beginning receivables are $150,000 while year-end receivables are $250,000, then receivable turnover is computed as follows:

$$\frac{\$1,200,00}{(\$150,000 + \$250,000) \div 2} = \frac{\$1,200,000}{\$200,000} = 6 \text{ times}$$

While the turnover figure furnishes a sense of the speed of collections and is valuable for comparison purposes, it is not directly comparable to the terms of trade that the enterprise normally extends. Such comparison is best made by converting the turnover into days of sales tied up in receivables.

Collection Period for Accounts Receivable

This measure, also known as *days sales in accounts receivable,* measures the number of days it takes, on average, to collect accounts (and notes) receivable. The number of days can be obtained by dividing the average accounts receivable turnover ratio discussed above into 360, the approximate round number of days in the year. Thus,

$$\text{Collection period} = \frac{360}{\text{Average accounts receivable turnover}}$$

Using the figures of the preceding example, the collection period is:

$$\frac{360}{6} = 60 \text{ days}$$

An alternative computation is to first obtain the average daily sales and then divide the *ending gross* receivable balance by it.

$$\text{Accounts receivable} \div \frac{\text{Sales}}{360}$$

The result will differ from the foregoing computation because the average accounts receivable turnover figure uses *average* accounts receivable, while this computation uses *ending* accounts receivable only; it thus focuses specifically on the latest accounts receivable balances. Using the figures from our example, the computation is:

$$\text{Average daily sales} = \frac{\text{Sales}}{360} = \frac{\$1,200,000}{360} = \$3,333$$

$$\frac{\text{Accounts receivable}}{\text{Average daily sales}} = \frac{\$250,000}{\$3,333} = 75 \text{ days}$$

Note that if the collection period computation would have used ending receivables rather than *average* receivables turnover, the identical collection period, that is, 75, could have been obtained as follows:

$$\frac{\text{Sales}}{\text{Accounts receivable (ending)}} = \frac{\$1,200,000}{\$250,000} = 4.8 \text{ times}$$

$$\frac{360}{\text{Receivables turnover}} = \frac{360}{4.8} = 75 \text{ days}$$

The use of 360 days is arbitrary because while receivables are outstanding 360 days (used for computational convenience instead of 365), the sales days of the year usually number less than 300. However, consistent computation of the ratio will make for valid period-to-period comparisons.

Evaluation

Accounts receivable turnover rates or collection periods can be compared to industry averages (see Chapter 2) or to the credit terms granted by the enterprise.

When the collection period is compared with the terms of sale allowed by the enterprise, the degree to which customers are paying on time can be assessed. Thus, if the average terms of sale in the illustration used above are 40 days, then an average collection period of 75 days reflects either some or all of the following conditions:

1. A poor collection job.
2. Difficulty in obtaining prompt payment from customers in spite of diligent collection efforts.
3. Customers in financial difficulty.

The first conclusion calls for remedial managerial action, while the last two reflect particularly on both the quality and the liquidity of the accounts receivable.

An essential analytical first step is to determine whether the accounts receivable are representative of company sales activity. Significant receivables may, for example, be lodged in the captive finance company of the enterprise. In that case, the bad debt provision may also relate to receivables not on company books.

It is always possible that an *average* figure is not representative of the receivables population it represents. Thus, it is possible that the 75-day average collection period does not represent an across-the-board payment tardiness on the part of customers but is rather caused by the excessive delinquency of one or two substantial customers.

The best way to investigate further an excessive collection period is to *age* the accounts receivable in such a way that the distribution of each account by the number of days past due is clearly apparent. An aging schedule in a format such as given below will show whether the problem is widespread or concentrated:

Accounts receivable aging schedule

	Current	\ 0–30	31–60	61–90	Over 90
		Days past due			
	Current	*0–30*	*31–60*	*61–90*	*Over 90*
Accounts receivable					

The age distribution of the receivables will, of course, lead to better informed conclusions regarding the quality and the liquidity of the receivables as well as the kind of action that is necessary to remedy the situation. Another dimension of receivables classification is by quality ranges of credit agencies such as Dun & Bradstreet.

Notes receivable deserve the particular scrutiny of the analyst because while they are normally regarded as more negotiable than open accounts, they may be of poorer quality than regular receivables if they originated as an extension device for an unpaid account rather than at the inception of the original sale.

In assessing the quality of receivables, the analyst should remember that a significant conversion of receivables into cash, except for their use as collateral for borrowing, cannot be achieved without a cutback in sales volume. The sales policy aspect of the collection period evaluation must also be kept in mind. An enterprise may be willing to accept slow-paying customers who provide business that is, on an overall basis, profitable; that is, the profit on sales compensates for the extra use by the customer of the enterprise funds. This circumstance may modify the analyst's conclusions regarding the *quality* of the receivables but not those regarding their *liquidity*.

In addition to the consideration of profitability, an enterprise may extend more liberal credit in cases such as (1) the introduction of a new product, (2) a desire to make sales in order to utilize available excess capacity, or (3) special competitive conditions in the industry. Thus, the relationship between the level of receivables and that of sales and profits must always be borne in mind when evaluating the collection period. The trend of the collection period over time is always important in an assessment of the quality and the liquidity of the receivables.

Another trend that may be instructive to watch is that of the relationship between the provision for doubtful accounts and gross accounts receivable. The ratio is computed as follows:

$$\frac{\text{Provision for doubtful accounts}}{\text{Gross accounts receivable}}$$

An increase in this ratio over time may indicate management's conclusion that the collectibility of receivables has deteriorated. Conversely, a decrease of this ratio over time may lead to the opposite conclusion or may cause the analyst to reevaluate the adequacy of the provision for doubtful accounts.

Measures of accounts receivable turnover are, as we have seen in this section, important in the evaluation of liquidity. They are also important as measures of asset utilization, a subject that will be covered in Chapter 6.

MEASURES OF INVENTORY TURNOVER

Inventories represent in many cases a very substantial proportion of the current asset group. This is so for reasons that have little to do with an enterprise's objective of maintaining adequate levels of liquid funds. Reserves of liquid funds are seldom kept in the form of inventories. Inventories represent investments made for the purpose of obtaining a return. The return is derived from the expected profits that may result from sales. In most businesses, a certain level of inventory must be kept in order to generate an adequate level of sales. If the inventory level is inadequate, the sales volume will fall to below the level otherwise attainable. Excessive inventories, on the other hand, expose the enterprise to expenses such as storage costs, insurance, and taxes, as well as to risks of loss of value through obsolescence and physical deterioration. Moreover, excessive inventories tie up funds that can be used more profitably elsewhere.

Due to the risk involved in holding inventories as well as the fact that inventories are one step further removed from cash than receivables (they have to be sold before they are converted into receivables), inventories are normally considered the least liquid component of the current assets group. As is the case with most generalizations, this is not always true. Certain staple items, such as commodities, raw materials, and standard sizes of structural steel, enjoy broad and ready markets and can usually be sold with little effort, expense, or loss. On the other hand, fashion merchandise, specialized components, or perishable items can lose their value rapidly unless they are sold on a timely basis.

The evaluation of the current ratio, which includes inventories in its computation, must include a thorough evaluation of the quality as well as the liquidity of these assets. Here again, measures of turnover are the best overall tools available for this purpose.

Inventory Turnover Ratio

The inventory turnover ratio measures the average rate of speed with which inventories move through and out of the enterprise.

Computation   The computation of the average inventory turnover is as follows:

$$\frac{\text{Cost of goods sold}}{\text{Average inventory}}$$

Consistency of valuation requires that the cost of goods sold be used because, as is the case with inventories, it is stated principally at *cost*. Sales, on the other hand, normally include a profit. Although the cost of goods sold figure is now disclosed in most published income statements, the external analyst is still occasionally confronted with an unavailability of such a figure. In such a case, the sales figure must be substituted. While this results in a theoretically less valid turnover ratio, it can still be used for comparison and trend development purposes, especially if used consistently and when sharp changes in profit margins are not present.

The average inventory figure is most readily obtained as follows:

$$\frac{\text{Opening inventory} + \text{Closing inventory}}{2}$$

Further refinement in the averaging process can be achieved, where possible and necessary, by averaging quarterly or monthly inventory figures.

When an inventory turnover ratio is computed in order to evaluate the *level* of inventory at a certain date, such as the year-end inventory, the inventory figure in the denominator should be the figure as of that date rather than an average inventory figure.

Before a turnover ratio is computed, the analyst must carefully examine the composition of the inventory figure and make adjustments, such as those from LIFO to FIFO.

Days to Sell Inventory

Another measure of inventory turnover that is also useful in assessing purchasing policy is the required number of *days to sell inventory.* The computation that follows, that is,

$$\frac{360 \text{ days}}{\text{Average inventory turnover}}$$

measures the number of days it takes to sell the average inventory in a given year, and an alternative computation

$$\frac{\text{Ending inventory}}{\text{Cost of average day's sales}}$$

measures the number of days that are required to sell off the ending inventory, assuming the given rate of sales where the

$$\text{Cost of an average day's sales} = \frac{\text{Cost of goods sold}}{360}$$

Example of computations

Sales................	$1,800,000
Cost of goods sold	1,200,000
Beginning inventory	200,000
Ending inventory	400,000

$$\text{Inventory turnover} = \frac{\$1,200,000}{(\$200,000 + \$400,000) \div 2} = \frac{\$1,200,000}{\$300,000} = 4 \text{ times}$$

$$\text{Number of days to sell average inventory} = \frac{360}{4} = 90 \text{ days}$$

Alternatively, the computation based on ending inventory is as follows:

Step 1:

$$\frac{\text{Cost of goods sold}}{360} = \frac{\$1,200,000}{360} = \$3,333 \text{ (cost of average day's sales)}$$

Step 2:

$$\frac{\text{Ending inventory}}{\text{Cost of average day's sales}} = \frac{\$400,000}{\$3,333} = 120 \text{ days}$$

Interpretation of Inventory Turnover Ratios   The current ratio computation views its current asset components as sources of funds that can, as a means of last resort, be used to pay off the current liabilities. Viewed this way, the inventory turnover ratios give us a measure of the quality as well as of the liquidity of the inventory component of the current assets.

The quality of inventory is a measure of the enterprise's ability to use it and dispose of it without loss. When this is envisaged under conditions of forced liquidation, then recovery of cost is the objective. In the normal course of business, the inventory should, of course, be sold at a profit. Viewed from this point of view, the normal profit margin realized by the enterprise assumes importance because the funds that will be obtained, and that would theoretically be available for payment of current liabilities, will include the profit in addition to the recovery of cost. In both cases, costs of selling will reduce the net proceeds.

In practice, a going concern cannot use its investment in inventory for the payment of current liabilities because any drastic reduction in normal inventory levels will surely cut into the sales volume.

A rate of turnover that is slower than that experienced historically, or that is below that normal in the industry, would lead to the preliminary conclusion that it includes items that are slow moving because they are obsolete, in weak demand, or otherwise unsalable. Such conditions do, of course, cast doubt on the feasibility of recovering the cost of such items.

Further investigation may reveal that the slowdown in inventory turnover is due to a buildup of inventory in accordance with a future contractual commitment, in anticipation of a price rise, in anticipation of a strike or shortage, or for any number of other reasons that must be probed further.

The analyst should be aware of the "just-in-time" inventory management approach which aims to keep inventory levels as low as possible by carefully integrating the ordering, producing, selling, and distributing functions. The implementation of this approach will lead to increases in inventory turnover.

A better evaluation of inventory turnover can be obtained from the computation of separate turnover rates for the major components of inventory such as (1) raw materials, (2) work in process, and (3) finished goods. Departmental or divisional turnover rates can similarly lead to more useful conclusions regarding inventory quality. One should never lose sight of the fact that the total inventory turnover ratio is an aggregate of widely varying turnover rates of individual components.

The biggest problem facing the external analyst who tries to compute inventory turnover ratios by individual product components is obtaining the necessary detailed data. This data is, at present, rarely provided in published financial statements. It can, however, be obtained from companies willing to provide such information.

The turnover ratio is, of course, also a gauge of liquidity in that it conveys a measure of the speed with which inventory can be converted into cash. In this connection, a useful additional measure is the conversion period of inventories.

Conversion Period of Inventories   This computation adds the collection period of receivables to the days needed to sell inventories in order to arrive at the time interval needed to convert inventories into cash.

Using figures developed in our examples of the respective ratios above, we get:

	Days
Days to sell inventory	90
Days to collect receivables	60
Total conversion period of inventories	150

It would thus normally take 150 days to sell inventory on credit and to collect the receivables. This is a period identical to the *operating cycle* that we discussed earlier in this chapter.

The Effect of Alternative Methods of Inventory Management

In evaluating the inventory turnover ratio, the analyst must be alert to the influence that alternative accounting principles have on the determination of the ratio's components. The basic discussion on alternative accounting principles of inventory measurement is found in Chapter 5. It is obvious that the use of the LIFO method of inventory valuation may render both the turnover ratios as well as the current ratio practically meaningless. Information is usually found in published financial statements that enable the analyst to adjust the unrealistically low LIFO inventory valuation occurring in times of rising price levels so as to render it useful for inclusion in turnover ratio or the current ratio. Even if two companies employ LIFO cost methods for their inventory valuation computation of their ratios, using such inventory figures may nevertheless not be comparable because their respective LIFO inventory pools (bases) may have been acquired in years of significantly different price levels. The inventory figure enters the numerator of the current ratio and also the denominator because the inventory method utilized affects the income tax liability.

The analyst must also bear in mind that companies using the so-called natural year may have at their year-end an unrepresentatively low inventory level and that this may increase the turnover ratio to unrealistically high levels.

Prepaid Expenses

Prepaid expenses are expenditures made for benefits that are expected to be received in the future. Since most such benefits are receivable within a year or within an enterprise's operating cycle, they will conserve the outlay of current funds.

Usually, the amounts included in this category are relatively small compared to the size of the other current assets, and consequently no extensive discussion of their treatment is needed here. However, the analyst must be aware of the tendency of managements of enterprises with weak current positions to include in prepaid expenses deferred charges and other items of dubious liquidity. Such items must consequently be excluded from the computation of working capital and of the current ratio.

CURRENT LIABILITIES

In the computation of working capital and of the current ratio, current liabilities are important for two related reasons:

1. A basic objective of measuring the excess of current assets over current liabilities is to determine whether the latter are covered by current assets and what margin of safety is provided by the excess of such assets over current liabilities.
2. Current liabilities are deducted from current assets in arriving at the net working capital position.

In the computation of the current ratio, the point of view adopted toward current liabilities is *not* one of a continuing enterprise but rather of an enterprise in liquidation. This is so because in the normal course of operations, current liabilities are not paid off but are rather of a refunding nature. As long as the sales volume remains stable, purchases will also remain at a stable level, and that in turn will cause current liabilities to remain level. Increasing sales, in turn, will generally result in an increasing level of current liabilities. Thus, generally the trend and direction of sales is a good indication of the future level of current liabilities.

In assessing the quality of the current ratio, the nature of the current liabilities must be carefully examined.

Differences in the "Nature" of Current Liabilities

Not all liabilities represent equally urgent and forceful calls for payment. At one extreme we find liabilities for taxes of all kinds that must be paid promptly regardless of current financial difficulties. The powers of collection of federal and local government authorities are as well known as they are powerful.

On the other hand, current liabilities to suppliers with whom the enterprise has a long-standing relationship and who depend on, and value, the enterprise's business are of a very different degree of urgency. Postponement and renegotiation of such debts in times of financial stringency are both possible and common.

The "nature" of current liabilities in terms of our present discussion must be judged in the light of the degree of urgency of payment that attaches to them. It should be understood that if fund inflows from current revenues are viewed as sources of funds available for the payment of current liabilities, then labor costs and other current fund-requiring costs and expenses have a first call on sales revenues and that trade bills and other liabilities can be paid only after such recurring outlays have been met. This dynamic aspect of funds flow will be examined more closely in the chapter that follows.

The analyst must also be aware of unrecorded liabilities that may have a claim to current funds. Examples of these are purchase commitments and obligations under pensions and leases. Moreover, under long-term loan acceleration clauses, a failure to meet current installments of long-term debt may render the entire debt due and payable, that is, cause it to become current.

Days Purchases in Accounts Payable Ratio

A measure of the degree to which accounts payable represent current rather than overdue obligations can be obtained by calculating the *days purchases in accounts payable ratio.* This ratio is computed as follows:

$$\frac{\text{Accounts payable}}{\text{Purchases per day*}} = \text{Days purchases in accounts payable}$$

* Computed: Purchases/360.

The difficulty that the external analyst will encounter in computing this ratio is that normally purchases are not separately disclosed in published financial statements. For retailers a rough approximation of the amount of purchases can be obtained by adjusting the cost of goods sold figure for depreciation and other noncash-requiring charges as well as for changes in inventories. Thus:

$$\text{Purchases} = \frac{\text{Adjusted cost}}{\text{of goods sold}} + \frac{\text{Ending}}{\text{inventory}} - \frac{\text{Beginning}}{\text{inventory}}$$

The cost of goods sold figure may, however, contain significant cash charges, and this may reduce the validity of a computation that contains an approximation of purchases on credit.

INTERPRETATION OF THE CURRENT RATIO

In the foregoing sections, we have examined the means by which the quality and the liquidity of the individual components of the current ratio is measured. This evaluation is, of course, essential to an overall interpretation of the current ratio as an indicator of short-term liquidity and financial strength.

The analyst must, however, exercise great care if he wants to carry the interpretation of the current ratio beyond the conclusion that it represents an excess of current resources over current obligations as of a given point in time.

Examination of Trend

An examination of the trend of the current ratio over time can be very instructive. Two tools of analysis that were discussed in Chapter 4 are useful here. One is *trend analysis,* where the components of working capital as well as the current ratio would be converted into an index to be compared over time. The other is *common-size analysis,* by means of which the *composition* of the current asset group is examined over time. A historical trend and common-size comparison over time, as well as an intra-industry comparison of such trends, can also be instructive.

Interpretation of Changes over Time

Changes in the current ratio over time must, however, be interpreted with great care. They do not automatically imply changes in liquidity or operating results. Thus, for example, in a prosperous year an increased liability for taxes may result in a lowering of the current ratio. Conversely, during a business contraction, current liabilities may be paid off while there may be a concurrent involuntary accumulation of inventories and uncollected receivables causing the ratio to rise.

In times of business expansion, which may reflect operating successes, the enterprise may suffer from an expansion in working capital requirements, otherwise known as a prosperity squeeze with a resulting contraction of the current ratio.

As can be seen from this example, a doubling of current assets, accompanied by a quadrupling of current liabilities and an unchanged amount of working capital will lead to a halving of the current ratio. This is the effect of business expansion unaccompanied by an added capital investment.

	Year 1	Year 2
Current assets	$300,000	$600,000
Current liabilities ...	100,000	400,000
Working capital	$200,000	$200,000
Current ratio	3 : 1	1.5 : 1

Inflation can have a similar effect on a business enterprise in that it will lead to a substantial increase in all current items categories.

Possibilities of Manipulation

The analyst must be aware of the possibilities of year-end manipulation of the current ratio, otherwise known as window dressing.

For example, toward the close of the fiscal year, the collection of receivables may be pressed more vigorously, advances to officers may be called in for temporary repayment, inventory may be reduced to below normal levels, and normal purchases may be delayed. Proceeds from these steps can then be used to pay off current liabilities. The effect on the current ratio of the reduction of current liabilities through the use of current assets can be seen in the following example:

	Payoff of $50,000 in liabilities	
	Before	After
Current assets	$200,000	$150,000
Current liabilities ...	100,000	50,000
Current ratio	2 : 1	3 : 1

The accounting profession, sensing the propensity of managements to offset liabilities against assets, has strengthened its prohibitions against offsets by restricting them strictly to situations where the legal right to offset exists.

To the extent possible, the analyst should go beyond year-end measures and should try to obtain as many interim readings of the current ratio as possible, not only to guard against the practice of window dressing described above but also to gauge the seasonal changes to which the ratio is exposed. The effect of a strong current ratio in December on an assessment of current financial condition may be considerably tempered if it is discovered that at its seasonal peak in July the enterprise is dangerously close to a serious credit squeeze.

The Use of "Rules of Thumb" Standards

A popular belief that has gained considerable currency is that the current ratio can be evaluated by means of *rules of thumb*. Thus, it is believed that if the current ratio is 2 : 1 (or 200 percent), it is sound and anything below that norm is bad while the higher above that figure the current ratio is, the better.

This rule of thumb may reflect the lender's, and particularly the banker's, conservatism. The fact that it is down from the norm of 2.5 : 1 prevailing at the turn of the century may mean that improved financial reporting has reduced this size of the "cushion" that the banker and other creditors would consider as the minimum protection they need.

What the 2 : 1 standard means is that there are $2 of current assets available for each dollar of current liabilities or that the value of current assets can, on liquidation, shrink by 50 percent before it will be inadequate to cover the current liabilities. Of course, a current ratio much higher than 2 : 1, while implying a superior coverage of current liabilities, may also mean a wasteful accumulation of liquid resources which do not "carry their weight" by earning an appropriate return for the enterprise.

It should be evident by now that the evaluation of the current ratio in terms of rules of thumb is a technique of dubious validity. This is so for two major reasons:

1. As we have learned in the preceding sections, the quality of the current assets, as well as the composition of the current liabilities that make up this ratio, are the most important determinants in an evaluation of the quality of the current ratio. Thus, two companies that have identical current ratios may nevertheless be in quite different current financial condition due to variations in the quality of the working capital components.
2. The need of an enterprise for working capital varies with industry conditions as well as with the length of its own particular *net trade cycle.*

The Net Trade Cycle

An enterprise's need for working capital depends importantly on the relative size of its required inventory investment as well as on the relationship between the credit terms it receives from its suppliers as against those it must extend to its customers. These relationships, known as the trade cycle, are exemplified in Illustration 4 below:

ILLUSTRATION 4.   Assume a company shows the following data at the end of year 1:

Sales of year 1	$360,000
Receivables	40,000
Inventories*	50,000
Accounts payable†	20,000
Cost of goods sold (including depreciation of $30,000)	320,000

    * Beginning inventory was $100,000.
    † In this example we assume that these relate to only purchases included in cost of goods sold.

To find purchases per day:

Ending inventory	50,000
Cost of goods sold	320,000
	370,000
Less: Beginning inventory	(100,000)
Cost of goods purchased and manufactured	270,000
Less: Depreciation expense included in cost of goods sold	(30,000)
Purchases...........................	240,000

Purchases per day = 240,000 ÷ 360 = $666.67

Net trade cycle:

Number of days in:

$$\text{Accounts receivable} = \frac{40,000}{360,000 \div 360} = 40.00 \text{ days}$$

$$\text{Inventories} = \frac{50,000}{320,000 \div 360} = \underline{56.24} \text{ days}$$

$$96.24$$

$$\text{Less: Accounts payable} = \frac{20,000}{666.67} = \underline{30.00} \text{ days}$$

Net trade cycle (days)   66.24

Please note that in the above computations the numerator and denominator are stated on a consistent basis. Thus accounts receivable, which are expressed in terms of sales prices, are divided by sales per day. Inventories, which are stated at cost, are divided by cost of goods sold per day. Accounts payable are divided by purchases per day.

The company has 40 days of sales tied up in receivables. It keeps 56.24 days of goods sold in inventory. On the other hand, it receives only 30 days of purchases as credit from its suppliers. Thus, while the day measures are expressed on different bases, the approximation of the net trade cycle is computed on a consistent basis. The higher the net trade cycle the larger the investment in working capital required. A reduction in the number of days sales in receivables or cost of sales in inventories will lower working capital requirements. An increase in the days of purchases credit received from suppliers will have a similar effect.

The working capital requirements of a supermarket with its high inventory turnover and low outstanding receivables are obviously lower than those of a tobacco company with its slow inventory turnover.

Valid Working Capital Standards

Comparison with industry current ratios, as well as analyses of working capital requirements such as the net trade cycle analysis described above, can lead to far more valid conclusions regarding the adequacy of an enterprise's working capital than can a mechanical comparison of its current ratio to the 2 : 1 rule of thumb standard.

The amount of working capital needed by an enterprise is importantly determined by industry conditions and practices. In recent years, the average industrial company needed about 15 cents of working capital for every dollar of sales. But averages can be misleading, and therefore it is best to focus on specific industry conditions and standards as cases for comparison.

The Importance of Sales

In an assessment of the overall liquidity of current assets, the trend of sales is an important factor. Since it takes sales to convert inventory into receivables or cash, an uptrend in sales indicates that the conversion of inventories into more liquid assets will be easier to achieve than when sales remain constant. Declining sales, on the other hand, will retard the conversion of inventories into cash.

Common-Size Analysis of Current Assets Composition

The composition of the current asset group, which can be analyzed by means of common-size statements, is another good indicator of relative working capital liquidity.

Consider, for example, the following comparative working capital composition:

	Year 1		Year 2	
Current assets:				
Cash....................	$ 30,000	30%	$ 20,000	20%
Accounts receivable	40,000	40	30,000	30
Inventories	30,000	30	50,000	50
Total current assets	$100,000	100%	$100,000	100%

The simple illustration above shows, even without the computation of common-size percentages, that the liquidity of the current asset group has deteriorated in year 2 by comparison with year 1. However, the use of common-size percentage comparisons will greatly facilitate the evaluation of comparative liquidity, regardless of the size of the dollar amounts involved.

The Liquidity Index

The measurement of the comparative liquidity of current assets can be further refined through the use of a *liquidity index*. The construction of this index (first suggested by A. H. Finney) can be illustrated as follows:

Using the working capital figures from the common-size computation above, and assuming that the conversion of inventories into accounts receivable takes 50 days on average and that the conversion of receivables into cash takes an average of 40 days, the index is computed as follows:

Year 1

	Amount	×	Days removed from cash	=	Product dollar-days
Cash	$ 30,000		—		—
Accounts receivable	40,000		40		1,600,000
Inventories	30,000		90		2,700,000
Total	$100,000 *(a)*				4,300,000 *(b)*

$$\text{Liquidity index} = \frac{b}{a} = \frac{4,300,000}{\$100,000} = 43$$

Year 2

	Amount	× Days removed from cash	= Product dollar-days
Cash	$ 20,000	—	—
Accounts receivable	30,000	40	1,200,000
Inventories	50,000	90	4,500,000
Total	$100,000		5,700,000

$$\text{Liquidity index} = \frac{5,700,000}{\$100,000} = \underline{57}$$

The computation of the respective liquidity indexes for the years 1 and 2 tells what we already knew instinctively in the case of this simple example, that is, that the liquidity has deteriorated in year 2 as compared to year 1.

The liquidity index must be interpreted with care. The index is in itself a figure without significance. It gains its significance only from a comparison between one index number and another as a gauge of the period-to-period change in liquidity or as a company-to-company comparison of relative liquidity. Increases in the index signify a deterioration in liquidity while decreases signify changes in the direction of improved liquidity. The index that is expressed in days is a weighing mechanism and its validity depends on the validity of the assumptions implicit in the weighing process.

An additional popular technique of current ratio interpretation is to submit it to a somewhat sterner test.

ACID-TEST RATIO

This test is the acid-test ratio, also known as the *quick ratio* because it is assumed to include the assets most quickly convertible into cash.

The acid-test ratio is computed as shown in Exhibit 3–2.

The omission of inventories from the acid-test ratio is based on the belief that they are the least liquid component of the current asset group.

Exhibit 3–2

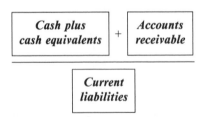

While this is generally so, we have seen in an earlier discussion in this chapter that this is not always true and that certain types of inventory can be more liquid than are slow-paying receivables. Another reason for the exclusion of inventories is the belief, quite often warranted, that the valuation of inventories normally requires a greater degree of judgment than is required for the valuation of the other current assets.

Since prepaid expenses are usually insignificant in relation to the other current assets, the acid-test ratio is sometimes computed simply by omitting the inventories from the current asset figure.

The interpretation of the acid-test ratio is subject to most of the same considerations which were discussed regarding the interpretation of the current ratio. Moreover, the acid-test ratio represents an even sterner test of an enterprise's liquidity than does the current ratio, and the analyst must judge what significance the omission of inventories has on the evaluation of liquidity.

OTHER MEASURES OF SHORT-TERM LIQUIDITY

The static nature of the current ratio that measures the relationship of current assets to current liabilities, at a given moment in time, as well as the fact that this measure of liquidity fails to accord recognition to the great importance that cash flows play in an enterprise's ability to meet its maturing obligations, has led to a search for more dynamic measures of liquidity.

Cash Flow Related Measures

Since liabilities are paid with cash, the relationship of cash provided by operations to current liabilities is significant.

The ratio of operating cash flow to current liabilities overcomes the weakness of the static current ratio in that its numerator represents a flow over time. Since operating cash flow encompasses a year it is appropriate for the current liabilities in the denominator to be the average for the period.

The ratio is computed:

$$\frac{\text{Cash flow from operations}}{\text{Average current liabilities}}$$

The computation for Campbell Soup for 1991 is as follows:

$$\frac{805.2 \;\boxed{64}}{(1,278 + 1298.1) \div 2 \;\boxed{45}} = 0.62$$

An empirical study[4] determined that a ratio of operating cash flow to current liabilities of 0.40 was common for healthy firms.

---

[4] C. Casey and N. Bartzcak, "Cash Flow—It's Not the Bottom Line," *Harvard Business Review,* July–August 1984, pp. 61–66.

THE CONCEPT OF FINANCIAL FLEXIBILITY

In addition to the tools of analysis of short-term liquidity with which we have dealt here and which lend themselves to quantification, there are important qualitative considerations that also have an important bearing on the short-term liquidity of an enterprise. These can be usefully characterized as depending on the financial flexibility of an enterprise.

Financial flexibility is characterized by the ability of an enterprise to take steps to counter unexpected interruptions in the flow of funds for reasons however unexpected. It means the ability to borrow from a variety of sources, to raise equity capital, to sell and redeploy assets, and to adjust the level and the direction of operations in order to meet changing circumstances.

The capacity to borrow depends on numerous factors and is subject to rapid change. It depends on profitability, stability, relative size, industry position, asset composition, and capital structure. It depends, moreover, on such external factors as credit market conditions and trends.

The capacity to borrow is important as a source of cash in time of need for cash and is also important when an enterprise must roll over its short-term debt. Prearranged financing or open lines of credit are more reliable sources of cash in time of need than is potential financing.

Other factors that bear on the assessment of the financial flexibility of an enterprise are the ratings of its commercial paper, bonds, and preferred stock; restrictions on the sale of its assets; the degree to which expenses are of a discretionary nature as well as the ability to respond quickly to changing conditions such as strikes, shrinking demand, or the cessation of sources of supply.

Financial flexibility is also important in the assessment of long-term solvency (see Chapter 5).

MANAGEMENT'S DISCUSSION AND ANALYSIS (MD&A)

Within the framework of its Integrated Disclosure System, the SEC requires an expanded management discussion and analysis of Financial Condition and Results of Operations. The "Financial Condition" section requires a discussion of liquidity factors—including known trends, demands, commitments, or uncertainties likely to have a material impact on the enterprise's ability to generate adequate amounts of cash. If a material deficiency in liquidity is identified, management must discuss the course of action it has taken or proposes to take in order to remedy the deficiency. In addition, internal and external sources of liquidity as well as any material unused sources of liquid assets must be identified and described.

Campbell Soup Company (Chapter 2, Appendix B) presents a "Liquidity and Capital Resources" section as part of its MD&A (see item 10).

Quaker Oats (Appendix to Chapter 10) presents its "Liquidity and Capital Resources MD&A discussion in item 142

Financial analysts should benefit significantly from a careful reading and evaluation of such required management discussion and analysis (see also Chapter 7).

Projecting Changes in Conditions or Policies

It is possible and often very useful to trace through the effects of changes in conditions and/or policies on the cash resources of an enterprise.

ILLUSTRATION 5.   Assume that the Prudent Company has the following account balances at December 31, Year 1:

	Debit	*Credit*
Cash	$ 70,000	
Accounts receivable	150,000	
Inventory	65,000	
Accounts payable		$130,000
Notes payable		35,000
Accrued taxes		18,000
Fixed assets	200,000	
Accumulated depreciation		43,000
Capital stock		200,000

The following additional information is available for Year 1:

Sales	$750,000
Cost of sales	520,000
Purchases	350,000
Depreciation	25,000
Net income	20,000

The company anticipates a growth of 10 percent in sales for the coming year. All corresponding revenue and expense items are also expected to increase by 10 percent, except for depreciation which will remain the same. All expenses are paid in cash as they are incurred during the year. The year 2 ending inventory will be $150,000. By the end of year 2, the company expects to have a notes payable balance of $50,000 and no balance in the accrued taxes account. The company maintains a minimum cash balance of $50,000 as a managerial policy.

I. Assume that the company is considering a change in credit policy so that the ending accounts receivable balance will represent 90 days of sales. What impact will this change have on the company's cash balance? Will it have to borrow?

This can be computed as follows:

Cash, January 1, Year 2		$ 70,000
Cash collections:		
Accounts receivable, January 1, Year 2	$150,000	
Sales	825,000	
	975,000	
Less: Accounts receivable, December 31, Year 2	206,250[a]	768,750
Total cash available		838,750
Cash disbursements:		
Accounts payable, January 1, Year 2	$130,000	
Purchases	657,000[b]	
	787,000	
Accounts payable, December 31, Year 2	244,000[c]	543,000
Notes payable, January 1, Year 2	35,000	
Notes payable, December 31, Year 2	50,000	(15,000)
Accrued taxes		18,000
Cash expenses[d]		203,500	749,500
		89,250
Cash balance desired		50,000
Cash excess		$ 39,250

Explanation:

[a] $\$825,000 \times \dfrac{90}{360} = \$206,250.$

[b] Year 2 cost of sales*: $\$520,000 \times 1.1 = \$572,000$

Ending inventory (given)	150,000
Goods available for sale	722,000
Beginning inventory	65,000
Purchases	$657,000

* which excludes depreciation.

[c] $\text{Purchases} \times \dfrac{\text{Old accounts payable}}{\text{Old purchases}} = \$657,000 \times \dfrac{\$130,000}{\$350,000}$

$= \$244,000$

[d] Gross profit ($\$825,000 - \$572,000$)....

		$253,000
Less: Net income	$24,500*	
Depreciation	25,000	49,500
Other cash expenses		$203,500

* 110 percent of $20,000 (Year 1 N.I.) + 10 percent of $25,000 (Year 1 depreciation).

II. What would the effect be if the change, instead of as in I, is to an *average* accounts receivable turnover of 4?

We compute this as follows:

Excess cash balance as computed above $39,250

Change from an *ending* to an *average* accounts receivable turnover will increase year-end accounts receivable balance to:

$$\frac{\$825,000}{4} = \$206,250 \times 2$$

$$= \$412,500 - \$150,000 = .. \$262,500^{(e)}$$

Less: Accounts receivable balance as above (I) 206,250   (cash
56,250 decrease)

Cash required to borrow $17,000

$(e) \dfrac{\text{Sales}}{\text{Average A/R turnover}} = \text{Average A/R};$

Ending A/R = [(Average A/R) × 2] − Beginning A/R

III. Assuming that in addition to the conditions prevailing in II above, suppliers require the company to pay within 60 days. What would be the effect on the cash balance?

The computation is as follows:

Cash required to borrow (from II above) .... $ 17,000

Ending accounts payable (I above) $244,000

Ending accounts payable under 60-day payment

$$= \text{Purchases} \times \frac{60}{360} = \$657,000 \times \frac{60}{360} = ... \quad 109,500$$

Additional disbursements required   134,500

Cash to be borrowed $151,500

QUESTIONS

1. Why is short-term liquidity so significant? Explain from the viewpoint of various parties concerned.
2. The concept of working capital is simple, that is, the excess of current assets over current liabilities. What are some of the factors that make this simple computation complicated in practice?
3. What are cash equivalents? How should an analyst value them in his or her analysis?
4. Can fixed assets be included in current assets? If so, explain the situation under which the inclusion may be allowed.
5. Some installment receivables are not collectible within one year. Why are they included in current assets?

6. Are all inventories included in current assets? Why or why not?

7. What is the theoretical justification for including prepaid expenses in current assets?

8. The company under analysis has a very small amount of current liabilities, but the long-term liabilities section shows a significant balance. In the footnote to the audited statements, it is disclosed that the company has a "revolving loan agreement" with a local bank. Does this disclosure have any significance to you?

9. Some industries are subject to peculiar financing and operating conditions that call for special consideration in drawing the distinction between what is *current* and what is *noncurrent*. How should the analyst recognize this in his evaluation of working capital?

10. Your careful computation of the working capitals of Companies A and B reveals that both have the same amount of working capital. Are you ready to conclude that the liquidity position of both is the same?

11. What is the current ratio? What does it measure? What are the reasons for its widespread use?

12. The holding of cash generally does not yield a return. Why does an enterprise hold cash at all?

13. Is there a relationship between the level of inventories and that of sales? Are inventories a function of sales? If there is a functional relationship between the two, is it proportional?

14. What are the major objectives of management in determining the size of inventory and receivables investment?

15. What are the theoretical limitations of the current ratio as a measure of liquidity?

16. If there are significant limitations attached to the current ratio as a measure of liquidity, what is the proper use of this tool?

17. What are cash ratios? What do they measure?

18. How do we measure the "quality" of various current assets?

19. What does the average accounts receivable turnover measure?

20. What is the collection period for accounts receivable? What does it measure?

21. A company's collection period is 60 days this year as compared to 40 days last year. Give three or more possible reasons for this change.

22. What is an accounts receivable aging schedule? What is its use in the analysis of financial statements?

23. What are the repercussions to an enterprise of *(a)* overinvestment or *(b)* underinvestment in inventories?

24. What problems would you expect to encounter in an analysis of a company using the LIFO inventory method in an inflationary economy? What effects do the price changes have *(a)* on the inventory turnover ratio and *(b)* on the current ratio?

25. Why does the "nature" of the current liabilities have to be analyzed in assessing the quality of the current ratio?

26. An apparently successful company shows a poor current ratio. Explain the possible reasons for this.

27. What is *window dressing?* Is there any way to find out whether the financial statements are window dressed or not?

28. What is the rule of thumb governing the expected size of the current ratio? What dangers are there in using this rule of thumb mechanically?
29. Describe the importance which the sales level plays in the overall current financial condition and liquidity of the current assets of an enterprise.
30. What is the liquidity index? What significance do the liquidity index numbers have?
31. What do cash flow ratios attempt to measure?
32. In addition to the tools of analysis of short-term liquidity that lend themselves to quantification, there are important qualitative considerations that also have an important bearing on the short-term liquidity of an enterprise. What are such considerations? And what are the SEC disclosure requirements that would help financial analysts in this regard?
33. What is the importance of projecting the effects of changes in conditions or policies on the cash resources of an enterprise?

Chapter 4

FUNDS FLOW ANALYSIS AND FINANCIAL FORECASTS

The preceding chapter examined the various measures that are derived from past financial statement data and that are useful in the assessment of short-term liquidity. The chapter that follows will focus on the use of similar data in an evaluation of longer-term solvency. The limitations to which these approaches are subject are due mainly to their static nature, that is, to their reliance on status reports, as of a given moment, of claims against an enterprise and the resources available to meet these claims.

An important and, in many cases, superior alternative to such static measures of conditions prevailing at a given point in time is the analysis and projection of more dynamic models of cash flows. Such models use the present only as a starting point, and while building on reliable patterns of past experience, utilize the best available estimates of future plans and conditions in order to forecast the future availability and disposition of cash.

The forecasting process is a difficult one and analysts must be aware of this. As Mark Twain once said: "The art of prophesy is very difficult, especially with respect to the future."

OVERVIEW OF CASH FLOW PATTERNS

Before we examine the methods by means of which cash flow projections are made, it would be useful to get a thorough understanding of the nature of cash flow. Exhibit 4–1 presents a diagram of the flow of cash through an enterprise.

The flow diagram focuses on cash. Cash (including cash equivalents) is the ultimate liquid asset. Almost all decisions to invest in assets or to incur costs require the immediate or eventual use of cash. This is why managements focus, from an operational point of view, on *cash* rather than on other concepts of liquid funds, such as working capital. The focus on the latter represents mainly the point of view of creditors who consider as part of the liquid assets pool other assets, such as receivables and

Exhibit 4–1 Flow of cash through an enterprise

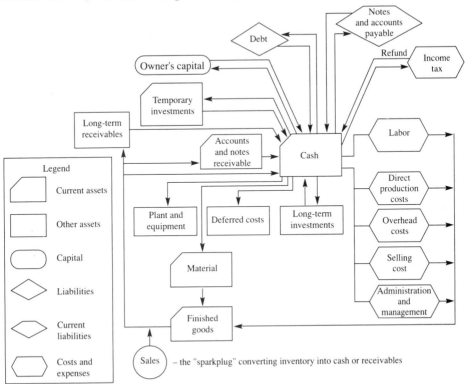

inventories, which are normally converted into cash within a relatively short time span.

Careful examination of the flows depicted in Exhibit 4–1 should contribute greatly to the reader's understanding of the importance of cash in an enterprise as well as the factors which cause it to be converted into assets and costs. The following factors and relationships are worthy of particular note:

Since the diagram focuses on cash flows only, assets, liabilities, and other items that are not directly involved, such as prepayments and accruals, as well as the income account, are not included in it. Some flows are presented in simplified fashion for an easier understanding of relationships. For example, accounts payable are presented as direct sources of cash, whereas in reality they represent a temporary postponement of cash payment for the acquisition of goods and services.

It is recognized that the holding of cash provides no return or a very low return and that in times of rising price levels, cash as a monetary asset is exposed to purchasing power loss. However, these

considerations aside, the holding of this most liquid of assets represents, in a business sense, the lowest exposure to risk. Management
must make the decision to invest cash in assets or costs, and such
a conversion increases risk because the certainty of ultimate recon-
version into cash is less than 100 percent. There are, of course, a
variety of risks. Thus, the risk involved in a conversion of cash into
temporary investments is lower than the risk involved in commit-
ting cash to long-term, long-payout assets such as plant, machinery,
or certain inventories. Similarly, the investment of cash in a
variety of assets and costs for the creation and marketing of a new
product involves serious risk regarding the recovery in cash of
amounts so committed. The short-term liquidity as well as the long-
term solvency of an enterprise depends on the recovery and realizability of such outlays.

The inflow and outflow of cash are highly interrelated. A failure of any
part of the system to circulate can affect the entire system. A cessation of sales affects the vital conversion of finished goods into
receivables or cash and leads, in turn, to a drop in the cash reservoir.
Inability to replenish this reservoir from sources such as owners'
capital, debt, or accounts payable (upper left-hand corner of diagram) can lead to a cessation of production activities that will result
in a loss of future sales. Conversely, the cutting off of expenses,
such as for advertising and marketing, will slow down the conversion of finished goods into receivables and cash. Longer-term block-
ages in the flows may lead to insolvency.

The diagram clarifies the interrelationship between profitability, income, and cash flow. The only real source of funds from operations
is sales. When finished goods, which for the sake of simplicity
represent the accumulation of *all* costs and expenses in the diagram,
are sold, the profit margin will enhance the inflow of liquid funds
in the form of receivables and cash. The higher the profit margin,
the greater the accretion of these funds.

Income, which is the difference between the cash and credit sales and
the cost of goods sold, can have a wide variety of effects on cash
flow. For example, the costs that flow from the utilization of plant
and equipment or from deferred charges generally do not involve
the use of cash. Similarly, as in the case of land sales on long-term
installment terms, the creation of long-term receivables through
sales reduces the impact of net income on cash flow. It can be readily
seen that adding back depreciation to net income creates only a
very crude measure of cash flow.

The limitation of the cash flow concept can be more clearly seen. As
cash flows into its reservoir, management has a *degree* of discretion
as to where to direct it. This discretion depends on the amount of

cash already committed to such outlays as dividends, inventory accumulation, capital expenditures, or debt repayment. The total cash inflow also depends on management's ability to tap sources such as equity capital and debt. With respect to noncommitted cash, management has, at the point of return of the cash to the reservoir, the discretion of directing it to any purpose it deems most important. It is this noncommitted cash flow segment that is of particular interest and importance to financial analysts. This noncommitted cash is also referred to as "free cash flow."

Under present accounting conventions, certain cash outlays, such as those for training, sales promotion, or for most research and development costs, are considered as period costs and are not shown as assets. These costs can, nevertheless, be of significant future value in either the increasing of sales or in the reduction of costs.

SHORT-TERM CASH FORECASTS

In the measurement of short-term liquidity, the short-term cash forecast is one of the most thorough and reliable tools available to the analyst.

Short-term liquidity analysis is of particular interest to management in the financial operations of an enterprise and to short-term credit grantors who are interested in an enterprise's ability to repay short-term loans. The analyst will pay particular attention to the short-term cash forecast when an enterprise's ability to meet its current obligations is subject to substantial doubt.

Realistic cash forecasts can be made only for relatively short time spans. This is so because the factors influencing the inflows and outflows of cash are many and complex and cannot be reliably estimated beyond the short term.

Importance of Sales Estimates

The reliability of any cash forecast depends very importantly on the forecast of sales. In fact, a cash forecast can never reach a higher degree of reliability than the sales forecast on which it is based. Except for transactions involving the raising of money from external sources or the investment of money in long-term assets, almost all cash flows relate to, and depend on, sales.

The sales forecast involves considerations such as:

1. The past direction and trend of sales volume.
2. Enterprise share of the market.
3. Industry and general economic conditions.

4. Productive and financial capacity.
5. Competitive factors.

These factors must generally be assessed in terms of individual product lines that may be influenced by forces peculiar to their own markets.

Pro Forma Financial Statements as an Aid to Forecasting

The reasonableness and feasibility of short-term cash forecasts can be checked by means of pro forma financial statements. This is done by utilizing the assumptions underlying the cash forecast and constructing, on this basis, a pro forma statement of income covering the period of the forecast and a pro forma balance sheet as at the end of that period. The ratios and other relationships derived from the pro forma financial statements should then be checked for feasibility against historical relationships that have prevailed in the past. Such relationships must be adjusted for factors that it is estimated will affect them during the period of the cash forecast.

Techniques of Short-Term Cash Forecasting

ILLUSTRATION 1. The Forward Corporation has recently introduced an improved product that has enjoyed excellent market acceptance. As a result, management has budgeted sales for the six months ending June 30, year 1, as follows:

	Estimated sales
January	100,000
February	125,000
March	150,000
April	175,000
May	200,000
June	250,000
Total	1,000,000

The cash balance at January 1, year 1, is $15,000, and the treasurer foresees a need for additional funds necessary to finance the sales expansion. She has obtained a commitment from an insurance company for the sale to them of long-term bonds as follows:

April	$50,000 (less $2,500 debt costs)
May	60,000

She also expects to sell real estate at cost: $8,000 in May and $50,000 in June. In addition, equipment with an original cost of $25,000 and a book value of zero was to be sold for $25,000 cash in June.

The treasurer considers that in the light of the expanded sales volume the following minimum cash balances will be desirable:

January	$20,000
February	25,000
March	27,000
April, May, and June	30,000

She knows that during the next six months she will not be able to meet her cash requirements without resort to short-term financing. Consequently, she approaches her bank and finds it ready to consider her company's needs. The loan officer suggests that in order to determine the cash needs and the sources of funds for loan repayment, the treasurer prepare a cash forecast for the six months ending June 30, year 1, and pro forma financial statements for that period.

The treasurer, recognizing the importance of such a forecast, proceeded to assemble the data necessary to prepare it.

The pattern of receivables collections based on experience was as follows:

Collections	Percent of total receivable
In month of sale	40
In the second month	30
In the third month	20
In the fourth month	5
Write-off bad debts	5
	100

On the basis of this pattern and the expected sales, the treasurer constructed Schedule A shown in Exhibit 4–2.

An analysis of past cost patterns resulted in the estimates of cost and expense relationships for the purpose of the cash forecast (Schedule B) shown in Exhibit 4–3.

It was estimated that all costs in Schedule B (exclusive of the $1,000 monthly depreciation charge) will be paid for in cash in the month incurred, except for material purchases that are to be paid 50 percent in the month of purchase and 50 percent in the following month. Since the product is manufactured to specific order, no finished goods inventories are expected to accumulate.

Exhibit 4–2

SCHEDULE A
Estimates of Cash Collections
For the Months January-June, Year 1

	January	February	March	April	May	June
Sales	$100,000	$125,000	$150,000	$175,000	$200,000	$250,000
Collections:						
1st month—40% .	40,000	50,000	60,000	70,000	80,000	100,000
2nd month—30%		30,000	37,500	45,000	52,500	60,000
3rd month—20% .			20,000	25,000	30,000	35,000
4th month—5% ..				5,000	6,250	7,500
Total cash						
collections ..	40,000	80,000	117,500	145,000	168,750	202,500
Write-offs—5%				5,000	6,250	7,500

Exhibit 4–3

SCHEDULE B
Cost and Expense Estimates for Six Months
Ending June 30, year 1

Materials	30% of sales
Labor	25% of sales
Manufacturing overhead:	
Variable	10% of sales
Fixed	$48,000 for six months (including $1,000 of depreciation per month)
Selling expenses	10% of sales
General and administrative expenses:	
Variable	8% of sales
Fixed	$7,000 per month

The raw materials inventory at the end of each month for the period January to June year 1 is expected to be as follows: $67,000, $67,500, $65,500, $69,000, $67,000, and $71,000, respectively. Raw materials inventory on January 1, year 1, was $57,000.

Schedule C (Exhibit 4–4) shows the pattern of payments of accounts payable (for materials).

Equipment costing $20,000 will be bought in February for notes payable that will be paid off, starting that month, at the rate of $1,000 per month. The new equipment will not be fully installed until sometime in August year 1.

Exhibit 4–5 presents the cash forecast for the six months ending June 30, year 1, based on the data given above. Exhibit 4–6 presents the pro

Exhibit 4–4

SCHEDULE C
Pro Forma Schedule of Cash Payments for Materials Purchases
For the Months January–June Year 1

	January	February	March	April	May	June
Materials purchased during month*	$40,000	$38,000	$43,000	$56,000	$58,000	$79,000
Payments:						
1st month—50% ...	20,000	19,000	21,500	28,000	29,000	39,500
2nd month—50% ..		20,000	19,000	21,500	28,000	29,000
Total payments ..	$20,000	$39,000	$40,500	$49,500	$57,000	$68,500

* These reconcile with material costs and changes in inventories.

forma income statement for the six months ending June 30, year 1. Exhibit 4–7 presents the actual balance sheet of The Forward Corporation as at January 1, year 1, and the pro forma balance sheet as of June 30, year 1.

The financial analyst should examine the pro forma statements critically and submit to feasibility tests the estimates on which the forecasts are based. The ratios and relationships revealed by the pro forma financial statements should be analyzed and compared to similar ratios of the past in order to determine whether they are reasonable and feasible of attainment. For example, the current ratio of The Forward Corporation increased from 2.6 on January 1, year 1, to 3.5 in the pro forma balance sheet as of June 30, year 1. During the six months ended June 30, year 1, a pro forma return on average equity of over 8 percent was projected. Many other significant measures of turnover, common-size statements, and trends can be computed. The reasonableness of these comparisons and results must be assessed. They can help reveal serious errors and inconsistencies in the assumptions that underlie the projections and thus help strengthen confidence in their reliability.

Differences between Short-Term and Long-Term Forecasts

The short-term cash forecast is, as we have seen, a very useful and reliable aid in projecting the state of short-term liquidity. Such a detailed approach is, however, only feasible for the short term, that is, up to about 12 months. Beyond this time horizon the uncertainties become so great as to preclude detailed and accurate cash forecasts. Instead of focusing on collections of receivables and on payments for labor and materials, the longer-term estimates focus on projections of net income and the resulting cash flow from operations as well as on other sources and uses of cash.

Exhibit 4–5

THE FORWARD CORPORATION
Cash Forecast
For the Months January–June Year 1

	January	February	March
Cash balance—beginning	$15,000	$20,000	$ 25,750
Add: Cash receipts:			
Collections of accounts receivable			
(Schedule A)	40,000	80,000	117,500
Proceeds from sale of real estate			
Proceeds from additional long-			
term debt			
Proceeds from sale of			
equipment			
Total cash available	$ 55,000	$100,000	$143,250
Less: Disbursements:			
Payments for:			
Materials purchases			
(Schedule C)	20,000	39,000	40,500
Labor	25,000	31,250	37,500
Fixed factory overhead	7,000	7,000	7,000
Variable factory overhead	10,000	12,500	15,000
Selling expenses	10,000	12,500	15,000
General and administrative ...	15,000	17,000	19,000
Taxes			
Purchase of fixed assets		1,000	1,000
Total disbursements	87,000	120,250	135,000
Tentative cash balance (negative) ..	(32,000)	(20,250)	8,250
Minimum cash balance required ...	20,000	25,000	27,000
Additional borrowing required ..	52,000	46,000	19,000
Repayment of bank loan			
Interest paid on balance			
outstanding at rate of 1/2% per			
month*			
Ending cash balance	$ 20,000	$ 25,750	$ 27,250
Loan balance	$ 52,000	$ 98,000	$117,000

* Interest is computed at the rate of 1/2 percent per month and paid on date of repayment which occurs at month end. Loan is taken out at beginning of month.

The projection of future statements of cash flow is best begun with an analysis of prior year cash statements. To these data can then be added all available information and estimates about the future needs for cash and the most likely sources of cash needed to cover such requirements.

April	May	June	Six-month totals
$ 27,250	$ 30,580	$ 30,895	$ 15,000
145,000	168,750	202,500	753,750
	8,000	50,000	58,000
47,500	60,000		107,500
		25,000	25,000
	$219,750	$267,330	$308,395	$959,250

(continued)

April	May	June	Six-month totals
$219,750	$267,330	$308,395	$959,250
49,500	57,000	68,500	274,500
43,750	50,000	62,500	250,000
7,000	7,000	7,000	42,000
17,500	20,000	25,000	100,000
17,500	20,000	25,000	100,000
21,000	23,000	27,000	122,000
		19,000	19,000
1,000	1,000	1,000	5,000
157,250	178,000	235,000	912,500
62,500	89,330	73,395	46,750
30,000	30,000	30,000	
—	—	—	117,000
30,000	58,000	29,000	(117,000)
1,920	435	145	2,500
$ 30,580	$ 30,895	$ 44,250	$ 44,250
$ 87,000	$ 29,000	—	—

ELECTRONIC SPREADSHEET PROGRAMS

The wide variety and sophistication of available electronic spreadsheet programs, and the ease of changing variables which they afford, can aid greatly in the preparation of pro forma statements. That ease and flexibility of use should not be confused with the fact that the quality of

Exhibit 4–6

THE FORWARD CORPORATION
Pro Forma Income Statement
For the Six Months Ending June 30, Year 1

		Source of estimate
Sales	$1,000,000	Based on sales budget (page 124)
Cost of sales:		
Materials	300,000	Schedule B
Labor	250,000	Schedule B
Overhead	148,000	Schedule B
	698,000	
Gross profit	302,000	
Selling expense	100,000	Schedule B
Bad debts expense	18,750	Schedule A
General and administrative		
expense	122,000	Schedule B
Total	240,750	
Operating income	61,250	
Gain on sale of equipment ..	25,000	
Interest expense	(2,500)	Exhibit 4–5, footnote
Income before taxes	83,750	
Income taxes	33,500	40% combined state and federal rate. Pay $19,000 in June and accrue balance.
Net income	$ 50,250	

projections is critically dependent on the validity of estimates and assumptions. The reasonableness of such assumptions is dependent on rigorous analysis and judgment rather than computer program manipulations.

ANALYSIS OF STATEMENTS OF CASH FLOWS

We shall now focus on the analysis of the SCF, paying particular attention to the value of such an analysis to a projection of future cash flows.

Exhibit 4–7

THE FORWARD CORPORATION
Balance Sheets

	Actual January 1, Year 1		Pro forma June 30, Year 1	
Assets				
Current assets:				
Cash	$ 15,000		$ 44,250	
Accounts receivable (net)	6,500		234,000	
Inventories—raw materials	57,000		71,000	
Total current assets		$ 78,500		$349,250
Real estate	58,000		—	
Fixed assets	206,400		201,400	
Accumulated depreciation	(36,400)		(17,400)	
Net fixed assets		228,000		184,000
Other assets		3,000		3,000
Deferred debt expenses				2,500
Total assets		$309,500		$538,750
Liabilities and Equity Capital				
Current liabilities:				
Accounts payable	2,000		41,500	
Notes payable	28,500		43,500	
Accrued taxes	—		14,500	
Total current liabilities		$ 30,500		$ 99,500
Long-term debt	15,000		125,000	
Common stock	168,000		168,000	
Retained earnings	96,000		146,250	
		279,000		439,250
Total liabilities and equity capital		$309,500		$538,750

In any analysis of financial statements, the most recent years are the most important because they represent the most recent experience. Since there is an inherent continuity in business events, it is this latest experience that is likely to have the greatest relevance to the projection of future results. So it is with the SCF.

It is important that the analyst obtain SCFs for as many years as possible.[1] This is particularly important in the case of an analysis of this statement since the planning and execution of plant expansions, of modernization schemes, of working capital increases as well as the financing of such activities by means of short- and long-term debt and by means

---

[1] Statements which have been presented in a different format in preceding years may have to be restated.

of equity funds is an activity that is likely to encompass many years. Thus, in order for the analyst to be able to assess management's plans and their execution, SCFs covering a number of years must be analyzed. In this way, a more comprehensive picture of management's financial habits can be obtained and an assessment of them made.

Because conditions vary so greatly from enterprise to enterprise, only a few useful generalizations regarding the thrust of such analysis are possible.

The analyst must first establish which the major sources of cash over the years were and what the major uses were to which cash was put. A common-size analysis of the SCF will aid in this year-to-year comparison. Detailed SCF often tend to obscure the major sources and uses of cash. In assessing overall trends and practices, it is best to cumulate the major sources and uses over a span of years, such as 5 or 10, because single fiscal periods are too short for purposes of reaching meaningful conclusions. Thus, for example, the financing of a major capital expansion may be accomplished years before it is in full swing.

In evaluating sources and uses of cash, the analyst should focus on questions such as these:

- Has the enterprise been able to finance fixed asset *replacements* from internally generated cash? Historical-cost as well as current-cost depreciation may be useful in this assessment. Many companies do not provide adequate information to enable the analyst to distinguish between replacement and capacity expansion.

- How have expansion and business acquisitions been financed?

- To what extent is the enterprise dependent on outside financing? How frequently is it required, and what form does it take?

- What does the company's need for cash and its access to cash suggest as implications for its dividend policy?

ILLUSTRATION OF THE ANALYSIS OF STATEMENTS OF CASH FLOWS

In this illustration, we shall analyze the statements of cash flow of Campbell Soup Company (see Exhibit 10–4), covering the six-year period ending July 28, 1991. Exhibit 10–15 presents these statements in common-size format.

During the six-year period the *major* sources of cash of Campbell Soup Company were operations $3010 million, long-term debt $854 million, and short-term debt $737 million. The major uses were plant purchases (net of sales) of $1647 million, business acquisitions (net of sales) of $718 million, and cash dividends of $649 million. During this period cash and cash equivalents increased by $24 million. Sources of cash from operations as a percentage of total sources averaged 48.5 percent and reached a low of 29 percent in 1989. Of these six years, 1991 was the most profitable, reflecting a recovery after two years of very poor results and of restructuring.

Over the six-year period, cash from operations covered handily net cash used in investing activities as well as most of dividends paid. The sharp declines in earnings in 1989 and 1990 were mitigated from a cash-flow point of view by the fact that restructuring charges of $682 million did not use cash.

An analysis of the SCF over the years is helpful as the basis of cash flow forecasts. A forecast of future SCF would have to take into consideration all above-discussed trends that the enterprise has exhibited, such as those relating to income, the elements that convert it to sources of cash from operations, fixed assets additions, and the relationship of sales to growth in operating working capital. The size of noncash adjustments, such as depreciation, depends on future depreciation policies and equipment acquisitions. The latter, as well as write-off methods to be used for tax purposes, will in turn determine the size of the deferred tax adjustments. The more we know about factors such as these the more reliable the forecast will be.

EVALUATION OF THE STATEMENT OF CASH FLOWS

The foregoing example of an analysis of the SCF illustrates the variety of information and insights that can be derived. Of course, the analysis of SCF is to be performed within the framework of an analysis of all the financial statements, and thus the conclusion reached from an analysis of one statement may be strengthened and corroborated by an analysis of the other financial statements.

There are some useful generalizations that can be made regarding the value of the analysis of the SCF to the financial analyst.

This statement enables the analyst to appraise the quality of management decisions over time, as well as their impact on the results of operations and financial condition of the enterprise. When the analysis encompasses a longer period of time, the analyst can evaluate management's response to the changing economic conditions as well as to the opportunities and the adversities which invariably present themselves.

Evaluation of the SCF analysis will indicate the purposes to which management chose to commit funds, where it reduced investment, the source from which it derived additional cash, and to what extent it reduced claims against the enterprise. Such an analysis will also show the disposition of earnings over the years, as well as how management has reinvested the internal cash inflow over which it had discretion. The analysis will also reveal the size and composition of cash from operations, as well as their pattern and degree of stability.

As depicted in Exhibit 4–1 earlier in this chapter, the circulation of cash in an enterprise involves a constant flow of cash and its periodic reinvestment. Thus, cash is invested in labor, material, and overhead costs, as well as in long-term assets, such as inventories and plant and equipment, which join the product-cost stream at a slower rate. Eventually, by the process of sales, these costs are converted back into accounts receivable and into cash. If operations are profitable, the cash recovered will exceed the amounts invested, thus augmenting the cash inflow or cash flow. Losses have, of course, the opposite effect.

What constitutes cash flow is the subject of considerable confusion. Generally, the cash provided by operations, that is, net income adjusted for items needed to convert it to a cash basis, is an index of management's ability to redirect funds away from areas of unfavorable profit opportunity into areas of greater profit potential. However, not all the cash provided by operations may be so available because of existing commitments for debt retirement, stock redemption, equipment replacement, and dividend payments. Nor is cash provided by operations the only potential cash inflow, since management can avail itself of external sources of capital in order to bolster its funds inflow. The components of the "cash from operations" figure hold important clues to the stability of that source of cash. Thus, for example, depreciation is a more stable element in the total than net income itself in that it represents a recovery by the enterprise of the investment in fixed assets out of selling prices even before a profit is earned. Cash recovered from depreciation must normally be reinvested in the productive assets used up. This is not the case with goodwill amortization. The recovery of this noncash charge does not have to be reinvested in the assets which have been amortized.

In evaluating the SCF, the analyst will judge a company's quality of earnings by the impact that changes in economic and industry conditions have on its flow of cash. The statement will also reveal noncash generating income that may have a bearing on the evaluation of earnings quality.

If in his estimates of future earnings potential the analyst foresees a need for additional capital, his analysis of the SCF will be directed toward a projection of the source from which cash will be obtained, and what dilution of earnings per share, if any, this will involve.

The analysis and evaluation of the SCF is, as the foregoing discussion suggests, an important early step in the projection of future SCFs.

PROJECTION OF STATEMENTS OF CASH FLOWS

No thorough model of an enterprise's future results is complete without a concurrent forecast of the amount of cash needed for the realization of the projections in the model as well as an assessment of the possible sources from which such cash can be derived.

If a future expansion of sales and profits is forecast, the analyst must know whether the enterprise has the "financial horsepower" to see such an expansion through, by means of internally generated cash and, if not, where the required cash is going to come from.

The projection of the SCF will start with a careful estimate of the expected changes in each individual category of assets and the cash that will be derived from or required by such changes. Some of the more important factors to be taken into consideration follow:

1. The net income expected to be generated by future results will be adjusted for noncash items, such as depreciation, depletion, deferred income taxes, and nonremitted earnings of subsidiaries and investees, in order to arrive at estimates of cash provided by operations.
2. The needs for operating working capital will be arrived at by estimating the required level of the individual working capital items such as receivables and inventories and reducing this by the expected levels of payables. Over the long term, working capital required to support a level of estimated sales can also be estimated on an aggregate or net basis. There is usually a relationship between incremental sales and the corresponding increment in required working capital amounts.
3. Sources of cash from disposals of assets, sales of investments, and the sale of stocks and bonds will be estimated.
4. Expected capital expenditures will be based on the present level of operations as compared with productive capacity, on an estimate of the future level of activity implied by the profit projections, as well as on current replacement cost data.
5. Mandatory debt retirement and desirable minimum levels of dividend payments will also be estimated.

ILLUSTRATION OF THE PROJECTION OF STATEMENTS OF CASH FLOWS

Based on the financial statements of the Campbell Soup Company (see Chapter 2, Appendix B) and on the preceding analysis we can prepare a forecast of the SCF of the Campbell Soup Company for 1992 and 1993 based on the following assumptions (all dollar amounts in millions):

1. Sales in 1992 will be $6350, and in 1993 $6800.
2. Net income 1992 will be as presented in the projected income statement for 1992 (Exhibit 10–16). For 1993, net income will be 7.9 percent of projected sales.
3. Net income for 1989 and 1990, which are used in the projecting

process, are before the net effect of divestitures, restructuring, and unusual charges of $260.8 in 1989 and $301.6 in 1990.

4. Depreciation and amortization in 1992 and 1993 will bear the same relationship to net income as the average depreciation and amortization during the 1989–91 period bore to the average net income over the same period.

5. Deferred income taxes will be in 1992 at a level that reflects the relationship of total 1990–91 deferred taxes to total 1990–91 net income. It will change in 1992 by the percentage change that 1993 estimated net income bears to 1992 estimated net income.

6. Other, net will be in 1992 at a level that reflects the relationship of total 1989–91 other, net to total 1989–91 net income. It will change in 1993 by the percentage change that 1993 estimated net income bears to 1992 estimated net income.

7. The level of operating working capital items, accounts receivable, inventory, and other current assets and liabilities (exclusive of cash and temporary investments) prevailing at fiscal year-end of 1992 and 1993 will be estimated as follows:

   a. Determine the percentage relationship between 1991 fiscal year-end operating working capital items and 1991 sales.

   b. Multiply the percentage relationship in *(a)* above by the estimated sales levels for 1992 and 1993, respectively.

8. The fiscal year-end level of cash and temporary investments is estimated to bear the same relationship to the estimated sales of the respective 1992 and 1993 years as does the fiscal year-end of cash and temporary investments in 1991 bear to sales in 1991.

9. All other amounts shown in the projected Statement of Cash Flows are estimated *(est.)* on the basis of the best available information, including situations where the moving average of the last six years is used.

Exhibit 4–8 presents the projected SCF for Campbell Soup for 1992 and 1993.

The Impact of Adversity

The projected SCF is useful not only in estimating the cash implications of future expansion and opportunity but also in assessing the impact on the enterprise of sudden adversity.

A sudden adversity will usually manifest itself in a serious interruption in the inflow of cash.

This can be brought about by such events as recessions, strikes, or the loss of a major customer or market. In this context, a projection of the

Exhibit 4–8

CAMPBELL SOUP COMPANY
Projected Statements of Cash Flows
($ millions)

	1993	1992
Cash flows from operating activities:		
Net earnings[a]	$540.0	$480.0
To reconcile net earnings to net cash provided by operating activities:		
Depreciation and amortization[b]	331.1	294.3
Deferred taxes[c]	30.0	26.7
Other, net[d]	65.5	58.3
(Increase) decrease in accounts receivable[e]	(38.2)	(12.4)
(Increase) decrease in inventories[f]	(51.2)	(16.6)
Net change in other current assets and liabilities[g]	85.9	27.9
Net cash provided by operating activities	963.1	858.2
Cash flows from investing activities:		
Purchases of plant assets[h]	(443.1)	(400.0)
Sale of plant assets (est.)[i]	31.5	28.4
Businesses acquired (est.)[i]	(85.3)	(77.0)
Sale of businesses (est.)[i]	25.5	23.0
Increase in other assets (est.)[i]	(53.9)	(48.6)
Net change in other temporary investments (est.)[i]	12.3	11.1
Net cash used in investing activities	(513.0)	(463.1)
Cash flows from financing activities:		
Long-term borrowings (est.)	132.0	142.3
Repayments of long-term borrowings[j]	(218.9)	(227.7)
Increase (decrease) in short-term borrowings[k]	(200.3)	(95.7)
Other short-term borrowings (est.)	131.2	122.9
Repayments of other short-term borrowings (est.)[l]	(140.4)	(200.0)
Dividends paid (est.)	(108.8)	(108.2)
Treasury stock purchases (est.)	(49.4)	(42.4)
Treasury stock issued (est.)	15.6	14.2
Other, net (est.)	9.1	10.4
Net cash provided (used in) financing activities	(429.9)	(384.2)
Effect of exchange rate changes on cash (est.)	(7.5)	(6.7)
Net increase (decrease) in cash and cash equivalents[m]	12.7	4.2
Cash and cash equivalents at the beginning of year[m]	183.1	178.9
Cash and cash equivalents at the end of year[m]	$195.8	$183.1

SCF would be a first step in the assessment of the defensive posture of an enterprise. The basic question to which such an analysis is directed is this: what can the enterprise do; and what resources, both internal and

(*continued on page 137*)

Exhibit notes:

Note: Some assumptions in the above projections may be considered as somewhat mechanical. They are presented here merely for purposes of illustration. In practice, more refined relationships may be calculated on the basis of detailed studies of past relationships.

(a) Projected net income for:
  −1992 is 7.6% of projected sales.
  −1993 is 7.9% of projected sales.

These projections are corroborated in the *Value Line Investment Survey* of February 21, 1992.

(b) Average percentage of depreciation and amortization to net income in 1989–91

$$\frac{\text{Total depreciation and amortization}}{\text{Total net income*}} = \frac{\$601.8}{\$981.4} = 61.32\%$$

Depreciation and amortization for 1992 = $480.0 × 0.6132 = $294.3
Depreciation and amortization for 1993 = $540.0 × 0.6132 = $331.1

(c) Average percent of deferred taxes to net income in 1990–91

$$\frac{\text{Total deferred taxes}}{\text{Total net income*}} = \frac{\$39.4 \boxed{59}}{\$707.5} = 5.57\%$$

Deferred taxes for 1992 = $480.0 × 0.0557 = $26.7
Percentage change of 1993 net income to 1992 net income =
  $540.0 / $480.0 = 112.5%
Deferred taxes for 1993 = $26.7 × 1.125 =. $30.0

(d) Average percent of other, net to net income in 1989–91:

$$\frac{\text{Total other, net}}{\text{Total net income*}} = \frac{\$119.1 \boxed{60}}{\$981.4} = 12.14\%$$

Other, net for 1992 = $480.0 × 0.1214 = $58.3
Percentage change of 1993 net income to 1992 net income = 112.5%
Other, net for 1993 = $58.3 × 1.125 = $65.5

(e) Percentage of year-end accounts receivable to sales in 1991:

$$\frac{\text{A/R } \boxed{33}}{\text{Sales } \boxed{13}} = \frac{527.4}{6204.1} = 8.5\%$$

Fiscal year end A/R in 1992 = 6350.0 × 0.085 = $539.8
Fiscal year end A/R in 1993 = 6800.0 × 0.085 = $578.0

Change in A/R in 1992 = $539.8 − $527.4 = $12.4 increase.
Change in A/R in 1993 = $578.0 − $539.8 = $38.2 increase.

Data in Chapter 10 indicate that over a 10-year period A/R had year-to-year increases over 9 years.

(f) Percentage of year-end inventories to sales in 1991:

$$\frac{\text{Inventories } \boxed{34}}{\text{Sales } \boxed{13}} = \frac{706.7}{6204.1} = 11.39\%$$

Fiscal year-end inventories in 1992 = 6350.0 × 0.1139 = $723.3
Fiscal year-end inventories in 1993 = 6800.0 × 0.1139 = $774.5

Change in inventories in 1992 = $723.3 − $706.7 = $16.6 increase.
Change in inventories in 1993 = $774.5 − $723.3 = $51.2 increase.

(g) Percentage of year-end net other current assets and liabilities (NOCACL) to sales in 1991:

$$\frac{\text{Total current liabilities } \boxed{45} - \text{Prepaid expenses } \boxed{35}}{\text{Sales } \boxed{13}} = \frac{\$1278.0 - \$92.7}{\$6204.1} = 19.11\%$$

Fiscal year-end NOCACL in 1992 = $6350.0 × 0.1911 = $1213.2
Fiscal year-end NOCACL in 1993 = $6800.0 × 0.1911 = $1299.1

Change in NOCACL in 1992 = $1213.2 − $1185.3 = $27.9 increase in liabilities.

Change in NOCACL in 1993 = $1299.1 − $1213.2 = $85.9 increase in liabilities.

(h) For 1992 see item $\boxed{11}$ of managements' discussion. . . .—statements of cash flows: Investing activities. For 1993: Percentage change in capital expenditures from 1991 to 1992:

$$\frac{\$400.0}{\$361.1 \ \boxed{65}} = 110.8\%$$

Projected capital expenditures = $400.0 × 110.8% = $443.1

(i) From (h) above, a percentage of 110.8% of last year balance is used also in relatively similar areas.

(j) See item $\boxed{172}$ and $\boxed{173}$, for maturity dates of LTD.

In 1993, $100.0 million due in 1996 at interest rate of 10.5% and redeemable in 1993, given that interest rates continue to fall which may call for refinancing.

(k) Net amount needed to balance the statement.

(l) For 1992, see item $\boxed{170}$, 13.99% Notes due 1992.

For 1993, estimated using average of 1987–1992.

(m) Cash and cash equivalents balance at the end of fiscal year is assumed to be related to the net sales of that year.

$$\text{For 1991} = \frac{\$178.9 \ \boxed{31}}{\$6204.1 \ \boxed{13}} = 2.88\%$$

For 1992 = $6350.0 × 0.0288 = $183.1
For 1993 = $680.0 × 0.0288 = $195.8

*

	For 1991		For 1990		For 1989	
Total net income =	$401.5	+	(4.4 + 301.6)	+	(13.1 + 260.8)	= $981.4
For 90 and 91 =	401.5	+	(4.4 + 301.6)			= $707.5

external, can it marshal to cope with a sudden and serious reduction in the inflow of cash?

The strategies and alternatives available to an enterprise faced with such adversities are ably examined and discussed in a work by Professor Donaldson. Dr. Donaldson defines financial mobility as the capacity to redirect the use of financial resources in response to new information about the company and its environment.[2] This concept is related to that of "financial flexibility" discussed in the preceding chapter.

---

[2] Gordon Donaldson, *Strategy for Financial Mobility* (Boston: Graduate School of Business Administration, Harvard University, 1969).

The projected SCF is an important tool in the assessment of the resources available to meet such "new information" as well as in planning the changes in financial strategy that this may require.

To the prospective credit grantor such an approach represents an excellent tool in the assessment of risk. In estimating the effects of, for example, a recession, on the future flow of cash he or she can trace through not only the potential shrinkage in cash inflows from operations but also the effects of such shrinkage on the uses of cash and on the sources from which they can be derived.

Published Financial Forecasts

The subject of published and/or audited financial forecasts is considered in Chapter 9.

The Cash Flow Adequacy Ratio

The purpose of this ratio is to determine the degree to which an enterprise generated sufficient cash from operations to cover capital expenditures, net investment in inventories, and cash dividends. To remove cyclical and other erratic influences, a five-year total is used in the computation of the ratio, thus:

$$\frac{\text{Five-year sum of cash from operations}}{\substack{\text{Five-year sum of capital expenditures, inventory} \\ \text{additions, and cash dividends}}}$$

The investment in the other important working capital item, receivables, is omitted on the theory that it can be financed primarily by short-term credit (i.e., growth in payables, and so forth). Only additions to inventories are counted. In years in which inventories decline the change counts as zero.

A ratio of 1 indicates that an enterprise has covered its needs based on attained levels of growth without the need for external financing. To the degree that the ratio falls below 1, internally generated cash may be inadequate to maintain dividends and current operating growth levels. This ratio may also reflect the effect of inflation on the fund requirements of an enterprise. The reading of this, like any other ratio, can provide no definitive answers and is only a pointer to further analysis and investigation.

Based on the data available in the financial statements of Campbell Soup (Chapter 2, Appendix B), we present here a five-year computation:

$$\frac{\text{5-year sum of sources of cash from operations}}{\substack{\text{5-year sum of capital expenditures, inventory} \\ \text{additions and cash dividends}}}$$

$$\frac{\$2545.8(a)}{\$2418.5(b) + \$117.1(c) + \$544.8(d)} = 0.83$$

(a) Cash from operations—Item 64
(b) Property additions—items 65 and 67
(c) Inventories—item 62
(d) Cash dividends—item 77

This computation indicates that for the five years ending in 1991, Campbell's cash from operations fell short of covering the three items in the denominator of the ratio. A six-year computation in Chapter 10 reveals a slightly more favorable ratio.

Cash Reinvestment Ratio

This ratio is useful in measuring the percentage of the investment in assets, which represents operating cash retained and reinvested in the enterprise for the replacement of assets and for growth in operations. The formula is:

$$\frac{\text{Cash provided by operations} - \text{Dividends}}{\text{Gross plant} + \text{Investment} + \text{Other assets} + \text{Working capital}}$$

A reinvestment rate of 8 to 10 percent is considered generally to be at a satisfactory level. The ratio for Campbell Soup (Chapter 2, Appendix B) for 1991 is:

$$\frac{\$805.2(e) - \$137.5(f)}{[\$2921.9 + \$477.6](g) + \$404.6(h) + [\$1518.5 - \$1278.0](i)} = 16.5\%$$

(e) Cash from Operations—Item 64
(f) Cash dividends—item 77
(g) Gross plant assets—items 158 thru 161
    Plus: Intangibles—items 163 and 164
(h) Other assets—item 39
(i) Total current assets—item 36
    Less: Total current liabilities—item 45

CONCLUSION

In the assessment of future liquidity, the use of cash inflows and outflows forecasts for the short term, and of projected SCF for the longer term, represent some of the most useful tools available to the financial analyst. In contrast to ratio measures of liquidity, these tools involve a detailed examination of sources and uses of cash. Such examination and estimation processes can be subjected to feasibility tests by means of pro forma statements and to the discipline inherent in the double-entry accounting system.

QUESTIONS

1. What is the primary difference between funds flow analysis and ratio analysis? Which is superior and why?
2. "From an operational point of view, management focuses on cash rather than working capital." Do you agree with the statement? Why or why not?
3. What is the relationship between inflows and outflows of cash?
4. Why is the short-term cash forecast important to the financial analyst?
5. What is the first step to be taken in preparing a cash forecast, and what considerations are required in such a step?
6. What are pro forma financial statements? How are they utilized in conjunction with funds flow projections?
7. What are the limitations of short-term cash forecasts?
8. If the usefulness of a short-term cash forecast is limited, what analytical approach is available to the financial analyst who wants to analyze future cash flows?
9. What questions will the analyst focus on in evaluating sources and uses of funds?
10. What useful information do you, as a financial analyst, expect to get from the analysis of past SCF (cash statement)?
11. What would a forecast of future SCF have to take into consideration?
12. What are the differences between short-term and long-term financial forecasts?
13. What analytical function does the common-size SCF serve?
14. Why is a projected SCF necessary when you have historical data which are based on actual performance?
15. If actual operations are seriously affected by unforeseen adversities, would a projected SCF still be useful?
16. "Cash flow per share" is sometimes used in common stock analysis in the same fashion as *earnings per share*. In financial analysis, shouldn't the former be used more often than the latter? Explain. (CFA)

Chapter 5

ANALYSIS OF CAPITAL STRUCTURE AND LONG-TERM SOLVENCY

The financial strength and stability of a business entity and the probability surrounding its ability to weather random shocks and to maintain its solvency in the face of adversity are important measures of risk associated with it. This evaluation of risk is critical because, as discussed in Chapter 1, the equity investor as well as the lender require returns that are commensurate with the levels of risk that each assumes. This and the preceding two chapters deal with the evaluation of the financial strength and viability of enterprises within different time frames.

KEY ELEMENTS IN THE EVALUATION OF LONG-TERM SOLVENCY

The process of evaluation of long-term solvency of an enterprise differs markedly from that of the assessment of short-term liquidity. In the latter, the time horizon is short and it is often possible to make a reasonable projection of cash flows. It is not possible to do this for the longer term, and thus the measures used in the evaluation of longer-term solvency are less specific but more all-encompassing.

There are a number of key elements involved in the evaluation of the long-term solvency of an enterprise. The analysis of capital structure is concerned with the types of capital funds used to finance the enterprise, ranging from "patient" and permanent equity capital to short-term funds that are a temporary, and, consequently, a much more risky source. There are different degrees of risk associated with the holding of different types of assets. Moreover, assets represent secondary[1] sources of security for lenders ranging from loans secured by specific assets to assets available as general security to unsecured creditors.

On a long-term basis, earnings and earning power (which implies the recurring ability to generate cash from operations in the future) are some

---

[1] When lending to going concerns, lenders should regard the liquidation of assets for the purpose of recovery of principal and interest as a measure of last resort and as an undesirable source of funds to rely on at the time credit is granted.

of the most important and reliable indicators of financial strength available. Earnings are the most desirable and reliable sources of cash for the longer-term payment of interest and repayment of principal. As a surrogate for cash generated by operations, earnings are the yardstick against which the coverage of interest and other fixed charges is measured. Moreover, a reliable and stable trend of earnings is one of the best assurances of an enterprise's ability to borrow in times of cash shortage and its consequent ability to extricate itself from the very conditions that lead to insolvency.

In addition to general measures of financial strength and long-term solvency, lenders rely on the protection afforded by loan covenants or the pledges of specific assets as security. All loan covenants define default and the legal remedies available when it occurs in order to give the lender the right to step in at an early stage. Most are designed to alert the lender to the deterioration in such key measures of financial health as the current ratio and the debt to equity ratio, against the issuance of further debt, or to ensure against the disbursement of resources through the payments of dividends above specified levels or through acquisitions. Of course, there can be no prohibition against operating losses, a core problem attending most cases of deterioration in financial condition. Thus, the existence of protective provisions cannot substitute for alertness and a continuous monitoring of the results of operations and of the financial condition of an enterprise in which long-term funds are at risk.[2]

The vast amount of public and private debt outstanding has led to standardized approaches to its analysis and evaluation. By far the most important is the rating of debt securities by rating agencies that is discussed in Appendix 5A to this chapter. Appendix 5B examines the use of ratios as predictors of failure.

In this chapter, we shall examine in further detail the tools and the measures available for the analysis of long-term solvency.

IMPORTANCE OF CAPITAL STRUCTURE

The capital structure of an enterprise consists basically of equity funds and debt. It is measured in terms of the relative magnitude of the various sources of funds of the enterprise. The inherent financial stability of an enterprise and the risk of insolvency to which it is exposed are importantly dependent on the sources of its funds as well as on the type of

---

[2] Lenders have learned that senior positions in the debt hierarchy do not always afford in practice the security they seem to afford in theory. Thus, subordinated debt is not akin to capital stock because subordinated creditors have a voice in determining whether a debtor should be rescued or be thrown into bankruptcy. This interdependence between junior and senior lenders has led some to the belief that one might as well buy the highest yielding obligation of an enterprise since any situation serious enough to affect the value of the junior security is likely to affect the senior security as well.

assets it holds and the relative magnitude of such asset categories. Exhibit 5–1 presents an example of the distribution of assets of an enterprise and the sources of funds used to finance their acquisition. It is evident from the diagram in Exhibit 5–1 that within the framework of equality prevailing between assets and liabilities plus capital, a large variety of combinations of assets and sources of funds used to finance them is possible.

ACCOUNTING PRINCIPLES

The amounts at which liabilities and equity accounts are shown on the financial statements are governed by the application of GAAP. The analyst must keep these principles in mind when analyzing the capital structure and its effect on long-term solvency. While it can be stated, as a broad generalization, that the accounting principles governing the measurement of liabilities and equities do not affect the analysis of financial statements as importantly as do those governing the measurement of assets, a study of the above-mentioned chapters will reveal aspects of real importance to the analyst.

Exhibit 5–1   Asset distribution and capital structure of an enterprise

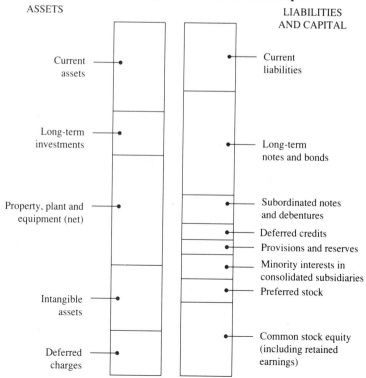

The relationship between liabilities and equity capital, the two major sources of capital in an enterprise, is always an important factor entering into the assessment of long-term solvency. Thus, an understanding of their nature is essential to the analyst. There are liabilities that are not fully reflected in the balance sheet, and there are accounts whose accounting classification as debt or equity should not be automatically accepted by the analyst. The proper decision of how to classify or deal with these depends on a thorough understanding of their nature and/or the particular conditions of issue to which they are subject.

Deferred Taxes

Most deferred credits, such as bond premiums, represent allocation accounts designed primarily to aid in the measurements of income. They do not present an important problem of analysis and are relatively insignificant in size. Deferred income items, such as subscription income received in advance, represent an obligation for future service and are, as such, clearly liabilities.

One type of deferred liability that is generally much more sizable, and consequently much more important, is *deferred income taxes.* This account is not a liability in the usual sense because the government does not have a definite short-term or even longer-term claim against the enterprise. Nevertheless, this account does represent in large measure the aggregate exhaustion in tax deductibility of assets and other items, over and above that recorded for book purposes, and this means that at some time in the future the deferred tax liability account (credit) will be used to reduce the higher income tax expense that corresponds to *increased* tax liabilities. Even if the likelihood of the deferred tax account "reversing" in the foreseeable future is quite good, there still remains the question of whether the time-adjusted present value of such future expected "reversals" should not be used instead of the nominal face value amount of the deferred credit. After all, most other liabilities on the balance sheet including pensions and leases are carried at present value. The higher the interest rates (cost of debt) applicable to an entity are, the more significant the impact of discounting to present value. In *SFAS 109* the board considered the issue of discounting deferred taxes and decided against discounting at the time.

To the analyst, the important question here is whether to treat the deferred tax account as a liability, as an equity item, or as part debt and part equity. The decision depends on the nature of the deferral, the past experience with the account (e.g., has it been constantly growing?), and the likelihood of future "reversal."

In making his or her judgment, the analyst must recognize that under normal circumstances, deferred tax liabilities will reverse, that is, become payable, when a firm shrinks in size. Generally, a shrinkage in size is attended by losses rather than by taxable income. In such circumstances, the drawing down of the deferred tax account is more likely to involve credits to tax loss carryforwards or carrybacks, rather than to the Cash account.

To the extent that such future "reversal" is only a remote possibility, as may be the case with timing differences due to accelerated depreciation, the deferred credit should be viewed as a source of funds of such long-term nature as to be classifiable as equity. On the other hand, if the possibility of a "drawing down" of the deferred tax account in the foreseeable future is quite strong, then the account, or a part of it, is more in the nature of a long-term liability. In classifying the deferred tax account as between debt and equity, the analyst must be guided by considerations such as the ones discussed above.

When the analyst decides to classify deferred tax credits as equity (either in whole or in part), the following *analytical* entry is appropriate:

Deferred Income Taxes—Current* X
Deferred Income Taxes—Noncurrent* .... Y
    Owners' Equity ....   Z
 * As applicable.

Long-Term Leases

Under *SFAS 13,* most financing long-term noncancelable leases must be shown as debt. While *SFAS 13* has tightened the rules considerably, companies can still find ways around them by the way leases are written and by other means. If the analyst concludes that leases that are not capitalized by the reporting entity should be capitalized, he can, for analytical purposes, book them as follows:

Leasehold Assets X
    Liabilities under Long-Term Leases ....   Y

Off-Balance-Sheet Financing

SFAS 13 has significantly curtailed one of the most significant and widely used methods of off-balance-sheet financing. However, in trying to determine the total debt to which an entity is subject, the analyst must be aware that some managements will attempt to understate debt and that new methods of doing this are constantly tried. A careful reading of footnotes and of management comments along with inquiries of management can shed light on the existence of unrecorded liabilities.

Liabilities for Pensions and for Other Postretirement Employee Benefits (OPEB)

SFAS 87 recognizes that if the fair value of pension assets falls short of the accumulated pension benefit obligation, a liability for pensions exists.

However, this liability does not take into consideration the *projected* benefit obligation which recognizes an estimate for future pay increases when pension plans base their benefits on future pay formulas. Analysts who judge such understatement as serious and who can estimate such understatement may want to adjust the pension liability for analytical purposes.

Companies can, on adoption of *SFAS 106,* recognize the unfunded OPEB obligation immediately or over as many as 20 years. Under the latter amortization option a company is, unlike under pension accounting, not required to record a minimum liability. Thus, the analyst will need to assess the present value of the unrecorded liability for OPEB.

There are distinctions between pension debt, as well as possibly OPEB liabilities, and other debt in that the former do not present as immediate a threat to force a company into bankruptcy as does the latter. Research into these differences also supports this view.[3] While the Pension Benefit Guaranty Corporation (PBGC) has the authority to take control of an underfunded plan and place a lien on company assets, for the protection of employee benefits, it has, so far, moved very cautiously in this area. The Internal Revenue Service also has established procedures under which companies in financial difficulty can obtain waivers to defer their contributions to a pension fund.

Unconsolidated Subsidiaries

The preferred method of presenting the financial statements of a parent and its subsidiary is in consolidated format. This is also the preferred method from the analyst's point of view for most analytical purposes, although separate financial statements of the consolidated entities are necessary in some cases, such as when the utilization of assets of a subsidiary (e.g., an insurance company or a bank) is not subject to the full discretion of the parent.

Information on unconsolidated subsidiaries may also be important because bondholders of such subsidiaries can look only to the latter's assets as security for their bonds. Moreover, bondholders of the parent company (particularly holding companies) may derive a significant portion of their fixed-charge coverage from the dividends of the unconsolidated subsidiaries. Yet, in the event of the subsidiary's bankruptcy, the parent bondholders may be in a junior position to the bondholders of the subsidiary.

When the financial statements of a subsidiary are not consolidated with the parent, consolidation may be undertaken as an analytical adjustment as follows:

---

[3] W. Landsman, "An Empirical Investigation of Pension Fund Property Rights," *The Accounting Review,* October 1986, pp. 662–91.

```
Subsidiary's Assets* ................................. X
     Subsidiary's Liabilities* ...........................     Y
     Parent's Investment in Subsidiary ....................     Z
```
* Using as much detail as is needed or is available.

If the subsidiary has unrecorded lease or pension liabilities, they too may be consolidated for purposes of analysis.

Provisions, Reserves, and Contingent Liabilities

Provisions such as for guarantees and warranties represent obligations to offer future service and should be classified as such. Generally speaking, reserves created by charges to income may also be considered as liabilities. However, general contingency reserves or reserves for very indeterminate purposes (most of which are now prohibited by *SFAS 5*) should not be considered as genuine liabilities.

The analyst must make a judgment regarding the probability of commitments or contingencies becoming actual liabilities and should then treat these items accordingly. Thus, guarantees of indebtedness of subsidiaries or others that are likely to become liabilities should be treated as such.

Minority Interests

Minority interests in consolidated financial statements represent the ownership interests of minority shareholders of the subsidiaries included in the consolidated group. These are not liabilities similar in nature to debt because they have neither mandatory dividend payment nor principal repayment requirements. Capital structure measurements concentrate on the mandatory payments aspects of liabilities. From this point of view, minority interests are more in the nature of outsiders' claims to a portion of the equity or an offset representing their proportionate ownership of assets.[4]

Convertible Debt

Convertible debt is generally classified among liabilities. However, if the conversion terms are such that the only reasonable assumption that can be made is that the debt will be converted into common stock, then it may be classified as equity for purposes of capital structure analysis.

---

[4] Minority interests are shown at book value. Thus, if the analyst wants to assess what the parent company would have to pay in order to acquire the minority interest, market rather than book values will be the determining factor.

Preferred Stock

Most preferred stock entails no absolute obligation for payment of dividends or repayment of principal, possessing thus the characteristics of true equity. However, preferred stock with a fixed maturity or subject to sinking fund requirements should, from an analytical point of view, be considered as debt.

Preferred stock with mandatory redemption requirements is akin to debt and should be considered as such by the analyst. This is so even though in some cases default by the company on the redemption provisions does not carry repercussions as severe as those flowing from the nonpayment of debt.

ADJUSTMENTS TO THE BOOK VALUE OF ASSETS

Because the owners' equity of an enterprise is measured by the excess of total assets over total liabilities, any analytical revision of asset book values (i.e., amounts at which assets are shown in the financial statements) will also result in a change in the amount of the owners' equity. For this reason, in assessing capital structure, the analyst must decide whether or not the book value amounts of assets are realistically stated. The following are examples of the need for possible adjustments. Different or additional adjustments may be needed depending on circumstances.

Recognition of Market Values

In industries such as mining, petroleum, timber, or other natural resources, or in real estate, the market value of assets can exceed significantly the historical costs carried on the balance sheets. Adjustments to market value of these assets will have a corresponding enhancing effect on equity capital. The higher values of these assets should also be reflected in increased earning power with a corresponding enhancing effect on the fixed-charge coverage ratio—an effect that is not dependent on analytical adjustments discussed here.

As will be seen below, some analysts use market values of the company's equity securities, rather than equity at book values, to adjust for the higher market values of assets. This is based on the assumption that the market is best able to reflect the value inherent in a company's total financial condition.

Inventories

Inventories carried at LIFO are generally understated in times of rising prices. The amount by which inventories computed under FIFO (which are closer to replacement cost) exceed inventories computed under LIFO is generally disclosed. Such disclosures should enable the analyst to adjust inventory amounts and the corresponding owners' equity amounts (after tax) to more realistic current costs or values.

Marketable Securities

Marketable securities are often stated at cost that may be below market value. Using parenthetical, footnote, or other information, the analyst can make an analytical adjustment increasing this asset to market value and owners' equity (after tax) by a corresponding amount.

Intangible Assets

Intangible assets and deferred items of dubious value that are included on the asset side of the balance sheet affect the computation of the total equity of an enterprise. To the extent that the analyst cannot evaluate or form an opinion on the present value or future utility of such assets, they may be excluded from consideration, thereby reducing the amount of equity capital (after tax) by the amounts at which such assets are carried. However, the arbitrary exclusion of all intangible assets from the capital base is an unjustified exercise in overconservatism.

The foregoing discussion related to the evaluation and the classification of debt and equity accounts. Let us now turn to an examination of the significance of capital structure in financial analysis.

THE SIGNIFICANCE OF CAPITAL STRUCTURE

The significance of capital structure is derived, first and foremost, from the essential difference between debt and equity.

The equity is the basic risk capital of an enterprise. Every enterprise must have some equity capital that bears the risk to which it is inevitably exposed. The outstanding characteristic of equity capital is that it has no guaranteed or mandatory return that must be paid out in any event and no definite timetable for repayment of the capital investment. Thus, capital that can be withdrawn at the contributor's option is not equity capital and has, instead, the characteristics of debt.[5] From the point of view of an enterprise's stability and exposure to the risk of insolvency, the outstanding characteristic of equity capital is that it is permanent, can be

_____

[5] For example, during the financial crisis that befell many brokerage houses in the late 1960s, it was discovered that much "equity" capital that was thought to lend strength to the enterprise and additional security to customers and creditors was in effect subject to withdrawal by owners. At the sign of real trouble, these owners withdrew their capital, thus compounding the financial problems even more.

counted on to remain invested in times of adversity, and has no mandatory requirement for dividends. It is such funds that an enterprise can most confidently invest in long-term assets and expose to the greatest risks. Their loss, for whatever reason, will not necessarily jeopardize the firm's ability to pay the fixed claims against it.

Both short-term and long-term debt, in contrast to equity capital, must be repaid. The longer the term of the debt and the less onerous its repayment provisions, the easier it will be for the enterprise to service it. Nevertheless, it must be repaid at certain specified times regardless of the enterprise's financial condition; and so must interest be paid in the case of most debt instruments. Generally, the failure to pay principal or interest will result in proceedings under which the common stockholders may lose control of the enterprise as well as part or all of their investment. Should the entire equity capital of the enterprise be wiped out by losses, the creditors may also stand to lose part or all of their principal and interest due.

It can be readily appreciated that the larger the proportion of debt in the total capital structure of an enterprise, the higher the resulting fixed charges and repayment commitments and the greater the probability of a chain of events leading to an inability to pay interest and principal when due.

To the investor in the common stock of an enterprise, the existence of debt represents a risk of loss of the investment, and this is balanced by the potential of high profits arising from financial leverage. Excessive debt may also mean that management's initiative and flexibility for profitable action will be stifled and inhibited. Leverage acts to magnify managerial mistakes. It can also increase risk already present because of such factors as commodity price fluctuations or technological obsolescence.

The creditor prefers as large a capital base as possible as a cushion that will shield against losses that can result from adversity. The smaller the relative capital base, or conversely, the larger the proportionate contribution of funds by creditors, the smaller is the creditors' cushion against loss and consequently the greater the risk of loss.

While there has been a considerable debate, particularly in academic circles, over whether the *cost of capital* of an enterprise varies with different capital structures, that is, with various mixes of debt and equity, the issue seems significantly clearer from the point of view of outsiders to the enterprise, such as creditors or investors, who must make decisions on the basis of conditions as they are. In the case of otherwise identical entities, the creditor exposes himself to greater risk if he lends to the company with 60 percent of its funds provided by debt (and 40 percent by equity capital) than if he lends to a similar company that derives, say, only 20 percent of its funds from debt.

Under the Modigliani-Miller thesis, the cost of capital of an enterprise in a perfect market is, except for the tax deductibility of interest, not affected by the debt to equity relationship.[6] This is so, they assert, because each individual stockholder can inject, by use of personally created leverage, his own blend of risk into the total investment position. Thus, under this theory, the advantage of debt will be offset by a markdown in a company's price-earnings ratio.

The degree of risk in an enterprise, as judged by the outside prospective investor is, however, a given; and our point of view, as well as our task here, is to measure the degree of risk residing in the capital structure of an enterprise.

REASONS FOR EMPLOYMENT OF DEBT

In addition to serving as an inflation hedge, a primary reason for the employment of debt by an enterprise is that up to a certain point, debt is, from the point of view of the ownership, a less expensive source of funds than equity capital. This is so for two main reasons:

1. The interest cost of debt is fixed,[7] and thus, as long as it is lower than the return that can be earned on the funds supplied by creditors, this excess return accrues to the benefit of the equity.
2. Unlike dividends, which are considered a distribution of profits, interest is considered an expense and is, consequently, tax deductible.

A further discussion of these two main reasons follows.

The Concept of Financial Leverage

Financial leverage means the inclusion in the capital structure of an enterprise of debt that pays a fixed return. Since no creditor or lender would be willing to put up loan funds without the cushion and safety provided by the owners' equity capital, this borrowing process is also referred to as "trading on the equity," that is, utilizing the existence of a given amount of equity capital as a borrowing base.

In Exhibit 5–2, a comparison is made of the returns achieved by two companies having identical assets and earnings before interest expense. Company X derives 40 percent of its funds from debt while Company Y has no debt. In year 1, when the average return on total assets is 12 percent, the return on the stockholders' equity of Company X is 16 percent. This higher return is due to the fact that the stockholders benefited from the excess return on total assets over the cost of debt. For Company

---

[6] F. Modigliani and M. Miller, "The Cost of Capital, Corporation Finance and the Theory of Investment," *American Economic Review,* June 1958, pp. 261–97.

[7] Except for debt subject to variable interest rates.

Exhibit 5–2 Trading on the equity—results under different earning assumptions (dollars in thousands)

	Assets	Debt payable	Stock-holders' equity	Income before interest and taxes	10 percent debt interest	Taxes(a)	Net income	Net income + (Interest) × (1 – Tax rate)	Return on Total assets(b)	Return on Stock-holders' equity(c)
Year 1:										
Company X	$1,000,000	$400,000	$ 600,000	$200,000	$40,000	$64,000	$ 96,000	$120,000	12.0%	16.0%
Company Y	1,000,000	—	1,000,000	200,000	—	80,000	120,000	120,000	12.0	12.0
Year 2:										
Company X	1,000,000	400,000	600,000	100,000	40,000	24,000	36,000	60,000	6.0	6.0
Company Y	1,000,000	—	1,000,000	100,000	—	40,000	60,000	60,000	6.0	6.0
Year 3:										
Company X	1,000,000	400,000	600,000	50,000	40,000	4,000	6,000	30,000	3.0	1.0
Company Y	1,000,000	—	1,000,000	50,000	—	20,000	30,000	30,000	3.0	3.0

(a) Assuming a 40 percent tax rate.

(b) $\dfrac{\text{Net income} + \text{Interest } (1 - 0.40)}{\text{Total Assets}}$.

(c) $\dfrac{\text{Net income}}{\text{Stockholders' equity}}$.

Y, the return on equity always equals the return on total assets. In year 2, the return on total assets of Company X was equal to the interest cost of debt and, consequently, the effects of leverage were neutralized. The results of year 3 show that leverage is a double-edged sword. Thus, when the return on total assets falls below the cost of debt, Company X's return on the equity is lower than that of debt-free Company Y.

The Effect of Tax Deductibility of Interest

The second reason given for the advantageous position of debt is the tax deductibility of interest. This can be illustrated as follows:

Assume the facts given in Exhibit 5–2 for year 2, and that the operating earnings of Company X and Company Y, $100,000 for each, are both of equal quality.[8] The results of the two companies can be summarized as follows:

	Company X	Company Y
Income before interest and taxes	$100,000	$100,000
Interest (10% of $400,000)	40,000	
Income before taxes	60,000	100,000
Taxes (40%)	24,000	40,000
Net income	36,000	60,000
Add back interest paid to bondholder	40,000	
Total return to security holders (debt and equity)	$ 76,000	$ 60,000

Disregarding leverage effects that are neutral in the above example, even if the return on assets is equal to the interest rate, the total amount available for distribution to the bondholders and stockholders of Company X is $16,000 higher than the amount available for the stockholders of Company Y. This is due to the lower total tax liability to which the security holders of Company X are subject.

It should be borne in mind that the value of the tax deductibility of interest is dependent on the existence of sufficient earnings. However, unrecovered interest changes can be carried back and carried forward as part of tax loss carryovers permitted by law.

Other Advantages of Leverage

In addition to the advantages accruing to equity stockholders from the successful employment of financial leverage and the tax deductibility of

---

[8] The concept of the quality of earnings is discussed in Chapter 9.

interest expenses, a sound longer-term debt position can result in other advantages to the equity owner. A rapidly growing company can avoid earnings dilution through the issuance of debt. Moreover, if interest rates are headed higher, all other things being equal, a leveraged company paying fixed interest rates will be more profitable than its nonleveraged competitor. The reverse is, of course, also true. There is, moreover, a financial benefit from advantageously placed debt because debt capital is not always available to an enterprise and the capacity to borrow may disappear should adverse operating results occur. Finally, in times of inflation, monetary liabilities will result in price-level gains.

Measuring the Effect of Financial Leverage

The effect of leverage on operating results is positive when the return on the equity capital exceeds the return on total assets. This difference in return isolates the effect that the return on borrowed money has on the return on the owner's capital. As was seen in the example in Exhibit 5–2, leverage is positive when the return on assets is higher than the cost of debt. It is negative when the opposite conditions prevail. The terms *positive* and *negative* are not used here in the strict algebraic sense.

The effect of financial leverage can be measured by the following formula:

$$\text{Financial leverage index} = \frac{\text{Return on common equity}}{\text{Return on total assets}}$$

Using the data in Exhibit 5–2, we compute the financial leverage indexes of Company X for years 1, 2, and 3 as follows:

Financial Leverage Index

$$\text{Year 1: } \frac{16.0}{12.0} = 1.33$$

$$\text{Year 2: } \frac{6.0}{6.0} = 1$$

$$\text{Year 3: } \frac{1.0}{3.0} = 0.33$$

In year 1, when the return on equity exceeded that on total assets, the index at 1.33 was positive. In year 2, when the return on equity equaled that on total assets, the index stood at 1, reflecting a neutralization of financial leverage. In year 3, the index, at 0.33, was way below 1.0, thus indicating the very negative effect of financial leverage in that year. The subject of return on investment is discussed in Chapter 6.

ILLUSTRATION OF COMPUTATION

The computation of a variety of ratios for Campbell Soup based on data in Chapter 2, Appendix B, and on data presented in Chapter 10 will be illustrated in the latter chapter as part of a comprehensive analysis.

In this and other chapters we will also be using the financial statements of Quaker Oats Company (also referred to as QO) as the basis for various illustrations so as to enrich the database on which we draw. The financial statements of QO are found in Appendix 10 and are also annotated with reference numbers for ease of identification of the data used.

The financial leverage index for Quaker Oats for 1991 is calculated as follows:

$$\frac{\text{Return on common equity}}{\text{Return on total assets}} = \frac{21.01\%}{8.61\%} = 2.44$$

with both returns calculated as follows:

Return on common equity:

$$\frac{\text{Net income} - \text{Preferred dividends}}{\text{Average common stockholders' equity}}$$

$$= \frac{\$205.8^{(a)} - \$4.3^{(b)}}{(\$901 + \$1,017.5)^{(c)} / 2} = 21.01\%$$

Return on total assets:

$$\frac{\text{Net income} + \text{Net interest expense} (1 - \text{Tax rate})}{\text{Average total assets}}$$

$$= \frac{\$205.8^{(a)} + \$101.9^{(d)} (1 - 0.34)^{(e)}}{(\$3,016.1 + \$3,326.1)^{(f)} / 2} = 8.61\%$$

[a] Net income—item $\boxed{11}$
[b] Preferred stock dividend—item $\boxed{111}$
[c] Common shareholders' equity—item $\boxed{91}$
[d] Interest expense (net)—item $\boxed{156}$
[e] 1—marginal tax rate
[f] Total assets—item $\boxed{69}$

THE FINANCIAL LEVERAGE RATIO

The financial leverage ratio measures the relationship between total assets and the common equity capital that finances them. It is expressed as:

$$\frac{\text{Total assets}}{\text{Common equity capital}}$$

The more assets that are financed on a given common equity capital base the higher the financial leverage ratio. As will be seen in Chapter 6, the financial leverage ratio is an element in the analytical disaggregation of the return on equity. Thus, in an enterprise that utilizes leverage profitably, a higher financial leverage ratio will enhance the return on equity. At the same time the risk inherent in a change in profitability is also greater.

The financial leverage ratio of Quaker Oats (Appendix to Chapter 10) for 1991 is computed as follows:

$$\frac{\text{Average total assets}}{\text{Average common equity}} = \frac{\boxed{69}\ (\$3,016.1 + \$3,326.1) \div 2}{\boxed{91}\ (\$901.0 + \$1,017.5) \div 2} = 3.31$$

QO's financial leverage ratio indicates that every dollar of common equity commands $3.31 in assets for the company.

MEASURING THE EFFECT OF CAPITAL STRUCTURE ON LONG-TERM SOLVENCY

From the foregoing discussion it is clear that the basic risk involved in a leveraged capital structure is the risk of running out of cash under conditions of adversity.

Debt involves a commitment to pay fixed charges in the form of interest and principal repayments. While certain fixed charges can be postponed in times of cash shortage, those associated with debt cannot be postponed without adverse repercussion to the ownership and also to the creditor groups.

Another important repercussion of excessive debt is a loss of financing flexibility (i.e., the ability to raise funds particularly in adverse capital markets).

LONG-TERM PROJECTIONS—USEFULNESS AND LIMITATIONS

If a shortage of cash required to service the debt is the most adverse possibility envisaged, then the most direct and most relevant measure of risk inherent in the leveraged capital structure of an enterprise would be a projection of future cash resources and flows that would be available to meet these cash requirements. These projections must assume the worst set of economic conditions that are likely to occur, since this is the most realistic and useful test of safety from the creditor's point of view. If only prosperous and normal times are to be assumed, then the creditor would not need his preferred position and would be better off with an equity position where the potential rewards are higher.

In Chapter 4, we concluded that detailed cash flow projections can be reliably made only for the short term. Consequently, they are useful only in the measurement of short-term liquidity.

The statement of cash flows (SCF) can be projected over a relatively longer term because such a projection is far less detailed than a projection of cash flows. However, as we saw in the discussion of such projections in the preceding chapter, this lack of detail as well as the longer time horizon reduces the reliability of such projections.

The short term is understood to encompass, generally, a period of up to one year. The longer term, however, is a much wider ranging period. Thus, it may include a solvency analysis with respect to a three-year term loan, or it may encompass the evaluation of risk associated with a 30-year bond issue. Meaningful projections covering the period over which the interest and principal of the term loan will be paid can still reasonably be made. However, a 30-year projection of funds flow covering the bond issue would be an unrealistic exercise. For this reason, longer-term debt instruments often contain sinking fund provisions that act to reduce the uncertain time horizon, and stipulations of additional security in the form of specific assets pledged as collateral. Moreover, they often contain provisions requiring the maintenance of minimum working capital levels or restrictions on the payment of dividends, all of which are designed to ensure against a deterioration in the financial ratios prevailing at the time the bonds are issued. They cannot, of course, prohibit adverse operating results—a major and severe cause of cash flow deficiencies.

Desirable as cash flow projections may be, their use for the extended longer term is severely limited. For this reason, a number of measures of long-term solvency have evolved that are more static in nature and are based on measures of capital structure as well as on asset and earnings coverage tests. These measures will be considered below.

CAPITAL STRUCTURE ANALYSIS— COMMON-SIZE STATEMENTS

A simple measure of financial risk in an enterprise is the composition of its capital structure. This can be done best by constructing a common-size statement of the liabilities and equity section of the balance sheet as shown in Exhibit 5–3.

An alternative way of analyzing capital structure with common-size percentages would be to focus only on the longer-term capital funds by excluding the current liabilities from total funds.

The advantage of a common-size analysis of capital structure is that it presents clearly the relative magnitude of the sources of funds of the enterprise, a presentation that lends itself readily to a comparison with similar data of other enterprises.

Exhibit 5–3   Liabilities and equity section—with common-size percentages

Current liabilities	$ 428,000	19.0%
Long-term debt	500,000	22.2
Equity capital:		
Preferred stock	400,000	17.8
Common stock	800,000	35.6
Paid-in capital	20,000	0.9
Retained earnings	102,000	4.5
Total equity capital	1,322,000	58.8
Total liabilities and equity capital	$2,250,000	100.0%

A variation of the approach of analyzing capital structure by means of common-size or component percentages is to analyze it by means of ratios.

CAPITAL STRUCTURE RATIOS

The basic ratio measurements of capital structure relate the various components of the capital structure to each other or to their total. Some of these ratios in common use are explained below.

TOTAL DEBT TO TOTAL CAPITAL (DEBT AND EQUITY)

The most comprehensive ratio in this area is that which measures the relationship between *total debt* (i.e., Current liabilities

+ Long-term debt + any other form of liability determined by the analyst to be debt, such as deferred income taxes and redeemable preferred stock) to *total capital* that in addition to total debt includes the stockholders' equity (inclusive of preferred stock). The ratio can thus be expressed as

$$\frac{\text{Total debt}}{\text{Total capital}} \text{ as defined above}$$

and can also be expressed as debt as a percentage of total capitalization (rather than the ratio of one to the other).

The 1991 debt to total capital ratio for Quaker Oats (Appendix to Chapter 10) is computed as follows:

$$\frac{\$926.9^{(a)} + \$701.2^{(b)} + \$115.5^{(c)} + \$366.7^{(d)}}{\$99.3^{(e)} + \$806.5^{(f)} + \$2,100.3^{(g)}} = \frac{\$2,110.3^{(g)}}{\$3,016.1} = 0.70$$

[a] Current liabilities—item $\boxed{78}$
[b] Long-term debt—item $\boxed{79}$
[c] Other liabilities—item $\boxed{80}$
[d] Deferred income taxes—item $\boxed{81}$
[e] Preferred stock outstanding—items $\boxed{82\text{-}84}$
[f] Shareholders' equity—items $\boxed{91\text{-}83}$
[g] Total debt (numerator)

The result can be expressed as a ratio of 0.70 or as debt being 70 percent of Quaker Oats's total capital (Debt + Equity).

Ratio of Total Debt to Total Equity Capital

An alternate measure of the relationship of debt to capital sources is the ratio of total debt (as defined above) to total equity capital only. Thus:

$$\frac{\text{Total debt}}{\text{Total stockholders' equity}}$$

This ratio for 1991 for Quaker Oats is computed as follows:

$$\frac{\$2,110.3^*}{\$99.3^* + \$806.5^*} = 2.33$$

* See above for derivation

This ratio means that QO's total debt is 2.33 times its equity capital or that the company borrowed from all sources $2.33 for every dollar of equity capital it has.

A reciprocal measure of the above is:

$$\frac{\text{Total stockholders' equity}}{\text{Total debt}}$$

For QO

$$\frac{\$905.8}{\$2,110.3} = 0.43$$

and this can be interpreted from the creditor's point of view as meaning that every dollar of debt is backed by only 43 cents of equity capital. This also clarifies the fact that the owners have a smaller stake in the enterprise than do all creditors.

Long-Term Debt/Equity Capital

This ratio measures the relationship of long-term debt to equity capital.[9] A ratio in excess of 1:1 indicates a higher long-term debt participation

---

[9] The term *long-term debt* usually includes *all* liabilities that are not current.

as compared to equity capital. This ratio is the familiar debt to equity ratio that is computed as follows:

$$\frac{\text{Long-term debt}}{\text{Equity capital}}$$

For QO, the 1991 long-term debt to stockholders' equity ratio is computed as follows:

$$\frac{\$2,110.3^{(a)} - \$926.9^{(b)}}{\$905.8^{(c)}} = 1.31$$

[a] Total debt.
[b] Total current liabilities.
[c] Stockholders' equity.
See above for derivation of amounts.

Confusion in Terminology

Analysts must be aware that in this area, as in many others, the popular name of a ratio may not convey precisely its meaning and, hence, the method of its computation. Before any measure or ratio is used, care must be taken that the method of its computation is thoroughly understood.

Short-Term Debt

The ratio of debt that matures over the short term to total debt is an important indicator of the short-run cash and financing needs of an enterprise. Short-term debt, as opposed to long-term debt or sinking fund requirements, is an indicator of enterprise reliance on short-term (mostly bank) financing. Moreover, short-term debt is subject to frequent changes in interest rates.

Equity Capital at Market Value

Accounting principles in current use place primary emphasis on historical costs rather than on current values.[10] Since the shareholders' capital is the residual of assets minus liabilities, this accounting can result in equity capital book value figures that are far removed from realistic market values.

One method of correcting this flaw in the stated equity capital amounts, particularly when they enter importantly into the computation of many of the ratios that we have considered above, is to restate them by converting the assets from historical cost to current market values. This may

---

[10] Starting with *SFAS 107* the FASB has moved to require the *disclosure* of the fair value of financial instruments.

be particularly important in the case of natural resource companies whose book values greatly understate the market value of their assets.

Although disclosure requirements affecting certain companies may provide analysts with some replacement cost data, we are still far from having complete market values available.

One way of overcoming the problem of giving recognition to market values is to compute the equity capital at current (or some kind of average) market value of the stock issues that comprise it. On the assumption that the valuation placed by the market on the equity capital recognizes the current values of assets and their earning power, this amount can then be used in the computation of the various debt to equity ratios.

A serious objection to this method is that stock prices fluctuate widely and may, particularly in times of overspeculation or market panic, not be representative of "true" values at a given moment. However, this argument can be countered with considerable evidence that the judgment of the marketplace is most of the time superior to that of other judgmental processes and that use of average market prices would solve the problem of temporary aberrations. Thus, the use of equity capital figures computed at current, or at average, market values has much to commend it. Being more realistic, they can improve the ratio measurements in which they are used and can provide a more realistic measure of the asset cushion that bondholders can count on.[11]

A persistent trend of equity at book value that is in excess of equity at market value can be interpreted as a sign of financial weakness and of restricted financial capability, affecting the ability to sell equity capital or even raise new debt capital. Conversely, an excess of market value of equity securities over book value is a strong protecting factor for bondholders and other creditors. It indicates an ability to raise equity capital at advantageous cost, which is an indicator of financial strength.

One important advantage of earnings-coverage ratios, as will be seen in the subsequent discussion of this subject, is that they are based on the earning power of assets rather than on the amount at which they are carried in the financial statements. Market values do, of course, give recognition to such earning power of an entity's assets. In that sense, ratio measures, such as debt to equity ratios, that use equity capital amounts at market value, are more consistent with earnings-coverage ratios than are ratios using historical book values.

---

[11] B. Graham, D. L. Dodd, and S. Cottle in their *Security Analysis,* 4th ed. (New York: McGraw-Hill, 1962), p. 361, suggest that the ratio of

$$\frac{\text{Market value of junior equity}}{\text{Par value of bonds}}$$

should not be less than 0.5 and can be used to corroborate earnings coverage measures. It would not be prudent to have to assume, they maintain, that the junior equity is undervalued by the market.

Using Quaker Oats' (see Appendix to Chapter 10) average common stock market price for 1991 we can compute:

$$\frac{\text{Total debt}}{\text{Common equity at market value} + \text{Preferred equity at book value}}$$

$$\frac{\$2,110,300,000^{(a)}}{76,328,721^{(b)} \times \$53.32^{(c)} + \$4,800,000^{(d)}} = \frac{\$2,110,300,000}{\$4,074,647,400} = 0.52$$

(a) Total debt—item $\boxed{78}$ + $\boxed{79}$ + $\boxed{80}$ + $\boxed{81}$
(b) Number of common stock outstanding—item $\boxed{85}$ – $\boxed{90}$
(c) Average stock price for 1991—item $\boxed{137}$ (range 64.88–41.75)
(d) Preferred stock at book value—item $\boxed{82}$ + $\boxed{83}$ + $\boxed{84}$

Market values of the equity capital can be important because they take into consideration the earnings power of assets, market values, and so on. If we compare the 0.52 that we get when using the market value of the equity to the 2.33 that was computed above when using the book values, we see that the market value ratio is far more favorable.

PREFERRED STOCK WITHIN THE CAPITAL STRUCTURE

Within the total stockholders' equity, preferred stock holds a preferential position with a prior claim on assets ahead of the common stock. Thus, it is instructive to compute the ratio of preferred stock to total stockholders' equity which is done as follows:

$$\frac{\text{Preferred stock at stated value (or liquidating value if higher)}}{\text{Total stockholders' equity}}$$

The ratio of preferred stock to total stockholders' equity would be computed as follows for Quaker Oats:

$$\frac{(1,282,051 - 10,089)^{(a)} \times \$78^{(b)}}{\$905.8^{(c)}} = \frac{\$99.2}{\$905.8} = 10.9\%$$

(a) Number of shares outstanding—item $\boxed{82}$ – $\boxed{84}$
(b) Liquidating value—item $\boxed{82}$
(c) Total shareholders' equity—item $\boxed{91}$ + $\boxed{82}$ + $\boxed{83}$ + $\boxed{84}$

The analyst must always consider how to treat preferred stock subject to mandatory redemption requirements. While such stock is akin to a liability more than to equity, it must be recognized that a failure to meet the redemption requirements may not have as dire a result on the entity's status as would a failure to meet a sinking fund requirement of debt.

THE ANALYTICALLY ADJUSTED RATIO OF LONG-TERM DEBT TO EQUITY

In our earlier discussion of the elements that enter into an entity's capital structure, we concluded that there are many types of analytical adjustments that the analyst may wish to make to the published financial data in computing debt to equity ratios. An illustration of the computation of the analytically adjusted long-term debt to equity ratio is given in Appendix C to this chapter.

INTERPRETATION OF CAPITAL STRUCTURE MEASURES

The common-size and ratio analyses of capital structure, which have been examined above, are all measures of risk inherent in the capital structure of an enterprise. The higher the proportion of debt, the larger the fixed charges of interest and debt repayment, the greater the likelihood of insolvency during protracted periods of earnings decline or other adversities.

One obvious value of these measures is that they serve as screening devices. Thus, when the ratio of debt to equity capital is relatively small, say, 10 percent or less, there is normally no need to be concerned with this aspect of an enterprise's financial condition; and the analyst may well conclude that time is better spent by directing attention to the more critical areas revealed by analysis.

Should an examination of the debt to equity ratios reveal that debt is indeed a significant factor in the total capitalization, then further analysis is necessary. Such an analysis will encompass many aspects of an enterprise's financial condition, results of operations, and future prospects.

An analysis of short-term liquidity is always important because before the analyst starts to assess long-term solvency he has to be satisfied about the short-term financial survival of the enterprise. Chapter 3 examines the analysis of short-term liquidity, and the analyst will use the tools discussed there to assess the situation and also to relate the size of working capital to the size of long-term debt. Loan and bond indenture covenants requiring the maintenance of minimum working capital ratios attest to the importance attached to current liquidity in ensuring the long-term solvency of an enterprise.

Additional analytical steps of importance will include an examination of debt maturities (as to size and spacing over time), interest costs, and other factors that have a bearing on the risk. Among those, the earnings stability of the enterprise and its industry as well as the kind of assets its resources are invested in are also important factors.

"EVENT" AND OTHER TYPES OF RISK

There are additional risks to which bondholders are exposed which are not always susceptible to measurement and which must be provided for by protective bond-indenture provisions or by other means.

One such risk is that the borrowing entity will issue significant additional numbers of bonds of equal or higher priority. This type of risk, referred to as *event risk,* has occurred recently, particularly in conjunction with leveraged buyouts, tender offers, and going-private transactions. Such transactions have resulted in serious declines in the value of outstanding bonds.

Additional risk of loss of value can impact bondholders when a borrower increases dividends to stockholders to unreasonable levels, invests in riskier assets, or jeopardizes bond security in other ways.

MEASURES OF ASSETS DISTRIBUTION

The type of assets an enterprise employs in its operations should determine to some extent the sources of funds used to finance them. Thus, for example, it is customarily held that fixed and other long-term assets should not be financed by means of short-term loans. In fact, the most appropriate source of funds for investment in such assets is equity capital, although debt also has a place in such financing especially in industries such as utilities that generally enjoy stable revenue sources. On the other hand, working capital, and particularly seasonal working capital needs, can be appropriately financed by means of short-term credit. The ratio of working capital to long-term debt should generally not fall below 1, and in most industries that are affected by the business cycle, a ratio below 1.5 to 2 may indicate weakness and vulnerability.

In judging the risk exposure of a given capital structure, the asset composition is one of the important factors to consider. This asset composition is best measured by means of common-size statements of the asset side of the balance sheet. For example, Exhibit 5–4 shows the common-size asset section of the balance sheet whose liabilities and equity section was presented in Exhibit 5–3.

Judging *only* by the distribution of assets and the related capital structure, it would appear that since a relatively high proportion of assets is current (61 percent), a 41 percent debt and current liabilities position

Exhibit 5–4   **Assets section—with common-size percentages**

Current assets:		
Cash	$ 376,000	16.7%
Accounts receivable (net)	425,000	18.9
Merchandise inventory	574,000	25.5
Total current assets	1,375,000	61.1
Investments	268,000	11.9
Land, property, and equipment (net)	368,000	16.4
Intangibles	239,000	10.6
Total assets	$2,250,000	100.0%

(see Exhibit 5–3) is not excessive. Other considerations and measurements may, however, change this conclusion.

Asset coverage is an important element in the evaluation of long-term solvency. Assets of value provide protection to holders of debt obligations both because of their earning power and because of their liquidation value. Additionally, they represent the bases on which an enterprise can obtain the additional financing that may be required to tie it over a period of financial stringency.

The relationship between asset groups and selected items of capital structure can also be expressed in terms of ratios.

Fixed assets to equity capital is a ratio that measures the relationship between long-term assets and equity capital. A ratio in excess of 1:1 means that some of the fixed assets are financed by means of debt.

Net tangible assets as a percentage of long-term debt is a measure of asset coverage of long-term obligations. It excludes assets of doubtful realizability or value and represents a measure of safety of debt based on liquidation of assets.

Total obligations to total net tangible assets (including net working capital) is another useful measure of the relationship between debt and the entity's investment in operating assets. An analysis of the property backing enjoyed by creditors is likely to be most useful in the case of companies, such as those in the natural resource field, where book values may be significantly understated.

If the financial structure ratios are such that they require further analysis, one of the best means for further investigation are tests that measure an enterprise's ability to service its debt requirements out of earnings. This is the area we shall turn to next.

CRITICAL IMPORTANCE OF "EARNING POWER"

One conclusion of our discussion of debt to equity ratios was that a major usefulness of these measurements lies in their function as a screening device, that is, a means of deciding whether the apparent risk inherent in the capital structure of an enterprise requires further investigation and analysis. An important limitation of the measurements of debt to equity relationships is that they do not focus on the availability of cash flows that are necessary to service the enterprise's debt. In fact, as a debt obligation is repaid, the debt to equity ratio tends to improve whereas the yearly amount of cash needed to pay interest and sinking fund requirements may remain the same or may even increase, as, for example, in the case of level payment debt loans with "balloon" repayment provisions or zero coupon bonds.

The long-term creditor must in the final analysis rely on the enterprise's earning power as the most reliable source of interest and principal repayments. While a highly profitable enterprise can in the short run be illiquid because of the composition of its assets, earning power is in the long run the major source of liquidity and of borrowing capacity.

MEASURES OF EARNINGS COVERAGE

Earnings-coverage ratios measure directly the relationship between debt-related fixed charges and the earnings available to meet these charges.[12] The concept of the basic earnings coverage of fixed-charges ratio is simple:

$$\frac{\text{Earnings available to meet fixed charges}}{\text{Fixed charges (as defined)}}$$

While the concept behind this measurement is simple and straight-forward, its practical implementation is complicated by the problem of defining what should be included in "earnings" and in "fixed charges."

Earnings Available to Meet Fixed Charges

Net income determined under the principles of accrual accounting is not the same thing as cash provided by operations. Specifically, certain items of income, such as undistributed earnings of subsidiaries and controlled companies or sales on extended credit terms, do not create cash. Similarly, certain expenses such as depreciation, amortization, depletion, and deferred income tax charges do not require the outlay of cash. On the other hand, it should be borne in mind that a parent company can determine the dividend policy of a controlled subsidiary.

Fixed-debt charges are paid out of cash rather than out of net income. Thus, the analyst must realize that an unadjusted net income figure may not be a correct measure of cash available to meet fixed charges.

The use of net income as an approximation of cash provided by operations may, in some instances, be warranted while in others it may significantly overstate or understate the amount actually available for the servicing of debt. Thus, the soundest approach to this problem lies not in generalizations but rather in a careful analysis of the noncash generating items included in income as well as the noncash requiring expenses charged to that income. Thus, for example, in considering depreciation as a noncash requiring expense, the analyst must realize that over the long run an enterprise must replace its plant and equipment.

---

[12] Fixed-charges-coverage ratios represent important inputs in bond-rating decisions. Bond indentures often specify that minimum levels of this ratio must be maintained before additional debt can be issued.

The problem of determining the amount of income to be included in fixed-charges-coverage ratios requires consideration of a number of additional factors:

1. *The treatment of extraordinary gains and losses.* As pointed out in the more comprehensive discussion of this subject in Chapter 9, extraordinary gains and losses enter into the determination of longer-term average earnings power. As such they must be recognized as a factor that may, over the longer term, contribute to or reduce the cash available to pay fixed charges. Any computation of earnings-coverage ratios utilizing average earnings figures must recognize the existence of extraordinary gains and losses over the years. This is particularly true of earnings-coverage ratios where what we measure is the risk of loss of sources of cash for payment of fixed charges.

2. *Preferred dividends* need not be deducted from net income because the payment of such dividends is not mandatory. However, in consolidated financial statements, preferred dividends of a subsidiary whose income is consolidated must be deducted because they represent a charge that has priority over the distribution of earnings to the parent.

3. Earnings that are attributed to *minority interests* are usually deducted from net income available for fixed charges even though minority shareholders can rarely enforce a cash claim under normal conditions. An exception arises where the consolidated subsidiary has fixed charges. In such instances, the coverage ratio should be computed on the basis of earnings before deducting minority interests.

If a subsidiary with a minority interest has a loss, the credit in the income statement that results from the minority's share in the loss should be excluded from consolidated earnings for purposes of the coverage ratio computation. The parent would, in most cases, meet fixed-charges obligations of its subsidiary to protect its own credit standing, whether or not legally obligated to do so.

4. *The impact of income taxes* on the computation of earnings-coverage ratios should always be carefully assessed. Since interest is a tax-deductible expense, it is met out of pre-tax income. Thus, the income out of which interest payments are met is pre-tax income. On the other hand, preferred dividends or sinking fund payments are not tax deductible and must be paid out of after-tax earnings.

5. *Add-back of fixed charges.* In order to determine the amount of pre-tax earnings available to meet specific fixed charges, those fixed charges that were deducted in arriving at pre-tax earnings must be added back to pre-tax income in the numerator of the ratio.

6. *The level of income* used in the computation of earnings-coverage ratios deserves serious consideration. The most important consideration here is: what level of income will be most representative of the amount that will actually be available in the *future* for the payment of debt-related fixed charges. An average figure of earnings from continuing operations

encompassing the entire range of the business cycle, and adjusted for any known factors that may change it in the future, is most likely to be the best approximation of the average source of cash from future operations that can be expected to become available for the payment of fixed charges. Moreover, if the objective of the earnings-coverage ratio is to measure the creditor's maximum exposure to risk, then the proper earnings figure to use is that achieved at the low point of the enterprise's business cycle.

Fixed Charges to Be Included

Having considered the amount of earnings that should be included in the earnings coverage, we shall now turn to an examination of the types of fixed charges that are generally includable in the computation of this ratio.

1. Interest Incurred

Interest incurred is the most direct and most obvious fixed charge that arises from the incurrence of indebtedness. Interest expense includes the amortization of deferred bond discount and premium. The bond discount and issue expenses represent the amount by which the par value of the bond indebtedness exceeded the proceeds from the bond issue. As such, the discount amortization represents an addition to the stated interest expense. The amortization of bond issue premium represents the reverse situation, and thus results in a reduction of interest expense over the period of amortization.[13]

If low coupon bonds have only a short period to run before maturity and it is likely that they will have to be refinanced with higher coupon bonds, it may be appropriate to incorporate in fixed charges the expected higher interest costs.

Interest on income bonds must be paid only as earned. Consequently, it is not a fixed charge from the point of view of the holder of fixed-interest securities. It must, however, be regarded as a fixed charge from the point of view of the income bond issuer.

When information disclosed is so vague or limited that it is impossible to determine the amount of interest incurred and interest capitalized, the amount of interest *incurred* can be approximated by referring to the mandatory disclosure of *interest paid* in the statement of cash flows. Interest incurred will differ from interest paid as disclosed due to changes in interest payable, because interest capitalized is often netted, because of interest discount and premium amortization, and possibly for other reasons. However, in the absence of other data, interest *paid* is a better approximation of interest incurred than any other amount.

---

[13] Bond discount and premium amortization, which are usually relatively insignificant in amount, do not, strictly speaking, require a current outlay of funds. They represent cost or income item allocations over the term of the loan.

2. Capitalized Interest

SFAS 34 requiring the capitalization of certain interest costs has greatly increased the practice of interest capitalization. Care must be taken to arrive at proper amounts in both the numerator and the denominator of the fixed-charges-coverage ratio.

Let us clarify where interest can be found in the income statement and the terminology that relates to it. Interest that the enterprise pays or is obligated to pay during a period is referred to as *interest incurred*. This is the amount we focus on as being covered by earnings. Interest incurred that is not immediately expensed but rather charged to some asset account is *interest capitalized*. Interest incurred less interest capitalized equals *interest expensed*. Since interest that is expensed is that which enters into the determination of pre-tax income, it should be added back to the pre-tax income found in the numerator of the ratio in order to arrive at pre-tax preinterest income. The denominator of the ratio will, however, include as a fixed-charge interest incurred whether capitalized or not.

Interest capitalized in one period will find its way into the income statements of subsequent periods in the form of costs such as depreciation or amortization. Such amortized interest that was previously capitalized must be added back to pre-tax income.[14] In effect, failure to add back such interest results in including earnings in the numerator *after* some interest costs rather than *before* interest, with a resulting understatement of the fixed-charges-coverage ratio. Since the FASB has not required the disclosure of the amount of previously capitalized interest that is amortized in a given period, analysts can obtain these amounts through voluntary disclosure by companies or they can sometimes derive them from other disclosures such as those relating to deferred taxes.

In item 156 Quaker Oats presents details of interest expense allocable to continuing operations, discontinued operations, as well as interest expense capitalized.

3. Interest Implicit in Lease Obligations

SFAS 13 requires the capitalization of most financing leases.

When a lease is capitalized, the interest portion of the lease payment is included in the interest expense on the income statement while most of the balance is usually considered as repayment of the principal obligation. A problem arises, however, when the analyst considers that certain leases that should have been capitalized are not so treated in the financial statements. The issue here actually goes beyond the pure accounting ques-

---

[14] SEC regulations require that different methods of computation apply to rate-regulated public utilities. In their case, the allowance for funds used during construction shall be added to gross income but not deducted from interest expense. Utilities may not add to earnings the amount of previously capitalized interest amortized during the period.

tion of whether capitalization is, or is not, appropriate. It stems rather from the fact that a long-term lease represents a fixed obligation that must be given recognition in the computation of the earnings-coverage ratio. Thus, even long-term leases that, from an accounting theory point of view, need not be capitalized may be considered as including fixed charges that have to be included in the coverage-ratio computation.[15]

The problem of extracting the interest portion of long-term lease payments is not a simple one. The external analysts can possibly obtain the rate of interest implicit in the lease, from an examination of the more extensive disclosure now available on the subject. Otherwise a rough rule of thumb, such as that interest represents one third of rentals, originally suggested by Graham and Dodd, may have to be used.[16] The SEC, which had encouraged use of this rule, no longer accepts it automatically and insists on a more reliable estimate of the portion of rentals that represent interest.[17] "Delay rentals" in the extractive industries represent payment for the privilege of deferring the development of properties and, being in the nature of not regularly recurring compensation to owners, are not considered as rentals includable in the earnings-coverage ratio.

As with the prohibition against the offsetting of interest income against interest expense, the general rule is that rental income should not be offset against rental expense when determining fixed charges. An exception is made, however, where the rental income represents a direct reduction in rental expense.

4. Preferred-Stock Dividend Requirements of Majority-Owned Subsidiaries

These are considered fixed charges because they have priority over the distribution of earnings to the parent. Items that would be or are eliminated in consolidation should not be considered fixed charges.

Income Tax Adjustment of Fixed Charges

Fixed charges that are not tax deductible must be tax adjusted. This is done by increasing them by an amount equivalent to the income tax that would be required to obtain an after-tax income sufficient to cover such

---

[15] In the discussion preceding the release of its 1982 revised regulations concerning the computation of the fixed-charges-coverage ratio, the SEC has reemphasized that "some long-term leases may narrowly miss the criteria for a capital lease but still have the characteristics of a financing transaction. The Commission does not believe that the presence of an interest factor is dependent upon the rental contract extending over any given period of time."

[16] Graham, Dodd, and Cottle, *Security Analysis,* 4th ed. (New York: McGraw-Hill, 1962), p. 344. (This rule was developed in a previous edition of this book.)

[17] SEC *Accounting Series Release 155* (now superseded), as well as discussion preceding the SEC's release of revised rules concerning the computation of the ratio in 1982.

fixed charges. The above preferred-stock dividend requirement is one example of such nontax-deductible fixed charges. The following adjustment is made to compute the "grossed-up" amount:

$$\frac{\text{Preferred-stock dividend requirements}}{1 - \text{Income tax rate}}$$

The tax rate to be used should be based on the relationship of the provision for income tax expense applicable to income from continuing operations to the amount of pre-tax income from continuing operations (i.e., the company's normal effective tax rate). The effective tax rate, rather than the statutory tax rate we normally use for this purpose, is used here in "grossing up," because this is the SEC's requirement.

Other Elements to be Included in Fixed Charges

The foregoing discussions concerned the determination of fixed financing charges, that is, interest and the interest portion of lease rentals. These are the most widely used measures of "fixed charges" included in conventional fixed-charges-coverage ratios such as those required by the SEC which we adopt as the standard required computation.

However, if the purpose of this ratio is to measure an enterprise's ability to meet fixed commitments that if unpaid could result in repercussions ranging all the way from financial embarrassment to insolvency, there are other fixed charges to be considered. The most important categories of such additional fixed charges that we shall consider here are principal repayment obligations such as sinking fund requirements, serial repayment provisions, and the principal repayment component of lease rentals. These items are not usually included as fixed charges, and the inclusion of some may be quite controversial. The inclusion of these fixed charges will not be illustrated here.

5. Principal Repayment Requirements

Principal repayment obligations are, from a cash-drain point of view, just as onerous as obligations to pay interest. In the case of rentals, the obligations to pay principal and interest must be met simultaneously.

A number of reasons have been advanced to indicate why the requirements for principal repayments are not given recognition in earnings-coverage ratio calculations:

1. The coverage of fixed-charges ratio is based on income. It is assumed that if the ratio is at a satisfactory level, it will be possible to refinance obligations as they become due or mature. Consequently, they may not have to be met from funds provided by earnings.

2. If the company has an acceptable debt to equity ratio it should be able to reborrow amounts equal to the debt repayments.
3. Another objection to the inclusion of sinking fund or other periodic principal repayment provisions in the calculation of the earnings-coverage ratio is that this may result in double counting, that is, the funds recovered by depreciation already provide for debt repayment. Thus, if earnings reflect a deduction for depreciation, then fixed charges should not include provisions for principal repayments.

   There is some merit to this argument if the debt was used to acquire depreciable fixed assets and if there is some correspondence between the pattern of depreciation charges and that of principal repayments. It must, moreover, be borne in mind that depreciation funds are recovered generally only out of profitable, or at least break-even, operations, and consequently this argument is valid only under an assumption of such operations.

   Our discussion of the definition of "earnings" to be included in the coverage-ratio calculations emphasized the importance of cash provided by operations as the measure of resources available to meet fixed charges. The use of this concept would, of course, eliminate the double-counting problem since nonfund-requiring charges such as depreciation would be added back to net income for the purpose of the coverage computations.

A more serious problem regarding the inclusion of debt repayment provisions among "fixed charges" arises from the fact that not all debt agreements provide for sinking fund payments or similar repayment obligations. Any arbitrary allocation of indebtedness over time would be an unrealistic theoretical exercise and would ignore the fact that to the extent that such payments are not required in earlier years, the immediate pressure on the cash resources of the enterprise is reduced. In the longer run, however, larger maturities as well as "balloon" payments will have to be met.

The most useful solution to this problem lies in a careful analysis and assessment of the yearly debt repayment requirements that will serve as the basis on which to judge the effect of these obligations on the long-term solvency of the enterprise. The assumption that debt can always be refinanced, rolled over, or otherwise paid off from current operations is not the most useful approach to the problem of risk evaluation. On the contrary, the existence of debt repayment obligations as well as the timing of their maturity must be recognized and included in an overall assessment of the long-term ability of the enterprise to meet its fixed obligations. The inclusion of sinking fund or other early repayment requirements in fixed charges is one way of recognizing the impact of such requirements on fund adequacy. Another method would, as a minimum, call for scheduling total debt repayment requirements over a period of 5 to 10 years into the future and relating these to after-tax funds expected to be available from operations.

6. Other Fixed Charges

While interest payments and debt repayment requirements are the fixed charges most directly related to the incurrence of debt, there is no logical justification to restrict the evaluation of long-term solvency only to these charges and commitments. Thus, a complete analysis of fixed charges that an enterprise is obliged to meet must include all long-term rental payment obligations[18] (not only the interest portion thereof) and particularly those rentals that must be met under any and all circumstances under noncancelable leases, otherwise known as "hell-and-high-water" leases.

The reason why short-term leases can be excluded from consideration as fixed charges is that they represent an obligation of limited duration, usually less than three years, and can consequently be discontinued in a period of severe financial stringency. Here, the analyst must, however, evaluate how essential the rented items are to the continuation of the enterprise as a going concern.

Other charges that are not directly related to debt but that may nevertheless be considered as long-term commitments of a fixed nature are long-term purchase contracts in excess of normal requirements not subject to cancellation and other similar obligations.

7. Guarantees to Pay Fixed Charges

Guarantees to pay fixed charges of unconsolidated subsidiaries or of unaffiliated persons (such as suppliers) should result in additions to fixed charges if the requirement to honor the guarantee appears imminent.

RATIO OF EARNINGS TO FIXED CHARGES

In its revised regulations concerning the "Ratio of Earnings to Fixed Charges," the SEC's concept of computing this ratio moved so close to our own that we present it on page 174 as the standard conventional[19] computation.

---

[18] Capitalized long-term leases affect income by the interest charge implicit in them as well as by the amortization of the property right. Thus, to consider the "principal" component of such leases as fixed charges (after income was reduced by amortization of the property right) may amount to double counting.

[19] Still in use but so simple as not to require elaboration here is the times-interest-earned ratio which considers only interest as a fixed charge to be covered, thus:

$$\frac{\text{Pretax income} + \text{Interest expense}}{\text{Interest expense}}$$

The key letters below explain items in the formula and will serve as a reference to computations as well as to the summary-amplifying notes which follow:

A Income before discontinued operations, extraordinary items, and cumulative effects of accounting changes.

B Interest incurred *less* interest capitalized.

C Is often included in interest expense.

D Since all financing leases are capitalized, the interest implicit in these is already included in interest expense—the interest portion of long-term operating leases is included on the theory that many long-term operating leases narrowly miss the criteria for a capital lease under *SFAS 13* but still have many of the characteristics of a financing transaction.

E Excluding in all cases items eliminated in consolidation. The dividend has to be increased to pre-tax earnings that would be required to cover such dividend requirements, that is:

$$\frac{\text{Preferred stock dividend requirements}}{100 \text{ percent} - \text{Income tax rate*}}$$

* Based on relationship between applicable actual income tax provision to income *before* income taxes, extraordinary items, and cumulative effect of accounting changes.

F Applies to nonutility companies only. In most cases, disclosure of this amount is not made.

G Minority interest in income of majority-owned subsidiaries that have fixed charges may be included in income.

H Whether expensed or capitalized.

The SEC's formula for computing the ratio is:

(Numerator)

(A) Pre-tax income from continuing operations *plus* (B) Interest expensed *plus* (C) Amortization of debt expense and discount or premium *plus* (D) Interest portion of operating rental expenses *plus* (E) Tax-adjusted preferred stock dividend requirements of majority-owned subsidiaries *plus* (F) Amount of previously capitalized interest amortized during the period *minus* (G) Undistributed income of less than 50-percent-owned persons (affiliates)

(Denominator)

(H) Total interest incurred *plus* (C) Amortization of debt expense and discount or premium *plus* (D) Interest portion of operating rental expenses *plus* (E) Tax-adjusted preferred stock dividend requirements of majority-owned subsidiaries

General

To reduce the complexity of the formula, two items (provisions) were left out:

1. In computing earnings, the *full* amount of losses of majority-owned subsidiaries should be considered.
2. Losses on investments in less than 50-percent-owned companies accounted for by the equity method should not be included in earnings *unless* the company has guaranteed the debt of the affiliate.

If the ratio of earnings to fixed charges is less than one, the amount of insufficiency of earnings to cover the fixed charges should be given (rather than a ratio).

Illustration of Earnings-Coverage-Ratio Calculations

Having discussed the various considerations that enter into the decision of what factors to include in the earnings-coverage-ratio computation, we will address ourselves now to the question of how the ratio is computed. The computation of the various coverage ratios will be based on the illustration in Exhibit 5–5.

Using the data in Exhibit 5–5 and letter references to the above formula, we compute the ratio of earnings to fixed charges as follows (dollars in thousands):

$$\frac{\$2,200 \text{ (A)} + \$700 \text{ (B and C)} + \$300 \text{ (D)} + \$80 \text{ (F)} - \$600 \text{ (G)} + \$200^*}{\$840 \text{ (H)} + \$60 \text{ (C)} + \$300 \text{ (D)}} = \underline{\underline{2.4}} \text{ times}$$

* The SEC permits the inclusion in income of the minority interest in the income of majority-owned subsidiaries that have fixed charges. This amount is added in order to reverse a similar deduction from income.

The ratio of earnings to fixed charges of Quaker Oats (see Appendix to Chapter 10), for 1991 can be computed as follows (letter references are to the formula above—dollars in millions):

$$\frac{\text{(A) } 411.5^{(a)} + \text{(B)}101.9^{(b)} + \text{(D)}14.8^{(c)}}{\text{(H)}103.8^d + \text{(D)}14.8^{(c)}} = 4.45$$

[a] Income from continuing operations before taxes—item [7].
[b] Interest expensed—item [156].
[c] One third of operating lease rentals or $\frac{1}{3}$ of $44.5 = $14.8. [154].
[d] Interest incurred $101.9 + 1.9 = 103.8 [156].

PRO FORMA COMPUTATIONS OF COVERAGE RATIOS

In cases where fixed charges yet to be incurred are to be recognized in the computation of the coverage ratio, as, for example, interest costs under a prospective incurrence of debt, it is quite proper to estimate the offsetting benefits that will ensue from such future inflows of cash and to include these estimated benefits in the pro forma income. Benefits to

Exhibit 5–5

THE LEVERED CORPORATION
Abbreviated Income Statement

Net sales		$13,400,000
Income of less than 50%-		
owned affiliates (all undistributed)		600,000
		14,000,000
Cost of goods sold	$7,400,000	
Selling, general, and administrative expenses	1,900,000	
Depreciation (excluded from above costs) (3)	800,000	
Interest expense (1)—net	700,000	
Rental expense (2)	800,000	
Share of minority interests in		
consolidated income*	200,000	11,800,000
Income before taxes		2,200,000
Income taxes:		
Current	800,000	
Deferred	300,000	1,100,000
Income before extraordinary items		1,100,000
Gain on sale of investment in land (net of $67,000		
tax)		200,000
Net income		$ 1,300,000
Dividends:		
On common stock	200,000	
On preferred stock	400,000	600,000
Earnings retained for the year		$ 700,000

* These subsidiaries have fixed charges.

Selected notes to the financial statements:
1. The interest expense is composed of the following:

Interest incurred (except items below)	$740,000
Amortization of bond discount	60,000
Interest portion of capitalized leases	100,000
Interest capitalized	(200,000)
Interest expense	$700,000

2. Interest implicit in noncapitalized leases amounts to $300,000.
3. Depreciation includes amortization of previously capitalized interest of $80,000.

Additional information (during year covered by Income Statement):

Increase in accounts receivable	$310,000
Increase in inventories	180,000
Increase in accounts payable	140,000
Decrease in accrued taxes	20,000

be derived from a prospective loan can be measured in terms of interest savings obtainable from a planned refunding operation, income from short-term investments in which the proceeds may be invested, or similarly reasonable estimates of future benefits.

The SEC will usually insist on the presentation of a pro forma computation of the ratio of earnings to fixed charges that reflects changes to be effected under prospective financing plans when the effect of the refinancing changes the historical ratio by 10 percent or more.

CASH FLOW COVERAGE OF FIXED CHARGES

The discussion earlier in this chapter pointed out that net income is generally not a reliable measure of cash provided by operations that is available to meet fixed charges. The reason is, of course, that fixed charges are paid with cash while net income includes items of revenue that do not generate cash as well as expense items which do not require the current use of cash. Thus, a better measure of fixed-charges coverage may be obtained by using in the numerator cash obtained by operations rather than net income. This figure can be obtained from the SCF.

Under this concept, the coverage ratio would be computed as follows:

$$\frac{\text{Pre-tax cash provided by operations} + \text{Fixed charges}}{\text{Fixed charges}}$$

Using the data in Exhibit 5–5 we compute the coverage ratio as follows:

Cash provided by operations (pre-tax):	
Pre-tax income	$2,200,000
Add (deduct) adjustments to cash basis:	
Depreciation	80,000
Deferred income taxes (already added back)	—
Amortization of bond discount	60,000
Share of minority interest in income..................	200,000
Undistributed income of affiliates	(600,000)
Increase in receivables	(310,000)
Increase in inventories	(180,000)
Increase in accounts payable	140,000
Decrease in accrued tax	(20,000)
Cash provided by operations (CFO)	$2,290,000

The fixed charges to be added back to pre-tax cash provided by operations of

	$2,290,000
Interest expensed (less bond discount added back above)	640,000
Interest portion of operating rental expense	300,000
Amount of previously capitalized interest amortized during period*	—
Total numerator	$3,230,000

* Assumed here to be included in depreciation (already added back).

Note that the numerator does not reflect a deduction of $600,000 (undistributed income of affiliates) because that figure, being a noncash providing item, was already deducted at arriving at pre-tax cash provided by operations. Similarly, the "share of minority interests in consolidated income" has already been added back in arriving at the pre-tax cash provided by operations figure.

The fixed charges in the denominator are computed as follows:

Interest incurred	$ 900,000
Interest portion of operating rentals	300,000
	$1,200,000

Thus, the ratio of pre-tax cash provided by operations to fixed charges is:

$$\frac{\$3,230,000}{\$1,200,000} = \underline{\underline{2.69}}$$

Quaker Oats' (see Appendix to Chapter 10) cash provided by operations to fixed charges ratio is computed as follows:

Numerator	$ millions
Cash provided by operating activities—item [31]	532.4
Add back	
Income tax expense (except deferred)[a]—item [158]	161.4
Interest expensed—item [156]	101.9
Amortization of previously capitalized interest (already added back)—presumably included in item [20]	—
Total numerator	795.7

Thus the ratio is

$$\frac{\$795.7}{\$103.8^{(b)} + \$14.8^{(c)}} = \underline{\underline{6.7}}$$

[a] Deferred tax already added back in computation of CFO.
[b] Interest incurred—item 156 (101.9 + 1.9).
[c] 1/3 of operating lease rentals of $44.5 154.

STABILITY OF "FLOW OF CASH FROM OPERATIONS"

Since the relationship between the "flow of cash from operations" to the fixed charges of an enterprise is so important to an evaluation of long-term solvency, it is important to assess the stability of that flow. This is done by a careful evaluation of the elements that comprise the sources of cash from operations. For example, the depreciation add-back to net income is a more stable element than is net income itself because the recovery of the depreciation cost from selling prices precedes the earning of any net income, and has thus a higher degree of probability of happening. Even in very competitive industries selling prices must, in the long run, reflect the cost of plant and equipment used up in production.

It should be noted that the depreciation add-back assumes that the cash-flow benefits of the recovery of depreciation from sales prices will be available to meet debt service. This, however, can be true only in the short run or in an emergency. In the long run such cash recovery must be dedicated to replacement of plant and equipment. This may not be true in the case of add-backs such as amortization of goodwill, which does not have to be replaced.

The stability of the change in the "current assets and current liabilities related to operations" component of cash from operations is more difficult to assess. This component is more strongly related to sales than to pre-tax income and may thus be more stable than the latter.

EARNINGS COVERAGE OF PREFERRED DIVIDENDS

In the evaluation of preferred stock issues, it is often instructive to calculate the earnings coverage of preferred dividends, much in the same way the interest or fixed-charges coverage of debt issues is computed. The computation of the earnings coverage of preferred dividends must include as charges to be covered by earnings all fixed charges that take precedence over the payment of preferred dividends.[20] As is the case with

---

[20] This is also the position of the SEC. Care must be exercised in comparing these coverage ratios because some analysts and financial services include only the preferred dividend requirements in the computation.

all fixed-charges-coverage computations, the final ratio depends on a definition of "fixed charges."

Since preferred dividends are not tax deductible, after-tax income must be used to cover them. Consequently, the basic formula for computing preferred dividend coverage is:

$$\frac{\text{Income before tax} + \text{Fixed charges*}}{\text{Fixed charges*} + \text{Preferred dividends} \times \left(\dfrac{1}{1 - \text{Tax rate}}\right)}$$

* Which *are* tax deductible.

To the formula we used earlier (see page 174) to compute the ratio of earnings to fixed charges for The Levered Corporation based on data in Exhibit 5–5, we now add the tax-adjusted preferred-dividend requirement in order to derive the preferred-dividend coverage ratio as follows (dollars in thousands):

$$\frac{\$2{,}200 \text{ (A)} + \$700 \text{ (B and C)} + \$300 \text{ (D)} + \$80 \text{ (F)} - \$600 \text{ (G)} + \$200^*}{\$840 \text{ (H)} + \$60 \text{ (C)} + \$300 \text{ (D)} + \$400 \left(\dfrac{1}{1 - 0.50}\right)^\dagger} = \underline{\underline{1.44}}$$

* Minority interest in income of majority-owned subsidiaries (see prior discussion).
† Tax-adjusted preferred dividend requirement.

If there are two or more preferred issues outstanding, a by-class coverage ratio can be computed by omitting the dividend requirements of the junior issue but always including all prior fixed charges and preferred dividends.

EVALUATION OF EARNINGS-COVERAGE RATIOS

The earnings-coverage ratio test is a test of the ability of an enterprise to meet its fixed charges out of current earnings. In a classic and pioneering analysis of investor experience in bonds, Hickman[21] found the following life span default rates at offering during 1900–1943 and their relationship to the Times-Charges-Earned Ratio:

---

[21] W. B. Hickman, *Corporate Bond Quality and Investor Experience* (Princeton, N.J.: Princeton University Press, 1958), also found (p. 11) that bonds with poor earnings coverage had a probability of default 17 times greater than those with good coverage.

Times-Charges-Earned Ratio	Default rate	Promised yield	Realized yield	Loss rate
3.0 and over	2.1	4.0	4.9	−0.9
2.0–2.9	4.0	4.3	5.1	−0.8
1.5–1.9	17.9	4.7	5.0	−0.3
1.0–1.4	34.1	6.8	6.4	0.4
Under 1.0	35.0	6.2	6.0	0.2

The correlation of the times-charges-earned ratio and the default rate is unmistakable.

The orientation toward earnings is a logical one because the bondholder or other long-term creditor, while interested in asset coverage or what can be salvaged in times of trouble, relies even more on the ability of the enterprise to stay out of trouble by meeting its obligations currently and as a going concern. Given the limited returns obtainable from debt instruments, an increase in the interest rate can rarely compensate the creditor for a serious risk of loss of principal. Thus, if the probability of the enterprise meeting its obligations as a going concern is not strong, then a creditor relationship can hardly be advantageous.

The coverage ratio is influenced by the level of earnings and by the level of fixed charges, which in turn depend importantly on the debt to equity relationship within the capitalization.

Importance of Earnings Variability

One very important factor in the evaluation of the coverage ratio is the pattern of behavior of cash flows over time, or the behavior of its surrogate—earnings. The more stable the earnings pattern of an enterprise or industry, the lower the relative earnings-coverage ratio that will be acceptable. Thus, a utility, which in times of economic downturn is likely to experience only a mild falloff in demand, can justify a lower earnings-coverage ratio than can a cyclical company, such as a machinery manufacturer, that may experience a sharp drop in sales in times of recession. Variability of earnings is, thus, an important factor in the determination of the coverage standard. In addition, the durability and the trend of earnings are important factors that must be considered apart from their variability.[22]

---

[22] Most factors that will affect an entity's equity securities will also affect its bonds. For example, when Consolidated Edison Company passed its dividend in 1974, its bonds plunged along with its common stock which was the security directly affected. The market, aside from taking its cue from this action, may also have concluded that the company's ability to sell equity securities as well as its overall financing flexibility had been impaired.

Importance of Method of Computation and of
Underlying Assumptions

The coverage standard will also depend on the method of computation of the coverage ratio. As we saw above, varying methods of computing the coverage ratio assume different definitions of "income" and of "fixed charges." It is reasonable to expect lower standards of coverage for the ratios that employ the most demanding and stringent definitions of these terms.

The SEC formula for computing the fixed-charges-coverage ratio that we have adopted here is based on income *before* discontinued operations, extraordinary items, and cumulative effects of accounting changes. While these exclusions impart a degree of stability to the earnings, they also remove from them important elements that must be considered as part of the operating experience of the entity. These elements should always be included in computing the *average* coverage ratio over a number of years.

The standards will also vary with the kind of earnings that are utilized in the coverage computation, that is, average earnings, the earnings of the poorest year, and so on. Moreover, the quality of earnings is an important consideration (see Chapter 9).

It is not advisable to compute earnings-coverage ratios under methods that are not theoretically sound and whose only merit is that they are conservative. Thus, using after-tax income in the computation of the coverage ratio of fixed charges that are properly deductible for tax purposes is not logical and introduces conservatism in the wrong place. Any standard of coverage adequacy must, in the final analysis, be related to the willingness and ability of the lender to incur risk.

Appendix 5A includes references to standards of fixed-charges-coverage ratios used by rating agencies in determining the ratings of individual debt securities.

CAPITAL STRUCTURE, LEVERAGED BUYOUTS, "JUNK BONDS," AND OTHER FINANCIAL "INNOVATIONS"

The reader may find it instructive to relate some recent developments in finance to the basic characteristics of risk inherent in a company's capital structure, as discussed above.

It is possible to increase the risks (as well as the potential rewards) of equity holders by increasing the degree of leverage of an entity. The leveraged buyout of a company accomplishes this by using increased leverage and other factors favorable to buyers such as the existence of undervalued assets which can be sold off for cash. Thus, in a leveraged buyout debt is used to take a company private and to buy out equity holders. The acquirors rely on cash flow to service the increased debt and on an anticipated sale of assets to reduce it. Also working to the advantage of debt issuers is the fact that interest on debt is tax deductible while dividends paid to equity holders are not.

A massive substitution of debt for equity (also referred to as decapitalization) inevitably results in a much riskier capital structure. Thus, many bonds used to finance such leveraged buyouts are referred to as "junk bonds." A junk bond, unlike its higher quality counterpart, is part of a highly risky capital structure and its interest payments are barely covered or poorly covered by earnings. Thus, economic adversity can easily jeopardize the payment of interest and principal on them. These bonds have more of the risk of equity than the safety of debt as their real characteristics.

Financial history has, time and again, proven to those who ignore its lessons that higher risk means higher probability of loss. That a highly speculative financial era has spawned risky securities is no surprise. The surprise is that so many refused to believe that the adjective *junk* when applied to bonds, meant what it implied. Similarly, zero coupon bonds, which defer all payment of interest to maturity, have great advantages if issued by the U. S. government. When issued, however, by those with less than impeccable credit credentials the risk inherent in zero coupon instruments is greatly increased because all interest as well as principal repayment is postponed into the far-off future. PIK Securities, standing for "payment in kind," pay interest by issuing additional debt. There the assumption must surely be that a debtor, too weak to pay interest currently, will somehow be strong enough to pay it much later.

While many novel approaches to the financing of companies have been tried and new words coined which stress form over substance, the basic truths about the relationships of risk and reward inherent in a capital structure remain unchanged.

THOROUGH ANALYSIS IS ESSENTIAL

The factors contributing to risks and the available tools of analysis discussed in this and the preceding chapters point to the need for care and thoroughly grounded analysis in the extension of credit.

Reliance on credit ratings, which will be discussed below, is basically a delegation of the analysis and evaluation function. It is very risky to place exclusive reliance on a single source of analysis, no matter how reputable, without forming some degree of independent judgment regarding the merit of a credit extension.

ILLUSTRATION 1. In June 1987, World of Wonder Inc. raised $80 million from the sale of convertible debentures by the highly reputable firm of Smith Barney Inc. Before even paying its first coupon, the company filed for protection from its creditors under Chapter 11 of the Bankruptcy Act. The bonds, which were initially sold for $1,000 each, traded for $75 after the filing.

APPENDIX 5A

THE RATING OF DEBT OBLIGATIONS

Over many years there has become established in the United States a comprehensive and sophisticated system for rating debt securities. Most ratings are performed by two highly regarded investment research firms, Moody's and Standard & Poor's (S&P).[23]

A bond credit rating is a composite expression of judgment about the creditworthiness of the bond issuer as well as the quality of the specific security being rated. A rating measures credit risk, that is, the probability of occurrence of developments adverse to the interests of the creditor.

This judgment of creditworthiness is expressed in a series of symbols that express degrees of credit risk. Thus, the top four rating grades of Standard & Poor's are:

AAA. Bonds rated AAA are highest-grade obligations. They possess the ultimate degree of protection as to principal and interest. Marketwise they move with interest rates, and hence provide the maximum safety on all counts.

AA. Bonds rated AA also qualify as high-grade obligations, and in the majority of instances differ from AAA issues only in small degree. Here, too, prices move with the long-term money market.

A. Bonds rated A are regarded as upper medium grade. They have considerable investment strength but are not entirely free from adverse effects of changes in economic and trade conditions. Interest and principal are regarded as safe. They predominantly reflect money rates in their market behavior, but to some extent, also economic conditions.

BBB. The BBB, or medium-grade category is borderline between definitely sound obligations and those where the speculative element begins to predominate. These bonds have adequate asset coverage and normally are protected by satisfactory earnings. Their susceptibility to changing conditions, particularly to depressions, necessitates constant watching. Marketwise, the bonds are more responsive to business and trade conditions than to interest rates. This group is the lowest that qualifies for commercial bank investment.

---

[23] Ratings are also performed by Duff and Phelps and by Fitch Investors Service. Many institutions also develop their own "in house" ratings.

There is a lower range of ratings ranging from BB which are lower medium grade all the way to the D category representing bonds in default.

The major reason why debt securities are widely rated while equity securities are not lies in the fact that there is a far greater uniformity of approach and homogeneity of analytical measures used in the evaluation of creditworthiness than there can be in the evaluation of the future market performance of equity securities. Thus, the wide agreement on what is being measured in credit risk analysis has resulted in a widespread acceptance of and reliance on published credit ratings.

The criteria that enter into the determination of a rating have never been precisely defined, and they involve both quantitative measures (e.g., ratio analysis) as well as qualitative factors such as market position and management quality. The major rating agencies refuse to be pinned down on what precise mix of factors enter into their rating process (which is a committee decision) because it is both art and science and also because to do so would cause endless arguments about the validity of the many judgmental factors that enter into a rating decision.

We can then see that in arriving at ratings these agencies must undertake analyses along the lines discussed throughout this book, the differences being mainly in the vast number of debt issues covered and the standardization of approaches which this entails. The following description of factors entering the rating process is based on published sources as well as on discussions with officials of the rating agencies.

THE RATING OF CORPORATE BONDS

In rating an industrial bond issue, the rating agency will focus on the issuing company's asset protection, financial resources, earning power, management, and the specific provisions of the debt security.

Also of great importance are size of firm, market share, industry position, susceptibility to cyclical influences,[24] and other broad economic factors.

Asset protection is concerned with measuring the degree to which a company's debt is covered by the value of its assets. One measure is net tangible assets to long-term debt. At S&P, an industrial needs a ratio of 5 to 1 to get an AAA rating, a ratio of over 4 to 1 to qualify for an AA rating, 3 to 3.5 to 1 for an A, and about 2.5 to 1 for a BBB rating.

Understated assets, such as those of companies in the natural resource or real estate fields, are generally accorded recognition in the rating process.

The long-term debt as a percentage of total capitalization calls for a ratio of under 25 percent for an AAA, around 30 percent for an AA, 35 percent for an A, and about 40 percent for a BBB rating.

---

[24] There are, for example, no AAA-rated companies in the steel or paper industries.

Other factors entering the consideration of asset protection include the determination of book value, the makeup of working capital, the quality and age of property, plant, and equipment as well as questions of off-balance-sheet financing and unrecorded liabilities.

Financial resources encompass, in particular, such liquid resources as cash and other working capital items. Quality measures here include the collection period of receivables and inventory turnover. These are judged by means of industry standards. The use of debt, both short term and long term, as well as the mix between the two is also investigated.

Future earning power and the resulting cash-generating ability is a factor of great importance in the rating of debt securities because the level and the quality of future earnings determine importantly an enterprise's ability to meet its obligations. Earning power is generally a more reliable source of security than is asset protection.

A prime measure of the degree of protection afforded by earning power is the fixed-charges-coverage ratio. To qualify for consideration for an AAA rating, an industrial company's earnings should cover its interest and rental charges after taxes above five to seven times, for an AA rating above four times, for an A rating over three times, and a BBB over two times.

Another measure of debt service paying ability is cash flow (from operations) to total funded debt. It should be 65 percent or more for an AAA, 45 to 60 percent for an AA, 35 to 45 percent for an A, and 25 to 30 percent for a BBB rating.

Management abilities, philosophy, depth, and experience always loom importantly in any final rating judgment. Through interviews, field trips, and other analyses, the raters probe into the depth and breadth of management, as well as into its goals, the planning process, and strategies in such areas as research and development, product promotion, new product planning, and acquisitions.

The specific provisions of the debt security are usually spelled out in the bond indenture. What is analyzed here are the specific provisions in the indenture that are designed to protect the interests of bondholders under a variety of future conditions. Included in consideration here are, among others, conditions for issuance of future debt issues, specific security provisions such as mortgaging, sinking fund and redemption provisions, and restrictive covenants.

As can be seen, debt rating is a complex process involving quantitative as well as qualitative factors, all of which culminate in the issuance of a single quality rating. The weights that may be assigned to each factor will vary among analysts, but the final conclusion will generally represent the composite judgment of several experienced raters.

THE RATING OF MUNICIPAL SECURITIES

Buyers of municipal bonds depend for their security of principal and interest on factors that are quite different from those that determine the quality of corporate debt. Hence, the processes of analysis differ.

Municipal securities, those issued by state and local governmental authorities, comprise a number of varieties. Many are general obligation bonds backed by the full faith and credit of the governmental unit that issues them. Others are special tax bonds that are limited in security to a particular tax that will be used to service and retire them. Then there are revenue bonds secured only by revenues of municipal enterprises. Other categories comprise housing authority bonds, tax anticipation notes, and so forth. Although the amount of information provided to buyers of municipal bonds is of very uneven quality there are moves to correct this, primarily by way of legislation.

Raters require a great variety of information from issuers of municipal debt. In the case of general obligation bonds, the basic security rests on the issuer's ability and willingness to repay the debt from general revenues under a variety of economic conditions.[25] The fundamental revenue source is the taxing power of the local municipality. Thus, the information they require includes current population and the trend and composition of population, the largest 10 taxpayers, the current market value of taxable properties, the gross indebtedness, and the net indebtedness (i.e., after deducting self-sustaining obligations, sinking fund, etc.), recent annual reports, budgets, and estimates of capital improvement and future borrowing programs, as well as an overall description of the area's economy.

While rating techniques have the same objectives as in the case of corporate bonds, the ratios used are adapted to the specific conditions that exist with respect to municipal debt obligations. Thus, debt as a percentage of market value of real estate is an important indicator: 10 percent is considered high while 3–5 percent is on the low side. Annual debt service of 10 percent of total revenue is considered comfortable while percentages in the high teens are considered as presenting a warning sign. Per capita debt of $400 or less is considered low while debt in the $900 to $1,000 area is considered excessive and, hence, a negative factor. Tax delinquencies should generally not exceed 3–4 percent.

Other factors of interest include unfunded pension liabilities as well as the trend of indebtedness. A steady increase in indebtedness is usually a danger sign. As in all cases of debt rating, the factor of management, though largely intangible and subject to measurement only through ultimate results, is of critical importance.

---

[25] The decision of New York State's highest court to overturn the New York City Moratorium on its notes strengthens the meaning of the concept of "full faith and credit." Said Chief Justice C. J. Breitel: "A pledge of the city's faith and credit is both a commitment to pay and a commitment of the city's revenue generating powers to produce the funds to pay . . . that is the way both words 'faith' and 'credit' are used and they are not tautological."

LIMITATIONS OF THE RATING PROCESS

As valuable and essential as the rating process is to buyers of the thousands upon thousands of bond issues of every description, the limitations of this standardized procedure must also be understood.[26] As is true in any phase of security analysis, the analyst who can, through superior analysis, improve on what is conventionally accepted stands to benefit accordingly. As was seen in Chapter 1, this is even more true in the case of debt securities than in the case of equity securities.

Bond ratings cover a wide range of characteristics, and they consequently present opportunities for those who can identify these differences within a rating classification. Moreover, rating changes generally lag the market, and this presents additional opportunities to the analyst who with superior skill and alertness can identify important changes before they become generally recognized.

References

"The Rating Game." New York: The Twentieth Century Fund, 1974.

H. C. Sherwood. *How Corporate and Municipal Debt Is Rated: An Inside Look at Standard & Poor's Rating System.* New York: John Wiley & Sons, 1976.

Corporate Bond Ratings: An Overview. New York: Standard & Poor's Corporation, 1978.

D. F. Hawkins, B. A. Brown, W. J. Campbell. "Rating Industrial Bonds." Morristown, N.J.: Financial Executives Research Foundation, 1983.

"The Ratings Game," *Institutional Investor,* August 1991, p. 73.

APPENDIX 5B

RATIOS AS PREDICTORS OF BUSINESS FAILURE

The most common use to which financial statement ratios are put is to use them as pointers in the direction of further investigation and analysis. Some investigation and experimentation has been undertaken to determine to what extent ratios can be used as predictors of failure. As such they could provide valuable additional tools in the analysis of long-term solvency.

The basic idea behind bankruptcy prediction models is that through observation of the trend and behavior of certain ratios of various firms

---

[26] As the huge defaults of the Washington Public Power Supply System Project 4 and 5 bonds have shown, good ratings can be withdrawn and can evaporate quickly. It appears that in this case the rating agencies paid more attention to legal obligations than to the economic underpinnings of these issues.

before failure, those characteristics in ratios that predominate in failing firms can be identified and used for prediction purposes. The expectation is that signs of deterioration observed in ratio behavior can be detected early enough and clearly enough so that timely action can be taken to avoid substantial risk of default and failure.

Empirical Studies

Among the earliest studies to focus on the behavior of ratios prior to the failure of firms were those of Winakor and Smith who studied a sample of 183 firms that experienced financial difficulties for as long as 10 years prior to 1931, the year when they failed.[27] Analyzing the 10-year trend of 21 ratios, they concluded that the ratio of net working capital to total assets was among the most accurate and reliable indicator of failure.

Fitzpatrick analyzed the three- to five-year trends of 13 ratios of 20 firms that had failed in the 1920–29 period.[28] By comparing them to the experience of a control group of 19 successful firms, he concluded that all of his ratios predicted failure to some extent. However, the best predictors were found to be the return on net worth and the net worth to total debt ratio.

Merwin studied the experience of a sample of 939 firms during the 1926–36 period.[29] Analyzing an unspecified number of ratios he found that three ratios were most sensitive in predicting "discontinuance" of a firm as early as four to five years before such discontinuance. The three ratios were the current ratio, net working capital to total assets, and net worth to total debt. They all exhibited declining trends before "discontinuance" and were at all times below estimated normal ratios.

Focusing on the experience of companies that experienced defaults on debt and bank credit difficulties, Hickman studied the experience of corporate bond issues during 1900–43 and reached the conclusion that the times interest earned ratio and the net profit-to-sales ratio were useful predictors of bond issue defaults.[30]

In a study using more powerful statistical techniques than used in its predecessors, Beaver found that financial ratios proved useful in the prediction of bankruptcy and bond default at least five years prior to such failure. He determined that ratios could be used to distinguish

---

[27] Arthur Winakor and Raymond F. Smith, *Changes in Financial Structure of Unsuccessful Firms,* Bureau of Business Research (Urbana, Ill.: University of Illinois Press, 1935).

[28] Paul J. Fitzpatrick, *Symptoms of Industrial Failures* (Washington, D.C.: Catholic University of America Press, 1931); and Paul J. Fitzpatrick, *A Comparison of the Ratios of Successful Industrial Enterprises with Those of Failed Companies* (Washington, D.C.: The Accountants Publishing Co., 1932).

[29] Charles L. Merwin, *Financing Small Corporations in Five Manufacturing Industries, 1926–36* (New York: National Bureau of Economic Research, 1942).

[30] W. Braddock Hickman, *Corporate Bond Quality and Investor Experience* (Princeton, N.J.: Princeton University Press, 1958), pp. 395–431.

correctly between failed and nonfailed firms to a much greater extent than would be possible by random prediction.[31]

Among his conclusions were that both in the short term and the long term, cash flow to total debt ratios were the best predictors, capital structure ratios ranked second, liquidity ratios third, while turnover ratios were the worst predictors.

In an investigation of the ability of ratios to predict bond-rating changes and bond ratings of new issues, Horrigan found that the rating changes could be correctly predicted to a much greater extent by the use of ratios than would be possible through random prediction.[32]

Altman extended Beaver's univariate analysis to allow for multiple predictors of failure.[33] Altman used multiple discriminant analysis (MDA) that attempts to develop a linear function of a number of explanatory variables to classify or predict the value of a qualitative dependent variable; for example, bankrupt or nonbankrupt. Twenty-two financial ratios, based on data one period before bankruptcy, were examined, and Altman selected five of these to be included in his final discriminant function: working capital/total assets (liquidity), retained earnings/total assets (age of firm and cumulative profitability), earnings before interest and taxes/total assets (profitability), market value of equity/book value of debt (financial structure), and sales/total assets (capital turnover rate).

Altman used the above five ratios to construct the Z-score which is currently the best known bankruptcy prediction model:

$$\text{Z-score} = 1.2 \left[\frac{\text{Net working capital}}{\text{Total assets}} \right] + 1.4 \left[\frac{\text{Retained earnings}}{\text{Total assets}} \right]$$

$$+ 3.3 \left[\frac{\text{Earnings before interest and taxes}}{\text{Total assets}} \right] + 0.6 \left[\frac{\text{Market value of equity}}{\text{Book value of liabilities}} \right]$$

$$+ 1.0 \left[\frac{\text{Sales}}{\text{Total assets}} \right]$$

Experience with the Z-score model led Altman to conclude that Z-scores of less than 1.81 indicate a high probability of bankruptcy while Z-scores above 3.00 indicate a low probability of bankruptcy.

[31] William H. Beaver, "Financial Ratios as Predictors of Failure," *Empirical Research in Accounting, Selected Studies, 1966,* Supplement to *Journal of Accounting Research* 4, pp. 71–127.

[32] James O. Horrigan, "The Determination of Long-Term Credit Standing with Financial Ratios," *Empirical Research in Accounting, Selected Studies, 1966,* Supplement to *Journal of Accounting Research* 4, pp. 44–62.

[33] Edward Altman, "Financial Ratios, Discriminant Analysis, and the Prediction of Corporate Bankruptcy," *Journal of Finance* 22 (September 1968), pp. 589–609.

Conclusions

The above research efforts, while pointing out the significant potential that ratios have as predictors of failure, nevertheless indicate that these tools and concepts are in an early stage of development.

The studies focused on experience with failed firms *after the fact*. While they presented evidence that firms that did not fail enjoyed stronger ratios than those that ultimately failed, the ability of ratios alone to predict failure has not been conclusively proved. Another important question yet to be resolved is whether the observation of certain types of behavior by certain ratios can be accepted as a better means of the analysis of long-term solvency than is the integrated use of the various tools described throughout this work. Further research may show that the use of ratios as predictors of failure will best complement and precede, rather than replace, the rigorous financial analysis approaches suggested in this work. However, as screening,[34] monitoring, and attention-directing devices they hold considerable promise.

APPENDIX 5C

ILLUSTRATION OF THE COMPUTATION OF THE ANALYTICALLY ADJUSTED LONG-TERM DEBT TO EQUITY RATIO

The conventional long-term debt to equity ratio is expressed as

$$\frac{LTD}{OE}$$

The formula that follows incorporates other analytical adjustments which can be made:

$$\frac{LTD + NFL}{OE + NDT + FIFOA + MSA}$$

where:

LTD = Long-term debt consists of all long-term liabilities inclusive of noncurrent deferred taxes judged *likely* to reverse and other noncurrent liabilities.

NDT = Noncurrent deferred taxes—which are judged as *unlikely* to reverse in the foreseeable future.

---

[34] Banks have for years been using credit scoring for personal loans, which gives weight to creditworthiness characteristics such as income, employment, and homeownership. But for loans above $10,000–$25,000, banks no longer rely on the mass-production techniques of credit scoring.

OE   = Owners' equity (including minority interests).
FIFOA = Excess of disclosed FIFO value of ending inventory over
           reported LIFO amount.
MSA   = Excess of market value of marketable securities over cost.
NFL   = Present value of noncapitalized financial leases.

Using the 1991 data of Quaker Oats (see Appendix 10) we can compute
the analytically adjusted debt to equity ratio as follows:

$$\frac{701.2^{(a)} + 115.5^{(b)} + 147^{(c)}}{806.5^{(d)} + 99.3^{(g)} + 220^{(e)} + 18.9^{(f)}} = \frac{963.7}{1144.7} = 0.84$$

$^{(a)}$ Long-term debt—item $\boxed{79}$.
$^{(b)}$ Other liabilities—$\boxed{80}$.
$^{(c)}$ 40% of deferred income taxes $\boxed{81}$ assumed liability portion.
$^{(d)}$ Shareholders' equity $\boxed{91}$–$\boxed{83}$.
$^{(e)}$ 60% of deferred income taxes $\boxed{81}$-assumed equity portion.
$^{(f)}$ Excess of mostly average cost over LIFO $\boxed{143}$.
$^{(g)}$ Preferred stock outstanding—items $\boxed{91}$–$\boxed{83}$.

Not all the items in the formula described earlier were found or were
disclosed in Quaker Oat's report.

QUESTIONS

1. Generally speaking, what are the key elements in the evaluation of long-
   term solvency?
2. How should deferred income taxes be treated in the analysis of capital
   structure?
3. In the analysis of capital structure how should lease obligations that have
   not been capitalized be treated? Under what conditions should they be
   considered the equivalent of debt?
4. What is off-balance-sheet financing? Name some examples.
5. What are liabilities for pensions? What factors should analysts assessing
   total pension obligations of the firm take into consideration?
6. When will information on unconsolidated subsidiaries be important to the
   analysis of long-term solvency?
7. How would you classify (i.e., equity or liability) the items that follow?
   State your assumptions and reasons.
   a. Minority interest in consolidated financial statement.
   b. General contingency reserve for indefinite purpose.
   c. Reserve for self-insurance.
   d. Guarantee for product performance on sale.
   e. Convertible debt.
   f. Preferred stock.
8. a. Why might the analyst need to adjust the book value of assets?
   b. Give three examples of the need for possible adjustments.
9. Why is the analysis of capital structure important?
10. What is meant by "financial leverage," and in what case(s) is such leverage
    most advantageous?

11. In the evaluation of long-term solvency why are long-term projections necessary in addition to a short-term analysis? What are some of the limitations of long-term projections?

12. What is the difference between common-size analysis and capital structure ratio analysis? Why is the latter useful?

13. The amount of equity capital shown on the balance sheets, which is based on historical cost, at times differs considerably from realizable market value. How should a financial analyst allow for this in the analysis of capital structure?

14. Why should the analyst compute the ratio of preferred stock to total stockholders' equity? How should preferred stock with mandatory redemption requirements be treated?

15. Why is the analysis of assets distribution necessary?

16. What does the earnings-coverage ratio measure and in what respects is it more useful than other tools of analysis?

17. For the purpose of earnings-coverage-ratio computation, what are your criteria for inclusion of an item in "fixed charges"?

18. The company under analysis has a purchase commitment of raw materials under a noncancelable contract that is substantial in amount. Under what conditions would you include the purchase commitment in the computation of fixed charges?

19. Is net income generally a reliable measure of funds available to meet fixed charges?

20. Company B is a wholly owned subsidiary of Company A. The latter is also Company B's principal customer. As potential lender to Company B, what particular facets of this relationship would concern you most? What safeguards, if any, would you require?

21. Comment on the statement: "Debt is a supplement to, not a substitute for, equity capital."

22. A company in need of additional equity capital decides to sell convertible debt, thus postponing equity dilution and ultimately selling its shares at an effectively higher price. What are the advantages and disadvantages of such a course of action?

23. *a.* What is the basic function of restrictive covenants in long-term debt indentures (agreements)?

   b. What is the function of provisions regarding:
      (1) Maintenance of minimum working capital (or current ratio)?
      (2) Maintenance of minimum net worth?
      (3) Restrictions on the payment of dividends?
      (4) Ability of creditors to elect a majority of the board of directors of the debtor company in the event of default under the terms of the loan agreement?

24. What is your opinion on the use of ratios as predictors of failure? Your answer should recognize the empirical research that has been done recently in this area.

25. Dogwood Manufacturing, Inc., a successful and rapidly growing company, has always had a favorable difference between the rate of return on its assets and the interest rate paid on borrowed funds. Explain why the

company should *not* increase its debt to the 90-percent level of total capitalization and thereby minimize any need for equity financing. (CFA)

26. Why are debt securities widely rated while equity securities are not?
27. On what aspects do the rating agencies focus in rating an industrial bond? Elaborate.
28. *a.* Municipal securities comprise a number of varieties. Discuss.
    b. What factors are considered in the rating of municipal securities?
29. Can the analyst improve on a rating judgment? Discuss.

Chapter 6

ANALYSIS OF RETURN ON INVESTMENT AND OF ASSET UTILIZATION

DIVERSE VIEWS OF PERFORMANCE

In this age of increasing social consciousness, there exist many views of what the basic objectives of business enterprises are or should be. There are those who will argue that the main objective of a business enterprise should be to make the maximum contribution to the welfare of society of which the enterprise is capable. That includes, aside from the profitable production of goods and services, consideration of such immeasurables as absence of environmental pollution and a contribution to the solution of social problems. Others, who adhere to the more traditional *laissez faire* school, maintain that the major objective of a business enterprise organized for profit is to increase the wealth of its owners and that this is possible only by delivering to society (consumers) that which it wants. Thus, the good of society will be served.

An extended discussion of these differing points of view on performance is beyond the purpose of this book. Since the analysis of financial statements is concerned with the application of analytical tools to that which can be measured, we shall concentrate here on those measures of performance that meet the objectives of financial analysis as outlined in Chapter 1. In that context, performance is the source of the rewards required to compensate investors and lenders for the risks that they are assuming.

CRITERIA OF PERFORMANCE EVALUATION

There are many criteria by which performance can be measured. Changes in sales, in profits, or in various measures of output are among the criteria frequently utilized.

No one of these measurements, standing by itself, is useful as a comprehensive measure of enterprise performance. The reasons for this are easy to grasp. Increases in sales are desirable only if they result in increased profits. The same is true of increases in volume of production. Increases in profits, on the other hand, must be related to the capital that is invested in order to attain these profits.

IMPORTANCE OF RETURN ON INVESTMENT (ROI)

The relationship between net income and the capital invested in the generation of that income is one of the most valid and most widely recognized measures of enterprise performance. In relating income to invested capital, the ROI measure allows the analyst to compare it to alternative uses of capital as well as to the return realized by enterprises subject to similar degrees of risk. The investment of capital can always yield some return. If capital is invested in government bonds, the return will be relatively low because of the small risk involved. Riskier investments require higher returns in order to make them worthwhile.[1] The ROI measure relates income (reward) to the size of the capital that was needed to generate it.

MAJOR OBJECTIVES IN THE USE OF ROI

Economic performance is the first and foremost purpose of business enterprise. It is, indeed, the reason for its existence. The effectiveness of operating performance determines the ability of the enterprise to survive financially, to attract suppliers of funds, and to reward them adequately. ROI is a prime measure of economic performance. The analyst uses it as a tool in three areas of great importance:

1. An indicator of managerial effectiveness.
2. A measure of an enterprise's ability to earn a satisfactory return on investment.
3. A method of projecting earnings.

However, the discussion later in this chapter will show that ROI is not a completely reliable measure of an enterprise's ability to reward its owners—the suppliers of its equity capital.

An Indicator of Managerial Effectiveness

The earning of an adequate or superior return on funds invested in an enterprise depends first and foremost on the resourcefulness, skill, ingenuity, and motivation of management. Thus, the longer-term ROI is of great interest and importance to the financial analyst because it offers a prime means of evaluating this indispensible criterion of business success: the quality of management.

---

[1] See Chapter 1 for an examination of the importance of the evaluation of risk and return in investing and lending decisions.

A Measure of Enterprise Ability to Earn a Satisfactory ROI

While related to managerial effectiveness, this measure is a far more reliable indicator of long-term financial health than is any measure of current financial strength based only on balance sheet relationships. For this reason, ROI is of great importance and interest to longer-term creditors as well as to equity investors.

A Method of Projecting Earnings

A third important function served by the ROI measure is that of a means of earnings projection. The advantage of this method of earnings projection is that it links the amount of earnings that it is estimated an enterprise will earn to the total invested capital. This adds discipline and realism to the projection process, which applies to the present and expected capital investment the return that is expected to be realized on it. The latter will usually be based on the historical and incremental rates of return actually earned by the enterprise and adjusted by projected changes, as well as on expected returns on new projects.

The rate of ROI method of earnings projection can be used by the analyst as either the primary method of earnings projection or as a supplementary check on estimates derived from other projection methods.

Internal Decision and Control Tool

While our focus here is on the work of the external financial analyst, mention should be made of the very important role that ROI measures play in the individual investment decisions of an enterprise as well as in the planning, budgeting, coordination, evaluation, and control of business operations and results.

It is obvious that the final return achieved in any one period on the total investment of an enterprise is composed of the returns (and losses) realized by the various segments and divisions of which it is composed. In turn, these returns are made up of the results achieved by individual product lines, projects, and so forth.

The well-managed enterprise exercises rigorous control over the returns achieved by each of its "profit centers" and rewards its managers on the basis of such results. Moreover, in evaluating the advisability of new investments of funds in assets or projects, management will compute the estimated returns it expects to achieve from them and use these estimates as a basis for its decision.[2]

---

[2] Managements' emphasis on these techniques has been challenged. In their article "Managing Our Way to Economic Decline" in the *Harvard Business Review* of July–August 1980, Professors R. Hayes and W. Abernathy argue that this preoccupation with ROI and the related discounted cash flow measures has led to an emphasis on short-term profits at the expense of long-term risk taking based on improved technology.

BASIC ELEMENTS OF ROI

The basic concept of ROI is relatively simple to understand. However, care must be used in determining the elements entering its computation because there exist a variety of views, which reflect different objectives, of how these elements should be defined.

The basic formula for computing ROI is as follows:

$$\frac{\text{Income}}{\text{Investment}}$$

We shall now examine the various definitions of *investment* and of the related *income.*

Defining the Investment Base

There is no one generally accepted measure of capital investment on which the rate of return is computed. The different concepts of investment reflect different objectives. Since the term *return on investment (ROI)* covers a multitude of concepts of investment base and income, there is need for more specific terms to describe the actual investment base used.

Total Assets   Return on total assets is perhaps the best measure of the *operating efficiency* of an enterprise. It measures the return obtained on *all* the assets entrusted to management. By removing from this computation the effect of the method used in financing the assets, the analyst can concentrate on the evaluation or projection of operating performance.

Modified Asset Bases   For a variety of reasons, some ROI computations are based not on total assets but rather on an adjusted amount.

One important category of adjustments relates to "unproductive" assets. In this category, assets omitted from the investment base include idle plant, facilities under construction, surplus plant, surplus inventories and surplus cash, intangible assets, and deferred charges. The basic idea behind these exclusions is not to hold management responsible for earning a return on assets that apparently do not earn a return. While this theory may have validity in the use of ROI as an internal management and control tool, it lacks merit when applied as a tool designed to evaluate management effectiveness on an overall basis. Management is entrusted with funds by owners and creditors, and it has discretion as to where it wants to invest them. There is no reason for management to hold on to assets that bring no return. If there are reasons for keeping funds invested in such assets, then there is no reason to exclude them from the investment base. If the long-run profitability of an enterprise is benefited by keeping funds invested in assets that have no return or a low return in the interim, then the longer-term ROI should reflect such benefits. In conclusion, it can be said that from the point of view of an enterprise evaluation by the external analyst, there is rarely any justification to omit assets from the investment base merely because they are not productively employed or do not earn a current return.

The exclusion of intangible assets from the investment base is often due to skepticism regarding their value or their contribution to the earning power of the enterprise. Under generally accepted accounting principles (GAAP), intangibles are carried at cost. However, if the cost exceeds their future utility, they must be written down or else the analyst should at least find an uncertainty reference regarding their carrying value included in the auditor's opinion. The exclusion of intangible assets from the asset (investment) base must be justified on more substantial evidence than a mere lack of understanding of what these assets represent or an unsupported suspicion regarding their value.

Depreciable Assets in the Investment Base   An important difference of opinion prevails with respect to the question of whether depreciable assets should be included in the investment base at original cost or at an amount net of the accumulated allowances for depreciation.

One of the most prominent advocates of the inclusion of fixed assets at gross amount in the investment base for purposes of computing the ROI was the management of E. I. du Pont de Nemours Company which pioneered the use of ROI as an internal management tool.

In a pamphlet describing the company's use of the ROI method in the appraisal of operating performance, this point of view is expressed as follows:

> *Calculation of return on investment.* Return on investment as presented in the chart series is based upon *gross* operating investment and earnings *net* of depreciation.
>
> Gross operating investment represents all the plant, tools, equipment and working capital made available to operating management for its use; no deduction is made for current or other liabilities or for the reserve for depreciation. Since plant facilities are maintained in virtually top productive order during their working life, the depreciation reserve being considered primarily to provide for obsolescence, it would be inappropriate to consider that operating management was responsible for earning a return on only the net operating investment. Furthermore, if depreciable assets were stated at net depreciated values, earnings in each succeeding period would be related to an ever-decreasing investment; even with stable earnings, Return on Investment would continually rise, so that comparative Return on Investment ratios would fail to reveal the extent of trend of management performance. Relating earnings to investment that is stable and uniformly compiled provides a sound basis for comparing the

"profitability of assets employed" as between years and between investments.

In the case of any commitment of capital—e.g., an investment in a security—it is the expectation that in addition to producing earnings while committed, the principal will eventually be recovered. Likewise, in the case of funds invested in a project, it is expected that in addition to the return earned while invested, the working capital will be recovered through liquidation at the end of the project's useful life and the plant investment will be recovered through depreciation accruals. Since earnings must allow for this recovery of plant investment, they are stated net of depreciation.[3]

It is not difficult to take issue with the above reasoning. It must, however, be borne in mind that the Du Pont system is designed for use in the internal control of separate productive units as well as for the control of operating management. Our point of view here is, however, that of evaluating the operating performance of an enterprise taken as a whole. While by an enterprise operating at a profit, the recovery of capital out of sales and revenues (via depreciation) can be disregarded in the evaluation of a *single* division or segment, it cannot be disregarded for an enterprise taken as a whole because such recovery is reinvested somewhere within that enterprise even if it is not reinvested in the particular segment that gave rise to the depreciation and that is evaluated for internal purposes. Thus, for an enterprise taken as a whole, the "net of depreciation" asset base is a more valid measure of investment on which a return is computed. This is so for the reasons given above and also because the income that is usually related to the investment base is net of the depreciation expense.

The tendency of the rate of return to rise as assets are depreciated is offset by the retention of capital recovered by means of depreciation, on which capital a return must also be earned. Moreover, maintenance and repair costs rise as equipment gets older, thus tending to offset the reduction, if any, in the asset base.

Among other reasons advanced in support of the use of fixed assets at their gross amount is the argument that the higher amounts are designed to compensate for the effects of inflation on assets expressed in terms of historical cost. Price-level adjustments can validly be made only within the framework of a complete restatement of all elements of the financial statements. Crude "adjustments," such as using the gross asset amount, are apt to be misleading and are generally worse than no adjustments at all.

Long-Term Liabilities plus Equity Capital   The use of long-term liabilities plus equity capital as the investment base differs from the "total

[3] American Management Association, *Executive Committee Control Charts,* AMA Management Bulletin No. 6, 1960, p. 22.

assets" base only in that current liabilities are excluded as suppliers of funds on which the return is computed. The focus here is on the two major suppliers of longer-term funds, that is, long-term creditors and equity shareholders. In this context, working capital required to support operations is regarded as the excess of current assets over current liabilities.

Shareholders' Equity   The computation of return on shareholders' equity measures the return accruing to the owners' capital. As was seen in the discussion of financial leverage in Chapter 5, this return reflects the effect of the employment of debt capital on the owners' return. Since preferred stock, while in the equity category, is usually nevertheless entitled only to a fixed return, it is also omitted from the calculation of the final return on equity computation.

Book versus Market Values in the Investment Base

Return on asset calculations are most commonly based on book values appearing in the financial statements rather than on market or fair values that are, in most cases, analytically more significant and relevant. Also, quite often, a return is earned by enterprises on assets that either do not appear in the financial statements or are significantly understated therein. Examples of such assets are intangibles such as patents, trademarks, expensed research and development (R&D) costs, advertising and training costs, and so forth. Other excluded assets may include leaseholds and the value of natural resources discovered.

One avenue to the use of such data is to rely on the valuation that the market places on the equity securities of the enterprise in order to approximate fair values. Thus, we can substitute the market value of equity securities and debt for the book value of total assets in computing a proper investment base.

Difference between Investor's Cost and Enterprise Investment Base

For purposes of computing the ROI, a distinction must be drawn between the investment base of an enterprise and that of an investor. The investor's investment base is, of course, the price paid for his or her equity securities. Except for those cases in which he or she acquired such securities at book value, the investment base is going to differ from that of the company in which he or she has invested. In general, the focus in ROI computations is on the return realized by the enterprise rather than the return realized on the investment cost of shareholders. Later in this chapter we will focus on the measurement of results achieved by the latter.

Averaging the Investment Base

Regardless of the method used in arriving at the investment base, the return achieved over a period of time is always associated with the investment base that was, on average, actually available to the enterprise over that period of time. Thus, unless the investment base did not change significantly during the period, it will be necessary to average it.

The most common method of averaging for the external analyst is that of adding the investment base at the beginning of the year to that at the end of the year and dividing their total by two. Care must, however, be used in employing this method of averaging. Companies in some industries choose a "natural" rather than the calendar business year. Thus, for example, in retailing, the natural business year ends when inventories are at their lowest (e.g., January 31 after the holiday selling season) and when it is easiest to count them. In such case, averaging two year-ends may yield the *lowest* rather than the average amount of assets employed.

In such or similar cases, more accurate methods of averaging, where the data are available, are to average by month-end balances, that is, adding the month-end investment bases and dividing the total by 12, or to average on a quarterly basis.

Relating Income to the Investment Base

In the computation of ROI, the definition of return (income) is dependent on the definition of the investment base.

If the investment base is defined as comprising total assets, then income *before* interest expense is used.[4] The exclusion of interest from income deductions is due to its being regarded as a payment for the use of money to the suppliers of debt capital in the same way that dividends are regarded as a reward to suppliers of equity capital. Before deductions for interest or dividends, income is used when it is related to total assets or to long-term debt plus equity capital (assuming most of the interest expense is on long-term obligations).

The income of a consolidated entity that includes a subsidiary that is partially owned by a minority interest usually reflects a deduction for the minority's share in that income. The consolidated balance sheet, however, includes all the assets of such a subsidiary, that is, those belonging to the parent as well as those belonging to the minority. Because the investment in the denominator includes all the assets of the consolidated entity, the income (in the numerator) should include all the income (or loss), not just the parent's share. For this reason, the minority's share of earnings

---

[4] Interest expense means interest incurred less interest capitalized. In theory, the amount of previously capitalized interest currently amortized and included in expenses should also be added back to income.

(or loss) must be added back to income in computing return on total assets. When the denominator is the equity capital only, the minority share in income (or loss) need not be added back if equity capital excludes minority interest.

When the return on the equity capital is computed, net income *after* deductions for interest and preferred dividends is used. If the preferred dividends are cumulative, they are deducted in arriving at the balance of earnings accruing to the common stock, whether these dividends were declared or not.

The final ROI must always reflect all applicable costs and expenses and that includes income taxes. Some computations of ROI nevertheless omit deductions of income taxes. One reason for this practice is the desire to isolate the effects of tax management from those of operating performance. Another reason is that changes in tax rates affect comparability over the years. Moreover, companies that have tax loss carryforwards find that the deduction of taxes from income adds confusion and complications to the ROI computations.

It must, however, be borne in mind that income taxes reduce the final return and that they must be taken into consideration particularly when the return on shareholders' equity is computed. Later in this chapter we discuss the disaggregation of ROI where one element is the tax burden borne by the entity

ADJUSTING THE COMPONENTS OF THE ROI FORMULA

In computing any measure or ratio, the analyst uses the amounts in the financial statements only as starting points. As was seen in the discussion in Chapter 5 on the adjustment of the debt to equity ratios, some amounts need analytical adjustment and some amounts not found in the financial statements need to be included in the adjusted computation. Reference to the discussion in Chapter 5 will reveal that some of the items discussed therein, such as adjustment of inventory amounts, may affect the ROI computation while others, such as reclassification of deferred taxes, may not. Moreover, some adjustments, such as those relating to inventory amounts, affect both the numerator and the denominator of the formula, thus moderating the net effect on the ratio.

The computation of ROI under the various concepts of "investment base" discussed above will now be illustrated by means of the data contained in Exhibits 6–1 and 6–2. The computations are for year 9 and are based on figures rounded to the nearest million dollars.

Return on Total Assets   Applying the basic formula to the data of American Company for year 9 we get:

Exhibit 6–1

AMERICAN COMPANY
Statement of Income
For Years Ended December 31, year 8 and year 9
(in thousands)

	Year 8	Year 9
Net sales	$1,636,298	$1,723,729
Costs and expenses	1,473,293	1,579,401
Operating income	163,005	144,328
Other income net	2,971	1,784
	165,976	146,112
Interest expense*	16,310	20,382
Income before tax	149,666	125,730
Provision for federal and other taxes on		
income	71,770	61,161
Net income	77,896	64,569
Less dividends:		
Preferred stock	2,908	2,908
Common stock	39,209	38,898
	42,117	41,806
Net income reinvested in the business	$ 35,779	$ 22,763

* In year 9, interest on long-term debt was $19,695.

$$\frac{\text{Net income} + \text{Interest expense} \times (1 - \text{Tax rate}) + \text{Minority interest in earnings}}{(\text{Beginning total assets} + \text{Ending total assets}) \div 2}$$

$$= \frac{\$65 + \$20\,(1 - 0.40) + 0^*}{(\$1,334 + \$1,372) \div 2} = 0.057, \text{ or } 5.7 \text{ percent}$$

* No minority interest in this case.

   The tax adjustment of the interest expense recognizes that interest is a tax-deductible expense and that if the interest cost is excluded, the related tax benefit must also be excluded from income. The *tax rate* we use is the approximate *marginal* or corporate tax rate of 40 percent because the tax incidence with respect to any one item (such as interest expense) can be measured by the marginal tax rate. In computing the fixed-charges-coverage ratio (see Chapter 5), we use the *effective* tax rate because we have adopted the SEC's computation which requires its use.
   The assets have been averaged by using the year-end figures for total assets. As discussed earlier, this method of computing the average may yield misleading results in some cases.

Exhibit 6–2

AMERICAN COMPANY
Statements of Financial Position
As at December 31, year 8 and year 9
(in thousands)

	Year 8	Year 9
Assets		
Current assets:		
Cash	$ 25,425	$ 25,580
Eurodollar time deposits and temporary cash		
investments	38,008	28,910
Accounts and notes receivable—net	163,870	176,911
Inventories	264,882	277,795
Total current assets	492,185	509,196
Investments in and receivables from		
nonconsolidated subsidiaries	33,728	41,652
Miscellaneous investments and receivables........	5,931	6,997
Funds held by trustee for construction	6,110	
Land, buildings, equipment, and timberlands—net ..	773,361	790,774
Deferred charges to future operations	16,117	16,452
Goodwill and other intangible assets	6,550	6,550
Total assets	$1,333,982	$1,371,621
Liabilities		
Current liabilities:		
Notes payable to banks—principally Eurodollar ..	$ 7,850	$ 13,734
Accounts payable and accrued expenses	128,258	144,999
Dividends payable	10,404	10,483
Federal and other taxes on income	24,370	13,256
Long-term indebtedness payable within one year	9,853	11,606
Total current liabilities	180,735	194,078
Long-term indebtedness	350,565	335,945
Deferred taxes on income	86,781	101,143
Total liabilities	618,081	631,166
Capital		
Preferred, 7% cumulative and noncallable, par value		
$25 per share; authorized 1,760,000 shares	41,538	41,538
Common, par value $12.50 per share; authorized		
30,000,000 shares	222,245	222,796
Capital in excess of par value	19,208	20,448
Earnings reinvested in the business	436,752	459,515
Less: Common treasury stock	(3,842)	(3,842)
Total capital	715,901	740,455
Total liabilities and capital	$1,333,982	$1,371,621

Return on Modified Asset Bases   Since our discussion earlier in the chapter came to the conclusion that in normal circumstances most of the modifications in the amount of total assets are not logically warranted, no illustrations of such computation will be given.

Return on Long-Term Liabilities plus Equity Capital

$$\frac{\text{Net income } + \text{ Interest expense* } \times (1 - \text{ Tax rate}) + \text{ Minority interest in earnings}}{\text{Average long-term liabilities } + \text{ equity capital}}$$

Using the data in Exhibits 6–1 and 6–2 for year 9:

$$\frac{\$65 + \$20* (1 - 0.40) + 0}{(\$437 + \$716 + \$437 + \$740) \div 2} = 0.066, \text{ or } 6.6 \text{ percent}$$

* On long-term debt ($19,695 rounded).

Decisions of how to classify items such as deferred taxes as between debt and equity will have to be made by the analyst using the considerations already discussed in Chapter 5. It should be noted that deferred taxes on income are included here among the long-term liabilities. In the computation of return on long-term liabilities and equity capital, the question of how to classify deferred taxes does not really present a problem because in this computation both debt and equity are aggregated anyway. The problem of classification becomes more real in computing the return on shareholders' equity. In the examples that follow, we assume circumstances where deferred taxes are considered to be more in the nature of long-term liability than equity. In many cases, the classification decision can have a significant effect on the return computation.

Return on Stockholders' Equity   The basic computation of return on the equity excludes from the investment base all but the common stockholders' equity.

$$\frac{\text{Net income } - \text{ Preferred dividends}}{\text{Average common stockholders' equity}}$$

Using data in Exhibits 6–1 and 6–2 for year 9:

$$\frac{\$65 - \$3}{(\$674 + \$699) \div 2} = 9 \text{ percent}$$

The higher return on shareholders' equity as compared to the return on total assets reflects the positive workings of financial leverage.

Should it be desired, for whatever reason, to compute the return on total stockholders' equity, the investment base would include the preferred shareholders' equity, while net income would not reflect a deduction for preferred dividends. The formula[5] would then be:

$$\frac{\text{Net income}}{\text{Average total shareholders' equity (common and preferred)}}$$

Where convertible debt sells at a substantial premium above par and is clearly held by investors for its conversion feature, there is justification for treating it as the equivalent of equity capital. This is particularly true when the company can choose at any time to force conversion of the debt by calling it.

Analysis and Interpretation of ROI

Earlier in the chapter we mentioned that ROI analysis is particularly useful to the analyst in the areas of evaluation of managerial effectiveness, enterprise profitability, and as an important tool of earnings projection.

The evaluation of ROI and the projection of earnings by means of ROI analysis are complex processes requiring thorough analysis. The reason for this is that the ROI computation usually includes components of considerable complexity.

Components of the ROI Ratio If we focus first on return on total assets, we know that the primary formula for computing this return is:

$$\frac{\text{Net income + Interest} \times (1 - \text{Tax rate})^*}{\text{Average total assets}}$$

* Omitting the add-back of minority interest in earnings in order to simplify the discussion does not impair its validity.

For purposes of our discussion and analysis, let us look at this computation in a simplified form:

$$\frac{\text{Net income}}{\text{Total assets}}$$

---

[5] The return on common stockholders' equity may also be computed thus:

$$\frac{\text{Earnings per share}}{\text{Book value per share}}$$

But the results will often not be identical because the earnings per share computation includes adjustments for common stock equivalents, etc.

Since sales are a most important yardstick in relation to which profitability is measured and are, as well, a major index of activity, we can recast the above formula as follows:

$$\frac{\text{Net income}}{\text{Sales}} \times \frac{\text{Sales}}{\text{Total assets}}$$

The relationship of net income to sales measures operating performance and profitability. The relationship of sales to total assets is a measure of asset utilization or turnover, a means of determining how effectively (in terms of sales generation) the assets are utilized. It can be readily seen that both factors, profitability as well as asset utilization, determine the return realized on a given investment in assets.

Profitability and asset utilization are, in turn, complex ratios that normally require thorough and detailed analysis before they can be used to reach conclusions regarding the reasons for changes in the return on total assets.

Exhibit 6–3 presents the major factors that influence the final return on total assets. In the next section, we shall be concerned with the interaction of profitability (net income/sales) and of asset utilization or turnover (sales/total assets) that in Exhibit 6–3 is regarded as the first level of analysis of the return on total assets. As can be seen from Exhibit 6–3, the many important and complex factors that, in turn, determine profitability and asset utilization represent a second level of analysis of the return on total assets. Chapters 7 and 8 will take up the analysis of results of operations, and Chapter 9 will deal with the evaluation and projection of earnings. The analysis of asset utilization will be discussed in subsequent sections of this chapter.

Relationship between Profitability and Asset Turnover   The relationship between return on total assets, profitability, and capital turnover (utilization) is illustrated in Exhibit 6–4, which indicates that when we multiply profitability (expressed as a percentage) by asset utilization (expressed as a turnover) we obtain the return on total assets (expressed as a percentage relationship).

Company X realizes its 10 percent return on total assets by means of a relatively high profit margin and a low turnover of assets. The opposite is true of Company Z, while Company Y achieves its 10 percent return by means of a profit margin half that of Company X and an asset turnover rate twice that of Company X. It is obvious from Exhibit 6–4 that there are many combinations of profit margins and turnover rates that can yield a return on assets of 10 percent.

In fact, as can be seen from Exhibit 6–5, there exist an infinite variety of combinations of profit margin and asset turnover rates that yield a 10 percent return on assets. The chart in the exhibit graphically relates asset turnover (vertical axis) to profitability (horizontal axis).

Exhibit 6–3

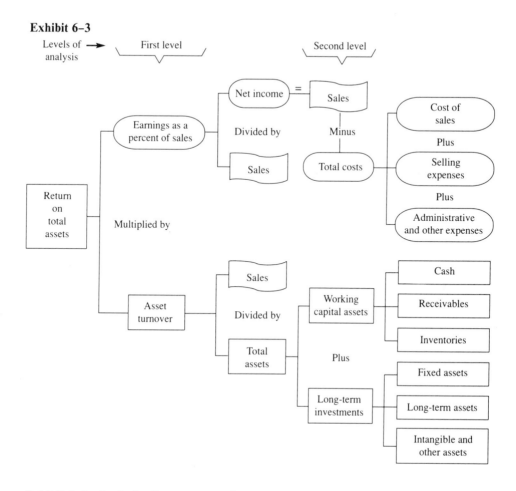

Levels of analysis → First level ... Second level

Exhibit 6–4   Analysis of return on total assets

	Company X	Company Y	Company Z
1. Sales	$5,000,000	$10,000,000	$10,000,000
2. Net income	500,000	500,000	100,000
3. Total assets	5,000,000	5,000,000	1,000,000
4. Profit as percent of sales $\left(\frac{2}{1}\right)$	10%	5%	1%
5. Asset turnover $\left(\frac{1}{3}\right)$	1	2	10
Return on total assets (4 × 5)	10%	10%	10%

The curve, sloping from the upper left area of low profit margins and high asset turnover rates, traces out the endless combinations of profitability and asset turnover rates that yield a 10 percent return on total

Exhibit 6–5

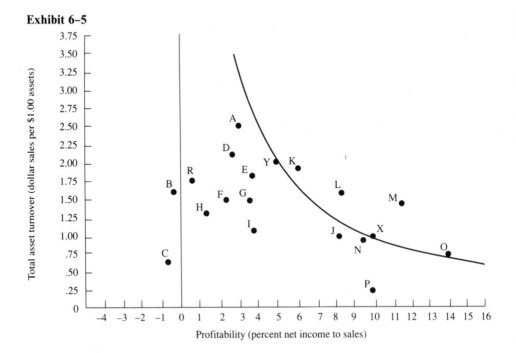

assets. The data of Companies X and Y (from Exhibit 6–4) are represented by dots on the graph, while the data of Company Z cannot be fitted on it since the full curve has not been shown. The other lettered dots represent the profit-turnover combination of other companies within a particular industry. This clustering of the results of various companies around the 10 percent return on assets slope is a useful way of comparing the return of many enterprises within an industry and the major two elements that comprise them.

The chart in Exhibit 6–5 is also useful in assessing the relative courses of action open to different enterprises that want to improve their respective returns on investments.

Companies B and C must, of course, restore profitability before the turnover rate becomes a factor of importance. Assuming that all the companies represented in Exhibit 6–5 belong to the same industry and that there is an average representative level of profitability and turnover in it, Company P will be best advised to pay first and particular attention to improvement in its turnover ratio, while Company R should pay foremost attention to the improvement of its profit margin. Other companies, such as Company I, would best concentrate on both the turnover and the profit margin aspects of ROI improvement.

While the above analysis treats profitability and turnover as two independent variables, they are, in fact, interdependent. As will be seen from the discussion of break-even analysis in Chapter 8, when fixed expenses are substantial, a higher level of activity (turnover) will tend to increase the profit margin because within a certain range of activity, costs increase proportionally less than sales. In comparing two companies within an industry, the analyst, in evaluating the one having the lower asset turnover, will make allowance for the potential increase in profitability that can be associated with a projected increase in turnover that is based primarily on an expansion of sales.

Analysis of return on total assets can reveal the weaknesses as well as the potential strengths of an enterprise. Assume that two companies in the same industry have returns on total assets as follows:

	Company A	Company B
1. Sales	$ 1,000,000	$20,000,000
2. Net income	100,000	100,000
3. Total assets	10,000,000	10,000,000
4. Profitability $\left(\dfrac{2}{1}\right)$	10%	0.5%
5. Turnover of assets $\left(\dfrac{1}{3}\right)$	0.1 times	2 times
Return on investment (4 × 5)	1%	1%

Both companies have poor returns on total assets. However, remedial action for them lies in different areas, and the analyst will concentrate on the evaluation of the feasibility of success of such improvement.

Company A has a 10 percent profit on sales that, let us assume, is about average for the industry. However, each dollar invested in assets supports only 10 cents in sales, whereas Company B gets $2 of sales for each dollar invested in its assets. The analyst's attention will naturally be focused on Company A's investment in assets. Why is its turnover so low? Are there excess assets that yield little or no return or are there idle assets that should be disposed of? Or, as often is the case, are the assets inefficiently or uneconomically utilized? Quite obviously, Company A can achieve more immediate and significant improvements by concentrating on improving turnover (by increasing sales, reducing investment, or both) than by striving to increase the profit margin beyond the industry average.

The opposite situation prevails with respect to Company B where attention should first be focused on the reasons for the low profit margin and to the improvement of it as the most likely avenue of success in increasing ROI. The reasons for low profitability can be many, including inefficient equipment and production methods, unprofitable product lines, excess capacity with attendant high fixed costs, excessive selling or administrative costs, and so on.

The company with the low profitability may discover that changes in tastes and in technology have resulted in an increased investment in assets being needed to finance a dollar of sales. This means that in order to maintain its return on assets, the company must increase its profit margin or else production of the product is no longer worthwhile.

There is a tendency to regard a high profit margin as a sign of high earnings quality. It is necessary to emphasize the importance of return on capital as the ultimate test of profitability. The following table compares during a given year the similar profit margins of five companies with their respective returns on capital:

	Profit margin as percent of sales	Profit as percent of capital
Whirlpool	5.3	17.1
Corn Products	5.9	12.0
Goodyear	5.5	9.6
U.S. Plywood	5.5	8.0
Distillers Seagram	5.0	6.7

It is evident that in the case of these five companies, which have similar profit margins, the rate of capital turnover made the difference in the return on capital performance, and this must be taken into account by the analyst. Thus, a supermarket chain will be content with a net profit margin of 1 percent or less because it has a high rate of turnover due to a relatively low investment in assets and a high proportion of leased assets (such as stores and fixtures). Similarly, a discount store will accept a low profit margin in order to obtain a high rate of asset turnover (primarily of inventories). On the other hand, capital-intensive industries such as steels, chemicals, and autos, which have heavy investments in assets and resulting low asset turnover rates, must achieve high net profit margins in order to offer investors a reasonable return on capital.

In most cases, the focus on single-year rates of return are apt to be misleading. The cyclical nature of many industries cause such swings in profitability that some years' profits may appear exorbitant while others barely are sufficient to justify the related investment. Such enterprises can only be validly evaluated on the basis of average returns over a number of years covering a full economic cycle.

ANALYSIS OF ASSET UTILIZATION

As is graphically illustrated in Exhibit 6–3, the return on total assets depends on (1) getting the largest profit out of each dollar of sales and (2) obtaining the highest possible amount of sales per dollar of invested capital (net assets). Throughout this work we use sales and revenues as synonymous concepts.

The intensity with which assets are utilized is measured by means of asset turnover ratios.[6] That utilization has as its ultimate measure the amount of sales generated since sales are in most enterprises the first and essential step to profits. In certain special cases, such as with enterprises in developmental stages, the meaning of turnover may have to be modified in recognition of the fact that most assets are committed to the development of future potential. Similarly, abnormal supply problems and strikes are conditions that will affect the state of capital utilization and, as such, will require separate evaluation and interpretation.

Evaluation of Individual Turnover Ratios

Changes in the basic turnover ratio that enters the determination of the ROI calculation, that is,

$$\frac{\text{Sales}}{\text{Total assets}}$$

can be evaluated meaningfully only by an analysis of changes in the turnover rates of individual asset categories and groups that comprise the total assets.

Sales to Cash   As was seen in the discussion in Chapter 3, cash and cash equivalents are held primarily for purposes of meeting the needs of day-to-day transactions as well as a liquidity reserve designed to prevent the shortages that may arise from an imbalance in cash inflows and outflows. In any type of business, there is a certain logical relationship between sales and cash level that must be maintained to support it.

Too high a rate of turnover may be due to a cash shortage that can ultimately result in a liquidity crisis if the enterprise has no other ready sources of funds available to it.

Too low a rate of turnover may be due to the holding of idle and unnecessary cash balances. Cash accumulated for specific purposes or

---

[6] P. F. Drucker in *Managing in Turbulent Times* (New York: Harper & Row, 1980) writes: "In the United States the General Electric Co., for example, does not owe its leadership position primarily to technological achievement. What sets it apart from Westinghouse, its closest competitor and the industry's number two, is above all productivity of capital. GE gets about twice as much work out of a dollar as Westinghouse does."

known contingencies may result in temporary decreases in the rate of turnover.

The basic trade-off here is between liquidity and the tying up of funds that yield no return or a very modest return.

Sales to Receivables   Any organization that sells on credit will find that the level of its receivables is a function of sales. A relatively low rate of turnover here is, among other reasons, likely to be due to an over-extension of credit, to an inability of customers to pay, or to a poor collection job.

A relatively high rate of turnover may indicate a strict credit extension policy or a reluctance or inability to extend credit. Determining the rate of turnover here is the trade-off between sales and the tying up of funds in receivables.

Sales to Inventories   The maintenance of a given level of sales generally requires a given level of inventories. This relationship will vary from industry to industry depending on the variety of types, models, colors, sizes, and other classes of varieties of items that must be kept in order to attract and keep customers. The length of the production cycle as well as the type of item (e.g., luxury versus necessity; perishable versus durable) has a bearing on the rate of turnover.

A slow rate of turnover indicates the existence of problems such as overstocking, slow-moving or obsolete inventories, overestimating of sales, or a lack of balance in the inventory. Temporary problems such as strikes at important customers may also be responsible for such a condition.

A higher than normal rate of turnover may mean an underinvestment in inventory that can result in lack of proper customer service and in loss of sales.

In this case, the trade-off is between tying up funds in inventory, on one hand, and sacrificing customer service and sales, on the other.

Sales to Fixed Assets   While the relationship between property, plant, and equipment and sales is a logical one on a long-term basis, there are many short-term and temporary factors that may upset this relationship. Among these factors are conditions of excess capacity, inefficient or obsolete equipment, multishift operations, temporary changes in demand, and interruptions in the supply of raw materials and parts.

It must also be remembered that increases in plant capacity are not gradual but occur, instead, in large increments. This too can create temporary and medium-term changes in the turnover rates. Often, leased facilities and equipment, which do not appear on the balance sheet, will distort the relationship between sales and fixed assets.

The trade-off here is between investment in fixed assets with a correspondingly higher break-even point, on one hand, and efficiency, productive capacity, and sales potential, on the other.

Sales to Other Assets In this category, we find among others, such assets as patents and deferred charges or other costs. While the direct relationship between these individual categories of assets and current sales levels may not be evident, no assets are held or should be held by an enterprise unless they contribute to sales or to the generation of income. In the case of deferred R&D costs, the investment may represent the potential of future sales. In the evaluation of rates of asset utilization, the analyst must allow for such factors.

Sales to Short-Term Liabilities The relationship between sales and short-term trade liabilities is a predictable one. The amount of short-term credit that an enterprise is able to obtain from suppliers depends on its needs for goods and services, that is, on the level of activity (e.g., sales). Thus, the degree to which it can obtain short-term credit depends also importantly on the level of sales. This short-term credit is relatively cost-free and, in turn, reduces the investment of enterprise funds in working capital.

Use of Averages

Whenever the level of a given asset category changes significantly during the period for which the turnover is computed, it is necessary to use averages of asset levels in the computation. The computation then becomes

$$\frac{\text{Sales}}{(\text{Asset at beginning of period} + \text{Asset at end of period}) \div 2}$$

To the extent that data are available and the variation in asset levels during the period dictates it, the average can be computed on a monthly or quarterly basis.

Other Factors to Be Considered in Return on Asset Evaluation

The evaluation of the return on assets involves many factors of great complexity. As will be seen from the discussion in Chapter 9, the inclusion of extraordinary gains and losses in single-period and average net income must be evaluated. The effects of price-level changes on ROI calculations must be taken into account by the analyst.

In analyzing the trend of return on assets over the years, the effect of acquisitions accounted for as poolings of interest must be isolated and their chance of recurrence evaluated. The effect of discontinued operations must be similarly evaluated.

The external analyst will not usually be able to obtain data on ROI by segments, product lines, or divisions of an enterprise. However, where his bargaining power or position allows him to obtain such data, they can make a significant contribution to the accuracy and reliability of the analysis.

A consistently high return on assets is the earmark of an effective management and can distinguish a growth company from one experiencing merely a cyclical or seasonal pickup in business.

An examination of the factors that comprise the return on assets will usually reveal the limitations to which their expansion is subject. Neither the profit margin nor the asset turnover rate can expand indefinitely. Thus, an expanding asset base via external financing and/or internal earnings retention will be necessary for further earnings growth.

Return on Shareholders' Equity

Up to now we have examined the factors affecting the return on total assets. However, of great interest to the owner group of an enterprise is the return on the stockholders' equity. The rate of return on total assets and that on the stockholders' equity differ because a portion of the capital with which the assets are financed is usually supplied by creditors who receive a fixed return on their capital or, in some cases, no return at all. Similarly, the preferred stock usually receives a fixed dividend. These fixed returns differ from the rate earned on the assets (funds) that they provide, and this accounts for the difference in returns on assets and those on stockholders' equity. This is the concept of financial leverage that was already discussed in Chapter 5.

ANALYSIS OF RETURN ON COMMON STOCKHOLDERS' EQUITY (ROCSE)

The ROCSE can be disaggregated into the following elements that facilitate its analysis:

$$\frac{\text{Net income} - \text{Preferred dividends}}{\text{Average common stockholders' equity}} = \frac{\text{Net income} - \text{Preferred dividends}}{\text{Sales}} \times \frac{\text{Sales}}{\text{Average total assets}} \times \frac{\text{Average total assets}}{\text{Average common stockholders' equity}}$$

Descriptively, we can express this formula as follows:

$$\begin{array}{c} \text{Rate of return} \\ \text{on CSE} \end{array} = \begin{array}{c} \text{Net income margin} \\ \text{after preferred} \\ \text{dividends} \end{array} \times \begin{array}{c} \text{Asset} \\ \text{turnover} \\ \text{ratio} \end{array} \times \begin{array}{c} \text{Common} \\ \text{stockholders'} \\ \text{leverage ratio} \end{array}$$

The net income margin represents the portion of the sales dollar that is left for the common shareholder after providing for all costs and claims (e.g., those of the preferred shareholders). The asset turnover was discussed above. The common stockholders' leverage ratio measures the extent to which total assets are financed by common stockholders. The larger this ratio is the smaller the proportion of assets financed by common stockholders and the greater the extent of leverage. Leverage can also be measured by means of the financial leverage index as was illustrated in Chapter 5.

Using the data in Exhibits 6–1 and 6–2 of the American Company, we can compute the disaggregated ROCSE for year 9 as follows (dollars in millions):

$$\frac{\$65 - \$3}{(\$674 + \$699) \div 2} = \frac{\$65 - \$3}{\$1,724}$$

$$\times \frac{\$1,724}{(\$1,334 + \$1,372) \div 2} \times \frac{(\$1,334 + \$1,372) \div 2}{(\$674 + \$699) \div 2} \text{ or}$$

	Net income margin after preferred dividends	Assets turnover ratio	Common stockholders' leverage ratio
Rate of return on CSE			
9% =	3.6%	× 1.27 ×	1.97

There is another useful way to look at the disaggregated ROCSE of American Company. Each dollar of common equity was used as the basis for borrowing 97 cents in various ways by means of long-term debt and short-term credit and considering, for simplicity's sake, deferred taxes as interest-free debt.

This $1.97 was able to generate $2.50 in sales because assets (which equal total capital plus total debt) are turning over (i.e., generating sales) at a rate of 1.27 (i.e., $1.97 × 1.27 = $2.50).

The $2.50 in sales earned a net margin after all costs and preferred dividends of 3.6 percent thus resulting in a return on the common stockholders' investment of 9 percent ($2.50 × 3.6%).

A further refinement can be introduced into this analysis by disaggregating the net income margin into its *pre-tax* component and its tax retention component. When the *pre-tax* profit margin is multiplied by 1 – effective tax rate paid by the company (i.e., the retention rate), we get the net income profit margin. This analysis separates the pre-tax margin, a measure of operating effectiveness, from the retention rate, a measure of tax-management effectiveness. This segregates one more factor contributing to the return on equity.

In the example of American Company the net income margin of 3.6% can be disaggregated as follows:

$$\frac{\text{Pre-tax earnings less}}{\text{Sales}} \times \frac{\text{Net Income} - \text{Preferred dividends}}{\text{Pre-tax earnings less}}$$
$$\frac{\text{Preferred dividends}}{\text{Preferred dividends}}$$

$$= \frac{126 - 3}{1724} \times \frac{65 - 3}{126 - 3}$$

$$= 7.1\% \times 50.4\%* = 3.6\%$$

* This is the retention rate, that is, the percentage of pre-tax income remaining after taxes.

ILLUSTRATION OF ANALYSIS OF RETURN ON TOTAL ASSETS AND ON EQUITY

Based on the financial statements of Campbell Soup (Appendix B to Chapter 2), we will now illustrate the analysis of various returns.

Return on Total Assets (ROTA)

$$\frac{\text{Net income } \boxed{28} + [\text{Interest expense } \boxed{18} \times (1 - \text{Tax rate})] + \text{Minority interest in income } |25}{\text{Average total assets } \boxed{39A}}$$

For 1991 (millions)

$$\frac{401.5 + 116.2\,(1 - 0.34) + 7.2}{(4,149.0 + 4,115.6)/2} = \frac{485.4}{4,132.3} = 11.75\%$$

Disaggregated

$$\frac{\text{Net income} + \text{Interest}}{\frac{(1 - \text{Tax interest}) + \text{Minority interest}}{\text{Sales}}} \times \frac{\text{Sales}}{\text{Average total assets}}$$

$$= \frac{\$485.4}{\$6,204.1} \times \frac{\$6,204.1}{\$4,132.3}$$

or

$$\underset{0.078}{\text{Profit margin}} \times \underset{1.5}{\text{Asset turnover}} = \underset{11.75\%}{\text{ROTA}}$$

Return on Common Stockholders' Equity (RCSE)

$$\frac{\text{Net income } \boxed{28} - \text{Preferred dividends}}{\text{Average common equity* } \boxed{54} \boxed{176}}$$

* Including 50% of deferred taxes which is assumed to be equity.

For 1991

$$\frac{401.5}{[(1,793.4 + 129.3) + (1,691.8 + 117.5)]/2} = \frac{401.5}{1,866} = 21.52\%$$

Disaggregated

$$\frac{\text{Net income } - \text{ Preferred dividends}}{\text{Sales } \boxed{13}} \times \frac{\text{Sales}}{\text{Average total assets}}$$

$$\times \frac{\text{Average total assets}}{\text{Average common equity}} = \text{ROCSE}$$

For 1991

$$\frac{401.5}{6,204.1} = \underline{\underline{6.47\%}} \quad \frac{6,204.1}{4,132.3} = \underline{\underline{1.50}} \quad \frac{4,132.3}{1,866.0} = \underline{\underline{2.22}}$$

	Net income margin		Asset turnover ratio		Common stockholders' leverage ratio		ROCSE
or	6.47%	×	1.50	×	2.22		= 21.52%

The 1991 net income margin of Campbell can be further disaggregated as follows:

$$\frac{\text{Pre-tax earnings}}{\text{Sales}} \times \frac{\text{Net earnings}}{\text{Pre-tax earnings}}$$

$$= \frac{667.4 \ \boxed{26}}{6204.1} \times \frac{401.5 \ \boxed{28}}{667.4}$$

=	Pre-tax profit margin		Tax retention rate	
	10.8%	×	60.2%	= 6.5%

For a comparative analysis of these ratios with those of preceding years please refer to the Return on Investment section of Campbell Soup's comprehensive analysis in Chapter 10.

This type of analysis over a period of time can be very instructive. If the ROCSE has declined, then it would be important to know which of these factors is most responsible for such a decline. Similarly, the areas of the most likely improvement in the ROCSE can be assessed by means of such analysis. Assuming that leverage is already high and that it would not be prudent to increase it, then the areas of improvement would be the profit margin and/or the asset turnover. The likelihood of improvements in these factors depends on industry conditions, competition, and similar influences. Is the profit margin high or low in comparison with what is achieved within the company's industry? How fast an asset turnover can be reasonably achieved in this industry? These are the considerations which the analyst will focus on in the analysis of changes in the ROCSE.

Expanded Disaggregation of ROCSE

We can introduce *interest burden* and the *tax rate* (or tax retention) into this disaggregation as follows:

EBIT = Net income $401.5 + Interest $116.2 + Taxes $265.9 $\boxed{27}$
     = $783.6

(Preferred dividends would be deducted if applicable)

Revenues = same as sales
ATA = average total assets
ACE = average common equity
ETR = effective tax rate = 265.9 $\boxed{27}$ ÷ 667.4 $\boxed{226}$ = 0.398

Disaggregation Formula

$$\frac{EBIT}{Revenues} \times \frac{Revenues}{ATA} - \frac{Interest}{ATA} \times \frac{ATA}{ACE}$$

$$\times (100 - ETR) = \frac{NI^*}{ACE} = ROCSE$$

* Net income—by definition *after tax.*

Additional Factors Disaggregated

$\dfrac{Interest}{ATA}$ = known as *interest burden* (the higher the interest burden the lower the ROCSE)

$(100 - ETR)$ = *Tax retention* (the higher the tax retention the higher the ROCSE).

For Campbell 1991

$$\left(\frac{783.6}{6,204.1} \times \frac{6,204.1}{4,132.3} - \frac{116.2}{4,132.3}\right) \times \frac{4,132.3}{1,866.0} \times (1.000 - 0.398)$$

$$= (0.126 \times 1.50 - 0.028) = 0.161 \times 2.22 \times 0.602 = \underline{\underline{0.2149^*}}$$

* Or 21.49%—difference with preceding calculation due to rounding.

Equity Growth Rate

The equity growth rate by means of *earnings retention* can be calculated as follows:

$$\frac{\text{Net income}^* - \text{Dividend payout}}{\substack{\text{Average common} \\ \text{shareholders' equity}}}$$

= Percent increase in common equity

* Minus preferred dividend requirements.

This is the growth rate due to the retention of earnings and assumes a constant dividend payout over time. It indicates the possibilities of earnings growth without resort to external financing. These increased funds, in turn, will earn the rate of return that the enterprise can obtain on its assets and thus contribute to growth in earnings.

For the American Company (Exhibits 6–1 and 6–2), the equity growth rate can be computed for year 9 as follows:

$$\frac{\$65 - \$3 - \$39^*}{(\$674 + \$699) \div 2} = 3.4 \text{ percent}$$

* Common stock dividends.

Sustainable Growth Rate

The internal growth of a business entity depends on: (1) the earnings retained and reinvested in the entity and (2) the rate of return earned on the earnings retained. Thus, the sustainable growth rate is

$$(1 - \text{payout rate}) \times \text{ROCSE}$$

For American Company (Exhibits 6–1 and 6–2) the sustainable growth rate for year 9 is:

$$\text{Dividend payout rate} = \frac{41,806}{64,569} = 0.65$$

Earnings retention rate × ROCSE = Sustainable growth rate

$$(1 - 0.65) \times 0.09 = 0.058 \text{ or } 5.8\%$$

Due to a significant earnings drop from year 8 to year 9 with a steady dividend payout as well as a decline in the ROCSE, the sustainable growth rate declined year to year. In estimating future growth rates it is best to average the sustainable growth rates over a number of years and to consider projected changes in expected earnings retention rates as well as in projected ROCSE.

Analysis of Financial Leverage Effects

The effect that each noncommon equity capital source has on the return on the common equity can be analyzed in detail. Using the data of American Company that was included in Exhibits 6–1 and 6–2 earlier in this chapter, we can undertake such an analysis as follows:

An analysis of the American Company balance sheet as at December 31, year 9[7] discloses the following major sources of funds (in thousands):

Current liabilities (exclusive of current portion of long-term debt)		$ 182,472
Long-term debt....................	$335,945	
Current portion	11,606	347,551
Deferred taxes		101,143
Preferred stock		41,538
Common stockholders' equity		698,917
Total investment or total assets ..		$1,371,621

The income statement for year 9 includes (in thousands):

Income before taxes	$125,730
Income taxes	61,161
Net income	64,569
Preferred dividends......................	2,908
Income accruing to common shareholders	$ 61,661
Total interest expense	$ 20,382
Assumed interest on short-term notes (5%)	687
Balance of interest on long-term debt	$ 19,695

[7] A year-end based analysis (rather than one based on average for the year amounts) is used here in order to simplify the computations.

The return on total assets is computed as follows:

$$\frac{\text{Net income} + \text{Interest} \times (1 - \text{Tax rate})}{\text{Total assets (year-end)}}$$

$$= \frac{\$64,569 + \$20,382 \ (1 - 0.40)}{\$1,371,621} = 5.6 \text{ percent}$$

The 5.56 percent return represents the average return on all assets employed by the company. To the extent that suppliers of capital other than the common stockholders get a lower reward than an average of 5.56 percent, the common equity benefits by the difference. The opposite is true when the suppliers of capital receive more than a 5.56 percent reward in year 9.

Exhibit 6–6 presents an analysis showing the relative contribution and reward of each of the major suppliers of funds and their effect on the returns earned by the common stockholders.

As can be seen from Exhibit 6–6, the $9,806,000 accruing to the common equity from use of current liabilities is largely due to its being free of interest costs. The advantage of $7,646,000 accruing from the use of long-term debt is substantially due to the tax deductibility of interest.

Exhibit 6–6   Analysis of composition of return on shareholders' equity (approximate computations in thousands of dollars)

Category of fund supplier	Fund supplied	Earnings on fund supplied at rate of 5.56 percent	Payment to suppliers of funds	Accruing to (detracting from) return on common stock
Current liabilities	$ 182,472	$10,218	$ 412[a]	$ 9,806
Long-term debt	347,551	19,463	11,817[b]	7,646
Deferred taxes	101,143	5,664	none	5,664
Preferred stock	41,538	2,326	2,908[c]	(582)
Earnings in excess of compensation to suppliers of funds				22,534
Add: Common stockholders' equity	698,917	39,139		39,139
Totals	$1,371,621	$76,810	$15,137	
Total income (return) on stockholders' equity				$61,673[d]

[a] Interest cost of $687 less 40 percent tax.
[b] Interest cost of $19,695 less 40 percent tax.
[c] Preferred dividends—not tax deductible.
[d] Slight differences with statement figures are due to rounding.

Since the preferred dividends are not tax deductible, the unimpressive return on total assets of 5.56 percent resulted in a disadvantage to the common equity of $582,000. The value of tax deferrals can be clearly seen in this case where the use of cost-free funds amounted to an annual advantage of $5,664,000.

We can now carry this analysis further (dollars in thousands).

The return on the common stockholders' equity is as follows:

$$\frac{\text{Net income less preferred dividends}}{\text{Common stockholders' equity}} = \frac{\$61,673^*}{\$698,917} = 8.8 \text{ percent}$$

* Ties in with total income accruing to common stockholders in Exhibit 6–6.

The net advantage that the common equity reaped from the working of financial leverage (Exhibit 6–6) is $22,534.

As a percentage of the common stockholders' equity, this advantage is computed as follows:

$$\frac{\begin{array}{c}\text{Earnings in excess of compensation}\\ \text{to outside suppliers of funds}\end{array}}{\text{Common stockholders' equity}} = \frac{\$22,534}{\$698,917} = 3.22 \text{ percent}$$

The return on common stockholders' equity can now be viewed as being composed as follows:

Return on assets	5.60%
Leverage advantage accruing to common equity	3.22
Return on common equity	8.82%

RETURN ON EQUITY VERSUS RETURN ON SHAREHOLDER INVESTMENT

As was pointed out in the preceding discussion, return on common shareholder's equity (ROCSE) measures the relationship of new income (attributable to common shareholders) to common equity at book value. However, that measure does not indicate how shareholders have fared in terms of return on *their* investment (i.e., the price they paid for common stock).

Shareholders don't buy at book value; in fact they often pay at a multiple of book value. Consider the following assumptions (data per share):

Company net income	$ 6
Dividends	2
Earnings retained	4
Book value...................................	$60
Ratio of market value to book value	2
Market valuation of retained earnings	$ 4

$$\text{ROCSE } \frac{6}{60} = 10\%$$

$$\text{Return on stockholder investment } \frac{\$2 + \$4}{2 \times \$60} = 5\%$$

Thus, the price paid by the investor plays a decisive role in determining *his* or *her* return on investment. A price below book value would have the opposite effect.

In this example we assume that the market accords at least *full* valuation to the earnings retained by the entity. This, as the study discussed below reveals, can hardly be taken for granted. Therefore, the additional factor to be considered is how the market values the earnings that have been retained by the entity.

If a company earns $1,000 then the shareholders will benefit (1) from the portion of earnings paid out as dividends, say $300, and (2) the value the market places on the retained earnings (RE) of $700, assumed here to be $900 over a period of time. Thus:

Shareholder enrichment =

$$\frac{\$300 \text{ (dividend)} + \$900 \text{ (change in market value associated with \$700 increase in retained earnings)}}{\$1,000 \text{ in earnings}}$$

$$= \frac{\$1,200}{\$1,000} = 1.20$$

which means that each dollar earned by the company enriched shareholders by $1.20 (ignoring tax effects).

This concept of shareholder enrichment was used by Ben C. Ball, Jr. in a remarkable study[8] which examined the 50 largest mature companies for the 1970–84 period and came to the surprising conclusion that many companies' profits don't find their way to shareholders as either dividends or higher stock value over time.

Mr. Ball found that ROCSE does not correlate with Return on Stockholders Investment (ROSI) expressed as

$$\text{ROSI} = \frac{\text{Dividends} + \text{Market value}}{\text{Number of shares} \times \text{Share price (cost)}}$$

Using the above concept of Shareholder Enrichment he related it to Net earnings as follows:

$$\text{Measure of shareholder benefit (MSB)} = \frac{\text{Shareholder enrichment}}{\text{Net earnings}}$$

---

[8] "The Mysterious Disappearance of Retained Earnings," *Harvard Business Review*, July–August 1987.

His findings were that of the companies examined, the MSB of Schlumberger was 346 percent (i.e., its shareholders were enriched by $3.46 for each dollar the company earned) while over the same time the shareholders of General Electric and General Motors were enriched by only 54 cents and 53 cents, respectively, for each dollar earned. At the low-end extreme shareholders of Xerox lost $1.19 for each dollar the company earned.

On average, the relationship of Change in market value/Increase in retained earnings was only 84 percent. That means that an investor holding a portfolio of the stocks included in the Ball study did not benefit from 16 percent of the earnings of these companies retained during the market period under study.

It is obvious that the additional factor not considered by ROCSE, but which affects stockholders significantly, is the judgment of the market and its valuation of retained earnings. If shareholder enrichment falls below net income it means that the market's discounting of the value of earnings retained actually offsets the value of dividends.

It is also obvious that the ROCSE measure falls short in measuring shareholder return because it omits the crucial market valuation mechanism (judgment) on which shareholder returns are so importantly dependent. Thus, as was discussed earlier, the decision set concerned with the valuation of equity securities must include, in addition to financial statement analysis, considerations such as the market valuation mechanism. This mechanism is at the heart of the distinction which sophisticated analysts draw between a company and its stock. A company may be among the best-managed entities in its industry as determined by measures such as ROCSE. It may nevertheless be a bad investment at a given point in time because it is seriously overvalued by the market. Conversely, a poorly performing company may, because of its unrealistically low market valuation, be a good investment at the time.

QUESTIONS

1. Why is return on investment (ROI) one of the most valid measures of enterprise performance? How is this measure used by the financial analyst?
2. How is ROI used as an internal management tool?
3. Discuss the validity of excluding "nonproductive" assets from the asset base used in the computation of ROI. Under what circumstances is the exclusion of intangible assets from the asset base warranted?
4. Why is interest added back to net income when the ROI is computed on total assets?
5. Under what circumstances may it be proper to consider convertible debt as equity capital in the computation of ROI?
6. Why must the minority interest's share in net income be added back when ROI is computed on total assets?

7. Why must the net income figure used in the computation of ROI be adjusted to reflect the asset base (denominator) used in the computation?
8. What is the relationship between ROI and sales?
9. Company A acquired Company B because the latter had a record of profitability (net income to sales ratio) exceeding that of its industry. After the acquisition took place, a major stockholder complained that the acquisition resulted in a low ROI. Discuss the possible reasons for his complaint.
10. Company X's profitability is 2 percent of sales. Company Y has a turnover of assets of 12. Both companies have ROIs of 6 percent that are considered unsatisfactory by industry standards. What is the asset turnover of Company X and what is the profitability ratio of Company Y? What action would you advise to the managements of the respective companies?
11. What is the purpose of measuring the asset utilization of different asset categories?
12. What factors enter into the evaluation of the ROI measures?
13. How is the equity growth rate computed? What does it signify?
14. *a.* How do the rate of return on total assets and that on stockholders' equity differ?
    b. What are the components of the rate of return on common stockholders' equity and what do they represent?
15. *a.* What is *equity turnover* and how is it related to the rate of return on equity?
    b. "Growth in per share earnings generated from an increase in equity turnover probably cannot be expected to continue indefinitely." Do you agree or disagree? Explain briefly, bringing out in your answer the alternative causes of an increase in equity turnover. (CFA)

Chapter 7

ANALYSIS OF RESULTS OF OPERATIONS—I

THE SIGNIFICANCE OF INCOME STATEMENT ANALYSIS

The income statement presents in summarized fashion the results of operations of an enterprise. These results, in turn, represent the major reason for the existence of a profit-seeking entity, and they are important determinants of its value and its solvency.

As was brought out in the discussion of objectives of financial analysis in Chapter 1, some of the most important decisions in security analysis and credit evaluation are based on an evaluation of income statements. To the security analyst, income is often the single most important determinant of security values, and hence the measurement and the projection of income are among the most important analytical objectives. Similarly, to the credit grantor, income and cash provided by operations are the most natural as well as the most desirable source of interest and principal repayment. In almost all other aspects of financial analysis, the evaluation and projection of operating results assume great importance.

THE MAJOR OBJECTIVES OF INCOME ANALYSIS

In the evaluation of the income of an enterprise, the analyst is particularly interested in an answer to the following questions:

1. What is the relevant net income of the enterprise and what is its quality?
2. What elements in the income statement can be used and relied upon for purposes of earnings forecasting?
3. How stable are the major elements of income and expense and what is their trend?
4. What is the "earning power" of the enterprise?

These questions will be examined in this and in the two chapters that follow.

What Is the Relevant Net Income of the Enterprise?

Based on the simple proposition that net income is the excess of revenues over costs and expenses during an accounting period, many people, including astute professional analysts, are exasperated at the difficulties they encounter in their search for the "true earnings" or the "real earnings" of an enterprise.

Why, they ask, should it be possible for so many different "acceptable" figures of "net income" to flow out of one set of circumstances? Given the economic events that the enterprise experienced during a given period, is there not only *one* "true" result, and is it not the function of accountancy to identify and measure such result?

Those who have studied this book will know why the answer to the last question must be "no." In this chapter, dealing with the analysis of income, it is appropriate to summarize *why* this is so.

Net Income Is Not a Specific Quantity   Net income is not a specific flow awaiting the perfection of a flawless meter with which it can be precisely measured. There are a number of reasons for this:

1. The determination of income is dependent on estimates regarding the outcome of future events. This peering into the future is basically a matter of judgment involving the assessment of probabilities based on facts and estimates.

While the judgment of skilled and experienced professionals, working on the basis of identical data and information, can be expected to fall within a narrow range, it will nevertheless *vary* within such a range. The estimates involve the allocation of revenues and costs as between the present and the future. Put another way, they involve the determination of the future utility and usefulness of many categories of unexpired costs and of assets as well as the estimation of future liabilities and obligations.

2. The accounting standards governing the determination and measurement of income at any given time are the result of the cumulative experience of the accounting profession, of regulatory agencies, of businessmen, and others. They reflect a momentary equilibrium that is based partly on knowledge and experience and partly on the compromise of widely differing interests and views on methods of measurement. While the accounting profession has moved to narrow the range of acceptable alternative measurement principles, alternatives nevertheless remain; and their complete elimination in the near future is unlikely.

3. Beyond the problem of honest differences in estimation and other judgments, as well as of the variety of alternative acceptable principles, is also the problem arising from the diverse ways in which the judgments and principles are applied.

Theoretically, the independent professional accountant should be concerned first and foremost with the fair presentation of the financial statements. He should make accounting a "neutral" science that gives expression and effect to economic events but does not itself affect the results presented. To this end, he should choose from among alternative principles those most applicable to the circumstances and should disclose all facts, favorable and adverse, that may affect the user's decision.

In fact, the accounting profession as a whole has not yet reached such a level of independence and detachment of judgment. It is subject to the powerful pressures on the part of managements who have, or at least feel that they have, a vital interest in the way in which results of operations are presented. The auditors are most vulnerable to pressures in those areas of accounting where widely differing alternatives are equally acceptable and where accounting theory is still unsettled. Thus, they may choose the lowest level of acceptable practice rather than that which is most appropriate and fair in the circumstances. Although relatively less frequent, cases of malpractice and collusion in outright deception by independent accountants nevertheless still surface from time to time.

The analyst cannot ignore these possibilities, and must be aware of them and be ever alert to them. It calls for constant vigilance in the analysis of audited data, particularly when there is reason to suspect a lack of independence and objectivity in the application of accounting principles.

In addition to the above reasons that are inherent in the accounting process, there exists another reason why there cannot be such a thing as an absolute measure of "real earnings." It is that financial statements are general-purpose presentations designed to serve the diverse needs of many users. Consequently, a single figure of "net income" cannot be relevant to all users, and that means that the analyst must use this figure and the additional information disclosed in the financial statements and elsewhere as a starting point and adjust it so as to arrive at a "net income" figure that meets his or her particular interests and objectives.

ILLUSTRATION 1.   To the buyer of an income-producing property, the depreciation expense figure that is based on the seller's cost is not relevant. In order to estimate the net income that can be derived from such property, depreciation based on the expected purchase price of the property must be substituted.

ILLUSTRATION 2.   To the analyst who exercises independent judgment and uses knowledge of the company he is analyzing and the industry of which it is a part, the reported net income marks the start of his analysis. He adjusts the net income figure for changes in income and expense items that he judges to be warranted. These may include, for example, estimates of bad debts, of depreciation, and of research costs as well as the treatment of gains and losses that are labeled extraordinary. Comparisons with other companies may call for similar adjustments so that the data can be rendered comparable.

From the above discussion it should be clear that the determination of a figure of net income is, from the point of view of the analyst, secondary to the objective of being able to find in the income statement all the disclosures needed in order to arrive at an income figure that is relevant for the purpose at hand.

The questions regarding the quality of earnings, of what elements in the income statement can be relied on for forecasting purposes, of what the stability and the trend of the earning elements are, and finally, of what the "earning power" of the enterprise is, will all be considered in Chapter 9.

We shall now proceed to examine the specific tools that are useful in the analysis of the various components of the income statement.

ANALYSIS OF COMPONENTS OF THE INCOME STATEMENT

The analysis of the income statements of an enterprise can be conceived as being undertaken at two levels: (1) obtaining an understanding of the accounting standards used and of their implication and (2) using the appropriate tools of income statement analysis.

Accounting Standards Used and Their Implication

The analyst must have a thorough understanding of the standards of income, cost, and expense accounting and measurement employed by the enterprise. Moreover, since most assets, with the exception of cash and receivables actually collectible, represent costs deferred to the future, the analyst must have a good understanding of the standards of asset and liability measurement employed by the enterprise so that he or she can relate them to the income accounting of the enterprise as a means of checking the validity of that accounting. Finally, he or she must understand and assess the implications that the use of one accounting principle, as opposed to another, has on the measurement of the income of an enterprise and its comparison to that of other enterprises.

Tools of Income Statement Analysis

The second level consists of applying the appropriate tools of analysis to the components of the income statement and the interpretation of the results shown by these analytical measures. The application of these tools is aimed at achieving the objectives of the analysis of results of operations mentioned earlier, such as the projection of income, the assessment of its stability and quality, and the estimation of earning power.

The remainder of this chapter will be devoted to an examination of these tools and to the interpretation of the results achieved through their use.

THE ANALYSIS OF SALES AND REVENUES

The analysis of sales and revenues is centered on answers to these basic questions:

1. What are the major sources of revenue?
2. How stable are these sources and what is their trend?
3. How is the earning of revenue determined and how is it measured?

Major Sources of Revenue

Knowledge of major sources of revenues (sales) is important in the analysis of the income statement particularly if the analysis is that of a multimarket enterprise. Each major market or product line may have its own separate and distinct growth pattern, profitability, and future potential.

The best way to analyze the composition of revenues is by means of a common-size statement that shows the percentage of each major class of revenue to the total. This information can also be portrayed graphically on an absolute dollar basis as shown in Exhibit 7–1.

Exhibit 7–1   Analysis of sales by product line over time

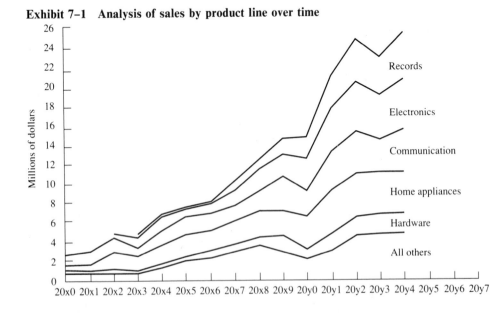

Chapter 10 contains a summary of segmental information of Campbell Soup and item 97 of its financial statements contains Geographic Area Information.

FINANCIAL REPORTING BY DIVERSIFIED ENTERPRISES

The user of the financial statements of diversified enterprises faces, in addition to the usual problems and pitfalls of financial analysis, the problem of sorting out and understanding the impact that the different individual segments of the business have on the sum total of reported results of operations and financial condition. The author of an important study in the reporting by diversified companies has defined a conglomerate company as follows:

> ... one which is so managerially decentralized, so lacks operational integration, or has such diversified markets that it may experience rates of profitability, degrees of risk, and opportunities for growth which vary within the company to such an extent that an investor requires information about these variations in order to make informed decisions.[1]

Reasons for the Need for Data by Significant Enterprise Segments

The above definition suggests some of the most significant reasons why financial analysts require as much information and detailed data as possible about the various segments of an enterprise. The analysis, evaluation, projection, and valuation of earnings requires that these be broken down into categories that share similar characteristics of variability, growth potential, and risk. Similarly, the asset structure and the financing requirements of various segments of an enterprise can vary significantly and thus require separate analysis and evaluation. Thus, the credit grantor may be interested in knowing which segments of an enterprise provide cash and which are net users of cash.

The composition of an enterprise, the relative size and profitability of its various segments, the ability of management to make profitable acquisitions, and the overall performance of management represents additional important information that the analyst seeks from its segmented data.[2] As will be seen from the discussion in Chapter 9, among the best ways

---

[1] R. K. Mautz, "Identification of the Conglomerate Company," *Financial Executive,* July 1967, p. 26.

[2] D. W. Collins in a study of 150 multisegment firms found that "SEC product-line revenue and profit disclosures together with industry sales projections published in various government sources provide significantly more accurate estimates of future total-entity sales and earnings than do those procedures that rely totally on consolidated data." *Journal of Accounting Research,* Spring 1976, pp. 163–77.

to construct an earnings forecast is to build the projections, to the extent possible, segment by segment.

The evaluation of the growth potential of earnings requires that as much information as possible be obtained about the different product lines or segments that make up the aggregate earnings. Rappaport and Lerner have illustrated the use of a segmented earnings contribution matrix that may prove useful in an assessment of earnings quality and growth potential, as well as in the valuation of aggregate earnings.[3] These are shown in Exhibits 7–2 and 7–3.

Disclosure of "Line of Business" Data

The degree of informative disclosure about the results of operations and the asset base of segments of a business can vary widely. Full disclosure would call for providing detailed income statements, statements of financial position, and statements of cash flow (SCF) for each significant segment. This is rarely found in practice because of the difficulty of obtaining such breakdowns internally, and also because of management's reluctance to divulge information that could harm the enterprise's

Exhibit 7–2 Earnings contribution and growth rates by industry segments

Industry	Earnings contributions (in thousands)	Growth rate of earnings contribution over the past three years
Leisure time:		
1. Camp equipment	$100	11%
2. Fishing equipment	50	2
3. Boats	72	15
4. Sporting goods	12	3
	234	
Agribusiness:		
1. Milk processing	85	2
2. Canning	72	8
3. Chicken farming	12	15
	169	
Education:		
1. Text publishing	40	3
2. Papers and supplies	17	6
	57	
Total	$460	

---

[3] A. Rappaport and E. M. Lerner, *A Framework for Financial Reporting by Diversified Companies* (New York: National Association of Accountants, 1969), pp. 18–19.

Exhibit 7-3 Segmented earnings contribution matrix

	Growth rate (in percent)			
Industry	0–5	5–10	10–15	Total
Leisure time	$ 62	$ 0	$172	$234
Agribusiness	85	72	12	169
Education	40	17	0	57
Total	$187	$89	$184	$460

competitive position. Short of the disclosure of complete financial statements by business segment, a great variety of partial detail has been suggested.

Income Statement Data

Revenues Only   In most enterprises, this should not present great difficulties.

Gross Profit   This involves complex problems of interdivisional transfer pricing as well as allocation of indirect overhead costs.

Contribution Margin   Contribution margin reporting (see also Chapter 8) is based on assigning to each segment the revenues, costs, and expenses for which that segment is solely responsible. It is a very useful concept in management accounting, but for purposes of public reporting of segment data, it presents problems because there are no generally accepted methods of cost allocation and, consequently, they can vary significantly from company to company and even within one enterprise. Disclosure of allocation methods, while helpful, will not remove all the problems facing the user of such data.

Net Income (after full cost allocation)   The further down the income statement reporting by segment occurs, the more pervasive and the more complex the allocation procedures become. Reporting segment net income would require allocating all joint expenses to each specific business activity on some rational basis, even though they may not be directly related to any particular one.

Balance Sheet Data

A breakdown by segments of assets employed is needed in an assessment of the efficiency of operations by segment, in the evaluation of segmental management, as well as in the computation of divisional return on investment.

In most companies, only certain assets, such as plant and equipment, inventories, and certain intangibles, are identified directly with a specific segment. An allocation of all assets would have to be arbitrary since in many enterprises cash, temporary investments, and even receivables are centralized at the group or corporate headquarters level.

Research Studies

Interest in the subject of reporting by diversified companies has sparked research efforts into the types of disclosures that are necessary and feasible and the problems related thereto.[4] A most extensive research effort was that undertaken by Professor R. K. Mautz,[5] and the FASB published an extensive *Discussion Memorandum* on the subject.

Statement of Financial Accounting Standards 14

In *SFAS 14* (1976), "Financial Reporting for Segments of a Business Enterprise," the Board established requirements for disclosures to be made in company financial statements concerning information about operations in different industries, foreign operations, export sales, and major customers.

The *Statement* recognizes that evaluation of risk and return is the central element of investment and lending decisions. Since an enterprise operating in various industry segments or geographic areas may have different rates of profitability, degrees and types of risk, and opportunities for growth, disaggregated information will assist analysts in analyzing the uncertainties surrounding the timing and amount of expected cash flows—and hence the risks—related to an investment in or a loan to an enterprise that operates in different industries or areas of the world.

The *Statement* requires companies to report in their annual financial statements the revenues, operating profit (revenue less operating expenses), and identifiable assets of each significant industry segment of their operations. Certain other related disclosures are required. *SFAS 14* does not prescribe methods of accounting for transfer pricing or cost allocation. However, it does require that the methods in use be disclosed.

---

[4] See Morton Backer and Walter B. McFarland, *External Reporting for Segments of a Business* (New York: National Association of Accountants, 1968). Also see Robert T. Sprouse, "Diversified Views about Diversified Companies," *Journal of Accounting Research* 7, no. 1 (Spring 1969), pp. 137–59; and A. Rappaport and E. H. Lerner, *A Framework for Financial Reporting by Diversified Companies* (New York: National Association of Accountants, 1969).

[5] R. K. Mautz, *Financial Reporting by Diversified Companies* (New York: Financial Executives Research Foundation, 1968).

A segment is regarded as significant, therefore reportable, under the *Statement* if its sales, operating profit, or identifiable assets are 10 percent or more of the related combined amounts for all of a company's industry segments.[6] To ensure that the industry segments for which a company reports information represent a substantial portion of the company's overall operations, the *Statement* requires that the combined sales of all segments for which information is reported shall be at least 75 percent of the company's total sales. The *Statement* also suggests 10 as a practical limit to the number of industry segments for which a company reports information. If that limit is exceeded it may be appropriate to combine certain segments into broader ones to meet the 75 percent test with a practical number of segments.

Under *SFAS 14,* if a company derives 10 percent or more of its revenue from sales to any single customer, that fact and the amount of revenue from each such customer also must be disclosed.

The *Statement* provides guidelines for determining a company's foreign operations and export sales and for grouping operations by geographic areas. Information similar to that required for industry segments also is required for a company's operations in different geographic areas of the world.

SEC Reporting Requirements

The SEC took an early lead in requiring disclosure of sales and profit information by lines of business. Following promulgation of *SFAS 14,* the SEC, by means of *FRR* No. 1 Section 503, conformed SEC reporting requirements to those of the *Statement.* However, the SEC reporting requirements, incorporated in Regulation S-K, differ from *SFAS 14* in that it requires that segment revenue, operating profit, and asset information be presented for three years. Moreover, an additional narrative description is called for in Regulation S-K covering the registrant's business by reportable segments including information on competition, dependence on a few customers, principal products and services, backlog, sources and availability of raw materials, patents, research and development (R&D) costs, number of employees, and the seasonality of the business.

---

[6] Specifically, an industry segment is significant if in the latest period for which statements are presented:

1. Its revenue is 10 percent or more of the *combined* revenue of all industry segments; or
2. Its operating profit (loss) is 10 percent or more of the greater of *(a)* the combined operating profit of all segments that did not incur a loss, or *(b)* the combined operating loss of all segments that did incur a loss; or
3. Its identifiable assets are 10 percent or more of the combined identifiable assets of all industry segments.

Implications for Analysis

The increasing complexity of diversified business entities and the loss of identity that acquired companies suffer in the published financial statements of conglomerates have created serious problems for the financial analyst.

The disclosure requirements of *SFAS 14* as well as those of the SEC increased the amount of segmental information available for analysis. However the analyst will have to be very careful in his assessment of the reliability of the data on which he bases his conclusions.

The more specific and detailed the information provided is, the more likely it is to be based on extensive allocations of costs and expenses. Allocation of common costs, as practiced for internal accounting purposes, is often based on such concepts as "equity," "reasonableness," and "acceptability to managers." These concepts have often little relevance to the objective of financial analysis.

Bases of allocating joint expenses are largely arbitrary and subject to differences of opinions as to their validity and precision. Some specific types of joint expenses that fall into this category are general and administrative expenses of central headquarters, R&D costs, certain selling costs, advertising, interest, pension costs, and federal and state income taxes.

There are, at present, no generally accepted principles of cost and expense allocation or any general agreement on the methods by which the costs of one segment should be transferred to another segment in the same enterprise. Moreover, the process of formulating such principles of reaching such agreement has barely begun. The analyst who uses segmented data must bear these limitations firmly in mind.

ILLUSTRATION 3.   Companies generally do not disclose internal accounting practices, which they are not obligated to disclose, unless it is in their interest to do so. The management of Murray Ohio Manufacturing Company found it to its advantage to disclose, in federal court, that its annual report did not give the true story as far as actual profit or loss by product line was concerned. Management admitted to understating losses in its bicycle division by many millions of dollars as part of an effort to fend off hostile takeover advances by a Swedish company. Murray Ohio feared that the option of closing a heavily losing bicycle division would appeal to the potential acquirer. The company simply chose not to allocate $17 million in corporate overhead to its bicycle division.

This case provides a rare glimpse into the murky area of overhead allocation and to many possibilities companies have to provide misleading segmental information if they choose to do so.

In *SFAS 14*, the Board has, in effect, recognized the above-described limitations and realities. Consequently, the disclosure of profit contribution (revenue less only those operating expenses that are directly traceable to a segment), which was proposed in the exposure draft issued for public comment, was not required in the final *Statement*. Similarly, the Board concluded that revenue from intersegment sales or transfers shall be accounted for on whatever basis is used by the enterprise to price intersegment sales or transfers. No single basis was prescribed or proscribed.

Moreover, the Board concluded that certain items of revenue and expense either do not relate to segments or cannot always be allocated to segments on the basis of objective evidence, and consequently, there is no requirement in *SFAS 14* that net income be disclosed for reportable segments. The Board also noted in the *Statement* that "determination of an enterprise's industry segments must depend to a considerable extent on the judgment of the management of the enterprise."

The implication for analysts of this lack of firmer guidelines and definitions is that segmental disclosures are and must be treated as "soft" information that is subject to manipulation and preinterpretation by managements. Consequently, such data must be treated with a healthy degree of skepticism, and conclusions can be derived from them only through the exercise of great care as well as analytical skill.

STABILITY AND TREND OF REVENUES

The relative trend of sales of various product lines or revenues from services can best be measured by means of trend percentages as illustrated in Exhibit 7–4.

Sales indexes of various product lines can be correlated and compared to composite industry figures or to product sales trends of specific competitors.

Important considerations bearing on the quality and stability of the sales and revenues trend include:

1. The sensitivity of demand for the various products to general business conditions.
2. The ability of the enterprise to anticipate trends in demand by the introduction of new products and services as a means of furthering

Exhibit 7–4 **Trend percentage of sales by product line (year 1 = 100)**

	Year 1	Year 2	Year 3	Year 4	Year 5
Product A	100	110	114	107	121
Product B	100	120	135	160	174
Product C	100	98	94	86	74
Service A	100	101	92	98	105

sales growth and as replacement of products for which demand is falling.

3. Degree of customer concentration (now required to be disclosed by *SFAS 14*), dependence on major customers, as well as demand stability of major customer groups.[7]
4. Degree of product concentration and dependence on a single industry.
5. Degree of dependence on relatively few star salesmen.
6. Degree of geographical diversification of markets.

ILLUSTRATION 4.   Micron Products Inc., reported sales to major customers as follows:

> Sales to three major customers amounted to approximately 32 percent, 25 percent and 11 percent of the Company's net sales.
> Sales to the Company's foreign customers amounted to approximately 15 percent and 13 percent of the Company's net sales.

MANAGEMENT'S DISCUSSION AND ANALYSIS OF FINANCIAL CONDITION AND RESULTS OF OPERATIONS

A significant concept of disclosure from the analyst's point of view was instituted by the SEC, further broadened in 1980, and is now codified in *FRR* No. 1 Section 501. The disclosures that are required are of an interpretative or explanatory nature that is necessary to enable investors to understand and evaluate significant period-to-period changes in the various items that report the enterprise's financial condition and results of operations. In *FRR 36* (1989) the SEC elaborated further on examples of satisfactory MDA disclosures.

Management's Discussion and Analysis of Financial Condition and Results of Operations (MDA) requirements, which are part of the SEC's integrated disclosure system, now require three years of income statements and focus on (*in addition* to results of operations) liquidity, capital resources, and the impact of inflation. These latter topics are discussed in Chapters 3, 4, and 5.

In the area of results of operations, MDA must cover revenue and expense components that are needed for understanding of results by the reader, major unusual or infrequent events that materially affect reported income from continuing operations, trends or uncertainties that have affected or are likely to affect results, and impending changes in cost/revenue relationships such as increases in materials or labor costs. MDA

---

[7] *Statement on Auditing Standards (SAS) 6* (AICPA) requires disclosure of the economic dependency of a company on one or more parties with which it transacts a significant volume of business, such as a sole or major customer, supplier, franchisor, distributor, borrower, or lender.

must also include a discussion of the extent to which material increases in revenues are attributable to increases in prices or to increases in volume or amount of goods or services being sold or to the introduction of new products or services as well as a discussion of the impact of inflation and changing prices on the registrant's revenues and on income from continuing operations.

Overall, the SEC desires that MDA's emphasis be redirected from operations to financial results; that forward-looking information should, if possible, be included; and the discussion should focus on trends and implications that are not evident from an examination of the financial statements.[8]

Campbell Soup Company (Chapter 2, Appendix B) presents its MDA in items 2 to 12.

IMPLICATIONS FOR ANALYSIS

In its instructions to MDA requirements, the SEC states that the purpose of the discussion and analysis is to provide investors and others with information relevant to an assessment of the financial condition and results of operations of the registrant as determined by evaluating the amounts and the certainty of cash flows from operations and from outside sources.

Even more so than under the previous requirements, the instructions for preparation of MDA make it clear that managements have a great deal of discretion on how to communicate to the reader and what to stress in such communications. The aim is meaningful disclosure in narrative form by those in charge of operations who are really in a position to know and who can supply significant additional details not usually found in the financial statements. The results will depend on management's attitudes and objectives.

While analysts must be aware that much information included in MDA is likely to be "soft" in nature, it must be borne in mind that in reporting in accordance with SEC requirements, managements cannot risk being careless or deceptive in their statements in such financial filings.

On balance, the analyst will have here much information that is valuable, that provides added insights, and that cannot readily be obtained

---

[8] In *FRR* No. 1 Section 501, the SEC released the staff's assessment of disclosures contained in MDA sections of annual reports. Examples cited in the release cover areas such as impact on pre-tax income of closing unprofitable facilities; effect of LIFO inventory liquidation on pre-tax income; changes in revenues by segment; forward-looking information; cash flow from operations on a trend basis; available sources of liquidity; known or reasonably likely liquidity deficiencies; and impact of inflation on sales, cost of sales, assets, and liabilities. *FRR 36* (1989) covers, among others, trends, demands, commitments, events, and uncertainties as well as year-to-year changes, segment data discussion, and analysis of cash flows.

in other ways. Thus, without having to take them at face value, the analyst can nevertheless use these disclosures as valuable analytical supplements for both the information that they provide and the insights into the thinking and the attitude of managements which they afford.

METHODS OF REVENUE RECOGNITION AND MEASUREMENT

Some methods of revenue recognition are more conservative than others. The analyst must understand the income recognition methods used by the enterprise and their implications as well as the methods used by companies with which the results of the enterprise under analysis are being compared. A foremost consideration is whether the revenue recognition method in use accurately reflects an entity's economic performance and earnings activities.

QUESTIONS

1. What are the major objectives of income analysis?
2. Why can "net income" not be a single specific quantity?
3. Two levels can be identified in the analysis of the income statement. Name them.
4. Why is knowledge of major sources of revenue (sales) of an enterprise important in the analysis of the income statement?
5. Why are information and detailed data about the segments of diversified enterprises important to financial analysts?
6. Disclosure of various types of information by "line of business" has been proposed. Comment on the value of such information and the feasibility of providing it in published financial statements.
7. What are the major provisions of *SFAS 14?*
8. To what limitations of public segmental data must the analyst be alert?
9. Which important considerations have a bearing on the quality and the stability of a sales and revenue trend?
10. How were the requirements for additional disclosures of an interpretive or explanatory nature in the form of Management's Discussion and Analysis of Financial Condition and Results of Operations (MDA) changed in 1980?
11. Cite some of the examples of the types of subjects that should be covered in the MDA.
12. What are the objectives of discussions required by the revised MDA?

Chapter 8

ANALYSIS OF RESULTS OF OPERATIONS—II

This chapter continues the discussion of the analysis of results of operations begun in the preceding chapter.

ANALYSIS OF COST OF SALES

In most enterprises,[1] the cost of goods or services sold is, as a percentage of sales, the single most significant cost category. The methods of determining cost of sales encompass a wide variety of alternatives. Moreover, there is, particularly in unregulated industries, no agreed-to uniform cost classification method that would result in a clear and generally accepted distinction among such basic cost and expense categories as cost of sales, administrative, general, sales, and financial expenses. This is particularly true in the classification of general and administrative expenses. Thus, in undertaking cost comparisons, the analyst must be ever alert to methods of classification and the effect they can have on the validity of comparisons within an enterprise or among enterprises.

GROSS PROFIT

The excess of sales over the cost of sales is the gross profit or gross margin. It is commonly expressed as a percentage:

Sales	$10,000,000	100%
Cost of sales	7,200,000	72
Gross profit	$ 2,800,000	28%

---

[1] Exceptions can be found, for example, in some land sales companies where selling and other costs may actually exceed the cost of land sold.

The gross profit percentage or gross margin is a very important operating ratio. In the above example, the gross profit is $2,800,000, or 28 percent of sales. From this amount, all other costs and expenses must be recovered and any net income that is earned is the balance remaining after all expenses. Unless an enterprise has an adequate gross profit, it can be neither profitable nor does it have an adequate margin with which to finance such essential future-directed discretionary expenditures as research and development and advertising. Gross profit margins vary from industry to industry depending on such factors as competition, capital investment, and the level of costs other than direct costs of sales that must be covered by the gross profit.

Factors in the Analysis of Gross Profit

In the analysis of gross profit, the analyst will pay particular attention to:

1. The factors that account for the variation in sales and costs of sales.
2. The relationship between sales and costs of sales and management's ability to control this relationship.

ANALYSIS OF CHANGES IN GROSS MARGIN[2]

A detailed analysis of changes in gross margin can usually be performed only by an internal analyst because it requires access to data such as the number of physical units sold, unit sales prices, as well as unit costs. Such data are usually not provided in published financial statements. Moreover, unless the enterprise sells a single product, this analysis requires detailed data by product line. The external analyst, unless he or she has special influence on the company analyzed, will usually not have access to the data required for the analysis of gross margin.

Despite the above limitations to which gross margin analysis is subject, it is instructive to examine its process so that the elements accounting for variations in gross margin can be more fully understood.

EXAMPLE OF ANALYSIS OF CHANGE IN GROSS MARGIN

Company A shows the following data for two years:

---

[2] In this discussion, the terms *gross profit* and *gross margin* are used interchangeably. Some writers reserve the term *gross margin* for situations where the cost of goods sold excludes overhead costs, that is, direct costing. This is not the intention here.

	Unit of measure	Year ended December 31		In- crease	De- crease
		Year 1	Year 2		
1. Net sales	Thousands of dollars	$657.6	$687.5	$29.9	
2. Cost of sales	Thousands of dollars	237.3	245.3	8.0	
3. Gross margin	Thousands of dollars	420.3	442.2	21.9	
4. Units of product sold	Thousands	215.6	231.5	15.9	
5. Selling price per unit (1 ÷ 4)	Dollars	$ 3.05	$ 2.97		$0.08
6. Cost per unit (2 ÷ 4)	Dollars	1.10	1.06		0.04

Based on the above data, Exhibit 8–1 presents an analysis of the changes in gross margin of $21,900 from year 1 to year 2.

This analysis is based on the principle of focusing on one element of change at a time. Thus, in Exhibit 8–1, the analysis of variation in sales involves the following steps:

Step 1: We focus on the year-to-year change in volume while *assuming* that the unit selling price remained unchanged at the former, year 1, level. Since both the volume change (15.9) and the unit selling price ($3.05) are positive, the resulting product ($48.5) is positive.

Step 2: We focus next on the change in selling price that represents a year-to-year decrease (−$0.08) and *assume* the volume (215.6) to be unchanged from the prior year level so as to single out the change due to price change. Algebraically, here the multiplication of a negative (price change) by a positive (volume) results in a negative product (−$17.2).

Step 3: We must now recognize that the *assumptions* used in steps 1 and 2 above, that is, that the volume remained unchanged while the unit price changed and vice versa, are temporary expedients used to single out major causes for change. To complete the computation, we must recognize that by making these assumptions we left out the *combined* change in volume and unit price. The change in volume of 15.9 represents an *increase* and, consequently, is *positive*. The unit selling price change represents a *decrease* (−$0.08) and hence is *negative*. As a result, the product is negative (−$1.3).

Exhibit 8-1

COMPANY A
**Statements Accounting for Variation in Gross Margin
between Year 1 and Year 2 (in thousands)**

I. *Analysis of variation in sales*
1. Variation due to change in volume of products sold:
    Change in volume (15.9) × year 1 unit selling price $48.5
    ($3.05) . . . .
2. Variation due to change in selling price:
    Change in selling price (−$0.08) × year 1 sales volume   −17.2
    (215.6) . . . .
                                                                        ─────
                                                                        31.3
3. Variation due to combined change in sales volume (15.9)   − 1.3
    and unit sales price (−$0.08) . . . .   ─────
    Increase in net sales 30.0*

II. *Analysis of variation in cost of sales*
1. Variation due to change in volume of products sold:
    Change in volume (15.9) × year 1 cost per unit ($1.10) . . .   17.5
2. Variation due to change in cost per unit sold:
    Change in cost per unit (−$0.04) × year 1 sales volume   − 8.6
    (215.6) . . . .   ─────
                                                                        8.9
3. Variation due to combined change in volume (15.9) and cost   − 0.6
    per unit (−$0.04) . . . .   ─────
    Increase in cost of sales 8.3*

    Net variation in gross margin $21.7*

    * Differences are due to rounding.

Step 4: Adding up the—

Variation due to volume change	$48.5
Variation due to price change	−17.2
Combined change of volume and unit price	− 1.3
We account for the causes behind the sales increase	$30.0

The analysis of variation in the cost of sales follows the same principles.

Interpretation of Changes in Gross Margin

The analysis of variation in gross margin is useful in identifying major causes of change in the gross margin. These changes can consist of one or a combination of the following factors:

1. Increase in sales volume.
2. Decrease in sales volume.

3. Increase in unit sales price.
4. Decrease in unit sales price.
5. Increase in cost per unit.
6. Decrease in cost per unit.

The presence of the "combined change of volume and unit sales price" and the "combined volume and unit cost" in the analysis presents no problem in interpretation since their amount is always minor in relation to the main causative factors of change.

The interpretation of the results of the analysis of gross margin involves the identification of the major factors responsible for change in the gross margin and an evaluation of the reasons for change in the factors. Such an analysis can also focus on the most feasible areas of improvement (i.e., volume, price, or cost) and the likelihood of realizing such improvements. For example, if it is determined that the major reason for a decline in gross margin is a decline in unit sales prices and that it reflects a situation of overcapacity in the enterprise's industry with attendant price cutting, then the situation is a serious one because of the limited control management has on such a development. If, on the other hand, the deterioration in the gross margin is found to be due to an increase in unit costs, then this may be a situation over which management can exercise a larger measure of control and, given its ability to do so, an improvement is a more likely possibility.

BREAK-EVEN ANALYSIS

The second level of cost analysis is importantly concerned with the relationship between sales and the cost of sales but goes beyond that segment of the income statement. This level encompasses break-even analysis and is concerned with the relationship of sales to most costs, including, but not limited to, the cost of sales.

Concepts underlying Break-Even Analysis

The basic principle underlying break-even analysis is the behavior of costs. Some costs vary directly with sales while others remain essentially constant over a considerable range of sales. The first category of costs is classified as *variable* while the latter are known as *fixed* costs.

The distinction among costs according to their behavior can be best understood within the framework of an example. In order to focus first on the basic data involved and on the technique of break-even analysis, we shall examine it by means of a simple illustration:

An enterprising graduate student saw an opportunity to sell pocket calculators at a financial analysts' convention due to take place in her hometown. Upon inquiry, she learned that she would have to get a vendor's license from the convention organizing committee at a cost of $10 and that the rental of a room in which to sell would amount to $140. The cost of calculators was to be $3 each with the right to return any that were not sold. The student decided that $8 was the proper sales price per calculator and wondered whether the undertaking will be worthwhile. As a first step she decided to compute the number of calculators she will have to sell in order to break even.

Equation Approach

We start from the elementary proposition that:

$$\text{Sales} = \text{Variable cost} + \text{Fixed costs} + \text{Profit (or} - \text{Loss)}$$

Since at break-even there is neither gain nor loss, the equation is:

$$\text{Sales} = \text{Variable cost} + \text{Fixed costs}$$

If we designate the number of calculators that must be sold to break even as X, we have

$$\$8X = \$3X + \$150$$

where:

Sales = Unit sales price ($8) $\times X$
Variable costs = Variable cost per unit ($3) $\times X$
Fixed costs = License fee ($10) + Rental ($140)

These costs are fixed because they will be incurred regardless of the number of calculators sold.

Solving the equation we get:

$$\$5X = \$150$$
$$X = 30 \text{ units or calculators to be sold to break even}$$

In this example, the number of calculators to be sold is important information because the student needs to assess the likelihood of obtaining the size of demand that will make her venture profitable. This approach is, however, limited to a single product enterprise.

If, as is common in business, an enterprise sells a mix of goods, the unit sales break-even computation becomes impracticable and the focus is on dollar sales. This would be the situation if our student sold stationery and books in addition to calculators.

This more prevalent break-even computation can be illustrated with the data already given.

If we designate the dollar sales at break even as Y, we get:

$$Y = \text{Variable-cost percentage } Y + \text{Fixed costs}$$
$$= 0.375Y + \$150$$
$$0.625Y = \$150$$
$$Y = \$240 \text{ (sales at break even)}$$

In this computation, the variable-cost percentage is the ratio of variable costs ($3) to sales price ($8). This means that each dollar of sales entails an incurrence of $0.375 for variable costs, or 37.5 percent of the sales price.

Graphic Presentation

Exhibit 8–2 portrays the results attained above in graphic form. A graph drawn to scale will yield a solution approximating in accuracy that obtained by the formula method. Moreover it portrays under one set of assumptions not only the break-even point but also a whole range of profitable operations above that point as well as the losses below it.

Contribution Margin Approach

Another technique of break-even analysis that can produce additional insights into the relationship of sales, costs, and profits is the contribution margin approach. It will be illustrated here by means of the foregoing pocket calculator example.

Exhibit 8–2   Calculator illustration—break-even chart

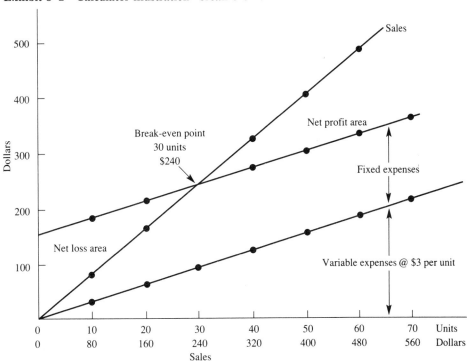

The contribution margin is what is left of the net sales price after deduction of the variable costs. It is from this margin that fixed costs must first be met and after that a profit earned.

$$
\begin{array}{ll}
\text{Sales price per calculator} \dots\dots\dots\dots\dots & \$8 \\
\text{Variable costs per calculator} \dots\dots\dots\dots & \underline{3} \\
\text{Unit contribution margin} \dots\dots\dots\dots\dots & \underline{\underline{\$5}}
\end{array}
$$

Since each unit (calculator) sold contributes \$5 to overhead and for profit, the break-even point in units is

$$
\frac{\text{Fixed costs}}{\text{Unit contribution margin}} = \frac{\$150}{\$5} = 30 \text{ units}
$$

Thus, after 30 units are sold, the fixed costs are covered and each additional unit sale yields a profit equal to the unit contribution margin, that is, \$5.

If, as is more usual, the break-even point is to be expressed in dollars of sales, the formula involves use of the contribution margin ratio rather than the unit contribution margin. The contribution margin ratio is a percentage relationship computed as follows:

$$
\frac{\text{Unit contribution margin}}{\text{Unit sales price}} = \frac{\$5}{\$8} = 0.625, \text{ or } 62.5 \text{ percent}
$$

The calculator problem dollar break-even point can now be calculated as follows:

$$
\frac{\text{Fixed costs}}{\text{Contribution margin ratio}} = \frac{\$150}{0.625} = \$240
$$

The contribution margin is an important tool in break-even analysis, and its significance will be the subject of further discussion later in this section.

Pocket Calculator Problem—Additional Considerations

The break-even technique illustrated above lends itself to a variety of assumptions and requirements. The following are additional illustrations, all using the original data of our example, unless changed assumptions are introduced:

ILLUSTRATION 1.   Assume that our student decided that in order to make the venture worthwhile she requires a net profit of $400. How many calculators must be sold to achieve this objective?

$$\text{Sales} = (\text{Variable cost percent})(\text{sales}) + \text{Fixed costs} + \text{Profit}$$
$$S = 0.375S + \$150 + \$400$$
$$0.625S = \$550$$
$$S = \$880$$
$$\frac{\$880}{\$8} = 110 \text{ units}$$

ILLUSTRATION 2.   Assume that the financial analysts' convention committee offered to provide the student with a room free of charge if she agreed to imprint on the calculators the Financial Analysts Society's seal. However, this would increase the cost of calculators from $3 to $4 per unit. Under the original assumptions, the break-even point was 30 calculators. What should it be if the student accepts the committee's proposal?

Here we have a reduction of fixed costs by $140 and an increase in variable costs of $1 per unit.

If X be the number of calculators sold at break-even point, then:

$$\text{Sales} = \text{Variables costs} + \text{Fixed costs}$$
$$\$8X = \$4X + \$10$$
$$\$4X = \$10$$
$$X = 2.5 \text{ calculators (rounded to 3)}$$

This proposal obviously involves a much lower break-even point and hence reduced risk. However, the lower contribution margin will at higher sales levels reduce total profitability. We can determine at what level of unit sales the original assumption of a $3 per unit variable cost and $150 fixed cost will equal the results of the $4 per unit variable cost and $10 fixed costs.

Let X be the number of units (calculators) sold, then:

$$\$4X + \$10 = \$3X + \$150$$
$$\$1X = \$140$$
$$X = 140 \text{ calculators}$$

Thus, if more than 140 calculators are sold, the alternative that includes the $3 variable cost will be more profitable.

Having examined the break-even analysis technique and some types of decisions for which it is useful, we will now turn to a discussion of the practical difficulties and the theoretical limitations to which the approach is subject.

Break-Even Technique—Problem Areas and Limitations

The intelligent use of the break-even technique and the drawing of reasonably valid conclusions therefrom depends on a resolution of practical difficulties and on an understanding of the limitations to which the techniques are subject.

Fixed, Variable, and Semivariable Costs   In the foregoing simple examples of break-even analysis, costs were clearly either fixed or variable. In the more complex reality found in practice, many costs are not so clearly separable into fixed and variable categories. That is, they either do not stay constant over a considerable change in sales volume or respond in exact proportion to change in sales.

We can illustrate this problem by reference to the costs of a food supermarket. As was discussed above, some costs will remain fixed within a certain range of sales. Rent, depreciation, certain forms of maintenance, utilities, and supervisory labor are examples of such fixed costs. The level of fixed costs can, of course, be increased by a simple management decision unrelated to the level of sales; for example, the grocery manager's salary may be increased.

Other costs, such as the cost of merchandise, trading stamps, supplies, and certain labor will vary closely with sales. These costs are truly variable. Certain other costs may, however, contain both fixed and variable elements in them. Examples of such *semivariable* costs are repairs, some materials, indirect labor, fuel, utilities, payroll taxes, and rents that contain a minimum payment provision and are also related to the level of sales. Break-even analysis requires that the variable component of such expenses be separated from the fixed component. This is often a difficult task for the management accountant and an almost impossible task for the outside analyst to perform without the availability of considerable internal data.

Simplifying Assumptions in Break-Even Analysis   The estimation of a variety of possible results by means of break-even calculations or charts requires the use of simplifying assumptions. In most cases, these simplifying assumptions do not destroy the validity of the conclusions reached. Nevertheless, in reaching such conclusions, the analyst must be fully aware of these assumptions and of their possible effect.

The following are some of the more important assumptions implicit in break-even computations:

1. The factors comprising the model actually behave as assumed, that is:
   a. That the costs have been reasonably subdivided into their fixed and variable components.
   b. That variable costs fluctuate proportionally with volume.
   c. That fixed costs remain fixed over the range relevant to the situation examined.
   d. That unit selling prices will remain unchanged over the range encompassed by the analysis.
2. In addition, there are certain operating and environmental assumptions that emphasize the static nature of any one break-even computation. It is assumed:

a. That the mix of sales will remain unchanged.
b. That efficiency of operations will remain constant.
c. That prices of cost factors will not change.
d. That the only factor affecting costs is volume.
e. That beginning and end-of-period inventory levels will remain substantially unchanged.
f. That there is no substantial change in the general price level during the period.

The formidable array of assumptions enumerated above points out the susceptibility of break-even computations to significant error. Not all the assumptions are, however, equally important, or, if not justified, will have an equal impact on the validity of conclusions. For example, the assumption that the selling price will not change with volume is contrary to economic theory and often is contrary to reality. Thus, the sales line is a curved rather than a linear function. However, the degree of error will depend on the actual degree of deviation from a strict linear relationship. Another basic assumption is that volume is *the* major, if not the only, factor affecting costs. We know, however, that strikes, political developments, legislation, and competition, to name a few other important factors, have a decided influence on costs. The analyst must, consequently, keep these simplifying assumptions firmly in mind and be aware of the dynamic factors that may require modifications in conclusions.

Break-Even Analysis—Uses and Their Implications

The break-even approach can be a useful tool of analysis if its limitations are recognized and its applications are kept in proper perspective.

The emphasis on the break-even, that is, zero profit, point is an unfortunate distortion of the objective of this type of analysis. Instead, the break-even situation represents but one point in a flexible set of projections of revenues and of the costs that will be associated with them under a given set of future conditions.

The managerial applications of break-even analysis are many. It is useful, among others, in price determination, expense control, and in the projection of profits. Along with standard cost systems it gives management a basis for pricing decisions under differing levels of activity. In conjunction with flexible budgets, it represents a powerful tool of expense control. The break-even chart is also a useful device with which to measure the impact of specific managerial decisions, such as plant expansion and new product introduction or of external influences, on the profitability of operations over various levels of activity.

To financial analysts, the function of profit projections is one of major importance. Moreover, the ability to estimate the impact of profitability of various economic conditions or managerial courses of action is also an extremely important one. Both of these are importantly aided by break-even analysis. The intelligent use of this technique and a thorough understanding of its operation are the factors that account for its importance to the external financial analyst.

Illustration of Break-Even Technique Application   Exhibit 8–3 presents the break-even chart of the Multi-Products Company at a given point in time. It is subject to the various assumptions that were discussed above including that relating to the ability to separate costs into their fixed and variable components.

At break even, a very condensed income statement of Multi-Products Company will be as follows:

Sales		$1,387,000
Costs:		
Variable	$887,000	
Fixed	500,000	1,387,000
Net income		–0–

The variable-cost percentage is $887/$1,387, or about 64 percent. The contribution margin ratio is 36 percent (100 − variable-cost percentage of 64). The variable-cost percentage means that on average, out of every

Exhibit 8–3   Multi-Products Company break-even chart—all operations

dollar of sales 64 cents go to meet variable costs, that is, costs that would not be incurred if the sale did not occur. The contribution margin ratio is basically the complement of the variable-cost percentage.

Break-even point:
Sales $1,387,000
Units 1,156,000
Average selling price per unit $1.20

This indicates that each dollar of sales generates a contribution of 36 cents toward meeting fixed expenses and the earning of a profit beyond the break-even point. The contribution margin earned on sales of $1,387,000 is just sufficient to cover the $500,000 in fixed costs. Quite obviously, the lower the fixed costs, the less sales it would take to cover them and the lower the resulting break-even point. In the most unlikely event that the Multi-Products Company would have no fixed costs, that is, all costs varied directly with sales, the company would have no break-even point, that is, it would start making a profit on the very first dollar of sales.

The break-even chart reflects the sale of a given mix of products. Since each product has different cost patterns and profit margins, any significant change in the product mix will result in a change in the break-even point and consequently in a change in the relationship between revenues, costs, and results. Although Exhibit 8–3 shows the number of units on the sales (volume) axis, this figure and the average selling price per unit are of limited significance because they represent averages prevailing as a result of a given mix of products.

The importance of a relatively stable sales mix to the successful application of break-even analysis suggests that this technique cannot be usefully employed in cases where the product mix varies greatly over the short term. Nor, for that matter, can break-even analysis be usefully applied in cases where there are sharp and frequent fluctuations in sales prices or in costs of production, such as raw materials.

Exhibit 8–3 indicates that given the existing mix of products, the present level of fixed costs of $500,000 can be expected to prevail up to a sales level of approximately $2,400,000. This is the point at which 100 percent of theoretical capacity will be reached. The break-even point is at 60 percent of capacity, while the current level of sales is at about 75 percent of capacity. This means that when the 100 percent capacity level is reached, the fixed costs may have to undergo an upward revision. If Multi-Products is reluctant to expand its capacity and thus increase its fixed costs and break-even point, assuming that variable costs do not decrease, it may have to consider other alternatives such as:

1. Forgoing an increase in sales.

2. Increasing the number of shifts, which could increase variable costs significantly.
3. Subcontracting some of its work to outsiders, thus forgoing some of the profit of increased activity.

Exhibit 8–3 also presents to the analyst at a glance the company's present position relative to the break-even point. The current level of sales of $1,800,000 is about $413,000 above the break-even point. This is also known as the *safety margin,* that is, the margin that separates the company from a no-profit condition. This concept can be expanded to indicate on the chart at what point the company will earn a desired return on investment (ROI), at what point the common dividend may be in jeopardy, and at what point the preferred dividend may no longer be covered by current earnings.

It is obvious that the data revealed by a reliably constructed break-even chart or by the application of break-even computations are valuable in profit projection, in the assessment of operating risk, as well as in an evaluation of profit levels under various assumptions regarding future conditions and managerial policies.

Analytical Implications of Break-Even Analysis

From the above discussion of a specific situation, such as that illustrated in Exhibit 8–3, we will now turn to a more general review of conclusions that can be derived from break-even analysis.

The Concept of Operating Leverage   Leverage and fixed costs go together. As we have seen in Chapter 5, financial leverage is based on fixed costs of funds for a portion of the resources used by the enterprise. Thus, earnings above that fixed cost magnify the return on the residual (or equity) funds and vice versa.

The fixed costs of a business enterprise, in the sense in which we have discussed them so far in this chapter, form the basis of the concept of operating leverage. Until an enterprise develops a volume of sales that is sufficient to cover its fixed costs, it will incur a loss. Once it has covered the fixed costs, further increments in volume will result in more than proportionate increases in profitability. The following will illustrate the nature of operating leverage:

Illustration of the Working of Operating Leverage   In a given enterprise, the cost structure is as follows:

Fixed costs = $100,000
Variable-cost percentage = 60 percent

The following tabulation presents the profit or loss at successively higher levels of sales and a comparison of relative percentage changes in sales volume and in profitability:

Sales	Variable costs	Fixed costs	Profit (loss)	Percentage increase over preceding step	
				Sales	Profit
$100,000	$ 60,000	$100,000	$(60,000)	—	—
200,000	120,000	100,000	(20,000)	100%	—
250,000	150,000	100,000	—	25	—
300,000	180,000	100,000	20,000	20	Infinite
360,000	216,000	100,000	44,000	20	120%
432,000	259,200	100,000	72,800	20	65%

The working of operating leverage is evident in the above tabulation. Starting at break even, the first 20 percent sales increase resulted in an infinite increase in profits because they started from a zero base. The next 20 percent increase in sales resulted in a 120 percent profit increase over the preceding level, while the sales increase that followed resulted in a 65 percent profit increase over the preceding level. The effects of leverage diminish as the sales increase above the break-even level because the bases to which increases in profits are compared get progressively larger.

Leverage, of course, works both ways. It will be noted that a drop in sales from $200,000 to $100,000, representing a 50 percent decrease, resulted in a tripling of the loss.

One important conclusion from this to the analyst is that enterprises operating near their break-even point will have relatively larger percentage changes of profits or losses for a given change in volume. On the upside, the volatility will, of course, be desirable. On the downside, however, it can result in adverse results that are significantly worse than those indicated by changes in sales volume alone.

Another aspect is operating *potential,* sometimes erroneously referred to as leverage, which derives from a high level of sales accompanied by very low profit margins. The potential here, of course, is the room for improvements in profit margins. Even relatively slight improvements in profit margins, applied on a large sales level, can result in dramatic changes in profits. Thus, the popular reference to a semblance of leverage for what is really a potential for improvement.

Another aspect of the same *potential* occurs when the sales volume *per share* is large. Obviously an improvement in profitability will be translated into larger earnings per share improvements.

The Significance of the Variable-Cost Percentage

The volatility of profits is also dependent on the variable-cost percentage. The low-cost enterprise will achieve higher profits for a given increment in volume once break-even operations are reached than will the high variable-cost enterprise.

ILLUSTRATION 3.   Company A has fixed costs of $700,000 and a variable cost equal to 30 percent of sales. Company B has fixed costs of $300,000 and variable costs equal to 70 percent of sales. Assume that both companies have now reached sales of $1,000,000 and are, consequently, at break even. A $100,000 increment in sales will result in a profit of $70,000 for Company A and only in a profit of $30,000 for Company B. Company A has not only greater operating leverage but can, as a result, afford to incur greater risks in going after the extra $100,000 in sales than can Company B.

From the above example it is evident that the *level* of the break-even point is not the only criterion of risk assessment but that the analyst must also pay attention to the variable-cost ratio.

The Significance of the Fixed-Cost Level

Given a certain variable-cost percentage, the higher the fixed costs, the higher the break-even point of an enterprise. In the absence of change in other factors, a given percentage change in fixed costs will result in an equal percentage change in the break-even point. This can be illustrated as follows:

First break-even situation

Sales		$100,000
Variable expenses	$60,000	
Fixed costs	40,000	100,000
Profit		–0–

Second break-even situation—20 percent increase in fixed costs

Sales (increase of 20%)		$120,000
Variable expenses (60%)	$72,000	
Fixed costs ($40,000 + 20%)	48,000	120,000
		–0–

Thus, a fixed cost increase of 20 percent, with the variable-cost ratio remaining unchanged, resulted in a 20 percent increase in the break-even point.

An increase in the break-even point of an enterprise generally increases operational risk. It means that the enterprise is dependent on a higher volume of sales in order to break even. Looked at another way, it means that the enterprise is more vulnerable to economic downturns as compared to its situation with a lower break-even point. The substantial acquisition of the large-capacity Boeing 747 aircraft by the airlines provides an example of the effects of high break-even points. While these large aircraft lowered the variable cost per passenger, they relied also on a projected increase in the number of passengers. When this failed to materialize, the airlines' profit margins deteriorated swiftly with many of them going into the red. There are other repercussions to high levels of fixed costs. For example, a higher break-even point may mean that the enterprise has less freedom of action in fields such as labor relations. A high level of fixed costs makes strikes more expensive and subjects the enterprise to added pressure to submit to higher wage demands.

Often, added fixed costs in the form of automatic machinery are incurred in order to save variable costs, such as labor, and to improve efficiency. That can be very profitable in times of reasonably good demand. In times of low demand, however, the higher level of fixed costs sets in motion the process of reverse operational leverage discussed above, with attendant rapidly shrinking profits or even growing losses. High fixed costs reduce an enterprise's ability to protect its profits in the face of shrinking sales volume.

Investments in fixed assets, particularly in sophisticated machinery, can bring about increases in fixed costs far beyond the cost of maintaining and replacing the equipment. The skills required to operate such equipment are quite specialized and require skilled personnel which the enterprise may be reluctant to dismiss for fear of not being able to replace them when business turns up again. This converts what should be variable costs into de facto fixed costs.

While fixed costs are incurred in order to increase capacity or to decrease variable costs, it is often advisable to cut fixed costs in order to reduce the risks associated with a high break-even point. Thus, a company may reduce fixed costs by switching from a salaried sales force to one compensated by commissions based on sales. It can avoid added fixed costs by adding work shifts, buying ready-made parts, subcontracting work, or discontinuing the least profitable product lines.

In evaluating profit performance, past and future, of an enterprise, the analyst must always keep in mind the effect that the level of fixed costs can have on operating results under a variety of business conditions. Moreover, in projecting future results, the analyst must bear in mind that any given level of fixed costs is valid only up to the limits of practical capacity within a range of product mixes. Beyond such a point, a profit projection must take into consideration not only the increased levels of fixed costs required but also the financial resources that an expansion will require as well as the cost and sources of the funds that will be needed.

The Importance of the Contribution Margin

The analyst must be alert to the absolute size of an enterprise's contribution margin because operating leverage is importantly dependent on it. He must, moreover, be aware of the factors that can change this margin, that is, changes in variable costs as well as changes in selling prices.

While we have focused on the individual factors that affect costs, revenues, and profitability, in practice, changes result from a combination of factors. Projected increases in sales volume will increase profits only if costs, both fixed and variable, are controlled and kept within projected limits. Break-even analysis assumes that efficiency remains constant. However, experience teaches us that cost controls are more lax in times of prosperity than they are in times of recession. Thus, the analyst cannot assume constant efficiency any more than he or she can assume a constant product mix. The latter is also an important variable that must be watched by the analyst. Questions of why an enterprise realized lower profits on a higher volume of sales can often be explained, at least in part, by reference to changes in sales mix.

In spite of its important limitations, the break-even approach is an important tool of analysis to the financial analyst.

Its ability to aid the external analyst in performance evaluation and in profit projection makes its use worthwhile to him or her in spite of the laborious work that it often entails and the fragmentary and scarce amounts of information on which, of necessity, it must be based.

ANALYSIS OF THE RELATIONSHIP BETWEEN SALES, ACCOUNTS RECEIVABLE, AND INVENTORIES

The analysis of the relationship between sales and accounts receivable and sales and inventories holds important clues to the evaluation of contemporary results of operations as well as important implications regarding future results.[3]

Accounts Receivable We have discussed the relationship between accounts receivable and sales in Chapter 3 in the context of short-term liquidity, i.e., in the assessment of the quality (collectibility) of the receivables and their liquidity (the speed with which they are collected).

Another dimension is the relationship between sales and accounts receivable in the context of evaluating the reliability and quality of reported

---

[3] These analytical tools were developed and refined by Thornton L. O'Glove, author of the "Quality of Earnings Report," which is the source of the two illustrations that follow. For an excellent discussion of these tools as well as further examples, see Thornton L. O'Glove, *Quality of Earnings: The Investor's Guide to How Much Money a Company is Really Making* (New York: The Free Press, 1987).

earnings. If accounts receivable grow at a rate in excess of that of sales this abnormal relationship requires close investigation into its reasons. The possibility exists that present sales have been made, by means of various extraordinary incentives and/or by the extension of generous credit terms, at the expense of future sales. Such conditions may mean that present sales have borrowed from the future and a sales slowdown is possible. Such conditions can also lead to difficulties in receivable collections.

ILLUSTRATION 4. The following table shows the relationship of sales and accounts receivable of a toy company during successive quarters:

	($ in thousands)				
Three months ended	3/29/x6	3/30/x5	4/29/x4	4/30/x3	5/1/x2
Net sales	$199,128	$227,449	$175,346	$197,634	$290,388
percent change		−12.4%	29.7%	−11.3%	−31.9%
Accounts receivable	$271,446	$224,952	$190,217	$276,110	$328,332
percent change		20.6%	18.2%	−31.1%	−15.9%

In the quarter ended 3/29/x6, sales declined by 12.4 percent whereas accounts receivable increased by 20.6 percent, an imbalance that contrasts with the relationships prevailing in preceding quarters. This condition warrants further exploration and analysis.

Inventories   We have discussed the relationship of inventories to cost of goods sold in Chapter 3 as part of our consideration of short-term liquidity. Inventory turnover is an important measure of inventory quality, and as seen in Chapter 6, of asset utilization. The analysis of inventory components holds important clues to future sales as well as to operating activity. Thus, for example, when an increase in the finished goods component is accompanied by a decrease in raw materials and/or work-in-process, a slowdown in production is indicated.

ILLUSTRATION 5. The following is a tabulation of the sales and the inventory components of Burroughs Corporation for the quarters indicated.

	($ in thousands)				
Three months ended	3/31/x6	3/31/x5	3/31/x4	3/31/x3	3/31/x2
Net sales revenues	$ 762.7	$ 793.9	$ 689.8	$ 559.0	$ 560.0
Inventories:					
Finished equipment and supplies	$ 907.1	$ 830.6	$ 631.6	$ 677.9	$ 699.9
Work-in-process and raw materials	609.0	664.7	561.2	467.7	379.2
Total inventories	$1,516.1	$1,495.3	$1,192.8	$1,145.6	$1,079.1

This tabulation indicates that during the last two quarters finished goods inventories increased while work in process and raw materials declined, foreshadowing a possible production slowdown. An increase of inventories (especially the finished goods component) in the face of a decline in sales may also be indicative of a failure of sales to keep up with production—another reason for a future slowdown in production.

ADDITIONAL CONSIDERATIONS IN THE ANALYSIS OF COST OF SALES

Gross margin analysis focuses on changes in costs, prices, and volume. Break-even analysis, in turn, focuses on the behavior of costs in relation to sales volume and on management's ability to control costs in the face of rising and falling revenues. The effectiveness of these and other methods of cost analysis depends on the degree of data availability as well as on an understanding of the accounting principles that have been applied.

The ability of the analyst to make the rough approximations that are necessary to separate costs into fixed and variable components depends on the amount of detail available. Disclosure of major cost components such as materials, labor, and various overhead cost categories can be helpful. The more detailed the breakdowns of expense categories, the more likely is the analyst to be able to construct meaningful break-even estimates.

In the evaluation of the cost of sales and the gross margin, and particularly in its comparison with those of other enterprises, the analyst must pay close attention to distortions that may arise from the utilization of a variety of accounting principles. While this is true of all items of cost, attention must be directed particularly to inventories and to depreciation accounting. These two areas merit special attention not only because they represent costs that are usually substantial in amount but also because of the proliferation of alternative principles that may be employed in accounting for them.

DEPRECIATION

Depreciation is an important cost element particularly in manufacturing and service enterprises. It is mostly fixed in nature because it is computed on the basis of elapsed time. However, if its computation is based on production activity, the result is a variable cost.

Because depreciation is computed in most cases on the basis of time elapsed, the ratio of depreciation expense to income is not a particularly meaningful or instructive relationship. In the evaluation of depreciation expense, the ratio of depreciation to gross plant and equipment is more meaningful. The ratio is computed as follows:

$$\frac{\text{Depreciation expense}}{\text{Assets subject to depreciation}}$$

This ratio can, of course, be computed by major categories of assets. The basic purpose is to enable the analyst to detect changes in the composite rate of depreciation used by an enterprise as a means of evaluating its adequacy and of detecting attempts at income smoothing.

AMORTIZATION OF SPECIAL TOOLS AND SIMILAR COSTS

The importance of the cost of special tools, dies, jigs, patterns, and molds varies from industry to industry. It is of considerable importance, for example, in the auto industry where special tool costs are associated with frequent style and design changes. The rate of amortization of such costs can have an important effect on reported income and is important to the analyst in an assessment of that income as well as in its comparison with that of other entities within an industry. The ratios that can be used to analyze changes in the deferral and amortization policies of such costs are varied and focus on their relationship to sales and other classes of assets.

The yearly expenditure for special tools can be related to and expressed as a percentage of (1) sales and (2) net property and equipment.

The yearly amortization of special tools can be related to (1) sales, (2) unamortized special tools, and (3) net property and equipment.

A comparison of the yearly trend in these relationships can be very helpful in an analysis of the consistency of income reporting of a single enterprise. The comparison can be extended further to an evaluation of the earnings of two or more enterprises within the same industry. This approach is indicative of the type of analysis which various elements of cost lend themselves to.

MAINTENANCE AND REPAIRS COSTS

Maintenance and repairs costs vary in significance with the amount invested in plant and equipment as well as with the level of productive activity. They have an effect on the cost of goods sold as well as on other elements of cost. Since maintenance and repairs contain elements of both fixed and variable costs, they cannot vary directly with sales. Thus, the ratio of repairs and maintenance costs to sales, while instructive to compare from year to year or among enterprises, must be interpreted with care. To the extent that the analyst can determine the fixed and the variable portions of maintenance and repairs costs, the interpretation of their relationship to periodic sales will be more valid.

Repairs and maintenance are, to a significant extent, discretionary costs. That is, the level of expense can, within limits, be regulated by management for a variety of reasons including those aimed at the improvement of reported income or at the preservation of liquid resources. Certain types of repairs cannot, of course, be postponed without resulting breakdowns in productive equipment. But many types of preventive repairs and particularly maintenance can be postponed or skimped on with results whose effects lie mainly in the future. Thus, the level of repairs and maintenance costs both in relation to sales and to plant and equipment is of interest to the analyst. It has, of course, a bearing on the quality of income, a subject that we shall consider in the next chapter.

The level of repairs and maintenance costs is also important in the evaluation of depreciation expense. Useful lives of assets are estimated by the use of many assumptions including those relating to the upkeep and maintenance of the assets. If, for instance, there is a deterioration in the usual or assumed level of repairs and maintenance, the useful life of the asset will, in all probability, be shortened. That may, in turn, require an upward revision in the depreciation expense or else income will be overstated.

OTHER COSTS AND EXPENSES—GENERAL

Most, although not all, cost and expense items found in the income statement have some identifiable or measurable relationship to sales or revenues. This is so because sales are the major measure of activity in an enterprise except in instances when production and sales are significantly out of phase.

Two analytical tools whose usefulness is based, in part, on the relationship that exists between sales and most costs and expenses should be noted here:

1. The *common-size income statement* expresses each cost and expense item in terms of its percentage relationship to net sales. This relationship of costs and expenses to sales can then be traced over a number of periods or compared with the experience of other enterprises in the same industry. The analysis of Campbell Soup Company (see Chapter 10) contains an illustration of a common-size income statement covering a number of years.

2. The *index number analysis of the income statement* expresses each item in the income statement in terms of an index number related to a base year. In this manner, relative changes of income statement items over time can be traced and their significance assessed. Expense item

changes can thus be compared to changes in sales and to changes in related expense or revenue items. Moreover, by use of common-size balance sheets, percentage changes in income statement items can be related to changes in assets and liabilities. For example, a given change in sales would normally justify a commensurate change in inventories and in accounts receivable. Chapter 10 contains an illustration of an index number analysis.

Selling Expenses

The analysis of selling costs has two main objectives:

1. The evaluation over time of the relationship between sales and the costs needed to bring them about.
2. An evaluation of the trend and the productivity of future-directed selling costs.

The importance of selling costs in relation to sales varies from industry to industry and from enterprise to enterprise. In some enterprises, selling costs take the form of commissions and are, consequently, highly variable in nature, while in others, they contain important elements of fixed costs.

After allowing for the fixed and variable components of the selling expenses, the best way to analyze them is to relate them to sales. The more detailed the breakdown of the selling expense components is—the more meaningful and penetrating can such analysis be. Exhibit 8–4 presents an example of such an analysis.

Analysis of Exhibit 8–4 indicates that for the entire period selling costs have been rising faster than sales and that in year 4 they took 5.6 percent more of the sales dollar than they did in year 1. In this period, salesmen's salaries increased by 1.0 percent of sales, advertising by 3.6 percent of sales, and branch expenses by 2.2 percent of sales. The drop in delivery expense may possibly be accounted for by the offsetting increase in freight costs.

A careful analysis should be made of advertising costs in order to determine to what extent the increase is due to the promotion of new products or the development of new territories that will benefit the future.

When selling expenses as a percentage of sales show an increase, it is instructive to focus on the selling expense increase that accompanies a given increase in sales. It can be expected that beyond a certain level, greater sales resistance is encountered in effecting additional sales. That sales resistance or the development of more remote territories may involve additional cost. Thus, it is important to know what the percentage of selling expense to sales is or to new sales as opposed to old ones. This may have, of course, implications on the projection of future profitability.

Exhibit 8–4

SELLALL CORPORATION
Comparative Statement of Selling Expenses
(in thousands)

	Year 4		Year 3		Year 2		Year 1	
Sales	$1,269		$935		$833		$791	
Trend percentage . .		160.0%		118.0%		105.0%		100.0%
Selling expenses (percent are of sales):								
Advertising . . .	$ 84	6.6	$ 34	3.6	$ 28	3.4	$ 24	3.0
District branch expenses* . . .	80	6.3	41	4.4	38	4.6	32	4.1
Delivery expense (own trucks)	20	1.6	15	1.6	19	2.3	22	2.8
Freight-out . . .	21	1.7	9	1.0	11	1.3	8	1.0
Salesmen's salary expense	111	8.7	76	8.1	68	8.1	61	7.7
Salesmen's travel expense	35	2.8	20	2.1	18	2.2	26	3.3
Miscellaneous selling expense	9	0.7	9	1.0	8	0.9	7	0.9
Total	$ 360	28.4%	$204	21.8%	$190	22.8%	$180	22.8%

* Includes rent, regional advertising, etc.

If an enterprise can make additional sales only by increasing selling expenses, its profitability may suffer. Offsetting factors, such as those related to break-even operations or to economies of scale, must also be considered.

BAD DEBT EXPENSES

These expenses are often regarded as a cost of marketing. Since the size of the expense is importantly tied to the size of "allowance for doubtful accounts," it is best evaluated in terms of the relationship between that allowance and gross accounts receivable. The following analysis of the allowance for doubtful accounts of a toy company is an example of such an evaluation:

	Fiscal year 3—quarter ending		
	Aug. 1, year 2	*May 2, year 2*	*Jan. 31, year 2*
Allowance for doubtful accounts (in thousands) ..	$ 13,500	$ 15,600	$ 19,200
Gross receivables (in thousands)	343,319	223,585	179,791
Allowance as percent of gross receivables	3.93%	6.98%	10.68%

	Fiscal year 2—quarter ending		
	Aug. 2, year 1	*May 3, year 1*	*Feb. 2, year 1*
Allowance for doubtful accounts (in thousands) ..	$ 16,600	$ 15,000	$ 12,200
Gross receivables (in thousands)	331,295	215,660	172,427
Allowance as percent of gross receivables	5.01%	6.96%	7.07%

It is noteworthy that there was a significant decline in the company's allowance for doubtful accounts in relation to gross receivables in fiscal year 3 quarters as compared to similar quarters in the preceding year. The reasons can be varied, including improvement in the collectibility of receivables or inadequate provisions that result in understated bad debt expense. This analysis certainly calls for further investigation by the analyst.

Future-Directed Marketing Costs

Certain categories of sales promotion costs, particularly advertising, result in benefits that extend beyond the period in which they were incurred. The measurement of such benefits is difficult if not impossible, but it is a reasonable assumption that there is a relationship between the level of expenditures for advertising and promotion and the sales level, present and future.

Since expenditures for advertising and other forms of promotion are discretionary in nature, the analyst must carefully follow the year-to-year trend in these expenditures. Not only does the level of such expenditures have a bearing on future sales estimates, but it also indicates whether management is attempting to "manage" reported earnings. The effect of discretionary costs on the "quality" of earnings reported will be the subject of further discussion in the chapter that follows.

GENERAL, ADMINISTRATION, FINANCIAL, AND OTHER EXPENSES

Most costs in this category tend to be fixed in nature. This is largely true of administrative costs because such costs include significant amounts of salaries and occupancy expenditures. However, there may be some "creep" or tendency for increases in this category, and this is particularly true in prosperous times. Thus, in analyzing this category of expense, the analyst should pay attention to both the trend of administrative costs as well as to the percentage of total sales that they consume.

Financial Costs

Financial costs are, except for interest on short-term indebtedness, fixed in nature. Moreover, unless replaced by equity capital, most borrowed funds are usually refinanced. This is because of the long-term nature of most interest-bearing obligations. Included in these costs are the amortization of bond premium and discount as well as of debt issue expenses. A good check on an enterprise's cost of borrowed money as well as credit standing is the calculation of the average effective interest rate paid. This rate is computed as follows:

$$\frac{\text{Total interest cost}}{\text{Average total indebtedness subject to interest}}$$

Quaker Oats (Appendix to Chapter 10) average interest rate on liabilities subject to interest can be computed as follows for 1991 (dollars in millions):

$$\frac{\text{Interest incurred}}{\text{Liabilities subject to interest}} = \frac{104^{(a)}}{815^{(b)}} = \underline{\underline{12.8\%}}$$

[a] Total interest costs (before deduction for interest capitalized)—item $\boxed{156}$

[b] Short-term debt $\boxed{147}$	$ 81
Current portion of long-term debt $\boxed{148}$	33
Long-term debt $\boxed{148}$	701
Total liabilities subject to interest ($ millions)	$815

The average effective interest rate paid can be compared over the years or compared to that of other enterprises. It is also significant in that it sheds light on the credit standing of the enterprise.

Quaker Oats has a good discussion of debt in the "Liquidity and Capital Resources" section of its MDA (item $\boxed{142}$) as well as disclosure about weighted average interest rates on various debt categories $\boxed{147}$.

A measure of sensitivity to interest changes is obtained by determining the portion of debt that is tied to the prime rate. In periods of rising interest rates, a significant amount of debt tied to the prime rate exposes an enterprise to sharply escalating interest costs. Conversely, falling interest rates are a beneficial factor to such an enterprise.

"Other" Expenses

"Other" expenses are, of course, a nondescript category. The total amount in this category should normally be rather immaterial in relation to other costs. Otherwise, it can obscure substantial costs that, if revealed, may provide significant information about the enterprise's current and future operations. Nonrecurring elements may also be included in the "other expense" category, and this may add to the significance of this category to the analyst.

The analyst must also be alert to the tendency to offset "other" expenses against "other" income. Here, too, the major problem is one of concealment of important information and data. Here it is important that details of the major items comprising the offset amount be given or determined.

OTHER INCOME

Miscellaneous income items that are small in amount are usually of no significance to the analyst. However, since "other income" may include returns from various investments, it may contain information about new ventures and data regarding investments that are not available elsewhere. Such investments may, of course, have future implications, positive or negative, that exceed by far in significance the amounts of current income that are involved.

INCOME TAXES

Income taxes represent basically a sharing of profits between an enterprise and the governmental authorities by which they are imposed. Since most enterprises with which this book is concerned are organized in corporate form, we shall focus primarily on corporate income taxes.

Income taxes are almost always significant in amount and normally can amount to a substantial portion of a corporation's income before taxes. For this reason, the analyst must pay careful attention to the impact that income taxes have on net income.

Except for a lower rate on a first modest amount of income (e.g., $100,000), corporate income is taxed at a rate determined by law (presently 34 percent). Differences in the timing of recognition of income or expense items as between taxable income and book income should not influence the effective tax rate because of the practice of interperiod income tax allocation that aims to match the tax expense with the book income regardless of when the tax is paid.

The relationship between the tax accrual and the pre-tax income, otherwise known as the effective tax rate or tax ratio, will, however, be influenced by permanent tax differences.[4]

The effective tax rate or tax ratio is computed as follows:

$$\frac{\text{Income tax expense for period}}{\text{Income before income taxes}}$$

For Quaker Oats (Appendix to Chapter 10) the effective tax rate for 1991 is best computed as follows:

$$\frac{175.7^{(a)}}{411.5^{(b)}} = 42.7\%$$

(a) Provision for income taxes—item $\boxed{8}$.
(b) Income from continuing operations before income taxes—item $\boxed{7}$.

The 42.7 percent effective tax rate corresponds to that computed by the company (item $\boxed{158c}$) and is widely used.

It should be noted, however, that the above computation uses "income from continuing operations" rather than net income.

Thus, if it is desired to compute the effective tax rate incurred by the company on all items of income and loss during the period, including discontinued operations and other items, then a different computation is required which for QO is as follows for 1991:

Income (loss)	Before tax	Related tax	After tax
Income from continuing operations before income taxes and other items	$411.5 $\boxed{7}$	$175.7 $\boxed{8}$	$235.8 $\boxed{9}$
Loss from discontinued operations— ..	(50)	(20) $\boxed{144}$*	(30) $\boxed{10}$
Net income	$361.5*	$155.7*	$205.8 $\boxed{11}$

* Derived amount.

The effective tax rate based on all items included in net income now becomes

$$\frac{\$155.7}{\$361.5} = 43 \text{ percent}$$

---

[4] This term includes differences due to state and local taxes, foreign tax rate differentials, various tax credits, untaxed income, nonallowed expenses, etc.

Quaker Oats presents an unusual case of preferred dividends [12] resulting in a tax benefit of undisclosed amount. This kind of tax effect bypassing the determination of net income (like similar tax effects relating to stock options and found in equity accounts), must be considered when reconciling all tax-related accounts as a means of understanding a company's tax picture and of reconciling the amount of taxes paid (see further discussion below).

For purposes of evaluation of the level of earnings, the trend of earnings, as well as for net income projection, the analyst must know the reasons why the effective tax rate deviated from the normal or the expected. Income taxes are such an important element of cost that even relatively small changes in the effective tax rate can result in important changes in net income. Moreover, without an understanding of the factors that cause changes in the effective tax rate of a company, the analyst is missing an important element required in forecasting future net income.

FRR No. 1 Section 204 contains rules in which the SEC expanded significantly the required analytical disclosures concerning current and deferred income taxes. Most of these disclosure requirements were adapted by *SFAS 109,* which deals with the accounting for income taxes.

The analysis of these and other aspects of income tax disclosures are important to the analyst and will be discussed and illustrated in the section that follows.

ANALYSIS OF INCOME TAX DISCLOSURES

Objectives of the Analysis

The analysis of income tax disclosures may be undertaken with specific or specialized objectives in mind. However, the more general objectives of such an analysis are:

- To understand the tax accounting of the enterprise and its impact on income, on related assets and liabilities, as well as on the sources and uses of cash.

- To judge the adequacy of the enterprise's tax disclosure.

- To provide a basis for assessing the effect of taxes on future income and cash flows.

- To provide a basis for informed queries to be put to management in order to clear up questions arising during the analysis.

- To identify unusual gains or losses not otherwise disclosed but whose tax effect is highlighted or revealed during analysis.

- To evaluate the effectiveness of tax management by the enterprise.

Analytical Steps and Techniques

A. Establish a T-account for each tax-related account in the balance sheet and income statement.

A current tax liability and/or a current receivable for overpayment or tax refunds will almost always be found. In addition, there will be one or two deferred tax accounts (one current and one noncurrent) in the balance sheet.

Care must be taken to identify the income taxes (current and possibly deferred) that relate to each separate section of the income statement: (1) continuing operations, (2) discontinued operations, (3) extraordinary items, and (4) cumulative effect of change(s) in accounting principles. As discussed above, income tax effects can be found in items outside the income statement (e.g., QO's Preferred Dividend tax benefit [72]).

The analyst should be aware that information on income tax effects can be found in parenthetical notes to financial statements, in schedules such as those reconciling owner's equity, in sections containing management discussion, and in footnotes in general and particularly in those relating to income taxes.

B. A good next step is to attempt to reconstruct as best as is possible the summary entry by means of which the tax expense for the period was booked. It is easier to do this if the entry is divided into the current and the deferred portions of the tax expense.

C. After the opening and closing balances of all tax-related balance sheet T-accounts have been entered, the tax expense entries and income statement should be posted to the relevant tax-related accounts and data should be used to aid in as complete a reconstruction of these accounts as is possible.

The changes in the deferred tax accounts on the balance sheet should generally agree with the deferred tax expense for the period as shown in the income statement or in related footnotes. Noncash adjustments to net income and other information in the statement of cash flows (SCF) often can provide added insights. If all attempts at reconciliation fail, it is possible that a deferred tax account is buried or combined under some other caption in the balance sheet, or that the company made some undisclosed entries for purposes of correcting errors or for other reasons. In such a situation, the analyst can only identify the needed balancing amount and label it as such, realizing that the correctness of any conclusions regarding balancing (plugged) amounts in the reconciliation is subject to the validity of assumptions that have been made.

With regard to those deferred tax accounts which have not been fully reconciled, amounts needed to reconcile them should be transferred to the Current Taxes Payable account or the Tax Refunds Receivable account.

D. After using tax law, knowledge of tax accounting, and all the disclosures in the financial statements, as well as the assumptions required in the situation, the tax T-accounts should be fully reconstructed. At this point, the amount of taxes paid during the year is arrived at as a "plug" to the current Taxes Payable account. Conversely a credit "plug" represents a tax refund received.

It should be noted that the quality of the analysis will depend on the quality of disclosure found in the financial statements. A lack of good disclosure will require more analytical ingenuity such as the combining of certain accounts (such as current tax receivable and payable accounts). The analyst must also be aware that the acquisition or disposition of businesses during a period may result in related additions or deductions to balance sheet tax accounts. Thus, for example, the acquisition of a company may result in the assumption of its tax liabilities.

Illustration of Income Tax Analysis of Quaker Oats Company

Let us first analyze the changes in QO's 1991 income tax accounts. The *first* step is to draw a T-account for each tax-related balance sheet account and one for each income tax expense and tax effect account in the 1991 income statement. (All number references are to QO financial statements in Appendix 10.)

In the balance sheet we find the income tax payable account and a deferred income taxes—noncurrent account.

In the income statement we see the regular "provision for income taxes" [8] and below it all other items are shown (as they should be) net of tax. We find the tax effect of the loss on discontinued operations [10] in Note 2 [144].

Neither the tax effect nor the reasons for the tax deductability of preferred dividends [12] are disclosed. Assuming the marginal 34 percent tax rate we can compute the tax effect as follows:

$$\text{Let } X = \text{preferred dividends before income tax}$$
$$X(1 - 34\%) = 4.3 \quad [12]$$
$$X = 6.5$$

then,

$$6.5 - \text{tax effect} = 4.3$$
$$\text{Tax effect} = \$2.2$$

The *second* step is to enter the opening and ending balances in these accounts. Tax-related accounts in the income statements do not have opening balances and their ending balances are closed via the income

Income Tax Payable 75				Deferred Income Tax 81		
(c)	2.2	36.3	**BB**		327.7	**BB**
(b)	20.0	161.4	(a)		14.3	(a)
(d)	24.7				24.7	(d)
assumed						
paid	105.7					
		45.1	**EB**		366.7	**EB**

Income Tax Expense 8		Tax Effect—Discontinued Operations 144	
(a)	175.7	20.0	(b)

Tax Effect—Preferred Dividends	
2.2	(c)

statement to retained earnings. In the case of some analyses the opening balances may have to be derived by using changes shown in the Statement of Cash Flows.

The *third* step is to enter the tax-related activity during the year (here, 1991) into the T-accounts based on all available information and footnotes, particularly the tax footnote. This can be done through journal entries which are posted to the relevant T-accounts.

The total tax expense (including the tax effect of items shown net of tax) can be combined but it is generally easier to enter them separately as will be illustrated here:

```
(a) Income Tax Expense 158 .................... 175.7
        Income Tax Payable ......................         161.4 158
        Deferred Income Tax .....................          14.3 158

(b) Income Tax Payable ........................   20.0
        Tax Effect-Disc. Operation ...............         20.0 144

(c) Income Taxes Payable .......................    2.2*
        Tax Effect-Preferred Dividends ............          2.2
    * See preceding computation.
```

Having entered in the T-accounts all tax-related transactions, we must now determine whether these entries have in fact fully explained the changes in all related accounts except the Tax Payable account.

In this case we find that the change in the Deferred Income Taxes account has not been fully explained and this requires an entry as follows:

(d) Income Tax Payable 24.7
     Deferred Income Tax .... 24.7 Plug

    To transfer unexplained difference to the Taxes Payable account.

The best estimate of the taxes *paid* during the period can only be made after the changes in the balances of all tax-related accounts, except the Taxes Payable (or Taxes Receivable) account, have been fully accounted for. After this has been done—as in our example here—the amount of taxes paid (or received as a refund) is determined as a balancing figure (plug) in the Taxes Payable account. In our example the plug of $105.7 is on the debit side, indicating a tax payment. The amount of tax paid (or received as refund) should be reconciled, as far as disclosure permits, to the amount of tax payments disclosed in the Statement of Cash Flows.

    Quaker Oats discloses income taxes paid in 1991 of $88.7 million 159. This is considerably less than the $105.7 million suggested by the analysis above. Complete confidence in our understanding of the company's tax accounting would require that management explain the main reasons for the discrepancy.

Explaining the Tax Rate

At another level of analysis we can explain how Quaker Oats, with a 1991 pre-tax income from continuing operations of $411.5 (all dollar amounts in millions) provided $175.7 in tax expense of which $161.4 are current federal income taxes:

		Item source	$ Millions
Expected federal income tax at 34%	$411.5 × 0.34	7	$140
Add: State tax net of federal benefit	$411.5 × 0.041	158c	16.9
			156.9
Add permanent differences 158c			
Repatriation of foreign earnings	4.3		
Non-U.S. tax rate differential	8.2		
Miscellaneous (rounded)	6.3		18.8
			175.7
Less total deferred taxes			14.3
Total current federal, non-U.S. and state taxes		158	161.4

Focus on Pre-Tax Earnings

While the focus on net income and on earnings per share requires a thorough analysis of changes in the effective tax rate, it must be borne in mind that many analysts attach great importance to pre-tax earnings. This is due to the greater importance that is assigned to pre-tax operating results, which require management skills of a higher order, as compared with changes due to variations in the effective tax rate over which, it is assumed, management has comparatively more limited control.

THE OPERATING RATIO

The operating ratio is yet another intermediate measure in the analysis of the income statement. It measures the relationship between all operating costs and net sales and is computed as follows:

$$\frac{\text{Cost of goods sold + Other operating expenses}}{\text{Net sales}}$$

The ratio is designed to enable a comparison within an enterprise or with enterprises of the proportion of the sales dollar absorbed by all operating costs. Only other income and expense items as well as interest and income taxes are excluded from operating expenses.

In effect, this ratio represents but an intermediate step in the common-size analysis of the income statement. It is, in and of itself, not of great analytical significance because it is a composite of many factors that require separate analysis. These factors comprise the analysis of gross margin and of other major expense categories discussed earlier. Thus, the operating ratio cannot be properly interpreted without a thorough analysis of the reasons accounting for variations in gross margin and for changes in selling, general, administrative, and other costs.

Operating Income is generally defined as income before interest and taxes. It focuses on operating efficiency (expense control) as opposed to considerations such as optimum financing and tax management.

NET INCOME RATIO

The net income ratio is the relationship between net income and total revenues and is computed as follows:

$$\frac{\text{Net income}}{\text{Total revenues}}$$

It represents the percentage of total revenue brought down to net income. In addition to its usefulness as an index of profitability, the net income ratio represents, as was seen in Chapter 6, a main component of the computation of the return on investment (ROI).

Exhibit 8–5

CAMPBELL SOUP COMPANY
Statement Accounting for Variation in Average Net Earnings
Three-Year Period 1986–1988 (Average)
Compared to Three-Year Period 1989–1991 (Average)
(in millions)

			Percentage increase
Items tending to increase net income:			
Increase in net sales:			
Net sales (1989–1991)	$6,027.3		
Net sales (1986–1988)	4,548.7	$1,478.6	32.5%
Deduct: Increase in costs of products sold:			
Cost of products sold (1989–1991)	$4,118.4		
Cost of products sold (1986–1988)	3,218.7	$ 899.7	28.0%
Net increase in gross margin		578.9	
Increase (decrease) in interest income:			
Interest income (1989–1991)	$ 27.3		
Interest income (1986–1988)	30.0	($2.7)	(9.0)%
Total items tending to increase net income		576.2	
Items tending to decrease net income:			
Increase in marketing and sales expenses:			
Marketing and sales expenses (1989–1991)	$ 918.5		
Marketing and sales expenses (1986–1988)	634.6	$ 283.9	44.7%
Increase in administrative expenses:			
Administrative expenses (1989–1991) .	$ 283.2		
Administrative expenses (1986–1988) .	214.1	$ 69.1	32.3%
Increase in R & D expenses:			
R & D expenses (1989–1991)	$ 52.6		
R & D expenses (1986–1988)	44.6	$ 8.0	17.9%
Increase in interest expenses:			
Interest expenses (1989–1991)	$ 107.3		
Interest expenses (1986–1988)	53.9	$ 53.4	99.1%
Increase in other expenses:*			
Other expenses (1989–1991)	$ 32.2		
Other expenses (1986–1988)	5.0	$ 27.2	544.0%
Increase in income tax expenses:			
Income tax (1989–1991)	$ 178.1		
Income tax (1986–1988)	160.5	$ 17.6	11.0%
Total items tending to decrease net income		459.2	

Change in net effect of equity in earnings of
   affiliates and minority interests (MI):
   Equity in earnings of affiliates and MI
         (1989–1991) .... $ 2.7
   Equity in earnings of affiliates and MI
         (1986–1988) ....   3.6   ($0.9)   (25.0)%
Net increase in net income:[†]
   Net income (1989–1991) .... $ 367.0
   Net income (1986–1988) ....   250.9 $ 116.1   46.3%

* Including foreign exchange losses.
[†] Income before both divestitures, restructuring, and unusual charges; and cumulative effect of change in accounting for income taxes.

Statement Accounting for Variation in Net Income

In the analysis of year-to-year changes in net income, it is useful to separate the elements that contributed to an increase in net income from those that contributed to a decrease. A statement that does this and also indicates the percentage increase or decrease in these factors is the "statement accounting for variations in net income." Exhibit 8–5 presents such a statement for Campbell Soup based on its income statements included in Chapter 2, Appendix B, as well as on prior-year data taken from financial reports which are summarized as part of the comprehensive analysis of Campbell Soup in Chapter 10.

QUESTIONS

1. What are the most important elements in the analysis of gross profit?
2. What is the basic principle underlying break-even analysis? What are fixed costs? Variable costs? Semivariable costs?
3. Certain assumptions that underlie break-even computations are often referred to as simplifying assumptions. Name as many of these as you can.
4. In break-even computation, what is the *variable-cost percentage?* What is its relationship to the *contribution margin ratio?*
5. What alternatives to an increase in fixed costs can an enterprise consider when it approaches 100 percent of theoretical capacity?
6. What is operating leverage? Why do leverage and fixed costs go together? What are the analytical implications of operating leverage?
7. Of what analytical significance are *(a)* the break-even point and *(b)* the variable-cost ratio?
8. What is a useful measure of the adequacy of current provisions for depreciation?
9. To what factors can maintenance and repairs costs be meaningfully related?
10. What are the main objectives of an analysis of selling expenses?

11. How can bad debt expense be evaluated most meaningfully? To what can a decline in the allowance to doubtful accounts be attributed?
12. *a.* What is the tax ratio and how is it computed?
    b. What are the objectives of an analysis of income tax disclosures?

Chapter 9

THE EVALUATION AND PROJECTION OF EARNINGS

OBJECTIVES OF EARNINGS EVALUATION

In the preceding chapters, we examined the steps that have to be taken and the understanding that must be brought to bear on the analysis of the operating performance of an enterprise. This chapter will examine the additional considerations involved in the achievement of the major objectives of income statement analysis:

The evaluation of the quality of earnings.

Evaluation of the earnings level and trend.

The estimation of earning power.

The forecasting of earnings.

Monitoring performance and results.

EVALUATION OF THE QUALITY OF EARNINGS

The discussions in this book have pointed out that much of the accounting process of income determination involves a high degree of estimation. The income of an enterprise, as measured by the accounting process, is not a specific amount but can vary depending on the assumptions used and the various principles applied. Complicating these measurements still further is the fact that numerous accounting periods can receive benefits from a single cash outlay and that it may take a number of periods before a transaction results in the collection of all amounts due. For that reason, creditors, in particular, are greatly interested in the cash equivalent of reported earnings.

This distinction between accrual income and the related cash flows has led some of those uninitiated in the income determination process to doubt the validity of all accounting measurements. This, however, is an extreme and unwarranted position because, as any student of accounting should know, the concept of income is the result of a series of complex assumptions and conventions, and exists only as the creation and the approximation of this system of measurement. This system is always subject to reexamination and is, despite its shortcomings, still the most widely accepted method of income determination.

In examining the level of reported income of an enterprise, the analyst must determine the effect of the various assumptions and accounting principles used on that reported income. Beyond that he or she must be aware of the "accounting risk" as well as the "audit risk" to which these determinations are subject.

Over the years, and especially since the enactment of the Securities Acts of 1933 and 1934, and with improvement in the audit function in this country, the incidence of outright fraud and deliberate misrepresentation in financial statements has diminished markedly. But they have *not* been completely eliminated and probably never will. Nor can the analyst ever rule out the possibility of spectacular failures in the audit function. While each major audit failure tends to contribute to the improvement of regulation and of auditing, they have not prevented the recurrence of such failures as the security holders of McKesson & Robbins, of Seaboard Commercial Corporation, of H. L. Green, of Miami Window, of Yale Express, of BarChris Construction Company, of Continental Vending Company, of Mill Factors Corporation, of W. T. Grant, of Equity Funding Company, of Frigitemp, of ESM Government Securities, Drysdale Securities Corporation, Crazy Eddie Inc., Regina Company, and ZZZ Best Company, well know.

The analyst must always assess the vulnerability to failure and to irregularities of the company under analysis and the character and the propensities of its management, as a means of establishing the degree of risk that it will prove to be the exception to the general rule.

The evaluation of the earnings level and of the earnings trend is intimately tied in with the evaluation of management. The evaluation of the management group cannot be separated from the results that they have actually achieved. Whatever other factors may have to be considered, results over a period of time are the acid test of management's ability, and that ability is perhaps the most important intangible (i.e., unquantifiable) factor in the prediction of future results. The analyst must be alert to changes in the management group and must assess its depth, stability, and possible dependence on the talents of one or a few individuals.

The Concept of Earnings Quality

The concept of earnings quality arose out of a need to provide a basis of comparison among the earnings of different entities as well as from the need to recognize such differences in "quality" for valuation purposes. There is almost no general agreement on definitions of or on assumptions underlying this concept. The elements that comprise the "quality of earnings" can be classified as follows:

a. One type of factor that affects the quality of earnings is the accounting and computational discretion of management and that of the attesting accountants in choosing from among accepted alternative accounting principles. These choices can be liberal, that is, they can assume the most optimistic view of the future, or they can be conservative. Generally, the quality of conservatively determined earnings is higher because they are less likely to prove overstated in the light of future developments than those determined in a "liberal" fashion. They also minimize the possibility of earnings overstatement and avoid retrospective changes. LIFO inventory accounting in rising markets and accelerated depreciation methods are examples of conservative accounting methods. On the other hand, unwarranted or excessive conservatism, while contributing to the temporary "quality" of earnings, actually results in a lack of reporting integrity over the long run and cannot be considered as a desirable factor. Quite apart from the impact that these accounting choices have on the financial statements, they also hold important clues to management's propensities and attitudes.

b. The second type of factor affecting the quality of earnings is related to the degree to which adequate provision has been made for the maintenance of assets and for the maintenance and enhancement of present and future earning power. In most enterprises, there exists considerable managerial discretion over the size of income streams, and particularly over the reported amounts of costs and expenses. Discretionary types of expenses, such as repairs and maintenance, advertising, and research and development (R&D) costs can be varied for the sole purpose of managing the level of reported net income (or loss) rather than for legitimate operating or business reasons. Here, too, the analyst's task is to identify the results of management practices and to judge its motivations.

c. The third major factor affecting the quality of earnings is not primarily a result of discretionary actions of managements, although skillful management can modify its effects. It is the effect of cyclical and other economic forces on earnings, on the stability of their sources, and particularly on their variability. Variability of earnings is generally an undesirable characteristic, and, consequently, the higher the variability the lower the quality of these earnings.

The fairly broad tolerances within which generally accepted accounting principles (GAAP) can be applied have been discussed throughout this book. A consideration of other aspects that affect earnings quality follows.

Evaluation of Discretionary and Future-Directed Costs   Discretionary costs are outlays that managements can vary to some extent from period to period in order to conserve resources and/or to influence reported income. For this reason, they deserve the special attention of analysts who are particularly interested in knowing whether the level of expenses is in keeping with past trends and with present and future requirements.

Maintenance and Repairs   As was already discussed in the preceding chapter, management has considerable leeway in performing mainte-nance work and some discretion with respect to repairs. The analyst can relate these costs to the level of activity because they do logically vary with it. Two ratios are particularly useful in comparing the repair and maintenance levels from year to year:

$$\frac{\text{Repairs and maintenance}}{\text{Sales}}$$

This ratio relates the costs of repairs and maintenance to this most available measure of activity. In the absence of sharp inventory changes, sales are a good indicator of activity. If year-to-year inventory levels change appreciably, an adjustment may be needed whereby ending in-ventories at approximate selling prices are added to sales, and beginning inventories, similarly adjusted, are deducted from them.

The other ratio is:

$$\frac{\text{Repairs and maintenance}}{\substack{\text{Property, plant, and equipment (exclusive of land)} \\ \text{net of accumulated depreciation}}}$$

It measures repair and maintenance costs in relation to the assets for which these costs are incurred. Depending on the amount of information available to the analyst, the ratio of repair and maintenance costs to specific categories of assets can be developed. It should be noted that substandard repairs and maintenance on assets may require revisions in the assumptions of useful lives for depreciation purposes.

The absolute trend in repair and maintenance costs from year to year can be expressed in terms of index numbers and compared to those of related accounts. The basic purpose of all these measurements is to de-termine whether the repair and maintenance programs of the enterprise have been kept at normal and necessary levels or whether they have been changed in a way that affects the quality of income and its projection into the future.

ILLUSTRATION 1.   A review of the level of maintenance and repair expense of Campbell Soup (based on data in Appendix 4B and Chapter 23) reveals the following relationships:

	1991	1990	1989
Maintenance and repairs to net sales	2.8%	2.9%	3.1%
Maintenance and repairs to property, plant, and equipment—net*	12.2%	13.0%	13.1%

  * Omitting land and construction progress.

The decline in these ratios *may* require further analysis.

Advertising   Since a significant portion of advertising outlays has effects beyond the period in which it is incurred, the relationship between advertising outlays and short-term results is a tenuous one. This also means that managements can, in certain cases, cut advertising costs with no commensurate immediate effects on sales, although it can be assumed that over the longer term sales will suffer. Here again, year-to-year variations in the level of advertising expenses must be examined by the analyst with the objective of assessing their impact on future sales and consequently on the quality of reported earnings.

There are a number of ways of assessing the trend in advertising outlays. One is to convert them into trend percentages using a "normal" year as a base. These trend percentages can then be compared to the trend of sales and of gross and net profits. An alternative measure would be the ratio of

$$\frac{\text{Advertising expenses}}{\text{Sales}}$$

which, when compared over the years, would also indicate shifts in management policy.

ILLUSTRATION 2.   Review of the relationship of advertising expense to sales of Campbell Soup (Appendix 4B and analysis in Chapter 23) reveals that the percentage of advertising expenses to sales declined from 3.5 percent in 1990 to 3.1 percent in 1991. The analyst may want to inquire into the reasons for the longer-term decline because in 1986 this relationship was 4.1 percent.

The ratio of

$$\frac{\text{Advertising}}{\text{Total selling costs}}$$

must also be examined so as to detect shifts to and from advertising to other methods of sales promotion.

An analysis of advertising to sales ratios over several years will reveal the degree of dependence of an enterprise on this promotional strategy. Comparison of this ratio with that of other companies in the industry will reveal the degree of market acceptance of products and the relative promotional efforts needed to secure it.

Research and Development Costs   The significance and the potential value of R&D costs are among the most difficult elements of the financial statements to analyze and interpret. Yet they are important, not only because of their relative size but even more so because of their significance for the projection of future results.

R&D costs have gained an aura of glowing potential in security analysis far beyond that warranted by actual experience. Mentioned most frequently are some of the undeniably spectacular and successful commercial applications of industrial research in the post-World War II era in such fields as chemistry, electronics, photography, and biology. Not mentioned are the vast sums spent for endeavors labeled *research* which are expensed or written off while benefits from these fall far short of the original costs.

The analyst must pay careful attention to R&D costs and to the absence of such costs. In many enterprises, they represent substantial costs, much of them fixed in nature, and they can represent the key to future success or failure. We must first draw a careful distinction between what can be quantified in this area and, consequently, analyzed in the sense in which we consider analysis in this book, and what cannot be quantified and must, consequently, be evaluated in qualitative terms.

In the area of R&D costs, the qualitative element looms large and important. The definition of what constitutes "research" is subject to wide-ranging interpretations as well as to outright distortion. The label *research* is placed on activities ranging from those of a first-class scientific organization engaged in sophisticated pure and applied research down to superficial and routine product-and-market-testing activities.

Among the many factors to be considered in the evaluation of the quality of the research effort are the caliber of the research staff and organization, the eminence of its leadership, as well as the commercial results of their research efforts. This qualitative evaluation must accompany any other kinds of analysis. Finally, a distinction must be drawn between government- or outsider-sponsored research and company-directed research that is most closely identified with its own objectives. From the foregoing discussion it is clear that research cannot be evaluated on the basis of the amounts spent alone. Research outlays represent an expense or an investment depending on how they are applied. Far from guaranteeing results, they represent highly speculative ventures that depend on the application of extraordinary scientific as well as managerial skills for their success. Thus, spending on research cannot guarantee results and should not be equated with them.

Having considered the all-important qualitative factors on which an evaluation of R&D outlays depends, the analyst should attempt to determine as best he can how much of the current R&D outlays that have been expensed have future utility and potential.

From the point of view of the analyst, the "future potential" of R&D costs is a most important consideration. Research cost productivity can be measured by relating R&D outlays to:

1. Sales growth.
2. New product introductions.
3. Acquisition of plant and equipment (to exploit the results of research).
4. Profitability.

Another important aspect of R&D outlays is their discretionary nature. It is true that those enterprises that have established R&D departments impart a fixed nature to a segment of these costs. Nevertheless, they can be increased or curtailed at the discretion of managements, often with no immediate adverse effects on sales. Thus, from the point of view of assessing the quality of reported income, the analyst must evaluate year-to-year changes in R&D outlays. This can be done by means of trend percentage analysis as well as by means of analysis of ratios such as the ratio of

$$\frac{\text{R\&D outlays}}{\text{Sales}}$$

A careful comparison of outlays for R&D over the years will indicate to the analyst whether the effort is a sustained one or one that varies with the ups and downs of operating results. Moreover, "one shot" research efforts lack the predictability or quality of a sustained, well-organized longer-term research program.

Other Future-Directed Costs   In addition to advertising and R&D, there are other types of future-directed outlays. An example of such outlays are the costs of training operating, sales, and managerial talent. Although these outlays for the development of human resources are usually expensed in the year in which they are incurred, they may have future utility, and the analyst may want to recognize this in his or her evaluation of current earnings and of future prospects.

Balance Sheet Analysis as a Check on the Validity and Quality of Reported Earnings

The amounts at which the assets and liabilities of an enterprise are stated hold important clues to an assessment of both the validity as well as the quality of its earnings. Thus, the analysis of the balance sheet is an important complement to the other approaches of income analysis discussed in this chapter, and elsewhere in this book.

Importance of Carrying Amounts of Assets   The importance that we attach to the amounts at which assets are carried on the balance sheet is due to the fact that, with few exceptions such as cash, some investments, and land, the cost of most assets enters ultimately the cost stream of the income statement. Thus, we can state the following as a general proposition: Whenever assets are overstated, the cumulative income[1] is overstated because it has been relieved of charges needed to bring such assets down to realizable values.

It would appear that the converse of this proposition should also hold true; that is, that to the extent to which assets are understated, cumulative income is also understated. Two accounting conventions qualify this statement importantly. One is the convention of conservatism, which calls for the recognition of gains only as they are actually realized. Although there has been some movement away from a strict interpretation of this convention, in general most assets are carried at original cost even though their current market or realizable value is far in excess of that cost.

The other qualifying convention is that governing the accounting for business combinations. The pooling of interests concept allows an acquiring company to carry forward the old book values of the assets of the acquired company even though such values may be far less than current market values or the consideration given for them. Thus, the analyst must be aware of the fact that such an accounting will allow the recording of profits, when the values of such understated assets are realized, which represents nothing more than the surfacing of such hitherto understated assets. Since such profits have, in effect, previously been bought and paid for, they cannot be considered as representing either the earning power of the enterprise or an index of the operating performance of its management.

Importance of Provisions and Liabilities   Continuing our analysis of the effect of balance sheet amounts on the measurement of income, we can enunciate the further proposition that an understatement of provisions and liabilities will result in an overstatement of cumulative income because the latter is relieved of charges required to bring the provision or the liabilities up to their proper amounts. Thus, for example, an understatement of the provision for taxes, for product warranties, or for pensions means that cumulative income is overstated.

Conversely, an overprovision for present and future liabilities or losses results in the understatement of income or in the overstatement of losses. Provisions for future costs and losses that are excessive in amount represent attempts to shift the burden of costs and expenses from future income statements to that of the present.

---

[1] The effect on any one period cannot be the subject of generalization.

Bearing in mind the general propositions regarding the effect on income of the amounts at which assets and liabilities are carried in the balance sheet, the critical analysis and evaluation of such amounts represents an important check on the validity of reported income.

Balance Sheet Analysis and the Quality of Earnings   There is, however, a further dimension to this kind of analysis in that it also has a bearing on an evaluation of the quality of earnings. This approach is based on the fact that various degrees of risk attach to the probability of the future realization of different types of assets.

For example, the future realization of accounts receivable has generally a higher degree of probability than has the realization of, say, inventory or unrecovered tools and dies costs. Moreover, the future realization of inventory costs can, generally, be predicted with greater certainty than can the future realization of goodwill or of deferred start-up costs. The analysis of the assets carried in the balance sheet by risk class or risk category holds clues to and is an important measure of the quality of reported income. Stated another way, if the income determination process results in the deferral of outlays and costs which carry a high degree of risk that they may not prove realizable in the future, then that income is of a lower quality than income that does not involve the recording of such high-risk assets.

Effect of Valuation of Specific Assets on the Validity and Quality of Reported Income   In order to illustrate the importance of balance sheet analysis to an evaluation of reported income, let us now examine the effect of the valuation of specific assets on the validity and quality of that income.

Accounts Receivable   The validity of the sales figure depends on the proper valuation of the accounts receivable that result from it. This valuation must recognize the risk of default in payment as well as the time value of money. On the latter score, *APB Opinion 21* provides that if the receivable does not arise from transactions with customers or suppliers in the normal course of business under terms not exceeding a year, then, except for some other stated exceptions, it must be valued using the interest rate applicable to similar debt instruments. Thus, if the receivable bears an interest rate of 8 percent while similar receivables would, at the time, be expected to bear an interest rate of 12 percent, both the receivable and the sale from which it arose would be restated at the lower discounted amount.

The relative level of accounts receivable and its relationship to sales can hold clues to income quality. If an increase in accounts receivable represents merely a shifting of inventory from the company to its distributing middlemen because of aggressive sales promotion or costly incentives, then these sales accomplish nothing more than "borrowing from the future" and thus reduce earnings quality.

Inventories   Overstated inventories lead to overstated profits. Overstatements can occur due to errors in quantities, errors in costing and pricing, or errors in the valuation of work in process. The more technical the product and the more dependent the valuation is on internally developed cost records, the more vulnerable are the cost estimates to error and misstatement. The basic problem here arises when costs that should have been written off to expense are retained in the inventory accounts.

An understatement of inventories results from a charge-off to income of costs that possess future utility and that should be inventoried. Such an understatement of inventories results in the understatement of current income and the overstatement of future income.

Deferred Charges   Deferred charges such as deferred tooling or start-up and preoperating costs must be scrutinized carefully because their value depends, perhaps more than that of other assets, on estimates of future probabilities and developments. Experience has shown that often such estimates have proven overoptimistic or that they did not contain sufficient provisions for future contingencies. Thus, the risk of failure to attain expectations is relatively higher here than in the case of other assets.

The Effect of External Factors on the Quality of Earnings   The concept of earnings quality is so broad that it encompasses many additional factors that, in the eyes of analysts, can make earnings more reliable or more desirable.

In times of rising price levels, the inclusion of "inventory profits" or the understatement of expenses such as depreciation lowers in effect the reliability of earnings and hence their quality.

The quality of foreign earnings is affected by factors such as difficulties and uncertainties regarding the repatriation of funds, currency fluctuations, the political and social climate as well as local customs and regulation. With regard to the latter, the inability to dismiss personnel in some countries in effect converts labor costs into fixed costs.

Regulation provides another example of external factors that can affect earnings quality. The "regulatory environment" of a public utility affects the "quality" of its earnings. Thus, an unsympathetic or even hostile regulatory environment that causes serious lags in the obtaining of rate relief will detract from earnings quality because of uncertainty about the adequacy of future revenues.

The stability and reliability of earnings sources affect earnings quality. Defense-related revenues can be regarded as nonrecurring in time of war and affected by political uncertainties in peacetime.

Finally, some analysts regard complexity of operations and difficulties in their analysis (e.g., of conglomerates) as negative factors.

EVALUATION OF THE EARNINGS LEVEL AND TREND

The analyst will concentrate on identifying those elements in the income and cost streams that exhibit stability, proven relationships, and pre-dictability, and will separate them from those elements that are random, erratic, or nonrecurring and that, consequently, do not possess the ele-ments of stability required for a reasonably reliable forecast or for inclu-sion in an "earning power" computation.

The analyst must be on guard against the well-known tendency of managements to practice income smoothing, thus trying to give to the income and expense streams a semblance of stability that in reality they do not possess. This is usually done in the name of "removing distor-tions" from the results of operations, whereas what is really achieved is the masking of the natural and cyclical irregularities that are part of the reality of the enterprise's experience and with which reality it is the an-alyst's primary task to come to grips in order to assess the level of risk.

Factors Affecting the Level of Earnings

We have, so far, discussed the *qualitative* factors that may cause the analyst either to adjust the earnings number of a given period (generally, a year) or to adjust the valuation (e.g., the price-earnings multiple) ac-corded such earnings.

The next step in the determination of the *level* of earnings of a given period is to recast the published income statements in such a way that the stable, normal, and continuing elements in the income statement are separated and distinguished from random, erratic, unusual, or nonre-curring elements that require separate analytical treatment or consider-ation. Moreover, such recasting also aims at identifying those elements included in the income statement of a given period that should more properly be included in the operating results of one or more prior periods.

The Analytical Recasting and Adjustment of Income Statements

The income statement along with all other financial statements and data contained in management's report represent the logical starting point of the analysis. It is clear that reported income is but the *starting point* of analysis and that from the point of view of the intelligent analyst, the most desirable income statement is the one containing a maximum of meaningful disclosure rather than one containing built-in interpretations that channel us to specific conclusions.

Over the years, notable shifts have occurred in the thinking of the accounting profession regarding the function of the income statement. An early position was that items of gain or loss should be included or excluded from income on the basis of the accountant's interpretation of what "normal operations" are. This position has resulted in much controversy and criticism to the point where the profession has adopted the "clean surplus" approach of including all[2] items of gain and loss in the income of the period in which they occur and, with few exceptions, such as corrections of errors, has also taken a position against the restatement of prior period results.

Major Sources of Information   As a consequence, the analyst will find data needed for the analysis of the results of operations and for their recasting and adjustment in:

1. The income statement which is generally subdivided into the following:

   > Income from continuing operations.
   > Income from discontinued operations (which includes gain or
   >   loss from disposal).
   > Extraordinary gains and losses.
   > Cumulative effect of changes in accounting principles.

2. The other financial statements and the footnotes thereto.
3. Management's comments found throughout its published report.
4. "Management's Discussion and Analysis of Financial Condition and Results of Operations" as required by the SEC's disclosure system (see also Chapter 7).

The analyst may also find "unusual" items segregated within the income statement (generally on a pre-tax basis), but their disclosure is optional. Such disclosure may not include items that the analyst may regard as significant, noteworthy, or unusual; and, consequently, the analyst will consult all the above-mentioned sources as well as management, if possible, in order to obtain the needed facts. These will include facts that affect the comparability and the interpretation of income statements, such as product-mix changes, production innovations, strikes, and raw material shortages that may or may not be included in management's mandatory discussion and analysis of the results of operations.

The Recasting and Adjusting Procedure

Once the analyst has secured as much information as it is possible to obtain, the income statements of a number of years (generally at least five) should be recast and adjusted in such a way as to facilitate their

---

[2] It should be noted that a departure from this position occurred in *SFAS 52* where, with few exceptions, gains and losses on the translation of foreign currency financial statements of subsidiaries bypass income and are accumulated in a separate stockholders' equity account. To a more limited extent, *SFAS 12*, on accounting for marketable securities, also represented such a departure, as does *SFAS 87*, concerned with the accounting for pensions.

further analysis to evaluate the trend of earnings as well as to aid in determining the average earning power of the enterprise for the period. While this procedure can be accomplished in one statement, it is simpler and clearer to subdivide it into two distinct steps: (1) recasting and (2) adjusting.

The Recasting Process   The recasting process aims at a rearranging of the items within the income statement in such a way so as to provide the most meaningful detail and the most relevant format needed by the analyst. At this stage, the individual items in the income statement may be rearranged, subdivided, or tax effected, but the total must reconcile to the net income of each period as reported.

The analytical reclassification of items *within* a period will help in the evaluation of the earnings level. Thus, discretionary and other noteworthy expenses should be segregated. The same applies to net items such as equity in income or loss of unconsolidated subsidiaries or associated companies, which are usually shown net of tax. Items shown in the pretax category must be removed *together* with their tax effect if they are to be shown below normal "income from continuing operations."

Expanded tax disclosure enables the analyst to segregate factors that reduce taxes as well as those that increase them, thus enabling an analysis of the degree to which these factors are of a recurring nature. All material permanent differences and credits should be included. The analytical procedure involves computing taxes at the statutory rate (currently 34 percent) and deducting tax benefits such as arising from a variety of tax credits, capital gains rates, tax-free income, or lower foreign tax rates, and adding factors such as additional foreign taxes, nontax-deductible expenses, and state and local taxes (net of federal tax benefit). Immaterial items may be considered in one lump sum labeled "other."

Analytically recast income statements will contain as much detail as is needed for analysis and are supplemented by explanatory footnotes. Exhibit 9–1 presents the analytically recast income statements of Campbell Soup which are annotated with key numbers for ease of reference to the financial statements found in Appendix 2B. Data preceding 1990 are taken from company reports which are summarized in Chapter 10. Chapter 10 contains a discussion of and an integration of Exhibit 9–1.

The Adjustment Process   Based on data developed in the recast income statements as well as on other available information, certain items of income or loss are to be assigned by the analyst to the period to which they most properly belong.

The reassignment of extraordinary items or unusual items (net of tax) to other years must be done with care. Thus, the income tax benefit of the carryforward of operating losses should generally be moved to the

Exhibit 9-1

CAMPBELL SOUP COMPANY
Analytically Recast Income Statements
For Fiscal Years 1986 to 1991
(in millions)

Reference item		1991	1990	1989	1988	1987	1986
13	Net sales	$6,204.1	$6,205.8	$5,672.1	$4,868.9	$4,490.4	$4,286.8
19	Interest income	26.0	17.6	38.3	33.2	29.5	27.4
	Total revenue	6,230.1	6,223.4	5,710.4	4,902.1	4,519.9	4,314.2
	Costs and expenses:						
145	Cost of products sold (1)	3,727.1	3,893.5	3,651.8	3,077.8	2,897.8	2,820.5
144	Marketing and Selling expenses (2)	760.8	760.1	605.9	514.2	422.7	363.0
16	Advertising (2)	195.4	220.4	212.9	219.1	203.5	181.4
17	Repair and maintenance (1)	173.9	180.6	173.9	155.6	148.8	144.0
102	Administrative expenses	306.7	290.7	252.1	232.6	213.9	195.9
20	Research and development expenses	56.3	53.7	47.7	46.9	44.8	42.2
104	Stock price related incentive programs (3)	15.4	(0.1)	17.4	(2.7)	—	8.5
162A	Foreign exchange adjustment	0.8	3.3	19.3	16.6	4.8	0.7
103	Other, net (3)	(3.3)	(2.0)	(1.4)	(4.7)	(0.4)	(9.0)
	Depreciation (1)	194.5	184.1	175.9	162.0	139.0	120.8
	Amortization of intangible and other assets						
18	(3)	14.1	16.8	16.4	8.9	5.6	6.0
	Interest expense	116.2	111.6	94.1	53.9	51.7	56.0
	Total costs and expenses	5,557.9	5,712.7	5,266.0	4,480.2	4,132.2	3,930.0
23	Earnings before equity in earnings of affiliates and minority interests	672.2	510.7	444.4	421.9	387.7	384.2
24	Equity in earnings of affiliates	2.4	13.5	10.4	6.3	15.1	4.3
25	Minority interests	(7.2)	(5.7)	(5.3)	(6.3)	(4.7)	(3.9)

293

Ref							
26	Income before taxes	667.4	518.5	449.5	421.9	398.1	384.6
	Income taxes at statutory rate*	(226.9)	(176.3)	(152.8)	(143.5)	(179.1)	(176.9)
135	Income from continuing operations	440.5	342.2	296.7	278.4	219.0	207.7
	State taxes (net of federal tax benefit)	(20.0)	(6.6)	(3.8)	(11.8)	(8.6)	(8.0)
137	Investment tax credit	—	—	—	—	4.4	11.6 †
138	Nondeductible amortization of intangibles	(4.0)	(1.6)	(1.2)	(2.6)	(1.4)	—
	Foreign earnings not taxed or taxed at other than statutory federal rate	2.0	(2.2)	(0.2)	3.2	11.1	15.2
139	Other: Tax effects	(17.0)	(2.2)	(0.1)	(3.7)	7.5	(4.7)
	Alaska Native Corporation transaction	—	—	—	—	4.5	—
22	Divestitures, restructuring, and unusual charges	—	(339.1)	(343.0)	(40.6)	—	—
	Tax effect of divestitures, restructuring . . . etc. (4)	—	13.9	64.7	13.9	—	—
	Gain on sale of businesses (1988) and subsidiary (1987)	—	—	—	3.1	9.7	—
	Loss on sale of exercise equipment subsidiary, net of tax	—	—	—	—	(1.7)	—
	LIFO liquidation gain (1)	—	—	—	1.7	2.8	1.4
	Income before cumulative effect of accounting change	401.5	4.4	13.1	241.6	247.3	223.2
153A	Cumulative effect of accounting change for income taxes	—	—	—	32.5	—	—
28	Net income as reported	401.5	4.4	13.1	274.1	247.3	223.2
14	(1) Cost of products sold	4,095.5	4,258.2	4,001.6	3,392.8	3,180.5	3,082.8
144	Less: Repair and maintenance expenses	(173.9)	(180.6)	(173.9)	(155.6)	(148.8)	(144.0)
162A	Less: Depreciation(a)	(194.5)	(184.1)	(175.9)	(162.0)	(139.0)	(120.0)
153A	Plus: LIFO liquidation gain(b)				2.6	5.1	2.6
		3,727.1	3,893.5	3,651.8	3,077.8	2,897.8	2,821.4

		1991	1990	1989	1988	1987	1986
[15]	(2) Marketing and selling expenses	956.2	980.5	818.8	733.3	626.2	544.4
[145]	Less: Advertising	(195.4)	(20.4)	(212.9)	(219.1)	(203.5)	(181.4)
		760.8	960.1	605.9	514.2	422.7	363.0
[21]	(3) Other expenses (income)	26.2	14.7	32.4	(3.2)	(9.5)	5.5
[102]	Less: Stock price related incentive programs	(15.4)	0.1	(17.4)	2.7	—	(8.5)
[103]	Less: Amortization of intangible and other assets	(14.1)	(16.8)	(16.4)	(8.9)	(5.6)	(6.0)
	Less: Gain on sale of international businesses (1988) and sale of pet food Subsidiary (1987)	—	—	—	4.7	14.7	—
[104]	Other, net	(3.3)	(2.0)	(1.4)	(4.7)	(0.4)	(9.0)
[136]	(4) Tax effect of divestitures, restructuring and unusual charges at the statutory rate	—	115.3 [c]	116.6 [d]	13.9	—	—
	Nondeductible divestitures, . . . etc.	—	(101.4) [e]	(51.9) [f]	—	—	—
		—	13.9	64.7	13.9	—	—

	1991	1990	1989	1988	1987	1986
* Statutory federal tax rate	34%	34%	34%	34%	45%	46%

† Not disclosed for 1986

[a] Most of depreciation is assumed as to be included in cost of products sold.

[b] LIFO liquidation gain before tax. For 1988 = 1.7 / (1 − 0.34) = 2.58

[c] $339.1 [22] × 0.34 = $115.3

[d] $343.0 [22] × 0.34 = $116.6

[e] $179.4 [26] [136] × 0.565 [136] = $101.4

[f] $106.5 [26] [136] × 0.487 [136] = $51.9

year in which the loss occurred. The costs or benefits from the settlement of a lawsuit may relate to one or more preceding years. The gain or loss on disposal of discontinued operations will usually relate to the results of operations over a number of years.

If possible, all years under analysis should be placed on a comparable basis when a change in accounting principle or accounting estimate occurs. If, as is usually the case, the *new* accounting principle is the desirable one, prior years should, if possible, be restated to the new method, or a notation made regarding a lack of comparability in certain respects. This procedure will result in a redistribution of the "cumulative effect of change in accounting principle" to affected prior years. Changes in estimates can be accounted for only prospectively and GAAP prohibit prior year restatements except in specified cases. The analyst's ability to place all years on a comparable basis will depend on availability of information.

Before the trend in earnings can be evaluated it is necessary to obtain the best approximation possible of the adjusted earnings *level* of each year. All items in the income statement must be considered, and none can be excluded or "dropped by the wayside." Thus, if it is decided that an item in the income statement does not properly belong in the year in which it appears, it may be either:

1. Shifted (net of tax) to the result of another year or a number of other years, or
2. If it cannot be identified with another specific year or years, it should be included in the *average* earnings of the period under analysis. While the averaging process helps in the determination of average earning power, it is not helpful in the determination of earnings trend.

It must be realized that moving an item of gain or loss to another year or recording one's inability to assign an item to the proper year does not remedy the fact that the results of some prior year(s) have been misstated. For example, a damage award in one year for patent infringement means that prior years had suffered from lost sales or similar damage.

Exhibit 9–2 presents the analytically adjusted income statements of Campbell Soup based on data in Appendix 2B as well as data taken from earlier financial reports. A further reference to Exhibit 9–2 will be found in the comprehensive analysis of Campbell found in Chapter 10.

Analysts must recognize that characterizations of income or expense items as "unusual," "nonrecurring," "infrequent," or "extraordinary" or the inclusion in equity of certain transactions (e.g., under *SFAS 12* and *52*) are all attempts to reduce earnings volatility or to explain away certain components of income. Items excluded from income by FASB direction are generally not adjusted for. However, all remaining items are part of the lifetime income of an enterprise—they do enhance or diminish the owners' wealth and they are part of the earning power of the enterprise.

Exhibit 9–2

CAMPBELL SOUP COMPANY
Analytically Adjusted Income Statements 1986–1991
(in millions)

	1991	1990	1989	1988	1987	1986	Total
Net income as reported	$401.5	$ 4.4	$ 13.1	$274.1	$247.3	$223.2	$1,163.6
Divestitures, restructuring and unusual charges		339.1	343.0	40.6			
Tax effect of divestitures, restructuring, etc.		(13.9)	(64.7)	(13.9)			
Gain on sale of businesses (1988) and sale of subsidiary (1987), net of tax				(3.1)	(9.7)		
Loss on sale of exercise equipment subsidiary					1.7		
Alaska Native corporation transaction					(4.5)		
LIFO liquidation gain				(1.7)	(2.8)	(1.4)	
Cumulative effect of change in accounting for income taxes				(32.5)			
Adjusted net income for individual years	401.5	329.6	291.4	263.5	232.0	221.8	
Total net income for the period							1,163.6
Average earnings for the period							$ 193.9

Thus, while it may be analytically appropriate to omit such items from any one year, they belong in any computation of *average* earning power actually achieved.

Determining the Trend of Income over the Years

Having determined the size of a company's basic earnings as well as the factors that require adjustment before those earnings can be used as a basis for forecasts, the analyst will next determine the variability of these earnings, that is, changes in their size over the business cycle and over the longer term.

Evaluation of Earnings Variability   Earnings that fluctuate up and down with the business cycle are less desirable than earnings that display a larger degree of stability over such a cycle. The basic reason for this is that fluctuating earnings cause fluctuations in market prices. Earnings that display a steady growth trend are of the most desirable type. In the evaluation of earnings, the intelligent analyst realizes the limitations to which the earnings figure of any one year is subject. Therefore, depending on his specific purposes, he will consider the following earnings figures as improvements over the single-year figure:

1. *Average earnings* over periods, such as 5 to 10 years, smooth out erratic and even extraordinary factors as well as cyclical influences, thus presenting a better and more reliable measure of "earning power" of an enterprise.
2. *Minimum earnings* are useful in decisions, such as those bearing on credit extension, which are particularly sensitive to risk factors. They indicate the worst that could happen during a complete business cycle, based on recent experience.

The Importance of Earnings Trends   In addition to the use of single, average, or minimum earnings figures, the analyst must be alert to earnings trends. These are best evaluated by means of trend statements such as those presented on page 342. The relevant earnings numbers to be included in the trend analysis will be derived from adjusted income statements as exemplified in Exhibit 9–2. The earnings trend contains important clues to the nature of the enterprise (i.e., cyclical, growth, defensive) and the quality of its management.

Distortions of Trends   Analysts must be alert to accounting distortions that affect trends. Among the most important are changes in accounting principles and the effect of business combinations, particularly purchases. These must be adjusted for.

Some of the most common and most pervasive manipulative practices in accounting are designed to affect the presentation of earnings trends.

These manipulations are based on the assumptions, often true, that the trend of income is more important than its absolute size; that retroactive revisions of income already reported in prior periods have little, if any, market effect on security prices,[3] and that once a company has incurred a loss, the size of the loss is not as significant as the fact that the loss has been incurred.

These assumptions and the propensities of some managements to use accounting as a means of improving the appearance of the earnings trend has led to techniques that can be broadly described as income smoothing.

Income Smoothing and Income Distortion

A number of requirements must be met by the income-smoothing process so as to distinguish it from outright falsehoods and distortions.

The income-smoothing process is a rather sophisticated and insidious device. It does not rely on outright or patent falsehoods and distortions but rather uses the wide leeway existing in alternatively acceptable accounting principles and their interpretation in order to achieve its ends. Thus, income smoothing is performed within the framework of GAAP. It is a matter of form rather than one of substance. Consequently, it does not involve a real transaction (e.g., postponing an actual sale to another accounting period in order to shift revenue) but only a redistribution of credits or charges among periods. The general objective is to moderate income variability over the years by shifting income from good years to bad years, by shifting future income to the present (in most cases presently reported earnings are more valuable than those reported at some future date), or vice versa. Similarly, income variability can be moderated or modified by the shifting of costs, expenses, or losses from one period to another.

Income smoothing may take many forms. Hereunder are listed some forms of smoothing to which the analyst should be particularly alert:

1. Changing accounting methods or assumptions with the objective of improving or modifying reported results. For example, to offset the effect on earnings of slumping sales and of other difficulties, Chrysler Corporation revised upward the assumed rate of return on its pension portfolio, thus increasing income significantly. Similarly, Union Carbide improved results by switching to a number of more liberal accounting alternatives.
2. Misstatements, by various methods, of inventories as a means of redistributing income among the years. The Londontown Manufacturing Company case provides a classic example of such practices.[4]

---

[3] This was recognized by *APB Opinion 20* and later *SFAS 16*, which, with but two exceptions, forbids the retroactive restatement of prior year financial statements.

[4] Details can be found in an SEC decision issued October 31, 1963 (41 SEC 676–688).

Some of these practices were outside the framework allowed by GAAP.

3. The offsetting of extraordinary credits by identical or nearly identical extraordinary charges as a means of removing an unusual or sudden injection of income that may interfere with the display of a growing earnings trend.

4. The provision of reserves for future costs and losses as a means of increasing the adverse results of what is already a poor year and utilizing such reserves to relieve future years of charges against income that would otherwise be properly chargeable against it. (Abuses in this area are intended to be curtailed by *SFAS 5*.)

5. The substantial write-downs of operating assets (such as plant and equipment) or of intangibles (such as goodwill) in times of economic slowdown when operating results are already poor. The reason usually given for such write-downs is that carrying the properties at book value cannot be economically justified. (For example, CSX Corporation wrote off, as part of a restructuring, $533 million of marginal and unproductive assets.) Particularly unwarranted is the practice of writing down operating assets to the point at which a target return on investment (which management thinks it *should* earn) is realized.

6. Timing the inclusion of revenues and costs in periodic income in such a way as to influence the overall trend of income (or loss) over the years. (Examples are the timing of sales or other disposition of property, incurring and expensing of discretionary costs such as R&D, advertising, maintenance, etc.) This category, unlike most others, entails more than accounting choice in that it may involve the timing of actual business transactions. Thus, in recent years, Franklin Mint inflated sales and income by accelerating shipments to customers ahead of a schedule called for by customer subscription terms and booking these as sales immediately.

Income Smoothing and Income Distortion—Some Implications for Analysis

Motivation for Distortions   Human nature has a most powerful and pervasive effect on measurements which affect the analysis of financial statements. This is particularly true of earnings levels and trends which enter so importantly into investing and lending decisions. As experience has repeatedly shown (some of it illustrated in this work), there is almost no limit to the degree to which beleaguered and/or greedy owners, managers, or company employees will go to manipulate or distort reported earnings in order to achieve ends which serve their objectives and interests.

Companies in financial difficulties may be motivated to engage in such practices for what they see and justify as their battle for survival. Successful companies will go to great lengths to uphold a hard-earned and well-rewarded image of earnings growth by smoothing those earnings artificially. Moreover, compensation plans or other incentives based on earnings will motivate managements to accelerate the recognition of income by anticipating revenues or deferring expenses.

The following examples are additional to those given throughout this work:

THE H. J. HEINZ COMPANY CASE.   The case of H. J. Heinz Company has shown that even second-tier divisional executives, motivated by self-interest in meeting earnings targets and in smoothing earnings, can without the knowledge of top management engage in income manipulation. In this case, "hidden reserves" were created by prepaying for services not yet received, such as advertising, and by the improper recording of sales.

THE J. W. T. GROUP, INC., CASE.   This case did not seem to involve a desire for personal gain but consisted rather in falsifying of records in order to make the syndication department look good by meeting its profit goals.

The department purchased programming from independent producers and bartered the programs to television stations in return for future commercial time that was in turn used to build "time banks" for sale to agency clients. The accounting deception involved the creation of fictitious time banks, fictitious clients, and fictitious revenues over a period of four years. So successful was the computerized deception that for a time, management invested additional capital in the division, lured by the substantial, if fictitious, returns it appeared to earn.

THE McCORMICK CO. CASE.   The SEC took this company to task for, among other things, managing its earnings by asking its advertising agency to delay mailing invoices till later periods. The company agreed not to engage in such practices in the future.

Analysts must appreciate the great variety of incentives and objectives that lead managements and, at times, second-tier management without the knowledge of top management, to engage in practices ranging from smoothing to the outright falsification of income.

The smoothing of earnings is often achieved by first understating reported earnings. Thus, Firestone Tire and Rubber Company engaged in the practice of hiding income in secret accounts for the purpose of drawing on these during leaner years.

Some reputable academicians have even suggested that smoothing is justified if it can help a company report earnings closer to its true "earning power" level. Such is not the function of financial reporting. As we have repeatedly seen in this book, the analyst will be best served by a full disclosure of periodic results and the components that comprise them. It is up to the analyst to average, smooth, or otherwise adjust reported earnings in accordance with specific analytical purposes.

As a possible case of earnings smoothing and of overprovision of costs in order to benefit future years a discussion of General Motors' accounting may be instructive:

GENERAL MOTORS' (GM) ACCOUNTING. In 1987 GM reported that, based on a careful study, a revision of useful lives of plant and equipment resulted in a $1.2 billion reduction of depreciation and amortization charges that year. (See also Chapter 10.) The chairperson's message stated that "GM earned $3.6 billion for the year, up 21 percent from 1986 despite a 9 percent reduction in worldwide unit sales." However, without the $1.2 billion reduction in depreciation and amortization, as a result of the significant lengthening of estimated lives of assets, earnings would have *declined* rather than increased.

The 1987 accounting change came on the heels of a 1986 provision of $1.3 billion for plant closings and other restructurings. However, by the end of the decade only $0.5 billion has been charged against this provision leaving the rest to absorb costs in future years. When 1990 saw a change in leadership at GM, stockholders learned of another $2.1 billion charge to earnings to cover the costs of closing several plants, including closings which won't actually occur until years later. This sequence of accounting events left analysts puzzled about the veracity of GM's accounting and the motivation of its management. Such accounting greatly increases the difficulties in arriving at a reliable earnings trend over the years. Any reliable estimate of earning power must include in the averaging process charges and provisions of all kinds.

The accounting profession has earnestly tried to promulgate rules that discourage practices such as the smoothing of earnings. However, given the above-mentioned powerful propensities of companies and of their owners and employees to engage in such practices, analysts must realize that where there is a will to smooth or even distort earnings, ways to do so are available and will be found. Consequently, particularly in the case of companies where incentives to smooth are likely to be present, analysts should analyze and scrutinize accounting practices in order to satisfy themselves to the extent possible, regarding the integrity of the income reporting process.

Extraordinary Gains and Losses

The evaluation of current earnings levels, the determination of earnings trends as well as the projection of future earnings rely importantly on the separation of the stable elements of income and expense from those that are random, nonrecurring, and erratic in nature.

Stability and sustainability are important characteristics that enter significantly into the determination of earning power. Moreover, in making earnings projections, the forecaster relies also on repetitiveness of occurrence. Thus, in order to separate the relatively stable elements of income and expense of an enterprise from those that are random or erratic in nature, it is important, as a first step, to identify those gains and losses that are nonrecurring and unusual as well as those that are truly extraordinary.

This separation is a first step that is mostly preparatory in nature. Following it is a process of judgment and analysis that aims at determining how such nonrecurring, unusual, or truly extraordinary items should be treated in the evaluation of the level of present income and of management performance as well as in the projection of future results.

Significance of Accounting Treatment and Presentation   The value of any accounting treatment and presentation is largely dependent on its usefulness to those who make decisions on the basis of financial statements. Unfortunately, particularly in the area of the accounting for, and the presentation of, extraordinary gains and losses, the usefulness of this accounting has been impaired because of the great importance attached to it by those who report the results of operations and who are judged by them.

The accounting for, and the presentation of, extraordinary gains and losses has always been subject to controversy. Whatever the merits of the theoretical debate surrounding this issue, the fact remains that one of the basic reasons for the controversial nature of this topic is reporting management's great interest in it. Managements are almost always concerned with the amount of net results of the enterprise as well as with the manner in which these periodic results are reported. This concern is reinforced by a widespread belief that most investors and traders accept the reported net income figures, as well as the modifying explanations that accompany them, as true indexes of performance. Thus, extraordinary gains and losses often become the means by which managements attempt to modify the reported operating results and the means by which they try to explain these results. Quite often these explanations are subjective and are designed to achieve the impact and impression desired by management.

The accounting profession has tacitly, if not openly, recognized the role that the foregoing considerations play in the actual practice of reporting extraordinary gains and losses. Its last pronouncement on this subject has at least ensured a fuller measure of disclosure of extraordinary gains and losses and their inclusion in the income statement. This represents an improvement over prior pronouncements that, in an attempt to arrive at a "true" index of operating performance, sanctioned the exclusion of certain extraordinary gains and losses from the income statement.

Analysis and Evaluation   The basic objectives in the identification and evaluation of extraordinary items by the analyst are:

1. To determine whether a particular item is to be considered "extraordinary" for purposes of analysis, that is, whether it is so unusual, nonoperating, and nonrecurring in nature that it requires

special adjustment in the evaluation of current earnings levels and of future earning possibilities.

2. To decide what form the adjustment for items that are considered as "extraordinary" in nature should take.

Determining Whether an Item of Gain or Loss Is Extraordinary   The infirmities and shortcomings of present practice as well as the considerations which motivate it, lead to the inescapable conclusion that the analyst must arrive at an independent evaluation of whether a gain or loss should be considered as extraordinary, and if so, how to adjust for it.

In arriving at this decision, it is useful to subdivide items, commonly classified as unusual or extraordinary, into three basic categories:

a. Nonrecurring operating gains or losses. By "operating" we usually identify items connected with the normal and usual operations of the business. The concept of normal operations is more widely used than understood and is far from clear and well defined. Thus, in a company operating a machine shop, operating expenses would be considered as those associated with the work of the machine shop. The proceeds from a sale above cost of marketable securities held by the company as an investment of excess cash would be considered a nonoperating gain. So would the gain (or loss) on the sale of a lathe, even if it were disposed of in order to make room for one that would increase the productivity of the shop.

The concept of recurrence is one of frequency. There are no predetermined generally accepted boundaries separating the recurring event from the nonrecurring. An event (which in this context embraces a gain or loss) occurring once a year can be definitely classified as "recurring." An event, the occurrence of which is unpredictable and which in the past has either not occurred or occurred very infrequently, may be classified as nonrecurring. On the other hand, an event that occurs infrequently but whose occurrence is predictable raises some question as to its designation. An example of the latter would be the relining of blast furnaces. They last for many years; while their replacement is infrequent, the need for it is predictable. Some companies provide for their replacement by means of a reserve. Casualties do not, however, accrue in similar fashion.

Nonrecurring operating gains or losses are, then, gains or losses connected with or related to operations that recur infrequently and/or unpredictably.

In considering how to treat nonrecurring operating gains and losses, the analyst would do best to recognize the fact of inherent abnormality and the lack of a recurring annual pattern in business and treat them as belonging to the results of the period in which they are reported.

We must also address ourselves to the question of what should be considered as "normal operations." Thus, it is a bakery's purpose to bake bread, rolls, and cakes, but it is presumably outside its normal purpose to buy and sell marketable securities for gain or loss, or even to sell baking machinery that is to be replaced for the purpose of more efficient baking.

This narrow interpretation of the objectives of a business has undergone considerable revision in modern financial theory. Thus, rather than the "baking bread" or any other specific objective, the main objective and task of management is viewed as that of increasing the capital of the owners, or expressed differently, the enhancing of the value of the common stock. This, according to modern financial theory, can be accomplished by means of the judicious combination of an optimal financing plan and any mix of operations opportunities that may be available to achieve the desired purpose.

The analyst should not be bound by the accountant's concept of "normal operations," and thus he or she can usefully treat a much wider range of gains and losses as being derived from "operations." This approach reinforces our conclusion that from the point of view of analysis, most nonrecurring, *operating* gains and losses should be considered part of the operating results of the year in which they occur.

This approach is offered as a general guideline rather than as a mechanical rule. After examination of all attendant circumstances, the analyst may conclude that some such items require separation from the results of a single year. The relative size of an item could conceivably be a factor requiring such treatment. In this case, the best approach is to emphasize *average earnings* experience over, say, five years rather than the result of a single year. This approach of emphasizing average earnings becomes almost imperative in the case of enterprises that have widely fluctuating amounts of nonrecurring and other extraordinary items included in their results. After all, a single year is too short and too arbitrary a period on the basis of which to evaluate the earnings power of an enterprise or the prospects for future results. Moreover, we are all familiar with enterprises that defer expenses and postpone losses and come up periodically with a loss year that cancels out much of the income reported in preceding years.

ILLUSTRATION 3.   1991 was a year of particularly numerous reports of big charges to earnings for reorganization, redeployment, or regrouping. Companies taking substantial write-offs included, in billions, AT&T $2.6, Occidental Petroleum $2, Continental Airlines $1.8, Digital Equipment $1, and in millions, Columbia Gas System $765, General Dynamics $567, and Bethlehem Steel $550.

While the information supplied with such announcements seldom enables a careful analysis of years affected by such big charges there is no question but that they represent in significant measure revisions of previously reported results. Thus, in one stroke, the write-off corrects the overreporting of earnings over many years. The analyst must also be alert to indications that such charges may include "cushions" designed to relieve future results of charges properly attributable to them.

b. Recurring nonoperating gains or losses. This category includes items of a nonoperating nature that recur with some frequency. An example would be the recurring amortization of a "bargain purchase credit." Other possible examples are interest income and the rental received from employees who rent company-owned houses.

While items in this category may be classified as unusual in published financial statements, the narrow definition of *nonoperating* which they involve as well as their recurrent nature are good reasons why they should not be excluded from current results by the analyst. They are, after all, mostly the result of the conscious employment of capital by the enterprise, and their recurrence requires inclusion of these gains or losses in estimates designed to project future results.

c. Nonrecurring nonoperating gains or losses. Of the three categories, this one possesses the greatest degree of "abnormality." Not only are the events here nonrepetitive and unpredictable, but they do not fall within the sphere of normal operations. In most cases, these events are extraneous, unintended, and unplanned. However, they can rarely be said to be totally unexpected. Business is ever subject to the risk of sudden adverse events and to random shocks, be they natural or manmade. In the same manner, business transactions are also subject to unexpected windfalls. One good example in this category is the loss from damage done by the crash of an aircraft on a plant not located in the vicinity of an airport. Other, but less clear-cut, examples in this category may also include:

1. Substantial uninsured casualty losses that are not within the categories of risk to which the enterprise can reasonably be deemed to be subject.
2. The expropriation by a foreign government of an entire operation owned by the enterprise.
3. The seizure or destruction of property as a result of an act of war, insurrection, or civil disorders, in areas where this is totally unexpected.

It can be seen readily that while the above occurrences are, in most cases, of a nonrecurring nature, their relation to the operations of a business varies. All are occurrences in the regular course of business. Even the assets destroyed by acts of God were acquired for operating purposes and thus were subject to all possible risks.

Of the three categories, the third comes closest to meeting the criterion of being "extraordinary." Nevertheless, truly unique events are very rare. What looks at the time as unique may in the light of experience turn out to be the symptom of new sets of circumstances that affect and may continue to affect the earning power as well as the degree of risk to which an enterprise is subject.

The analyst must bear in mind such possibilities, but barring evidence to the contrary, items in this category can be regarded as extraordinary in nature and thus can be omitted from the results of operations of a *single* year. They are, nevertheless, part of the longer-term record of results of the enterprise.[5] Thus, they enter the computation of *average earnings,* and the propensity of the enterprise to incur such gains or losses must be considered in the projection of future average earnings.

The foregoing discussion has tried to point out that the intelligent classification of extraordinary items provides a workable solution to their treatment by the analyst. There are, however, other aspects of the evaluation of extraordinary items that must be considered here. One is the effect of extraordinary items on the resources of an enterprise; the other is their effect on the evaluation of management performance.

Effect of Extraordinary Items on Enterprise Resources   Every extraordinary gain or loss has a dual aspect. In addition to recording a gain (whether extraordinary or not), a business records an increase in resources. Similarly, a loss results in a reduction of resources. Since return on investment (ROI) measures the relationship of net income to resources, the incurrence of extraordinary gains and losses will affect this important measure of profitability. The more material the extraordinary item, the more significant that influence will be. In other words, if earnings and events are to be used to make estimates about the future, then extraordinary items convey something more than past performance. Thus, if an extraordinary loss results in the destruction of capital on which a certain return is expected, that return may be lost to the future. Conversely, an extraordinary gain will result in an addition of resources on which a future return can be expected.

This means that in projecting profitability and return on investment, the analyst must take into account the effect of recorded "extraordinary" items as well as the likelihood of the occurrence of future events that may cause extraordinary items.

Effect on Evaluation of Management   One implication frequently associated with the reporting of extraordinary gains and losses is that they have not resulted from a "normal" or "planned" activity of management and that, consequently, they should not be used in the evaluation of management performance. The analyst should seriously question such a conclusion.

What is "normal activity" in relation to management's deliberate actions? Whether we talk about the purchase or sale of securities, of other assets not used in operations, or of divisions and subsidiaries that definitely relate to operations, we talk about actions deliberately taken by

---

[5] Analysts must be aware that some financial services arbitrarily exclude some gains and losses from reported earnings. Thus, *The Value Line Investment Survey* decided to "exclude most nonrecurring gains and losses from reported earnings per share."

management with specific purposes in mind. Such actions require, if anything, more consideration or deliberation than do ordinary everyday operating decisions because they are most often unusual in nature and involve substantial amounts of money. They are true tests of management ability. The results of such activities always qualify or enhance the results of "normal" operations, thus yielding the final net results.

For example, Standard Oil Co. (Ohio) took an extraordinary charge of $1.15 billion in writing down its ill-fated investment in Kennecott. It is quite likely that the loss resulted in prior years' earnings being overstated.

Similarly, management must be aware of the risk of natural or man-made disasters or impediments in the course of business. The decision to engage in foreign operations is made with the knowledge of the special risks that this involves. The decision to insure or not is a normal operating decision. Nothing can really be termed completely unexpected or unforeseeable. Management does not engage, or is at least not supposed to engage, in any activity unconsciously; hence, whatever it does is clearly within the expected activity of a business. Every type of enterprise is subject to specific risks that are inherent in it, and managements do not enter such ventures blindly.

When it comes to the assessment of results that count and results that build or destroy value, the distinction of what is normal and what is not fades almost into insignificance. Management's beliefs about the quality of its decisions are nearly always related to the normalcy, or lack thereof, of surrounding circumstances. This can be clearly seen in the management report section of many annual reports. Of course, management has to take more time to explain failure or shortcomings than to explain success. Success hardly needs an explanation, unless it involves circumstances not likely to be repeated. Failure often evokes long explanations, and more often than not, unusual or unforeseeable circumstances are blamed for it. If only normal conditions had prevailed, everything would have been much better. But in a competitive economy, normal conditions hardly ever prevail for any length of time. Management is paid to anticipate and expect the unusual. No alibis are permitted. Explanations are never a substitute for performance. In this area the letters to shareholders of Berkshire Hathaway written by its chairman, Warren Buffet, are examples of lucidity and candor.

THE CONCEPT OF EARNING POWER

The best possible estimate of the *average* earnings of an enterprise, which can be expected to be sustained and to be repeated with some degree of regularity over a *span of future years,* is referred to as its earning power. Except in specialized cases, earning power is universally recognized as the single most important factor in the valuation of an enterprise. Most valuation approaches entail in one form or another the capitalization of earning power by a factor or multiplier that takes into account the cost of capital as well as future expected risks and rewards.

The importance of "earning power" is such that most analyses of the income and related financial statements have as one of their ultimate objectives the determination of its amount. Earning power is a concept of financial analysis, not of accounting. It focuses on stable and recurring elements and thus aims to arrive at the best possible estimate of repeatable average earnings over a span of future years. Accounting, as we have seen, can supply much of the essential information for the computation of earning power. However, the process is one involving knowledge, judgment, experience, and a time horizon, as well as a specialized investing or lending point of view, such as is described in Chapter 1.

Investors and lenders look ultimately to future cash flows as sources of rewards and safety. Accrual accounting, which underlies income determination, aims to relate sacrifices and benefits to the periods in which they occur. In spite of known shortcomings, this framework represents the most reliable and relevant indicator of longer-term future probabilities of *average* cash inflows and outflows presently known.

While in its objectives, valuation is *future* oriented, we must recognize that the most sound and realistic basis for estimating future conditions and probabilities is the actual track record of the enterprise's achievement in the most recent past. Not only does such an earning record over a representative span of years, usually encompassing an entire business cycle, represent what has in fact been achieved as the actual operating experience of the enterprise, but it also represents the operating model on the basis of which we can give effect to assumptions about future conditions that we expect to differ from those prevailing in the past.

In this context, it must be realized that valuation, whether it is performed for purposes of investment, taxation, or the adjudication of disputes as to value, is of such importance to the parties at interest that estimates, if they are made, must be most soundly based. Thus, any departure from actual experience must be carefully verified and justified. Our ability to pierce the veil of the future is limited indeed. As Bennian[6] stated it:

> It is impossible to make an economic forecast in which full confidence can be placed. No matter what refinements of techniques are employed, there still remain at least some exogenous variables. It is thus not even possible to say with certainty how likely our forecast is to be right. We must be brash enough to label a forecast as "most probable," but this implies an ability on our part to pin an approximate probability coefficient on a

---

[6] Edward G. Bennian, "Capital Budgeting and Game Theory," *Harvard Business Review,* November–December 1956, pp. 115–23.

forecast: 1.0 if it is virtual certainty, 0.0 if it is next to an impossibility, or some other coefficient between these extremes. But, again, since we have no precise way of measuring the probability of our exogenous variables behaving as we assume them to do, there is no assurance that the estimated probability coefficient for our forecast is anything like 100 percent correct.

It is for this reason that the courts and others have been reluctant, except in the most persuasive of circumstances, to substitute guesses about the future for the experience of the past, and, for this reason, *average* past earnings enter very importantly into the determination of earning power.

Earning Power Time Horizon

It can be readily recognized that one year represents too short and too arbitrary a time period for purposes of income measurement and evaluation. Because of the length of time required to assess the ultimate workout and the results of many investments and outlays, because of the ups and downs of the business cycle, and because of the presence of numerous nonrecurring and extraordinary factors, the earning power of an enterprise is best measured by means of average earnings realized over a number of years. Thus, while gains and losses may be unusual or extraordinary with respect to any one period, they are, nevertheless, still part of the enterprise's longer-term operating experience.

The period of time over which an earnings average should be calculated will vary with the industry of which the enterprise is part and with other special circumstances. However, in general, a from 5- to 10-year earnings average will smooth out many of the distortions and the irregularities that impair the significance of a single year's results. A five-year earnings average will, in most cases, be adequate to retain an emphasis on recent experience while avoiding the inclusion of years that may no longer be representative or relevant.

Our discussion of the analysis of the income statement has shown that the analysis must focus on the level of income for each year as well as on the *trend* of earnings over time. Trend is an important factor in valuation.

If the earnings are subject to a sustainable trend, the averaging process may have to be weighted so as to accord more weight to most recent earnings. Thus, in a five-year average computation, the last year may be given a weight of 5/15, the preceding year a weight of 4/15, and the first year a weight of 1/15.

The more representative the most recent enterprise experience and the nature of its operations are of what can be expected in the future, the more valid the averaging process is. Conversely, if there have been significant recent changes in the nature of the enterprise's operations, the averaging period may have to be shortened and/or greater emphasis may have to be placed on estimation of future conditions.

Adjustment of Reported Earnings per Share

In our discussion of the adjustment of earnings, we concluded that in determining the earning power of an enterprise, no item of income and expense should be excluded. Since every item of income or expense is part of the enterprise's operating experience, the question is only to what year items should be assigned or into what period of time they should be included when an average of earnings is computed.

For purposes of analysis or comparison, analysts may, however, wish to focus on an adjusted level of earnings for a short period, for example, for two years. This can be done by adding to, or removing from, reported earnings per share selected items of income or expense that were included therein. If this is to be done on a per share basis, every item must be adjusted for tax effect (by using the enterprise's effective tax rate unless the applicable tax rate is otherwise specified) and must be divided by the number of shares that are used in the basic computation of earnings per share.

The following example of such suggested analytical adjustments is adapted from a tabulation prepared by "The Quality of Earnings Report"[7] concerning the reported earnings of A. H. Robins Company.

Per share earnings impact

Item	year 2	year 1
Effective tax rate change	+$0.02	
Settlement of Hartz litigation	+0.07	+$0.57
Change to straight-line depreciation	+0.02	
Reserves for losses on Iranian assets	+0.02	−0.15
Loss on sale of divisions	−0.19	
Change to LIFO	−0.07	
Litigation settlements and expense	−0.09	−0.12
Foreign exchange translation	−0.03	−0.04
Above trend R&D expenditures	−0.11	
Higher percent allowance for doubtful accounts	−0.02	
± Per share earnings impact	−$0.38	+$0.26
Per share earnings as reported	*$1.01*	*$1.71*
Add back negative (−) impact to year 2	0.38	
Subtract positive (+) impact from year 1		*(0.26)*
Adjusted earnings per share	$1.39	$1.45

(+) Positive.
(−) Negative.

In the above tabulation, items that increased earnings are listed as positive (+) and items that diminished earnings are listed as negative

---

[7] Published by Reporting Research Corporation, Englewood Cliffs, N.J.

(−). Thus, in order to remove them from reported earnings, positive items are deducted while negative items are added back. The validity of each adjustment is, of course, a matter for the analyst's judgment.

THE FORECASTING OF EARNINGS

A major objective of income analysis is the forecasting of income. From an analytical point of view, the evaluation of the level of earnings is closely related to their forecast. This is so because a valid forecast of earnings involves an analysis of each major component of income and a considered estimate of its probable future size. Thus, some of the considerations discussed above are also applicable to earnings forecasting.

Forecasting must be differentiated from extrapolation. The latter is based on an assumption of the continuation of an existing trend and involves, more or less, a mechanical extension of that trend into the uncharted territory of the future.

Forecasting, on the other hand, is based on a careful analysis of as many individual components of income and expense as is possible and a considered estimate of their future size taking into consideration interrelationships among the components as well as probable future conditions. Thus, forecasting requires as much detail as is possible to obtain. In addition, the "stability" of the individual components must be assessed in terms of the likelihood of their future recurrence. This lends particular importance to the analysis of nonrecurring factors and of extraordinary items. Some of the mechanics of earnings forecasting were considered in Chapter 4 as part of the process of projecting short-term cash flows.

A financial or earnings projection differs from a forecast in that the assumptions used may not necessarily be the most probable, but rather the assumptions represent a condition that the projection desires to test.

Forecasting requires the use of an earnings record covering a number of periods. Repeated or recurring performance can be forecast with a better degree of confidence than can random events.

Forecasting also requires use of enterprise data by product line or segment wherever different segments of an enterprise are subject to different degrees of risk, possess different degrees of profitability, or have differing growth potentials.

For example, the tabulation of divisional earnings results, in the table below, indicates the degree to which the results of a component of an enterprise can be masked by the aggregate results.

Judgment on the earnings potential of the enterprise depends, of course, on the relative importance, as well as the future prospects, of segment B. The subject of product line reporting was discussed in Chapter 7.

	Earnings in millions			
	year 1	year 2	year 3	year 4
Segment A	$1,800	$1,700	$1,500	$1,200
Segment B	600	800	1,100	1,400
Total net income	$2,400	$2,500	$2,600	$2,600

Can Earnings be Forecast?

Statistical studies by Little,[8] and Little and Rayner[9] in England, and by Brealey[10] in the United States, documented the apparent random behavior of reported earnings. Since these studies showed that earnings growth occurs in an almost purely random fashion, the implication was drawn that earnings changes cannot be accurately forecasted. Here again we have the problem of deriving from the behavior of large aggregates conclusions about what can or cannot be done in individual cases. Operationally, such generalized conclusions are of very limited practical use.

Serious forecasting is not done by the naive extrapolation of past growth trends of earnings. It is done by a painstaking analysis of the *components* of earnings, the revenues, and the expenses, as well as of all factors that are known or are expected to alter these in the period of the forecast. No knowledgeable forecaster would work only with the earnings figure that is merely a net residual. Thus, it was reported[11] that Days Inns, a motel chain, has been including forecasts in its annual reports for years and that their accuracy was satisfactory to many users, including bankers. Nor is it hard to envisage highly accurate forecasts in such businesses as apartment buildings or hospitals. It is equally easy to find business categories where forecasting would be very difficult and unreliable.

A paper[12] that undertook a comprehensive review of the research on earnings forecasts concluded: "We feel that both the properties of earnings forecasts and the question of their value continues to be a fertile area of research." It is equally clear that those seriously interested in the earnings forecasting function will find the study of specific tools and conditions to be of considerably more value than the statistical study of large aggregates.

---

[8] I. M. D. Little, "Higgledy Piggledy Growth" (Oxford, Eng.: Oxford University Institute of Statistics, 1962).

[9] I. M. D. Little and Rayner, "Higgledy Piggledy Growth Again" (Oxford, Eng.: Basil Blackwell, 1966).

[10] Richard A. Brealey, *Introduction to Risk and Return from Commerce Stocks* (Cambridge, Mass.: MIT Press, 1983).

[11] *Forbes,* October 26, 1981, p. 189.

[12] A. R. Abdel-Khalik and R. B. Thompson, "Research on Earnings Forecasts: The State of the Art," *The Accounting Journal,* Winter 1977–78.

SEC Disclosure Requirements—Aid to Forecasting

The "Management's Discussion and Analysis of Financial Condition and Results of Operations" disclosure requirements of the SEC (see Chapter 7) contain a wealth of information on management's views and attitudes as well as on factors that can influence enterprise operating performance. Consequently, the analyst may find much information in these analyses to aid in the forecasting process. Moreover, while not requiring it, the SEC encourages the inclusion in these discussions of forward-looking information.

Elements in Earnings Forecasts

Granted that the decision maker is interested primarily in future prospects, the approach to assessing them must be based primarily on the present as well as on the past. While expected future changes in conditions must be given recognition, the experience of the present and the past form the base to which such adjustments are applied. In doing this, the analyst relies on the degree of continuity and perseverance of momentum that is the common experience of the enterprise and the industry of which it is part. Random shocks and sudden changes are always possible, but they can rarely be foreseen with any degree of accuracy.

The importance to the analyst of the underlying continuity of business affairs should not be overemphasized. One should not confuse the basis for the projection of future results, which the past record represents, with the forecast which is the end product. As a final objective, the analyst is interested in a projection of net income. Net income is the result of the offset of two big streams: (1) total revenues and (2) total costs.

Considering that net income represents most frequently but a relatively small portion of either stream, one can see how a relatively minor change in either of these large streams can cause a very significant change in net income.

A significant check on the reasonableness of an earnings projection is to test it against the return on invested capital which is implicit in the forecast. If the result is at variance with returns realized in the past and industry returns, the underlying assumptions must be thoroughly examined so that the reasons for such deviations can be pinpointed.

In terms of the framework examined in Chapter 6, the ROI depends on earnings that are a product of *management* and of *assets* that require funds for their acquisition.

1. Management. It is well known that it takes resourceful management to "breathe life" into assets by employing them profitably and causing their optimum utilization. The assumption of stability of relationships and trends implies that there has been no major change in the skill, the depth, and the continuity of the management group or a radical change in the type of business in which their skill has been proven by a record of successful performance.

2. Assets. The second essential ingredient to profitable operations is funds or resources with which the assets essential to the successful conduct of business are acquired. No management, no matter how ingenious, can expand operations and have an enterprise grow without an adequate asset base. Thus, continuity of success and the extrapolation of growth must be based on an investigation of the sources of additional funds that the enterprise will need and the effect of the method of financing on net income and earnings per share.

The financial condition of the enterprise, as was seen in Chapters 3 and 5, can have a bearing on the results of operations. A lack of liquidity may inhibit an otherwise skillful management, and a precarious or too risky capital structure may lead to limitations by others on its freedom of action.

The above factors, as well as other economic, industry, and competitive factors, must be taken into account by the analyst when forecasting the earnings of an enterprise. Ideally, in forecasting earnings, the analyst should add a lot of knowledge about the future to some knowledge of the past. Realistically the analyst must settle for a lot of knowledge about the past and present and only a limited knowledge of the future.

In evaluating earnings trends, the analyst relies also on such indicators of future conditions as capital expenditures, order backlogs, as well as demand trends in individual product lines.

It is important to realize that no degree of sophistication in the techniques used in earnings forecasting can eliminate the inevitable uncertainty to which all forecasts are subject. Even the best and most soundly based projections retain a significant probability of proving widely off the mark because of events and circumstances that cannot be foreseen.

The most effective means by which the analyst and decision maker can counter this irreducible uncertainty is to keep close and constant watch over how closely actual results conform to his forecasts. This requires a constant monitoring of results and the adjustment and updating of projections in the light of such results. The monitoring of earnings is considered later in this chapter.

Publication of Financial Forecasts

Recent years have witnessed intensified interest in publication by companies of forecasts of earnings and other financial data. The publication of forecasts in Britain in certain specialized situations as well as a belief that forecasts would be useful to investors were major factors behind this interest. This type of forecasting by insiders (i.e., management) is to be distinguished from forecasts made by financial analysts that are based on all the information that they can obtain.

Speagle, Clark, and Elgers have categorized assumptions underlying forecasted financial statements as (1) "ongoing assumptions relating to the forecast methodology, company operating characteristics, and so on; (2) standard assumptions bearing upon the continuity in accounting policy, company management, supply sources, etc.; and (3) transitory assumptions covering events in a particular year such as recapitalizations, labor settlements, new product introductions, facilities expansion, etc."[13]

The validity of any forecasted financial data depends to a high degree on the assumptions, both implicit and explicit, upon which the forecasting technique is based. The financial analyst who uses a management forecast as input to his own projections should pay first and primary attention to the assumptions on which it is based.

In early 1977, an advisory committee to the SEC recommended that the agency design procedures to encourage companies to make forecasts of their economic performance. Following this, the SEC deleted from its regulations a reference to predictions of "earnings" as possibly misleading in certain situations. Thus the Commission will no longer object to disclosure in filings with it of projections that are made in good faith and have a reasonable basis, provided that they are presented in appropriate form and are accompanied by information adequate for investors to make their own judgments. In 1978 the SEC issued "Guides for Disclosure of Projections of Future Economic Performance."

Following this up, in 1979 the SEC issued a rule intended to encourage companies to make public their financial forecasts by protecting them from lawsuits in case their predictions did not come true. These "safe harbor" rules against fraud charges will protect companies as long as their projections have a "reasonable basis" and are made in good faith. Because of practical legal considerations few companies have availed themselves of these "safe harbor" rules and published forecasts.

The interest in financial forecasts has resulted in a formal consideration of some of the issues by the AICPA which in 1975 issued two statements on the subject.[14]

These statements recommend, among others, that financial forecasts should be presented in a historical financial statement format and that they include regularly a comparison of the previous forecast with attained results.

Both statements recognize the primary importance that assumptions play in the reliability and creditability of a financial forecast. Consequently, those assumptions that management thinks most crucial or significant to the forecast—or are key factors upon which the financial results

---

[13] R. E. Speagle, J. J. Clark, and P. Elgers, *Publishing Financial Forecasts: Benefits, Alternatives, Risk* (Laventhol Krekstein Horwath & Horwath, 1974).

[14] "Guidelines for Systems for the Preparation of Financial Forecasts" and "Presentation and Disclosure of Financial Forecasts," AICPA, 1975. (Auditing implications are also being considered.)

of the enterprise depends—should be disclosed to provide the greatest benefit to users of forecasts. There ordinarily should be some indication of the basis or rationale for these assumptions.

In 1980, the Financial Forecasts and Projections Task Force of the AICPA issued a *Guide for a Review of a Financial Forecast.* This publication set forth the scope as well as the procedures to be followed by an accountant in reviewing a financial forecast and the method of reporting on such a review.

AUDITED FINANCIAL FORECASTS AND PROJECTIONS

In 1985, the AICPA's Auditing Standards Board issued its first Statement on Standards for Accountants' Services on Prospective Financial Information, entitled "Financial Forecasts and Projections." The Statement establishes standards for three types of services that independent accountants can render to clients for prospective financial statements: *(a)* compilation, *(b)* examination, and *(c)* application of agreed-upon procedures.

The Statement
- Defines a financial "forecast" and "projection."
- Establishes procedures and reporting standards for a compilation service on prospective financial statements.
- Establishes procedures and reporting standards for an examination service on prospective financial statements.
- Establishes standards for service to apply agreed-upon procedures to prospective financial statements.
- Prohibits an accountant from compiling, examining, or applying agreed-upon procedures to prospective financial statements that omit a summary of significant assumptions. Also prohibits the accountant from association with a "projection" when intended for other than limited use.

A *financial forecast* consists of ". . . prospective financial statements that present, to the best of the responsible party's knowledge and belief, an entity's expected financial position, results of operations, and changes in financial position." A financial forecast, then, reflects what is expected to happen if the entity follows its existing plans and if stated assumptions regarding its business and economic environment are reasonably accurate. It may be expressed either as a single set of expected results or in terms of a range of expected results.

A *financial projection* consists of ". . . prospective financial statements that present, to the best of the responsible party's knowledge and belief, given one or more hypothetical assumptions, an entity's expected financial position." Thus, a financial projection is helpful in evaluating the effects of alternative courses of action upon expected results. It may be expressed either as a single set of expected results or in terms of a range of expected results.

MONITORING PERFORMANCE AND RESULTS

The judgments of what the proper financial forecast of an enterprise is or what its earning power is, are based on estimates that hinge on future developments that can never be fully foreseen. Consequently, the best course of action is to monitor performance closely and frequently and to compare it with earlier estimates and assumptions. In this way, one can constantly revise one's estimates and judgments and incorporate the unfolding reality into earlier judgments and conclusions. One of the best ways of monitoring performance is to follow interim reports closely.

Interim Financial Statements

The need to follow closely the results achieved by an enterprise requires frequent updating of such results. Interim financial statements, most frequently issued on a quarterly basis, are designed to fill this need. They are used by decision makers as means of updating current results as well as in the prediction of future results.

If, as we have seen, a year is a relatively short period of time in which to account for results of operations, then trying to confine the measurement of results to a three-month period involves all the more problems and imperfections. For this and other reasons the reporting of interim earnings is subject to serious limitations and distortions. The intelligent use of reported interim results requires that we have a full understanding of these possible problem areas and limitations. The following is a review of some of the basic causes of these problems and limitations, as well as their effect on the determination of reported interim results.

Year-End Adjustments   The determination of the results of operations for a year requires a great many estimates, as well as procedures, such as accruals and the determination of inventory quantities and carrying values. These procedures can be complex, time-consuming, and costly. Examples of procedures requiring a great deal of data collection and estimation include estimation of the percentage of completion of contracts, determination of cost of work in process, the allocation of under- or overabsorbed overhead for the period, and the estimation of year-end inventory levels under the LIFO method. The complex, time-consuming, and expensive nature of these procedures can mean that they are performed much more crudely during interim periods and are often based on records that are less complete than are their year-end counterparts. The result inevitably is a less accurate process of income determination which, in turn, may require year-end adjustments that can modify substantially the interim results already reported.

Seasonality   Many enterprises experience at least some degree of seasonality in their activities. Sales may be unevenly distributed over the year, and so it may be with production and other activities. This tends to distort comparisons among the quarterly results of a single year. It also presents problems in the allocation of many budgeted costs, such as advertising, R&D, and repairs and maintenance. If expenses vary with sales, they should be accrued on the basis of expected sales for the full year. Obviously, the preparer of yearly financial statements has the benefit of hindsight that the preparer of interim statements does not. There are also problems with the allocation of fixed costs among quarters.

ILLUSTRATION 4.   The following is an example of adjustments that can result from seasonal variations: "Because of a seasonal production cycle, and in accordance with practices followed by the Company in reporting interim financial statements prior to year 4, $435,000 of unabsorbed factory overhead has been deferred at July 4, year 5. Due to uncertainties as to production and sales in year 4, $487,000 of such unabsorbed overhead was expensed during the first 6 months of the year."

APB Opinion 28

In its *Opinion 28,* the APB concluded that interim reports should be prepared in accordance with GAAP used in the preparation of the latest financial statements. Adopting mostly the point of view that a quarterly report is an integral part of a full year rather than a discrete period, it calls for the accrual of revenues and for the spreading of certain costs among the quarters of a year. For example, it sanctions the accrual of such year-end adjustments as inventory shrinkages, quantity discounts, and uncollectible accounts; but it prohibits the accrual of advertising costs on the ground that benefits of such costs cannot be anticipated. Losses cannot, generally, be deferred beyond the interim period in which they occur. LIFO inventory liquidations should be considered on an annual basis. Only permanent declines in inventory values are to be recorded on an interim basis. Moreover, the *Opinion* calls for the inclusion of extraordinary items in the interim period in which they occur.[15] Income taxes should be accrued on the basis of the effective tax rate expected to apply to the full year.

---

[15] *SFAS 3* specifies that "if a cumulative effect type accounting change is made in other

SEC Interim Reporting Requirements

The SEC took a relatively early and strong interest in interim reporting and as a result brought about very significant improvements in reporting and disclosure in this area. In 1972, it required quarterly reports (on Form 10-Q) and reports on current developments (Form 8-K), disclosure of separate fourth quarter results, and details of year-end adjustments.

In 1975, the SEC issued requirements (now in codification of *FRR,* Sections 301, 303, and 304) that served to expand substantially the content and the utility of interim reports filed with the Commission. The principal requirements include:

Comparative quarterly and year-to-date abbreviated income statement data—this information may be labeled *unaudited* and must also be included in annual reports to shareholders. (Small companies are exempted.)

Year-to-date statements of changes of cash flow.

Comparative balance sheets.

Increased pro forma information on business combinations accounted for as purchases.

Conformity with the principles of accounting measurement as set forth in professional pronouncements on interim financial reports. Increased disclosure of accounting changes with a letter from the registrant's independent public accountant stating whether or not he or she judges the changes to be preferable.

Management's narrative analysis of the results of operations, explaining the reasons for material changes in the amount of revenue and expense items from one quarter to the next. (See discussion in Chapter 7.)

Indications as to whether a Form 8-K was filed during the quarter—reporting either unusual charges or credits to income or a change of auditors.

Signature of the registrant's chief financial officer or chief accounting officer.

In promulgating these expanded disclosure requirements, the Commission indicated that it believed that these disclosures will assist investors in understanding the pattern of corporate activities throughout a fiscal period. It maintained that presentation of such quarterly data will

---

than the first interim period of an enterprise's fiscal year, no cumulative effect of the change shall be included in net income of the period of change. Instead, financial information for the pre-change interim periods of the fiscal year in which the change is made shall be restated by applying the newly adopted accounting principle to those pre-change interim periods."

supply information about the trend of business operations over segments of time which are sufficiently short to reflect business turning points.

Campbell Soup (Chapter 2, Appendix B) presents quarterly data in item 184 .

Implications for Analysis

While there have been some notable recent improvements in the reporting of interim results, the analyst must remain constantly aware that accuracy of estimation and the objectivity of determinations are and remain problem areas that are inherent in the measurement of results of very short periods. Moreover, the limited association of auditors with interim data, while lending some unspecified degree of assurance, cannot be equated to the degree of assurance that is associated with fully audited financial statements. SEC insistence that the professional pronouncements on interim statements (such as *APB Opinion 28*) be adhered to can offer analysts some additional comfort. However, not all principles promulgated by the APB on the subject of interim financial statements result in presentations useful to the analyst. For example, the inclusion of extraordinary items in the results of the quarter in which they occur will require careful adjustment to render them meaningful for purposes of analysis.

While the normalization of expenses is a reasonable intraperiod accounting procedure, the analyst must be aware of the fact that there are no rigorous standards or rules governing its implementation and that it is consequently subject to possible abuse. The shifting of costs between periods is generally easier than the shifting of sales; and, therefore, a close analysis of sales may yield a more realistic clue to a company's true state of affairs for an interim period.

Since the price of the common stock influences the computation of earnings per share, the analyst should in the evaluation of per share results be alert to the separation of these market effects from those related to the operating fundamentals of an enterprise.

Some problems of seasonality in interim results of operations can be overcome by considering in the analysis not merely the results of a single quarter, but also the year-to-date cumulative results which incorporate the results of the latest available quarter. This is the most effective way of monitoring the results of an enterprise and bringing to bear on its analysis the latest data on operations that are available.

QUESTIONS

1. Distinguish between income and cash flow. Why should there be a distinction between the two?

2. *a.* What is meant by *quality of earnings?* Why do analysts assess it?

   b. On what major elements does the quality of earnings depend?

3. *a.* What are discretionary costs?

   b. Of what significance are discretionary costs to an analysis of the quality of earnings?

4. *a.* Why is the evaluation of R&D costs important in the analysis and projection of income?

   b. What are some of the precautions required in analyzing R&D expenses?

5. *a.* What is the relationship between the carrying amounts of various assets and the earnings reported?

   b. What is the relationship between the amounts at which liabilities, including provisions, are carried and earnings are reported?

6. In what way is balance sheet analysis a check on the validity as well as the quality of earnings?

7. Comment on the effect which the "risk category" of an asset has on the quality of reported earnings.

8. Explain briefly the relationship between the quality of earnings and the following balance sheet items:

   a. Accounts receivable.

   b. Inventories.

   c. Deferred charges.

9. What is the effect of external factors on the quality of earnings?

10. What is the objective of recasting the income statement?

11. Where will the analyst find data needed for the analysis of the results of operations and for their recasting and adjustment?

12. What is the aim of the recasting process, and how is the recasting accomplished?

13. Describe the income statement adjustment process.

14. What is income smoothing? How can it be distinguished from outright falsehoods?

15. Name and explain three forms of income smoothing.

16. *a.* What factors and incentives motivate companies to engage in income smoothing?

   b. What are the implications for analysis?

17. Why are managements so greatly interested in the reporting of extraordinary gains and losses?

18. What are the basic objectives of the analyst in the identification and the evaluation of extraordinary items?

19. *a.* Into what categories can items which are described as unusual or extraordinary in the financial statements be usefully subdivided for purposes of analysis?

   b. Give examples of each such category.

   c. How should the analyst treat items in each category? Is such a treatment indicated under all circumstances? Explain.

20. What are the effects of extraordinary items on:

   a. Enterprise resources?

   b. The evaluation of managements?

21. Comment on the following statement:
    "Extraordinary gains or losses have not resulted from a 'normal' or 'planned' activity of management and, consequently, they should not be used in the evaluation of managerial performance."
    Do you agree?
22. What is the difference between forecasting and extrapolation of earnings?
23. How can SEC disclosure requirements aid in forecasting?
24. What are the categories of assumptions underlying forecasted financial statements? Give examples of each category. What is the importance of these assumptions to the financial analyst?
25. What is earning power? Why is it important?
26. *a.* What are interim financial statements used for?
    b. What accounting problems that are peculiar to interim statements must the analyst be aware of?
27. Interim financial reporting can be subject to serious limitations and distortions. Discuss some of the reasons for this.
28. What are the major disclosure requirements by the SEC with regard to interim reports? What are the objectives behind them?
29. What implications do interim reports hold for the financial analyst?

Chapter 10

COMPREHENSIVE ANALYSIS OF FINANCIAL STATEMENTS

THE METHODOLOGY OF FINANCIAL STATEMENT ANALYSIS

The marshaling, arrangement, and presentation of data for purposes of financial statement analysis can be standardized to some extent in the interest of consistency and organizational efficiency. However, the actual process of analysis must be left to the judgment of the analyst so that he or she may allow for the great diversity of situations and circumstances that are likely to be encountered in practice, and thus give full reign to his or her own initiative, originality, and ingenuity. Nevertheless, there are some useful generalizations and guidelines that may be stated as to a general approach to the task of financial statement analysis.

To begin with, financial statement analysis is oriented toward the achievement of definite objectives. In order that the analysis best accomplish these objectives, the first step is to define them carefully. The thinking and clarification leading up to such a definition of objectives is a very important part of the analytical process, for it ensures a clear understanding of objectives, that is, of what is pertinent and relevant and what is not, and thus also leads to avoidance of unnecessary work. This clarification of objectives is indispensable to an *effective* as well as to an *efficient* analysis; *effective,* in that, given the specifications, it focuses on the most important and most relevant elements of the financial statements; *efficient,* in that it leads to an analysis with maximum economy of time and effort.

ILLUSTRATION 1. The bank loan officer, dealing with a request for a short-term loan to finance inventory, may define his objective as assessing the intention and the ability of the borrower to repay the loan on time. Thus, the analyst can concentrate on what is needed to achieve this objective and need not, for instance, address himself to industry conditions that can affect the borrowing entity only over the longer term.

Once the objective of the analysis has been defined, the next step is the formulation of specific questions the answers to which are needed in the achievement of such objectives.

ILLUSTRATION 2. The loan officer in Illustration 1 now needs to define the critical criteria that will affect his decision. For instance, the question of the borrower's *willingness* to repay the short-term loan bears on his character; and financial statement analysis can reveal only the history of past loans granted it. Thus, tools other than financial statement analysis will have to be employed to get complete information on the borrower's character.

Among the other questions on which the loan officer will need information are the following:

1. What is the enterprise's short-term liquidity?
2. What will its sources and uses of cash be during the duration of the loan agreement?

Financial statement analysis can go far toward providing answers to such questions.

Having defined the objective and having translated it into specific questions and criteria that must be resolved, the analyst is ready for the third step in the analysis process. This is to decide which tools and techniques of analysis are the most appropriate, effective, and efficient ones to use in working on the particular decision problem at hand.

ILLUSTRATION 3. Following the sequence developed in Illustrations 1 and 2, the loan officer will now decide which financial statement analysis tools are the most appropriate to use in this case. He may choose one or more of the following:

1. Short-term liquidity ratios.
2. Inventory turnover measures.
3. Cash flow projections.
4. Analyses of changes in financial position.

These analyses will have to include estimates and projections of future conditions toward which most, if not all, financial analysis is oriented.

The fourth and final step in analysis is the interpretation of the data and measures assembled as a basis for decision and action. This is the most critical and difficult of the steps, and the one requiring the application of a great deal of judgment, skill, and effort. Interpretation is a process of investigation and evaluation, and of envisaging the reality that lies behind the figures examined. There is, of course, no mechanical substitute for this process of judgment. However, the proper definition of the problem and of the critical questions that must be answered, as well as the skillful selection of the most appropriate tools of analysis available in the circumstances, will go a long way toward a meaningful interpretation of the results of analysis.

ILLUSTRATION 4. Following the sequences of the first three examples above, the collection, by the loan officer, of the data described in Illustration 3 is, of course, not the end result of his analysis. These data must be integrated, evaluated, and interpreted for the purposes of reaching the basic decision of whether to make the loan and, if so, in what amount.

By way of analogy, the weather forecasting function provides an example of the difference between the availability of analytical data and its successful interpretation. Thus, the average listener to weather information does not know how to interpret barometric pressure, relative humidity, or wind velocity. What one needs to know is the weather forecast that results from an interpretation of these data.

The intelligent analyst and interpreter of financial statement data must always bear in mind that a financial statement is at best an abstraction of an underlying reality. Further mathematical manipulation of financial data can result in second, third, and even further levels of abstractions; and the analyst must always keep in mind the business reality behind the figures. No map of the Rocky Mountains can fully convey the grandeur of the terrain. One has to see them in order to appreciate them because maps, like financial statements, are, at best, abstractions. That is why security analysts must, at some point, leave the financial statements and visit the companies that they analyze in order to get a full understanding of the phenomena revealed by their analysis. This is particularly true because the static reality portrayed by the abstractions found in the financial statements cannot remain stable for very long. Reality is ever changing.

A recognition of the inherent limitations of financial data is needed for intelligent analysis. This does not detract from their importance because financial statements and data are the only means by which the financial realities of an enterprise can be reduced to a common denominator that is quantified and that can be mathematically manipulated and projected in a rational and disciplined way.

SIGNIFICANCE OF THE "BUILDING BLOCK" APPROACH TO FINANCIAL ANALYSIS

The six major building blocks of financial analysis that we have examined in this text are:

1. Short-term liquidity.
2. Funds flow.
3. Capital structure and long-term solvency.
4. Return on investment (ROI).
5. Asset utilization.
6. Operating performance.

The building block approach to financial statement analysis involves:

1. The determination of the major objectives that a particular financial analysis is to achieve.
2. Arriving at a judgment about which of the six major areas of analysis (i.e., our "building blocks") must be evaluated with what degree of emphasis and in what order of priority.

For example, the security analyst, in the evaluation of the investment merit of a particular issue of equity securities, may attach primary importance to the earning capacity and potential of the enterprise. Thus, the first building block of the analysis will be the evaluation of *operating performance* and the next, perhaps, *return on investment (ROI)*. A thorough analysis will, of course, require that attention be paid to the other four major areas of analysis, although with perhaps lesser degrees of emphasis; that is, depth. This attention to the other major areas of analysis is necessary in order to detect possible problem areas; that is, areas of potential risk. Thus, further analysis may reveal a liquidity problem arising from a "thin" working capital condition, or it may reveal a situation of inadequate capital funds that may stifle growth and flexibility. It is conceivable that these problem areas may reveal themselves to be so important as to overshadow the question of earning power, thus leading to a change in the relative emphasis that the analyst will accord to the main areas of his or her particular analysis.

While the subdivision of the analysis into six distinct aspects of a company's financial condition and performance is a useful approach, it must be borne in mind that these areas of analysis are highly interrelated. For example, the operating performance of an enterprise can be affected by the lack of adequate capital funds or by problems of short-term liquidity. Similarly, a credit evaluation cannot stop at the point where a satisfactory short-term liquidity position has been determined because existing or incipient problems in the "operating performance" area may result in serious drains of funds due to losses. Such drains can quickly reverse the satisfactory liquidity position that may prevail at a given point in time.

At the start of the analysis, the analyst will tentatively determine the relative importance of the areas that he or she will examine and the order in which they will be examined. This order of emphasis and priority may subsequently change in the light of the analyst's findings and as the analysis progresses.

THE EARMARKS OF GOOD FINANCIAL ANALYSIS

As we have noted, the foundation of any good analysis is a thorough understanding of the objectives to be achieved and the uses to which it is going to be put. Such understanding leads to economy of effort as well as to a useful and most relevant focus on the points that need to be clarified and the estimates and projections that are required.

In practice, rarely can all the facts surrounding a particular analysis be obtained, so that most analyses are undertaken on the basis of incomplete and inadequate facts and data. The process of financial analysis is basically one of reducing the areas of uncertainty—which can, however, never be completely eliminated.

A written analysis and report is not only a significant medium of communication to the reader but it also serves importantly to organize the thinking of the analyst as well as to allow him or her to check the flow and the logic of the presentation. The process of writing reinforces our thinking and vice versa. As we revise our words, we also refine our thoughts—and improvements in style lead, in turn, to the sharpening and improvement in the thinking process itself.

A good analysis separates clearly for the reader the interpretations and conclusions of the analysis from the facts and data upon which they are based. This not only separates fact from opinion and estimate but also enables the reader to follow the rationale of the analyst's conclusions and allows him to modify them as his judgment dictates. To this end, the analysis should contain distinct sections devoted to:

1. General background material on the enterprise analyzed, the industry of which it is a part, and the economic environment in which it operates.
2. Financial and other data used in the analysis as well as ratios, trends, and other analytical measures that have been developed from them.
3. Assumptions as to the general economic environment and as to other conditions on which estimates and projections are based.
4. A listing of positive and negative factors, quantitative and qualitative, by important areas of analysis.
5. Projections, estimates, interpretations, and conclusions based on the aforementioned data. (Some analyses list only the positive and negative factors developed by the analysis and leave further interpretations to the reader.)

A good analysis should start with a brief "Summary and Conclusion" section as well as a table of contents to help the busy reader decide how much of the report he wants to read and on which parts of it to concentrate.

The writer of an analytical report must guard against the all-too-common tendency to include irrelevant matter. For example, the reader need not know the century-old details of the humble beginnings of the enterprise under analysis nor should he be taken on a "journey" along all the fruitless byways and missteps that the analyst inevitably encountered in the process of ferreting out and separating the important from the insignificant. Irrelevant bulk or "roughage" can only serve to confuse and distract the reader of a report.

Ambiguities and equivocations that are employed to avoid responsibility or to hedge conclusions do not belong in a good analytical report. Finally, the writers of such reports must recognize that we are all judged on the basis of small details. Consequently, the presence of mistakes in grammar or of obvious errors of fact in a report can plant doubt in the reader's mind as to the competence of the author and the validity of the analysis.

SPECIAL INDUSTRY OR
ENVIRONMENTAL CHARACTERISTICS

In this book, the analysis of the various segments of financial statements was treated from the point of view of the ordinary commercial or industrial enterprise. The financial analyst must, however, recognize that there are industries with distinct accounting treatments that arise either from their specialized nature or from the special conditions, such as governmental regulation, to which they are subject. The analysis of the financial statements of such enterprise requires a thorough understanding of the accounting peculiarities to which they are subject, and the analyst must, accordingly, prepare himself for his task by the study and the understanding of the specialized areas of accounting that affect his particular analysis.

Thus, for example, the analysis of a company in the oil and gas industry requires a thorough knowledge of accounting concepts peculiar to that industry such as the determination of "cost centers," prediscovery costs, discovery costs, and the disposition of capitalized costs. There are particular problems in the treatment of exploratory, development, and other expenditures as well as in amortization and depletion practices.

Life insurance accounting, to cite another example, also requires specialized knowledge that arises from the peculiarities of this industry and from the regulation to which it is subject. There are special problems in the area of recognition of premium revenues, the accounting for acquisition costs of new business, and the determination of policy reserves.

Public utility regulation has resulted in specialized accounting concepts and problems of which every utility analyst must be aware. There are tax allocation problems resulting in differences among companies that "normalize" taxes versus those which "flow" them through. Then there are problems related to the adequacy of provisions for depreciation, and problems concerning the utility's "rate base" and the method by which it is computed.

As in any field of endeavor, specialized areas of inquiry require that specialized knowledge be brought to bear upon them. Financial analysis is, of course, no exception.

ILLUSTRATION OF A COMPREHENSIVE ANALYSIS OF FINANCIAL STATEMENTS—CAMPBELL SOUP COMPANY

The following analysis of the financial statements and other data of the Campbell Soup Company (Campbell) will serve as an illustration of this process.

Introduction

Campbell Soup Company is one of the world's largest and best-known food companies which manufactures prepared convenience foods for human consumption.

The company's operations are managed by three divisions; Campbell North America, Campbell Biscuit and Bakery, and Campbell International. Within each division there are groups and business units; as an example, within the Campbell North America division the major sectors are Soups, Convenience Meals, Grocery, Condiments, and the Canadian company operations.

The company's products are primarily for home use, but various items are also manufactured for restaurants, vending machines, and institutions. The company distributes its products through direct customers, including chain stores, wholesalers, and distributors that maintain central warehouses, institutional and industrial customers, convenience stores, club stores, and certain governmental agencies. In the United States, sales solicitation activities are conducted by subsidiaries and through independent brokers and contract distributors. No material part of the business is dependent upon a single customer. Shipments are made promptly by the company after receipt and acceptance of orders; therefore, there is no significant backlog of unfilled orders.

Exhibit 10–1 shows sales contribution by division for 1986 to 91. As can be seen, Campbell North America and International are the largest contributors of sales, accounting for 68.7 percent and 19.7 percent, respectively, in 1991.

Soup is the core business of Campbell U.S.A., with about 60 percent of the overall soup market, and the more recent introductions of dry, ramen noodle, and microwavable soups. Other Campbell Soup brands include ready-to-serve soups—"Home Cooking," "Chunky," and "Healthy Request." An integral part of the soup business is Swanson's canned chicken broth. Americans purchase more than 2.5 billion cans of

Exhibit 10–1

CAMPBELL SOUP COMPANY

	1991	1990	1989	1988	1987	1986
Sales contribution by division (in millions)						
Campbell North America:						
Campbell U.S.A.	$3,911.8	$3,932.7	$3,666.9	$3,094.1	$2,881.4	$2,910.1
Campbell Canada	352.0	384.0	313.4	313.1	312.8	255.1
	4,263.8	4,316.7	3,980.3	3,407.2	3,194.2	3,165.2
Campbell Biscuit and Bakery:						
Pepperidge Farm	569.0	582.0	548.4	495.0	458.5	420.1
International Biscuit	219.4	195.3	178.0	—	—	—
	788.4	777.3	726.4	495.0	458.5	420.1
Campbell International	1,222.9	1,189.8	1,030.3	1,036.5	897.8	766.2
Interdivision	(71.0)	(78.0)	(64.9)	(69.8)	(60.1)	(64.7)
Total sales	$6,204.1	$6,205.8	$5,672.1	$4,868.9	$4,490.4	$4,286.8
Percent of sales by division						
Campbell North America:						
Campbell U.S.A.	63.0%	63.4%	64.7%	63.6%	64.2%	67.9%
Campbell Canada	5.7	6.2	5.5	6.4	6.9	5.9
	68.7	69.6	70.2	70.0	71.1	73.8
Campbell Biscuit and Bakery:						
Pepperidge Farm	9.2	9.4	9.7	10.2	10.2	9.8
International Biscuit	3.5	3.1	3.1	—	—	—
	12.7	12.5	12.8	10.2	10.2	9.8
Campbell International	19.7	19.2	18.2	21.3	20.0	17.9
Interdivision	(1.1)	(1.3)	(1.2)	(1.4)	(1.3)	(1.5)
Total sales	100.0%	100.0%	100.0%	100.0%	100.0%	100.0%

Campbell's soups each year, and on average have nine cans in their pantry at any time during the year.

Fiscal 1991 was a successful transition year for Campbell. Major divestitures were completed and significant restructuring and reorganization projects were accomplished. Corporate goals concerning earnings, returns, and cash flows were exceeded. The North America and International divisions had exceptionally strong earnings results. The company entered fiscal 1992 with a reconfigured product portfolio, positioned well to support a continued strong financial performance. The strong margin growth had given Campbell an opportunity to increase consumer advertising which fostered the introduction of new products, line extensions, and continued revitalization of flagship products.

FINANCIAL STATEMENTS

The financial statements of Campbell Soup which are included in the 1991 annual report, along with the notes and commentaries contained therein and data from Form 10-K are presented in Chapter 2, Appendix B. Exhibits 10–2, 10–3, and 10–4 present summary financial statements for the six fiscal years ending in 1991.

The auditor's opinions on the financial statements have been unqualified for the past six years.

ADDITIONAL INFORMATION

Exhibit 10–5 presents growth rates, annually compounded, for periods as described. Most impressive is the growth in net income per share over the past five years (12.93%). Growth in sales per share over the most recent five-year period has been at a rate lower than that of net income. Equity per share growth in the latest 5-year period declined compared to the 10-year period. This, plus the two cells in the exhibit which show negative growth rates, is due to the significant divestitures and restructuring implemented in 1989 and 1990.

Exhibits 10–6 through 10–9 are based on the financial statements of Campbell.

FOCUS OF ANALYSIS

Based on the foregoing data and information, we are to analyze the financial statements of Campbell Soup Company with the following alternative points of view (objectives) in mind.

1. That of a bank which has been requested to make available to the

Exhibit 10–2

CAMPBELL SOUP COMPANY
Income Statements
For Years 1986 to 1991

	1991	1990	1989	1988	1987	1986
Net sales	$6,204.1	$6,205.8	$5,672.1	$4,868.9	$4,490.4	$4,286.8
Costs and expenses:						
Cost of product sold	4,095.5	4,258.2	4,001.6	3,392.8	3,180.5	3,082.7
Marketing and selling expenses	956.2	980.5	818.8	733.3	626.2	544.4
Administrative expenses	306.7	290.7	252.1	232.6	213.9	195.9
Research and development expenses	56.3	53.7	47.7	46.9	44.8	42.2
Interest expense	116.2	111.6	94.1	53.9	51.7	56.0
Interest income	(26.0)	(17.6)	(38.3)	(33.2)	(29.5)	(27.4)
Foreign exchange losses, net	0.8	3.3	19.3	16.6	4.8	0.7
Other expense (income)	26.2	14.7	32.4	(3.2)	(9.5)	5.5
Divestitures, restructuring, and unusual charge	0.0	339.1	343.0	40.6	0.0	0.0
Total costs and expenses	5,531.9	6,034.2	5,570.7	4,480.3	4,082.9	3,900.0
Earnings before equity in earnings of affiliates and minority interests	672.2	171.6	101.4	388.6	407.5	386.8
Equity in earnings of affiliates	2.4	13.5	10.4	6.3	15.1	4.3
Minority interests	(7.2)	(5.7)	(5.3)	(6.3)	(4.7)	(3.9)
Earnings before taxes	667.4	179.4	106.5	388.6	417.9	387.2
Taxes on earnings	265.9	175.0	93.4	147.0	170.6	164.0
Earnings before cumulative effect of accounting change	401.5	4.4	13.1	241.6	247.3	223.2
Cumulative effect of change in accounting for income taxes	0	0	0	32.5	0	0
Net earnings	$401.5	$4.4	$13.1	$274.1	$247.3	$223.2
Net earnings per share	$3.16	$0.03	$0.10	$2.12*	$1.90	$1.72
Weighted average shares outstanding	127.00	126.60	129.30	129.30	129.90	129.50

* Including $0.25 per share cumulative effect of change in accounting for income taxes

333

Exhibit 10–3

CAMPBELL SOUP COMPANY
Balance Sheets
For Years 1986 to 1991
(in millions)

	July 28, 1991	July 29, 1990	July 30, 1989	July 31, 1988	August 2, 1987	August 3, 1986
Assets						
Current assets						
Cash and cash equivalents	$ 178.90	$ 80.70	$ 120.90	$ 85.80	$ 145.00	$ 155.10
Other temporary investments, at cost which approximates market	12.80	22.50	26.20	35.00	280.30	238.70
Accounts receivable	527.40	624.50	538.00	486.90	338.90	299.00
Inventories	706.70	819.80	816.00	664.70	623.60	610.50
Prepaid expenses	92.70	118.00	100.40	90.50	50.10	31.50
Total current assets	1,518.50	1,665.50	1,601.50	1,362.90	1,437.90	1,334.80
Plant assets, net of depreciation	1,790.40	1,717.70	1,540.60	1,508.90	1,349.00	1,168.10
Intangible assets, net of amortization	435.50	383.40	466.90	496.60	—	—
Other assets	404.60	349.00	323.10	241.20	310.50	259.90
Total assets	$4,149.00	$4,115.60	$3,932.10	$3,609.60	$3,097.40	$2,762.80
Liabilities and Shareowners' Equity						
Current liabilities						
Notes payable	$282.20	$202.30	$271.50	$138.00	$93.50	$88.90
Payable to suppliers and others	482.40	525.20	508.20	446.70	374.80	321.70
Accrued liabilities	408.70	491.90	392.60	236.90	182.10	165.90
Dividend payable	37.00	32.30	29.70	—	—	—
Accrued income taxes	67.70	46.40	30.10	41.70	43.40	49.60
Total current liabilities	1,278.00	1,298.10	1,232.10	863.30	693.80	626.10

Long-term debt	772.60	805.80	629.20	525.80	380.20	362.30
Other liabilities, principally deferred income taxes	305.00	319.90	292.50	325.50	287.30	235.50
Shareowners' equity						
Preferred stock; authorized 40,000,000 sh.; none issued	—	—	—	—	—	—
Capital stock, $0.15 par value; authorized 140,000,000 sh.; issued 135,622,676 sh.	20.30	20.30	20.30	20.30	20.30	20.30
Capital surplus	107.30	61.90	50.80	42.30	41.10	38.10
Earnings retained in the business	1,912.60	1,653.30	1,775.80	1,879.10	1,709.60	1,554.00
Capital stock in treasury, at cost	(270.40)	(107.20)	(70.70)	(75.20)	(46.80)	(48.40)
Cumulative translation adjustments	23.60	63.50	2.10	28.50	11.90	(25.10)
Total shareowners' equity	1,793.40	1,691.80	1,778.30	1,895.00	1,736.10	1,538.90
Total liabilities and shareowners' equity	$4,149.00	$4,115.60	$3,932.10	$3,609.60	$3,097.40	$2,762.80

Exhibit 10–4

CAMPBELL SOUP COMPANY
Consolidated Statements of Cash Flows
For Years 1986 to 1991
(in millions)

	1991	1990	1989	1988	1987	1986	Total
Cash flows from operating activities:							
Net earnings	$401.5	$ 4.4	$ 13.1	$274.1	$247.3	$223.2	$1,163.6
To reconcile net earnings to net cash provided by operating activities:							
Depreciation and amortization	208.6	200.9	192.3	170.9	144.6	126.8	1,044.1
Divestitures and restructuring provision	—	339.1	343.0	17.6	—	—	699.7
Deferred taxes	35.5	3.9	(67.8)	13.4	45.7	29.0	59.7
Other, net	63.2	18.6	37.3	43.0	28.0	16.6	206.7
Cumulative effect of accounting change	—	—	—	(32.5)	—	—	(32.5)
(Increase) decrease in accounts receivable	17.1	(60.4)	(46.8)	(104.3)	(36.3)	(3.6)	(234.3)
(Increase) decrease in inventories	48.7	10.7	(113.2)	54.2	(3.9)	23.1	19.6
Net change in other current assets and liabilities	30.6	(68.8)	(0.6)	30.2	42.9	48.7	83.0
Net cash provided by operating activities	805.2	448.4	357.3	466.6	468.3	463.8	3,009.6
Cash flows from investing activities:							
Purchases of plant assets	(361.1)	(387.6)	(284.1)	(245.3)	(303.7)	(235.3)	(1,817.1)
Sale of plant assets	43.2	34.9	39.8	22.6	—	29.8	170.3
Businesses acquired	(180.1)	(41.6)	(135.8)	(471.9)	(7.3)	(20.0)	(856.7)
Sale of businesses	67.4	21.7	4.9	23.5	20.8	—	138.3
Increase in other assets	(57.8)	(18.6)	(107.0)	(40.3)	(50.1)	(18.0)	(291.8)
Net change in other temporary investments	9.7	3.7	9.0	249.2	(60.7)	(144.1)	66.8
Net cash used in investing activities	(478.7)	(387.5)	(473.2)	(462.2)	(401.0)	(387.6)	(2,590.2)

Cash flows from financing activities:

Long-term borrowings	402.8	12.6	126.5	103.0	4.8	203.9	853.6
Repayments of long-term borrowings	(129.9)	(22.5)	(53.6)	(22.9)	(23.9)	(164.7)	(417.5)
Increase (decrease) in short-term borrowings*	(137.9)	(2.7)	108.2	8.4	(20.7)	4.6	(40.1)
Other short-term borrowings	117.3	153.7	227.1	77.0	89.3	72.9	737.3
Repayments of other short-term borrowings	(206.4)	(89.8)	(192.3)	(87.6)	(66.3)	(88.5)	(730.9)
Dividends paid	(137.5)	(124.3)	(86.7)	(104.6)	(91.7)	(104.6)	(649.4)
Treasury stock purchases	(175.6)	(41.1)	(8.1)	(29.3)	—	—	(254.1)
Treasury stock issued	47.7	12.4	18.5	0.9	1.6	4.0†	85.1
Other, net	(0.1)	(0.1)	23.5	2.3	18.6	17.9	62.1
Net cash provided (used in) financing activities	(219.6)	(101.8)	163.1	(52.8)	(88.3)	(54.5)	(353.9)
Effect of exchange rate change on cash	(8.7)	0.7	(12.1)	(10.8)	(7.1)	(3.7)	(41.7)
Net increase (decrease) in cash and cash equivalents	98.2	(40.2)	35.1	(59.2)	(28.1)	18.0	23.8
Cash and cash equivalents at the beginning of year	80.7	120.9	85.8	145.0	173.1	155.1	760.6
Cash and cash equivalents at the end of year	178.9	80.7	120.9	85.8	145.0	173.1	784.4

* With less than three months maturities.
† 2.8 issued for a pooling of interest.

Exhibit 10–5

CAMPBELL SOUP COMPANY

Five-year growth rates*
(annually compounded)

Per share	1986–1991	1986–1988 to 1989–1991
Sales........................	8.09%	5.95%
Net income	12.93	−10.53
Dividends	11.50	6.69
Equity	3.55	0.53

Ten-year growth rates*
(annually compounded)

Per share	1981–1991	1981–1983 to 1989–1991
Sales........................	8.51%	7.22%
Net income	12.19	−0.44
Dividends	8.18	6.62
Equity	6.22	5.13

* Growth rates (annually compounded) are computed using the compound interest method.

$$\text{Future value } (FV) = \text{Present value} \quad (PV) \times \left(1 + \frac{r}{100}\right)^n$$

For example, net sales per share during 1986–1991 grew at a rate of:

$$PV = \$33.10$$
$$FV = \$48.85 \qquad FV = PV\left(1 + \frac{r}{100}\right)^n$$
$$n = 5 \qquad\qquad 48.8 = 33.1\left(1 + \frac{r}{100}\right)^5$$
$$r = \text{rate of growth} \qquad r = 8.09\%$$

company a line of credit (for short-term operating purposes) of up to $60 million.

2. That of an insurance company to whom the company wants to sell privately $50 million of 25-year bonds.
3. That of an investor considering a substantial investment in the company.

These diverse and broad points of view require that we analyze all major aspects of the company's financial condition and results of operations, that is:

1. Short-term liquidity.
2. Funds flow.
3. Capital structure and long-term solvency.

Exhibit 10-6

CAMPBELL SOUP COMPANY
Common Size Income Statements
For Years 1986 to 1991

	1991	1990	1989	1988	1987	1986
Net sales	100.00%	100.00%	100.00%	100.00%	100.00%	100.00%
Costs and expenses:						
Cost of products sold	66.01%	68.62%	70.55%	69.68%	70.83%	71.91%
Marketing and selling expenses ...	15.41	15.80	14.44	15.06	13.95	12.70
Administrative expenses	4.94	4.68	4.44	4.78	4.76	4.57
Research and development expenses ...	0.91	0.87	0.84	0.96	1.00	0.98
Interest expense	1.87	1.80	1.66	1.11	1.15	1.31
Interest income	(0.42)	(0.28)	(0.68)	(0.68)	(0.66)	(0.64)
Foreign exchange losses, net	0.01	0.05	0.34	0.34	0.11	0.02
Other expense (income)	0.42	0.24	0.57	(0.07)	(0.21)	0.13
Divestitures, restructuring, and unsual charge ...	—	5.46	6.05	0.83	—	—
Total costs and expenses	89.17%	97.23%	98.21%	92.02%	90.93%	90.98%
Earnings before equity in earnings of affiliates and minority interests	10.83%	2.77%	1.79%	7.98%	9.07%	9.02%
Equity in earnings of affiliates	0.04	0.22	0.18	0.13	0.34	0.10
Minority interests	(0.12)	(0.09)	(0.09)	(0.13)	(0.10)	(0.09)
Earnings before taxes	10.76%	2.89%	1.88%	7.98%	9.31%	9.03%
Taxes on earnings	4.29	2.82	1.65	3.02	3.80	3.83
Earnings before cumulative effect of accounting change	6.47%	0.07%	0.23%	4.96%	5.51%	5.21%
Cumulative effect of change in accounting for income taxes ..	—	—	—	0.67	—	—
Net earnings	6.47%	0.07%	0.23%	5.63%	5.51%	5.21%

Exhibit 10–7

CAMPBELL SOUP COMPANY
Common Size Balance Sheets
For Years 1986 to 1991

	July 28, 1991	July 29, 1990	July 30, 1989	July 31, 1988	August 2, 1987	August 3, 1986	Industry Composite
Current assets							
Cash and cash equivalents	4.31%	1.96%	3.07%	2.38%	4.69%	5.61%	3.4%
Other temporary investments, at cost which approximates market	0.31	0.55	0.67	0.97	9.05	8.64	16.5
Accounts receivable	12.71	15.17	13.68	13.49	10.94	10.82	38.6
Inventories	17.03	19.92	20.75	18.41	20.13	22.10	2.2
Prepaid expenses	2.23	2.87	2.55	2.51	1.62	1.14	
Total current assets	36.60%	40.47%	40.73%	37.76%	46.43%	48.31%	60.70%
Plant assets, net of depreciation	43.15	41.74	39.18	41.80%	43.55%	42.28%	21.0%
Intangible assets, net of amortization	10.50	9.32	11.87	13.76	–	–	
Other assets	9.75	8.48	8.22	6.68	10.02	9.41	18.3
Total assets	100.00%	100.00%	100.00%	100.00%	100.00%	100.00%	100.00%
Current liabilities							
Notes payable	6.80%	4.92%	6.90%	3.82%	3.02%	3.22%	6.7%
Payable to suppliers and others	11.63	12.76	12.92	12.38	12.10	11.64	10.2
Accrued liabilities	9.85	11.95	9.98	6.56	5.88	6.00	15.8
Dividend payable	0.89	0.78	0.76	–	–	–	
Accrued income taxes	1.63	1.13	0.77	1.16	1.40	1.80	
Total current liabilities	30.80%	31.54%	31.33%	23.92%	22.40%	22.66%	32.70%

Long-term debt	18.62%	19.58%	16.00%	14.57%	12.27%	13.11%	19.7%
Other liabilities, principally deferred income taxes	7.35	7.77	7.44	9.02	9.28	8.52	1.5
Shareowners' equity							
Preferred stock; authorized 40,000,000 sh.; none issued	—	—	—	—	—	—	
Capital stock, $0.15 par value; authorized 140,000,000 sh.; issued 135,622,676 sh.	0.49	0.49	0.52	0.56	0.66	0.73	
Capital surplus	2.59	1.50	1.29	1.17	1.33	1.38	
Earnings retained in the business	46.10	40.17	45.16	52.06	55.19	56.25	
Capital stock in treasury, at cost	-6.52	-2.60	-1.80	-2.08	-1.51	-1.75	
Cumulative translation adjustments	0.57	1.54	0.05	0.79	0.38	-0.91	
Total shareowners' equity	43.22%	41.11%	45.23%	52.50%	56.05%	55.70%	46.10%
Total liabilities and shareowners' equity	100.00%	100.00%	100.00%	100.00%	100.00%	100.00%	100.00%

Exhibit 10–8

CAMPBELL SOUP COMPANY
Trend Index of Selected Accounts
(1986 = 100)

	1991	1990	1989	1988	1987	1986
Cash and cash equivalents	115%	52%	78%	55%	93%	$ 155.1
Accounts receivable	176	209	180	163	113	299.0
Temporary investments	5	9	11	15	117	238.7
Inventory	116	134	134	109	102	610.5
Total current assets	114	125	120	102	108	1,334.8
Total current liabilities	204	207	197	138	111	626.1
Working capital	34	52	52	70	105	708.7
Plant assets, net	153	147	132	129	115	1,168.1
Other assets	156	134	124	93	119	259.9
Long-term debt	213	222	174	145	105	362.3
Total liabilities	192	198	176	140	111	1,223.9
Shareowners' equity	117	110	116	123	113	1,538.9
Net sales	145	145	132	114	105	4,268.8
Cost of products sold	133	138	130	110	103	3,082.7
Administrative and research						
expenses	157	148	129	119	109	195.9
Marketing and sales expenses ...	176	180	150	135	115	544.4
Interest expense	199	191	161	104	101	58.5
Total costs and expenses	142	155	143	115	105	3,900.0
Earnings before taxes	172	46	28	100	108	387.2
Net income	180	2*	6*	123	111	223.2

* Excluding the net effect of divestitures, restructuring, and unusual charges, will change these amounts to: 1990—137 and 1989—123

Exhibit 10–9

CAMPBELL SOUP COMPANY
Per Share Results

	1991	1990	1989	1988	1987	1986
Sales	$48.85	$47.88	$43.87	$37.63	$34.57	$33.10
Net income	3.16	0.03	0.10	2.12	1.90	1.72
Dividends	1.12	0.98	0.90	0.81	0.71	0.65
Book value (shareowners'						
equity)	14.12	13.09	13.76	14.69	13.35	11.86
Average shares outstanding						
(in millions)	127.0	129.6	129.3	129.4	129.9	129.5

4. Return on investment (ROI).
5. Asset utilization.
6. Operating performance.

In this analysis Industry Composite figures are used for comparison purposes. These are drawn primarily from Dun & Bradstreet Industry Norms and Key Business Ratios, and are based on composite financial statements constructed from the 1991 financial statements of companies included in the SIC classification 2033.

ANALYSIS OF SHORT-TERM LIQUIDITY

Exhibit 10–10 presents some important measures of short-term liquidity over the past six years along with comparative data.

The current ratio of the company in 1991 is at its lowest level in the last six years under analysis. At 1.19 it is relatively lower than the industry composite of 1.86. This is due in part to the rate of growth in current liabilities in recent years, where we find them double what they were in 1986, while current assets in 1991 are only 114 percent of the 1986 level. A substantial amount of notes payable were reclassified as long-term debt in 1990. This contributed to improvement of the current ratio. Exhibit 10–11 reveals that the cash and cash equivalents in 1991 represent a greater proportion of current assets (11.78%) than is the case with the industry composite (5.60%).

Campbell's acid-test ratio in the last three years (0.56) is only slightly below the 1991 industry composite (0.61). Exhibit 10–7 shows the relative variation between current assets included in the acid-test ratio and current liabilities of the company and those of the industry composite. As can be seen from Exhibits 10–7 and 10–11, inventories represent a much lower proportion of total assets (17%) and total current assets (46.5%) than they do for the industry (63.6% and 22%, respectively). Also, inventory turnover for Campbell in 1991 is 5.37 times versus 2.53 for the industry average. These are strong indicators that Campbell does not tie up a great amount of funds in inventory relative to the industry average. This conclusion is strengthened by looking at Exhibit 10–8, where inventory growth is much slower than growth in sales (116% vs. 145%). Further, these improvements in inventory management may be seen to be a result of Campbell's institution of the "just-in-time" inventory system particularly at the raw materials level. Exhibit 10–12 sets forth data on Campbell's inventories. Over the years there had been a decline in the proportion of raw materials to total inventories, a trend confirming the above conclusion.

The company uses the LIFO inventory method to account for approximately 70% of consolidated inventories in 1991 and 64% in 1990

Exhibit 10–10

CAMPBELL SOUP COMPANY
Short-Term Liquidity Analysis

Units		1991	1990	1989	1988	1987	1986	Industry composite
1. Ratio	Current ratio	1.19	1.28	1.30	1.58	2.07	2.13	1.86
2. Ratio	Acid-test ratio	0.56	0.56	0.56	0.70	1.10	1.11	0.61
3. Times	Accounts receivable turnover	10.77	10.68	11.07	11.79	14.08	15.13	8.37
4. Times	Inventory turnover	5.37	5.21	5.41	5.27	5.15	5.14	2.53
5. Days	Collection period for ending A/R	30.60	36.23	34.15	36.00	27.17	25.11	43.01
6. Days	Days to sell ending inventory	62.12	69.31	73.41	70.53	70.59	71.29	142.03
7. Days	Conversion period	92.72	105.54	107.56	106.53	97.76	96.40	185.32
8. Percent	Cash to current assets	11.78%	4.84%	7.55%	6.30%	10.14%	11.62%	5.60%
9. Percent	Cash to current liabilities	14.00%	6.22%	9.81%	9.94%	20.90%	24.77%	10.40%
10. Days	Liquidity index	59.87	72.62	72.55	71.46	52.29	52.07	130.62
11. M$'s	Working capital	240.50	367.40	369.40	499.60	744.10	708.70	54.33
12. Days	Average no. of days to pay accounts payable	46.03	46.56	46.20	49.30	44.25	39.33	
13. Days	Average net trade cycle	46.69	58.98	61.36	57.23	53.51	57.07	
14. Percent	Cash provided by operations to average current liabilities	62.51%	35.44%	34.10%	60.22%	71.36%	77.34%	

Notes:

For 1991 (in millions):

(3) $\dfrac{\text{Net sales } \boxed{13}}{\text{Average accounts receivable } \boxed{33}} = \dfrac{6{,}204.1}{(527.4 + 624.5)/2} = 10.77$ times

(4) $\dfrac{\text{Cost of products sold } \boxed{14}}{\text{Average inventory } \boxed{34}} = \dfrac{4{,}095.5}{(706.7 + 819.8)/2} = 5.37$ times

(5) $\dfrac{\text{Ending accounts receivable } \boxed{33}}{\text{Sales } \boxed{13} \ / \ 360} = \dfrac{527.4}{6{,}204.1/360} = 30.6$ days

(6) $\dfrac{\text{Ending inventory } \boxed{34}}{\text{Cost of products sold } \boxed{14} \ / \ 360} = \dfrac{706.7}{4{,}095.5/360} = 62.12$ days

(7) = (5) + (6)

(10)

	Days removed from cash		Product
Cash and temporary investments $\boxed{31}$ + $\boxed{32}$	$191.7 \times$	0 =	0
Accounts receivable $\boxed{33}$	$527.4 \times$	30.6 =	16138
Inventories $\boxed{34}$	$706.7 \times$	92.7 =	65511
Prepaid expenses $\boxed{35}$	$92.7 \times$	100^{*} =	9270
	1518.5		90919

* Assumed number.

Liquidity index $= \dfrac{90919}{1518.5} = 59.87$ days

(12) $\dfrac{\text{Accounts payable } \boxed{41}}{\text{Purchases per day}^{\dagger}} = \dfrac{482.4}{10.48} = 46.03$ days

† From Exhibit 10–12.

(13) Number of days' sales in:

Accounts receivable 30.60
Inventories 62.12
                                    92.72
Less: accounts payable 46.03
                                    46.69

(14) $\dfrac{\text{Cash from operation } \boxed{64}}{\text{Beginning + ending current liabilities } \boxed{45} \ \div \ 2} = \dfrac{805.2}{1{,}288} = 62.51$

345

Exhibit 10-11

CAMPBELL SOUP COMPANY
Common-Size Analysis of
Current Assets and Current Liabilities

	July 28, 1991	July 29, 1990	July 30, 1989	July 31, 1988	August 2, 1987	August 3, 1986	Industry composite
Current assets							
Cash and cash equivalents	11.78%	4.85%	7.55%	6.30%	10.09%	11.62%	5.60%
Other temporary investments, at cost which approximates market	0.84	1.35	1.64	2.57	19.49	17.88	—
Accounts receivable	34.73	37.50	33.59	35.72	23.57	22.40	27.18
Inventories	46.54	49.22	50.95	48.77	43.37	45.74	63.60
Prepaid expenses	6.11	7.08	6.27	6.64	3.48	2.36	3.62
Total current assets	100.00%	100.00%	100.00%	100.00%	100.00%	100.00%	100.00%
Current Liabilities							
Notes payable	22.08%	15.58%	22.04%	15.99%	13.48%	14.20%	20.49%
Payable to suppliers and others	37.75	40.46	41.25	51.74	54.02	51.38	31.19
Accrued liabilities	31.98	37.89	31.86	27.44	26.25	26.50	48.32
Dividend payable	2.89	2.49	2.41	—	—	—	
Accrued income taxes	5.30	3.58	2.44	4.83	6.25	7.92	
Total current liabilities	100.00%	100.00%	100.00%	100.00%	100.00%	100.00%	100.00%

Exhibit 10–12

CAMPBELL SOUP COMPANY
Inventory Data
(in millions)

	1991	1990	1989	1988	1987	1986
1. Beginning inventory	$ 819.8	$ 816.0	$ 664.7	$ 623.6	$ 610.5	$ 623.1
2. Plus: production inputs	3,982.4	4,262.0	4,152.9	3,433.9	3,193.6	3,070.1
3. Goods available for sale	4,802.2	5,078.0	4,187.6	4,057.5	3,804.1	3,693.2
4. Less: Ending inventory	706.7	819.8	816.0	664.7	623.6	610.5
4. Cost of products sold	4,095.5	4,258.2	4,001.6	3,392.8	3,180.5	3,082.7
5. Depreciation	208.6	200.9	192.3	170.9	144.6	126.8
6. (2) – (5) = Purchases	3,773.8	4,061.1	3,960.6	3,263.0	3,049.0	2,943.3
7. (6) / 360 = Purchases per day	$ 10.48	$ 11.28	$ 11.00	$ 9.06	$ 8.47	$ 8.18
Ending inventories:						
Raw materials, containers, and supplies	$ 342.3	$ 384.4	$ 385.0	$ 333.4	$ 333.6	$ 340.4
Finished products	454.0	520.0	519.0	412.5	372.4	348.1
	796.3	904.4	904.0	745.9	706.0	688.5
Less: Adjustment of inventories to LIFO	89.6	84.6	88.0	81.2	82.4	78.5
Total	$ 706.7	$ 819.8	$ 816.0	$ 664.7	$ 623.6	$ 610.5
Raw materials, containers, and supplies	43.0%	42.5%	42.6%	44.7%	47.3%	49.4%
Finished products	57.0	57.5	57.4	55.3	52.7	50.6
	100.0%	100.0%	100.0%	100.0%	100.0%	100.0%

Exhibit 10–13

CAMPBELL SOUP COMPANY
Inventory Data under FIFO
(in millions)

	1991	1990	1989	1988	1987	1986
Beginning inventory	$ 904.4	$ 904.0	$ 745.9	$ 706.0	$ 688.5	$ 707.0
Production inputs (same as under LIFO)	3,982.4	4,262.0	4,152.9	3,433.9	3,193.6	3,070.1
Goods available for sale	4,886.8	5,166.0	4,898.8	4,139.9	3,882.1	3,777.1
Less: Ending inventory	796.3	904.4	904.0	745.9	706.0	688.5
Cost of products sold (FIFO)	$4,090.5	$4,261.6	$3,994.8	$3,394.0	$3,176.1	$3,088.6
Cost of products sold (LIFO)	$4,095.5	$4,258.2	$4,001.6	$3,392.8	$3,180.5	$3,082.7
Effect of restatement to FIFO is to increase (decrease) cost of products sold by:	$ (5.0)	$ 3.4	$ (6.8)	$ 1.2	$ (4.4)	$ 5.9
Net of tax* effect of restatement to FIFO is to decrease (increase) net income by:	$ (3.3)	$ 2.2	$ (4.5)	$ 0.8	$ (2.4)	$ 3.2
* Tax rate	34.0%	34.0%	34.0%	34.0%	45.0%	46.0%

(disclosure in item $\boxed{153A}$). Exhibit 10–13 contrasts the effect on income resulting from the company's use of the LIFO method as opposed to the FIFO method. Normally, in times of rising prices LIFO income is lower than FIFO income. However, we see here that this was true in Campbell's case only every other year, 1987, 1989, and 1991. During the other years the opposite was true. This may be due to declining costs, and possibly inventory liquidation, at least in two of the three years. There is, of course, a limit to how much income can, over the years, benefit from LIFO liquidation.

The accounts receivable turnover has declined over the past six years, but it is still above the industry level in 1991 (Exhibit 10–10). In addition, Exhibit 10–8 shows that accounts receivable grew much faster than sales, and reached a peak in 1990 (209), then declined in 1991 (176). This may indicate a more aggressive credit policy in recent years to forestall the effects of the general state of economic recession.

As can be seen from Exhibit 10–10, the collection period for A/R deteriorated between 1986–90, then started to turn around in the right direction in 1991. The same, to a lesser degree, can be said about the number of days to sell inventory. However, the conversion period in 1991 is back to 92.7 days versus 96.4 days in 1986, due primarily to an enhanced inventory turnover, which causes Campbell to compare favorably in its conversion period against the industry norms.

Campbell has managed its current liabilities with varying results. Overall, the tendency over the last three years has been for the average days to pay A/P (Exhibit 10–10) to stay relatively stable. The company's average net trade cycle has fluctuated during the last six years. However, in 1991 it is back below the 1986 level of 46.7 (vs. 57 days), which corroborates the conclusion of improving liquidity.

ANALYSIS OF CASH FLOWS

This analysis has two main objectives:

1. To analyze the statement of cash flows (SCF) in order to assess the implications on longer term flows of cash (e.g., long-term solvency) and to discern cash flow patterns over time.
2. To supplement the static measures used to assess short-term liquidity by means of a short-term cash flow forecast.

We will start with an analysis of Cash Flow from Operations (CFO), that very important subset of total cash flows. Campbell presents cash flows from operations by the indirect method and so we recast these to the analytically more significant and useful inflow-outflow format (also known as the direct method), as shown in Exhibit 10–14.

Exhibit 10–14

CAMPBELL SOUP COMPANY
Analysis of Cash from Operations
Utilizing the Inflow-Outflow Format
(in millions)

	1991	1990	1989	1988	1987	1986
Inflows:						
Net sales	$6,204.1	$6,205.8	$5,672.1	$4,868.9	$4,490.4	$4,286.8
(Increase) decrease in accounts receivable	17.1	(60.4)	(46.8)	(104.3)	(36.3)	(3.6)
Cash collections on sales	6,221.2	6,145.4	5,625.3	4,764.6	4,454.1	4,283.2
Interest income	26.0	17.6	38.3	33.2	29.5	27.4
Total cash collections from operations	6,247.2	6,163.0	5,663.6	4,797.8	4,483.6	4,310.6
Outflows:						
Cost of products sold*	3,823.7	4,038.7	3,772.0	3,178.9	3,007.9	2,939.3
Marketing and sales expenses	956.2	980.5	818.8	733.3	626.2	544.4
Administrative expenses	306.7	290.7	252.1	232.6	213.9	195.9
Foreign exchange losses	0.8	3.3	19.3	16.6	4.8	0.7
Interest expense	116.2	111.6	94.1	53.9	51.7	56.0
Adjusted by: (Increase) decrease in deferred taxes	(35.5)	(3.9)	67.8	(13.4)	(45.7)	(29.0)
Research and development expenses	56.3	53.7	47.7	46.9	44.8	42.2
Other expenses (income)	26.2	14.7	32.4	19.8	(9.5)	5.5
Increase (decrease) in inventories	(48.7)	(10.7)	113.2	(54.2)	3.9	(23.1)
Net change in other current assets and liabilities	(30.6)	68.8	0.6	(30.2)	(42.9)	(48.7)
Income tax expense	265.9	175.0	93.4	147.0	170.6	164.0
Net effect of equity in earnings of affiliates and minority interests†	4.8	(7.8)	(5.1)	0.0	(10.4)	(0.4)
Total cash outflows for operations	5,442.0	5,714.6	5,306.3	4,331.2	4,015.3	3,846.8
Cash from operations	$ 805.2	$ 448.4	$ 357.3	$ 466.6	$ 468.3	$ 463.8

* Adjusted by items which don't effect cash. For 1991:

Cost of products sold as per IS (item 14)	$4095.5
Less: Depreciation and amortization as per SCF (item 57)	208.6
Less: Other, net as per SCF (item 60)	63.2
	$3823.7

† This is aggregated for convenience. It is also correct to include dividend receipts under "inflows."

This analysis reveals that CFO represents a steady and growing source of cash for Campbell especially in 1991 ($805 million). The interruption in this trend in 1989 is due primarily to the increase in inventories (113 millions) and the negative (decrease in) deferred taxes (68 millions). The increase in inventories is due to management's objective to improve customer service. As for the deferred taxes, the large amounts of restructuring and unusual charges which were not tax deductible resulted in credits to tax expense of about $78 million, but higher *current* tax liabilities. It is noteworthy that the sharp declines in net income in 1989 and 1990 had no effect on CFO, because the declines resulted from large restructuring and divestiture charges which had no cash effects in those years.

Cash outflows maintained an increasing trend throughout 1990. In 1991 outflows declined due mainly to a decline in cost of products sold, combined with relatively lower marketing and selling expenses, and a relatively higher decrease in inventories, and less payables. Those factors were partially offset by higher taxes and other expenses.

Overall, Campbell has been able to translate, over the years, its growing sales and lately its enhanced margin into a commensurately growing stream of operating cash flows.

Exhibit 10–15, on pages 354–355, presents the common-size consolidated statements of cash flows for the six years ending with 1991 as well as the composite of that period. This exhibit affords an interesting and instructive overview of the company's cash flow patterns over the past six years. Thus, temporary or erratic changes, such as caused by the relatively high usage of cash in investing activities in 1987 (62%), can be seen in perspective and are smoothed out by the aggregate figures for the six years shown in the "total" column.

Over the years, cash provided by operations constituted about half of all cash inflows. This, in conjunction with the fact that financing activities were mostly refinancing in nature (using only 7% of cash inflows) is a fair testimony to the soundness and the strength of Campbell's financial condition and financing practices.

Cash used for acquisition of assets and businesses represented, over the six-year period, about 50 percent of cash inflows and dividends about 12%. In summary, cash inflows from operations (56%) and net cash used in financing (7%) approximate the net cash used in investing activities (48%). Therefore, the cash position throughout the six-year period tended to stay even while fluctuating somewhat. It grew by less than half of one percent (0.44%) during the period.

A summary of cash inflows and outflows by major categories of activity is analytically instructive. From Exhibit 10–4, we can extract the following tabulation of cash inflows and outflows (in millions). (See the table on the following page):

Summary of Cash Inflows and Outflows by Major Category of Activity

	1991	1990	1989	1988	1987	1986	Total
From operations	$805.2	$448.4	$357.3	$466.6	$468.3	$463.8	$3,009.6
Investing activities	(478.7)	(387.5)	(473.2)	(462.2)	(401.0)	(387.6)	(2,590.2)
Financing activities	(219.6)	(101.8)	(163.1)	(52.8)	(88.3)	(54.5)	(353.9)
Increase (decrease) in cash	98.2	(40.2)	35.1	(59.2)	(28.1)	18.0	23.8

The remarkable picture that emerges from an analysis of Campbell's major cash flows is that throughout the six-year period cash from operations (CFO) has supported substantial investing outlays of about $2.6 billion, financing outlays (inclusive of dividends) of about $354 million, and a slight cumulative increase in cash. In 1987, 1988, and 1990 cash balances were drawn down to support investing and financing activities. Overall, especially with 1991 included, the CFO was adequate to fund all of the company's investing and financing needs leaving excess cash of $24 million.

Having considered the pattern of cash flows over recent years we can now turn to a short-term cash flow forecast which will supplement the static measures of short-term liquidity which were covered earlier.

A first step in the projection of CFO is the projection of earnings. Exhibit 10–16, on page 356, is a projected statement of earnings for Campbell for 1992. Sales are projected to be approximately 2.35 percent higher than 1991.[1]

Net earnings in fiscal 1992 are projected at $480.0 million, which is approximately 20 percent higher than in 1991. This increase reflects more the increase in operating margin than in sales. The profit margin expansion is primarily due to an easing in manufacturing costs, where labor cost has increased very modestly, lately, and the cost of metal food containers was considerably lower in the recent past, due to increased competitive conditions and greater capacity in the aluminum industry. In addition, financing costs are expected to decrease, benefiting from the decline in short-term interest rates. Campbell is also expected to enjoy additional favorable operating leverage as a result of a major restructuring program.

Expenses are calculated based on the assumptions stated in Exhibit 10–16. Taxes on earnings are estimated on the basis of the current federal statutory tax rate of 34 percent.

Exhibit 4–9, which presents a Projected Statement of Cash Flows for fiscal 1992 and fiscal 1993, is mainly based on the presentation above, in addition to its own set of assumptions. The projected statements indicate that, based on the assumptions as stated, Campbell is expected to finance the expected level of investments in plant assets and acquisition of businesses mainly from cash from operations, and even redeem some of its high coupon long-term debts. In fact, should these projections hold, Campbell will have enough free cash for dividends and other uses.

Exhibit 10–17 presents two additional measures of Campbell's cash flows. The purpose of the cash flow adequacy ratio is to evaluate the degree to which the company generated sufficient cash from operations to cover capital expenditures, investment in inventories, and cash dividends.

---

[1] The estimate is corroborated in *The Value Line Investment Survey* of February 21, 1992.

Exhibit 10–15

CAMPBELL SOUP COMPANY
Common-Size Consolidated Statements of Cash Flows*
For Years 1986 to 1991

	1991	1990	1989	1988	1987	1986	Total
Cash flows from operating activities:							
Net earnings	26.89%	0.54%	1.15%	25.14%	38.42%	27.88%	21.54%
To reconcile net earnings to net cash provided by operating activities:							
Depreciation and amortization	13.97	24.58	16.82	15.67	22.47	15.84	19.33
Divestitures and restructuring provisions	—	41.49	30.00	1.61	—	—	12.95
Deferred taxes	2.38	0.48	(5.93)	1.23	7.10	3.62	1.11
Other, net	4.23	2.28	3.26	3.94	4.35	2.07	3.83
Cumulative effect of accounting change	—	—	—	(2.98)	—	—	(0.60)
(Increase) decrease in accounts receivable	1.15	(7.39)	(4.09)	(9.57)	(5.64)	(0.45)	(4.34)
(Increase) decrease in inventories	3.26	1.31	(9.90)	4.97	(0.61)	2.89	0.36
Net change in other current assets and liabilities	2.05	(8.42)	(0.05)	2.77	6.67	6.08	1.54
Net cash provided by operating activities	53.92	54.86	31.25	42.80	72.76	57.94	55.72
Cash flows from investing activities:							
Purchases of plant assets	(24.18)%	(47.42)%	(24.85)%	(22.50)%	(47.19)%	(29.39)%	(33.64)%
Sale of plant assets	2.89	4.27	3.48	2.07		3.72	3.15
Businesses acquired	(12.06)	(5.09)	(11.88)	(43.28)	(1.13)	(2.50)	(15.86)
Sale of businesses	4.51	2.66	0.43	2.16	3.23	—	2.56
Increase in other assets	(3.87)	(2.28)	(9.36)	(3.70)	(7.78)	(2.25)	(5.40)
Net change in other temporary investment	0.65	0.45	0.79	22.86	(9.43)	(18.00)	1.24
Net cash used in investing activities	(32.06)	(47.41)	(41.39)	(42.39)	(62.31)	(48.42)	(47.95)

Cash flows from financing activities:

Long-term borrowings	26.97%	1.54%	11.07%	9.45%	0.75%	25.47%	15.80%
Repayments of long-term borrowings	(8.70)	(2.75)	(4.69)	(2.10)	(3.71)	(20.57)	(7.73)
Increase (decrease) in short-term borrowings	(9.23)	(0.33)	9.46	0.77	(3.22)	0.57	(0.74)
Other short-term borrowings	7.86	18.81	19.87	7.06	13.88	9.11	13.65
Repayments of other short-term borrowings	(13.82)	(10.99)	(16.82)	(8.03)	(10.30)	(11.06)	(13.53)
Dividends paid	(9.21)	(15.21)	(7.58)	(9.59)	(14.25)	(13.07)	(12.02)
Treasury stock purchases	(11.76)	(5.03)	(0.71)	(2.69)	—	—	(4.70)
Treasury stock issued	3.19	1.52	1.62	0.08	0.25	0.50	1.58
Other, net	(0.01)	(0.01)	2.06	0.21	2.89	2.24	1.15
Net cash provided (used in) financing activities	(14.71)	(12.46)	14.27	(4.84)	(13.72)	(6.81)	(6.55)
Effect of exchange rate change on cash	(0.58)%	0.09%	(1.06)%	(0.99)%	(1.10)%	(0.46)%	(0.77)%
Net increase (decrease) in cash and cash equivalents	6.58	(4.92)	3.07	(5.43)	(4.37)	2.25	0.44

* Common-size percentages are based on total cash inflows of all kinds = 100%. For 1991 the 100% is composed of:
CFO + Sale of plant assets + Sale of bus. + Decrease in temp. invest. + LT borrowings + ST borrowings + Treas. st. issued
53.92 + 2.89 + 4.51 + 0.65 + 26.97 + 7.86 + 3.19

Exhibit 10–16

CAMPBELL SOUP COMPANY
Projected Statement of Earnings
For Year Ended August 2, 1992
(in millions)

		Percent
Net sales*	$6,350.0	100.00%
Costs and expenses:†		
Cost of products sold	4,095.8	64.50
Marketing and selling expenses	990.6	15.60
Administrative expenses	308.0	4.85
Research and development expense	57.2	0.90
Interest expense	114.3	1.80
Interest income	(31.8)	−0.50
Other expense (income), including foreign		
exchange losses	88.9	1.40
Total costs and expenses	5,623.0	88.55%
Earnings before taxes‡	727.0	11.45
Taxes on earnings§	(247.0)	−3.89
Net earnings	$ 480.0	7.56%

* Projected at approximately 2.35 % higher than 1991 sales of $6,204.1. *The Value Line Investment Survey,* Feb. 21, 1992 release.

  † Based on the following assumptions:

    —Cost of products sold is expected to be 64.5% of 1992 sales. It is along the lines of the 1989–91 average and recognizes the enhancement in the gross margin in recent years, which resulted from the series of divestitures and restructurings.

    —Marketing and selling expenses are expected to be along the lines of the 1989–91 average with a slight increase due to increase in advertising.

    —Administrative expenses are expected to increase slightly from the 1989–91 average.

    —All other items are assumed to be approximately at the same relative level as 1989–91 average.

  ‡ Effects of equity in earnings of affiliates and minority interests are ignored as immaterial.

  § At the federal statutory rate of 34%.

Campbell's cash flow adequacy ratio for the six-year period is approximately 0.88, which means that funds generated from operations were not sufficient to cover the items in the denominator, and there was a need for external financing. However, this is an aggregate ratio and when we look at individual years, particularly 1991, we find that this problem did not show up in most years, except for 1987 and 1989.

The cash reinvestment ratio measures the percentage of the investment in assets that is being retained and reinvested in the enterprise for replacement of assets and for the growth in operations. Campbell's average reinvestment ratio is 11.8 percent for the six-year period. This reinvestment rate is at a satisfactory level. The 1991 reinvestment rate is at a

Exhibit 10–17

CAMPBELL SOUP COMPANY
Analysis of Cash Flow Ratios
(in millions)

(1) Cash flow adequacy ratio $= \dfrac{\text{6-year sum of sources of cash from operations}}{\substack{\text{6-year sum of capital expenditures, inventory} \\ \text{additions, and cash dividends}}}$

$= \dfrac{3,009.6}{(1817.1 + 856.7) + (113.2 + 3.9) + 649.4}$

$= 0.875$

(All amounts are per SCF)

(2) Cash reinvestment ratio $= \dfrac{\text{Cash provided by operations} - \text{Dividends}}{\text{Gross PPE} + \text{Investments} + \text{Other assets} + \text{W/C}}$

1986 to 1991 $= \dfrac{3009.6 - 649.4}{15,183.7 + 1,888.3 + 2,929.7} = 11.8\%$

1991 $= \dfrac{805.2 - 137.5}{2921.9 + 404.6 + 240.5} = 18.7\%$

1990 $= \dfrac{448.4 - 124.3}{2734.9 + 349.0 + 367.4} = 9.4\%$

1989 $= \dfrac{357.3 - 86.7}{2,543.0 + 323.1 + 369.4} = 8.4\%$

1988 $= \dfrac{466.6 - 104.6}{2539.7 + 241.2 + 499.6} = 11.0\%$

1987 $= \dfrac{468.3 - 91.7}{2355.1 + 310.5 + 744.1} = 11.0\%$

1986 $= \dfrac{463.8 - 104.6}{2089.1 + 259.9 + 708.7} = 11.7\%$

(Numerator amounts are per SCF and denominator amounts are per BS)

much higher level. This ratio has been at an acceptable level over the years except for 1989 and 1990 which is attributable to the decrease in cash from operations for reasons discussed earlier.

ANALYSIS OF CAPITAL STRUCTURE AND LONG-TERM SOLVENCY

Having examined the funds aspect of Campbell Soup's long-term solvency, we now turn to an examination of its capital structure and the risks inherent in it. Changes in the company's capital structure can be gauged by means of a number of measurements and comparisons.

Exhibit 10–18 details the capital structure of Campbell for the six years ended 1991. For analytical purposes half of the deferred taxes were considered as long-term liabilities and the other half as equity. Changes resulting from *SFAS 109,* "Accounting for Income Taxes," and currently applicable corporate tax rates, are likely to slow the growth in deferred taxes. Exhibit 10–19 presents a common-size analysis of the capital structure. In 1991, liabilities constituted 53 percent of total invested capital and equity the balance of 47 percent.

Exhibit 10–20 presents selected capital structure and long-term solvency ratios. The debt to equity ratios have increased markedly in the last three years of the six-year period, but remain below the industry average. The long-term debt component grew the most, which can be seen in Exhibit 10–8, where the trend index of long-term debt (213) has exceeded that of current liabilities (204), total liabilities (192), and especially shareowners' equity (117). However, Campbell's debt to equity ratios compare favorably to the industry composites, except in the case of long-term debt to equity, where in 1991, Campbell shows a ratio of 48 percent versus an industry composite of 43 percent. Furthermore, the analytically adjusted long-term debt to equity ratio does not differ significantly from its unadjusted counterpart. Generally, one can say that Campbell is moving away from the conservative capital structure it used to maintain in the past and turning to a more aggressive one. This is corroborated by a lower level of fixed charge coverage ratios measured by both earnings and cash from operations. The company's long-term debt is rated AA by the major rating agencies, down from the AAA rating the company enjoyed previously, but still a very favorable rating.

Overall, Campbell enjoys outstanding financial strength, ranking A+ according to *The Value Line Investment Survey* release of February 21, 1992. Further, according to the same source, Campbell ranks second in terms of "Safety" on a scale of 1(best) to 5(worst). The company's creditors continue to enjoy sound asset and earning power backing.

ANALYSIS OF RETURN ON INVESTMENT

Exhibit 10–21 presents selected return on investment ratios for Campbell. The return on total assets was essentially stable over the years 1986 to 1988 and declined sharply during fiscal 89 and fiscal 90. It did rebound strongly to 11.75 percent in 1991. The extremely low returns for 89 and 90 are due to substantial divestitures and restructuring charges. We must be alert to the fact that the exceptional improvement in 1991 may be due, in part, to the substantial write-offs of the previous years.

The 1991 RTA was composed of profit margin of 7.83%, and an asset turnover of 1.50. Both these components show improvement over their

Exhibit 10–18

CAMPBELL SOUP COMPANY
Analysis of Capital Structure
(in millions)

	1991	1990	1989	1988	1987	1986
Long-term liabilities:						
Notes payable	$ 757.8	$ 792.9	$ 610.3	$ 507.1	$ 358.8	$ 346.7
Capital lease obligation	14.8	12.9	18.9	18.7	21.4	15.6
Total long-term debt	772.6	805.8	629.2	525.8	380.2	362.3
Deferred income taxes*	129.3	117.6	109.0	140.3	124.0	99.6
Other long-term liabilities	23.0	28.5	19.6	15.6	15.8	16.3
Total long-term liabilities	924.9	951.9	757.8	681.7	520.0	478.2
Current liabilities†	1,278.0	1,298.1	1,232.1	863.3	693.8	626.1
Total liabilities	$2,202.9	$2,250.0	$1,989.9	$1,545.0	$1,213.8	$1,104.3
Equity capital:						
Common shareholders' equity	$1,793.4	$1,691.8	$1,778.3	$1,895.0	$1,736.1	$1,538.9
Minority interests	23.5	56.3	54.9	29.3	23.5	20.1
Deferred income taxes*	129.2	117.5	109.0	140.3	124.0	99.5
Total equity capital	1,946.1	1,865.6	1,942.2	2,064.6	1,883.6	1,658.5
Total liabilities and equity	$4,149.0	$4,115.6	$3,932.1	$3,609.6	$2,097.4	$2,762.8

* For analytical purposes 50 percent of deferred income taxes are considered debt and the balance equity.
† Including notes payable–current.

Exhibit 10–19

CAMPBELL SOUP COMPANY
Common-Size Analysis of Capital Structure

	1991	1990	1989	1988	1987	1986
Long-term liabilities:						
Notes payable	18.26%	19.27%	15.52%	14.05%	11.59%	12.55%
Capital lease obligation	0.36	0.31	0.48	0.52	0.69	0.56
Total long-term debt	18.62	19.58	16.00	14.57	12.28	13.11
Deferred income taxes*	3.12	2.86	2.77	3.88	4.00	3.61
Other long-term liabilities	0.55	0.69	0.50	0.43	0.51	0.59
Total long-term liabilities	22.29%	23.13%	19.27%	18.88%	16.79%	17.31%
Current liabilities†	30.80	31.54	31.34	23.92	22.40	22.66
Total liabilities	53.09%	54.67%	50.61%	42.80%	39.19%	39.97%
Equity capital:						
Common shareholders' equity	43.22	41.11	45.22	52.50	56.05	55.70
Minority interests	0.57	1.37	1.40	0.81	0.76	0.73
Deferred income taxes*	3.12	2.85	2.77	3.89	4.00	3.60
Total equity capital	46.91%	45.33%	49.39%	57.20%	60.81%	60.03%
Total liabilities and equity	100.00%	100.00%	100.00%	100.00%	100.00%	100.00%

* For analytical purposes 50 percent of deferred income taxes are considered debt and the balance equity.
† Including notes payable–current.

Exhibit 10–20

CAMPBELL SOUP COMPANY
Capital Structure and Long-Term Solvency Ratios

	1991	1990	1989	1988	1987	1986	Industry composite
1. Total debt to equity	1.13	1.21	1.02	0.75	0.64	0.67	1.17
2. Total debt to total debt plus equity	0.53	0.55	0.51	0.43	0.39	0.40	0.54
3. Long-term liabilities to equity	0.48	0.51	0.39	0.33	0.28	0.29	0.43
4. Analytically adjusted long-term liabilities to equity	0.46	0.50	0.38	0.33	0.27	0.28	
5. Total equity to total liabilities	0.88	0.83	0.98	1.34	1.56	1.50	0.86
6. Fixed assets to equity	0.92	0.92	0.79	0.73	0.72	0.70	0.46
7. Short-term liabilities to total liabilities	0.58	0.58	0.62	0.56	0.58	0.57	0.61
8. Ratio of earnings to fixed charges	5.16	2.14	1.84	6.06	6.41	6.28	
9. Cash from operations coverage of fixed charges	7.47	5.27	5.38	8.94	8.69	9.26	

Notes:

$$(1)\ 1991 = \frac{\text{Total liabilities*}}{\text{Equity capital*}} = \frac{2,202.9}{1,946.1} = 1.13$$

$$(2)\ 1991 = \frac{\text{Total liabilities*}}{\text{Total liabilities and equity } \boxed{55}} = \frac{2,202.9}{4,149.0} = 0.53$$

$$(3)\ 1991 = \frac{\text{Long-term liabilities*}}{\text{Equity capital*}} = \frac{924.9}{1,946.1} = 0.48$$

$$(4)\ 1991 = \frac{\begin{array}{c}\text{Long-term liabilities*} +\\ \text{Present value of lease obligations } \boxed{173} -\\ \text{Capitalized lease obligations } \boxed{172}\end{array}}{\begin{array}{c}\text{Equity capital*} +\\ \text{Excess of FIFO over LIFO inventory } \boxed{153}\end{array}} = \frac{924.9 + (21.5 - 14.8)}{1,946.1 + 89.6} = 0.46$$

$$(5)\ 1991 = \frac{\text{Equity capital*}}{\text{Total liabilities*}} = \frac{1,946.1}{2,202.9} = 0.88$$

$$(6)\ 1991 = \frac{\text{Plant assets } \boxed{37}}{\text{Equity capital*}} = \frac{1790.4}{1,946.1} = 0.92$$

$$(7)\ 1991 = \frac{\text{Current liabilities } \boxed{45}}{\text{Total liabilities*}} = \frac{1278.0}{2,202.9} = 0.58$$

$$(8)\ 1991 = \frac{\begin{array}{c}\text{Pre-tax income } \boxed{26} + \text{Interest expense } \boxed{18} +\\ \text{Interest portion of rent expense}^\dagger -\\ \text{Undistributed equity in earnings in affiliates } \boxed{24},\ \boxed{169A}\end{array}}{\begin{array}{c}\text{Interest incurred } \boxed{98} +\\ \text{Interest portion of rent expense}^\dagger\ \boxed{143}\end{array}} = \frac{667.4 + 116.2 + 20 - (2.4 - 8.2)}{136.9 + 20} = 5.16$$

$$(9)\ 1991 = \frac{\begin{array}{c}\text{Cash flows from operations } \boxed{64} +\\ \text{Current tax expense } \boxed{124A} + \text{Interest expense } \boxed{18} +\\ \text{Interest portion of rent expense}^\dagger\ \boxed{143}\end{array}}{\begin{array}{c}\text{Interest incurred } \boxed{98} +\\ \text{Interest portion of rent expense}^\dagger\ \boxed{143}\end{array}} = \frac{805.2 + 230.4 + 116.2 + 20}{136.9 + 20} = 7.47$$

* From Exhibit 10–18.
† 1/3 of rent expense under operating leases. For 1991: 1/3 of $59.7 $\boxed{143}$.

Exhibit 10–21

CAMPBELL SOUP COMPANY
Return on Investment Ratios

	1991	1990*	1989*	1988	1987	1986	Industry composite
1. Return on total assets (RTA)	11.75%	2.08%	2.13%	9.42%	9.57%	9.90%	9.20%
2. Return on equity**	21.52%	0.24%	0.67%	14.07%	14.14%	14.40%	19.80%
3. Return on long-term liabilities and equity	17.07%	3.04%	2.96%	12.27%	12.35%	12.90%	13.50%
4. Financial leverage index (times) (2) / (1)	1.83	0.12	0.31	1.49	1.48	1.46	2.15
5. Equity growth rate	13.85%	−6.30%	−3.67%	8.59%	8.79%	8.96%	—
** Disaggregation of return on equity:							
Net income margin	6.47%	0.07%	0.23%	5.63%	5.51%	5.10%	6.60%
	×	×	×	×	×	×	×
Assets turnover ratio	1.50	1.54	1.50	1.45	1.53	1.68	1.38
	×	×	×	×	×	×	×
Common stockholders' leverage	2.22	2.18	1.92	1.72	1.68	1.68	2.17
	21.52%	0.24%	0.67%	14.07%	14.14%	14.40%	19.80%

* Excluding the effect of divestitures, restructuring, and unusual charges, net of tax, of $301.6 million in 1990 and $260.8 million in 1989 will drastically change these ratios. For example, RTA for 1990 and 1989 will become 9.57% and 9.03%, respectively.

363

Notes:

(1) For 1991 RTA

$$= \frac{\text{Net income} + \text{Interest expense } (1 - \text{tax rate}) + \text{Minority interest (MI)}}{\text{Average total assets}}$$

$$= \frac{401.5 + 116.2\,(1 - 0.34) + 7.2}{(4{,}149.0 + 4{,}115.6)\,/\,2} = \underline{\underline{11.75\%}}$$

$$= \frac{\text{Net income} + \text{Interest expense } (1 - \text{TR}) + \text{MI}}{\text{Sales}} \times \frac{\text{Sales}}{\text{Average total assets}}$$

RTA disaggrated

$$= \left[\frac{401.5 + 116.2\,(1 - 0.34) + 7.2}{6{,}204.1} = \underline{\underline{7.83\%}} \right] \times \left[\frac{6{,}204.1}{(4{,}149.0 + 4{,}115.6)/2} = \underline{\underline{1.5}} \right] = \underline{\underline{11.75\%}}$$

$$= 6.6\% \times 1.4 = \underline{\underline{9.24\%}}$$

1991 Industry composite

(2) For 1991 Return on equity

$$= \frac{\text{Net income}}{\text{Average common equity*}} = \frac{401.5}{[(1{,}946.1 - 23.5) + (1{,}865.6 - 56.3)]\,/\,2} = \underline{\underline{21.52\%}}$$

$$= \frac{\text{Net income}}{\text{margin}} \times \frac{\text{Asset turnover}}{\text{ratio}} \times \frac{\text{Common stockholders'}}{\text{leverage ratio}}$$

Return on equity disaggregated

$$= \frac{401.5}{6{,}204.1} \times \frac{6{,}204.1}{(4{,}149.0 + 4{,}115.6)/2} \times \frac{(4{,}149.0 + 4{,}115.6)/2}{1865.95*}$$

$$= 6.47\% \times 1.50 \times 2.22 = \underline{\underline{21.52\%}}$$

(3) For 1991 Return on LTD and equity

$$= \frac{\text{Net income} + \text{Interest expense } (1 - \text{tax rate}) + \text{MI}}{\text{Average long-term liabilities}^{\dagger} + \text{Average equity}^{\dagger}}$$

$$= \frac{401.5 + 116.2\,(1 - .34) + 7.2}{(924.9 + 951.9)/2 + (1{,}946.1 + 1{,}865.6)/2} = \underline{\underline{17.07\%}}$$

(4) For 1991 Financial leverage index

$$= \frac{\text{Return on equity capital}}{\text{Return on total assets}} = \frac{21.52\%}{11.75\%} = \underline{\underline{1.83}}$$

(5) For 1991 Equity growth rate

$$= \frac{\text{Net income} - \text{Dividends paid}}{\text{Average common stockholders' equity}^{\dagger}} = \frac{401.5 - 137.5}{(1{,}946.1 + 1{,}865.6)\,/\,2} = \underline{\underline{13.85\%}}$$

* Including 50% of deferred taxes, which is assumed to be equity, and excluding minority interests (MI). See Exhibit 10–18.
† Including 50% of deferred taxes. See Exhibit 10–18.

counterparts in 1988 (comparison with 90 and 89 ratios is not meaningful). They compare also favorably with the industry yardsticks. The improvements in 1991 can be seen as, hopefully, early results of what Campbell's management intended to accomplish through the major restructuring, closings, and business reorganizations they undertook during 89 and 90. As a result of those restructuring programs and cost-cutting efforts, profit margins are widening. Previously, the company's returns had been held down by a number of poorly performing or ill-fitting businesses. Management has divested those lines, while streamlining and modernizing its manufacturing facilities.

Campbell's return on equity at 21.52 percent exceeds both the industry as well as the company's own recent experience. This is due to superior net income margin as well as leverage ratio. The greatly improved net income margin may have benefited from the rebound from the 1990 and 1989 depressed levels.

Referring to the disaggregation of Campbell's return on equity we notice that a major factor responsible for fluctuations in the return on equity over the years are changes in the net income margin. Over the six-year period, it recorded an extreme low of 0.07 percent in 1990 due to the substantial restructuring, and a high of 6.47 percent in 1991 possibly affected by the rebound absence of heavy charges, and *possibly* due to overprovisions in 1989 and 1990. The asset turnover declined slightly in 1987 from 1986, then stayed relatively level throughout the rest of the period but below the 1986 level. The leverage ratio improved gradually because of the company's increasingly leveraged capital structure.

Comparison of the disaggregated factors comprising Campbell's return on equity with those of the industry reveals the company's superior assets turnover and leverage ratios and a slightly inferior net income margin. Thus, the company's higher asset turnover (1.50) and higher leverage ratio (2.22) are primarily responsible for the return on equity of 21.52 percent compared to the industry's 19.8 percent. The increased leverage ratio had a cost in that it resulted in a lower credit rating for the company.

In 1991 Campbell was borrowing $1.22 on each dollar of equity. This considered 50 percent of deferred taxes as interest-free debt. The $2.22 in funds were able to generate $3.33 in sales because assets were turning over at a rate of 1.50 times. The $3.33 in sales were earning 6.47 percent in net income resulting in a return on equity of 21.52 percent.

The return on long-term liabilities and equity displays a relatively similar pattern to that of return on equity. In 1991, this ratio, at about 17 percent, compares very favorably with an industry composite of 13.5 percent.

The financial leverage index is positive and for the first three years, it was stable before declining in 89 and 90 for reasons discussed earlier. In 1991 it rebounded very strongly and showed material improvement over earlier years. This ratio confirms what we know from other evidence, that Campbell utilizes its debt profitably.

The equity growth rate has drastically improved in 1991 over earlier years, and stood at almost double the level of the first three years in the period under analysis. Because the company maintained its dividend payout while undergoing major costs of restructuring, this ratio turned negative in 1989 and 1990. The strong rebound in this ratio in 1991 bodes well for future growth in sales and earnings. A higher level of reinvestment frees the company from reliance on outside sources of capital to finance growth needs. In 1991, a net income of $401.5 million and dividends of $142.2 million was generating substantial funds for reinvestment and internally financed growth.

ANALYSIS OF ASSET UTILIZATION

As indicated in Exhibit 10–22, Campbell's total asset turnover has remained relatively stable over the years. However, this relative stability masks the significant changes of turnover within the component categories. The area of most significant fluctuation throughout the period is cash and cash equivalents. This can also be observed from Exhibit 10–8, which also shows a gradual elimination of temporary investments. In 1991, cash and cash equivalents increased by $98.2 million (Exhibit 10–4). This increase in cash is mostly from operations.

The accounts receivable turnover also showed a recent improvement over the last couple of years, due mainly to the decrease of $97.1 million in receivables in 1991. Management's desire to decrease inventories at every stage of the manufacturing process is not showing up, so far, in better overall turnover ratios.

The asset turnover ratios of Campbell do compare favorably to the industry in several key areas such as receivables, inventories, short-term liabilities, and most importantly working capital. As for cash and fixed assets it is not a favorable comparison, and with other assets the company approximates the industry. Overall, the sales to total assets ratio give the company an edge over the industry.

ANALYSIS OF OPERATING PERFORMANCE

Exhibit 10–23 indicates that Campbell's gross profit ratio is higher than that of the industry. However, the net income to sales ratio is slightly below the industry level. Still, Campbell's net income ratio has improved overall between 1986 and 1991 after the heavy costs of 1989 and 1990. Campbell's management has slimmed down overstaffed administrative ranks and unwieldy corporate divisions. Thus, in 1991 we can see early

CAMPBELL SOUP COMPANY
Asset Utilization Ratios

	1991	1990	1989	1988	1987	1986	Industry composite
1. Sales to cash and equivalents	34.7	76.9	46.9	56.8	31.0	27.6	40.6
2. Sales to receivables	11.8	9.9	10.5	10.0	13.2	14.3	8.4
3. Sales to inventories	8.8	7.6	7.0	7.3	7.2	7.0	3.6
4. Sales to working capital	25.8	16.9	15.4	9.8	6.0	6.1	4.9
5. Sales to fixed assets	3.5	3.6	3.7	3.2	3.3	3.7	6.6
6. Sales to other assets*	7.4	8.5	7.2	6.6	14.5	16.5	7.5
7. Sales to total assets	1.5	1.5	1.4	1.4	1.5	1.6	1.4
8. Sales to short-term liabilities	4.9	4.8	4.6	5.6	6.5	6.9	4.2

* Including intangible assets.

Exhibit 10–23

CAMPBELL SOUP COMPANY
Analysis of Profit Margin Ratios

	1991	1990	1989	1988	1987	1986	Industry composite
1. Gross profit to sales	34.00%	31.38%	29.45%	30.32%	29.17%	28.09%	29.30%
2. Operating income to net revenue	12.63%	4.69%	3.54%	9.09%	10.46%	10.34%	—
3. Net income to sales	6.47%	0.07%	0.23%	5.63%	5.51%	5.21%	6.60%

Notes:

(1) Gross profit to net sales $= \dfrac{\text{Net sales} - \text{Cost of products sold}}{\text{Net sales}}$

For 1991 $= \dfrac{6204.1 - 4{,}095.5}{6{,}204.1} = 34\%$

(2) Operating income to sales $= \dfrac{\text{Income before taxes and interest expenses}}{\text{Net sales}}$

For 1991 $= \dfrac{667.4 + 116.2}{6{,}204.1} = 12.63\%$

indications of tighter control over several areas of operating expenses. This should allow the company to continue improving the net income ratio and exceed its counterpart of the industry.

Exhibit 10–6 confirms the earlier observation about gross margin, where cost of products sold continue to decline (about 66 percent in 1991 versus 72 percent in 1986). This improvement in gross margin may continue over the coming years, but will not be easy to achieve. The key for a net income ratio that benefits from improving gross margins is ample control over administrative and marketing expenses.

The trend index analysis in Exhibit 10–8 shows that while sales in 1991 are at a level 145 percent higher than 1986, cost of products sold is at a level of 133 percent only, total costs and expenses at a level of 142, and net income at an impressive level of 180 compared to 1986. The important conclusion from all of these trends is the fact that sales, gross margin, and, in turn, net income are growing at a relatively faster rate than do costs and expenses.

Interest expense grew throughout the six-year period at a relatively lower rate than did total liabilities, except for 1991 (Exhibit 10–8). This indicates a lower cost of borrowing resulting primarily from lower interest rates even though Campbell now seems to be a more risky borrower as its debt to equity ratio is increasing.

From item $\boxed{1}$ of Campbell's 1991 annual report, included in Chapter 2, Appendix B, we can see that foreign operations contributed to 1991 operating earnings a total of $92.3 million from Campbell Canada, International Biscuit, and Campbell International. This total represents about 11.6 percent of total operating earnings. In 1990 and 1989 foreign operations contributed negatively to total earnings, as a result of the major restructuring in those years, reducing total operating earnings by 134.1 million in 1990 and by 82.3 million in 1989. These negative contributions were additional to losses from foreign currency translation of 3.8 million in 1990 and 20.0 million in 1989. This latter item in 1991 was insignificant, though positive. Overall, foreign operations continued throughout the years to represent roughly 20 percent of total operations (Exhibit 10–1). They will continue to exert a significant impact on Campbell's earnings.

Campbell's effective tax rate (item $\boxed{140}$) was 39.8 percent in 1991, 97.5 percent in 1990, and 87.7 percent in 1989. The extraordinarily high rates for 90 and 89 are mainly due to the large amounts of nondeductible divestitures, restructuring, and unusual charges, representing 56.5 and 48.7 percent of earnings before taxes, respectively (item $\boxed{135}$). Excluding the effect of these divestitures brings down the effective tax rate to about 40 percent.

The company is using substantial tax loss carryforward benefits of foreign subsidiaries and at the end of 1991 still has 77.4 million in unused tax loss carryforward benefits. About half will expire through 1996 and the rest will be available indefinitely. Most deferred taxes result from depreciation book/tax differences, pensions, and divestitures, restructuring, and unusual charges. The deferred tax due to depreciation differences stayed relatively high through 1990, then in 1991 declined to a low of $5.9 million.

Exhibit 10–24 indicates that accumulated depreciation as a percentage of gross plant assets has essentially remained fairly stable with some minor variations. The same can be said about the other two indicators in that exhibit. Thus, earnings quality seems not to have been affected in this area.

An analysis of discretionary costs, as it appears in Exhibit 10–25, shows that 1991 spending in each major category has decreased compared to most other previous years. This may possibly be evidence of more controlled spending and enhanced efficiencies.

Exhibit 8–5 analyzes the factors accounting for the variation in average net earnings over two three-year spans. This analysis is corroborative of some of the factors mentioned or discussed above. Gross margins increased, while on a relative basis, increases in marketing and selling expenses, interest expense, and other expenses outpaced the increase in sales by a big margin. However, administrative expenses and research and development expenses did not increase as much as sales. Statutory tax rates declined over the period thus holding down growth in tax expenses. Profitability increased because the increase in gross margin has, quantitatively, a much larger impact on the bottom line.

Exhibit 9–1 presents analytically recast income statements for the six fiscal periods ending in 1991 and discloses many elements already discussed above. Exhibit 9–2 presents Campbell's analytically adjusted income statements for the six fiscal periods ending in 1991. On an adjusted basis there is an increasing trend in net income from 1989 to 1990, which is in contrast to reported net income. The adjustments for divestitures, restructuring, and unusual charges do reveal a trend. However, the average earning power calculation for the six-year period must include all charges and stands at about $194 million.

SUMMARY AND CONCLUSIONS

This analysis has examined all facets of Campbell Soup Company's record of results of operations and financial position and has estimated the projected results and cash flows for one year. An analysis such as this, adjusted to fit the requirements of the specific situation and circumstances at hand, is an indispensable step in arriving at a decision. Nevertheless, essential as the data and information developed by this analysis are, it is not sufficient in most cases to arrive at a final conclusion. This is so because qualitative and other factors can have an important bearing on

Exhibit 10–24

CAMPBELL SOUP COMPANY
Analysis of Depreciation Data

	1991	1990	1989	1988	1987	1986
1. Accumulated depreciation as a percentage of gross plant assets*	44.6%	42.3%	43.1%	43.7%	46.6%	48.6%
2. Annual depreciation expenses as a percentage of gross plant assets	7.7%	7.7%	7.6%	6.9%	6.4%	6.4%
3. Annual depreciation expenses as a percentage of sales	3.1%	3.0%	3.1%	3.3%	3.1%	2.8%

Notes:

(1) For 1991 $= \dfrac{1{,}131.5 \ \boxed{162}}{758.7 \ \boxed{159} + 1{,}779.3 \ \boxed{160}} = 44.6\%$

(2) For 1991 $= \dfrac{194.5 \ \boxed{162A}}{758.7 \ \boxed{159} + 1{,}779.3 \ \boxed{160}} = 7.7\%$

(3) For 1991 $= \dfrac{194.5 \ \boxed{162A}}{6{,}204.1 \ \boxed{13}} = 3.1\%$

* Exclusive of land and projects in progress.

Exhibit 10–25

CAMPBELL SOUP COMPANY
Analysis of Discretionary Costs
(in millions)

	1991	1990	1989	1988	1987	1986
Net sales	$6,204.1	$6,205.8	$5,672.1	$4,868.9	$4,490.4	$4,286.8
Plant assets (net)*	1,406.5	1,386.9	1,322.6	1,329.1	1,152.0	974.1
Maintenance and repairs	173.9	180.6	173.9	155.6	148.8	144.0
Advertising	195.4	220.4	212.9	219.1	203.5	181.4
R & D	56.3	53.7	47.7	46.9	44.8	42.2
Percent of maintenance and repairs to sales	2.8%	2.9%	3.1%	3.2%	3.3%	3.4%
Percent of maintenance and repairs to plant	12.4	13.0	13.1	11.7	12.9	14.8
Percent of advertising to sales	3.1	3.6	3.8	4.5	4.5	4.2
Percent of R & D to sales	0.9	0.9	0.8	1.0	1.0	1.0

* Exclusive of land and projects in process.

the final evaluation. Only when all the factors, those developed by the analysis as well as the others, have been assembled can a decision be reached by the application of judgment.

For example, a *bank* that may be asked to extend short-term credit must take into consideration the character of the management, past loan experience, as well as the ongoing relationship with the loan applicant.

In addition to the foregoing intangibles, the long-term lender will focus on such matters as security arrangements, provisions that safeguard the solvency of the recipient of the loan, and events risks (see also Chapter 5).

The *equity investor* is, of course, interested in earning power and in earnings per share, but many considerations and judgments must be joined with these data before an investment decision is made. Thus, for instance, what earnings are, and what they are likely to be, is the product of financial analysis. At what price-earnings ratio they should be capitalized is a question for investment judgment. Similarly, the risk inherent in an enterprise, the volatility of its earnings, and the breadth and quality of the market for its securities are factors which must also be considered. They determine whether an investment fits into the investor's portfolio and whether it is compatible with his or her investment objectives.

Since the ultimate conclusions regarding problems, such as the lending and investing decision that we consider in this case, are based on more than the data and facts brought out by financial analysis alone, it follows that the most useful way to present the results of financial analysis is to summarize them by listing the most relevant and salient points which were developed by the analysis and which the decision maker should consider. This we shall do in this case.

The following are the main points that have been developed by our analysis of Campbell Soup Company.

Short-Term Liquidity

Campbell's short-term liquidity position is a mixed one. Both current and acid-test ratios do not compare favorably with the industry, while the cash position of the company compares very favorably with the industry. Moreover, both accounts receivable and inventory turnover ratios are higher than their counterparts of the industry. The company's conversion period is much lower than that of the industry.

The cash position of Campbell is strong and may allow for some cash to be used beyond operations, especially for acquisitions.

Cash Flows

With only 1989 as an exception, because of material increases in inventories, Campbell has generated substantial and increasing cash from operations in recent years. They represent over half of all cash inflows.

Purchases and acquisitions of plant assets represent outflows totaling about 50 percent of all cash inflows. Dividends required about 12 percent of cash inflows.

A cash forecast for 1992 and 1993, based on assumptions as stated, projects that Campbell is expected to finance the expected investments in plant assets from an increasing cash flow from operations and to require only relatively small additions to debt.

The cash flow adequacy ratio confirms the earlier conclusion that the company is generating sufficient cash from operations to cover the majority of their capital expenditures, net investment in inventories, and cash dividends. Campbell's average cash reinvestment ratio was at a good level of 16.5 percent over the last six-year period.

Capital Structure and Long-term Solvency

Compared to its industry, and by any other standard, Campbell has developed in recent years a less conservative capital structure. Total debt is about 53 percent of total invested capital, and long-term debt alone is about half of equity. However, both earnings-based and cash from operations-based, fixed-charge coverage ratios are at strong levels, with the exception of coverage based on earnings in 1989 and 1990, due to restructuring. These strong ratios attest to the significant protection enjoyed by the company's creditors. Further, the company is still having ample debt capacity and the market has accorded the company a superior credit rating (AA).

Return on Investment

The company's return on total assets over the years 1986–88 was essentially stable at about 9.5 percent. During 1989 and 90 it declined to a low of about 2 percent, due in a major way to divestitures, restructuring, and unusual charges. In 1991, the ratio rebounded back to a strong 11.75 percent, composed of a profit margin of 6.47 percent and an asset turnover of 1.50. This return, overall, compares favorably to the industry average return of 9.2 percent.

At 21.52 percent the return on equity, which suffered a setback in 1989 and 90, is also above the industry average of 19.8 percent. The determining factor of this ratio, beyond RTA elements, is the common stockholder's leverage, which stands at 2.22 in 1991. This leverage is at a relatively higher level than preceding years, due mainly to a more risky capital structure which Campbell is allowing in recent years.

Campbell's equity growth rate has increased drastically in 1991 over earlier years, due in a major part to strong and healthy earnings and a higher rate of earnings retention.

Asset Utilization

While Campbell's total asset turnover has remained relatively stable over the years, the turnover of cash and cash equivalents has fluctuated from year to year. Meanwhile, accounts receivable and inventories turnovers have improved and are above their industry counterparts. These improvements are due mainly to the continuous efforts of the company to reduce working capital through lower receivables and lower inventories, among other things.

Asset turnover compares favorably to that of the industry composite, despite the relatively low cash turnover and fixed assets turnover.

Operating Performance

While Campbell's gross profit ratio has been improving in recent years and is clearly above the industry average, its net income to sales ratio is not as advantageously placed. This is due mainly to more corporate operating expenses, and the fact that Campbell's management does not have as much control over those expenses as it ought to have. Recent developments indicate that the company is going to exercise tighter control over costs.

Market Measures

Exhibit 10–26 presents some market measures of Campbell. Except for the dividend payout ratio which is a measure reflecting management discretion, these measures reflect the impact of the market's valuation of the company's equity securities. The 1989 and 1990 earnings-per-share figures are adjusted to exclude the effect of the enormous amounts of divestitures, restructuring, and unusual charges, which if unadjusted make most of the market measures meaningless for analytical purposes.

Thus, while earnings per share increased from $1.72 in 1986 to $3.16 in 1991, the earnings yield declined for the same period, because of steadily increasing price earnings ratios over the years. These are due mainly to strong equity markets. Similarly, while dividends per share increased from $0.65 in 1986 to $1.12 in 1991, the dividend yield declined from 2.5 percent to 1.74 percent over the same period.

The decline in the earnings yield and the dividend yield over this period is attributable in a major way to the steady and significant expansion in price-earnings ratios over this period of time. Price-earnings ratios reflect the appreciation and confidence with which investors view a company's performance, and as our analysis indicates, Campbell's operating performance over this period was relatively superior, despite the temporary interruption in 1989 and 90. They do, however, also reflect exceptionally euphoric market conditions.

Exhibit 10–26

CAMPBELL SOUP COMPANY
Market Measures

	1991	1990*	1989*	1988	1987	1986
1. Price-earning ratio (range) ..	27–14	26–18	29–12	16–11	19–14	20–10
2. Earnings yield (percent)	4.91	4.53	4.91	7.45	6.20	6.61
3. Dividend yield (percent) ...	1.74	1.88	2.08	2.85	2.32	2.50
4. Dividend payout ratio (percent)	35.44	41.53	42.45	38.21	37.37	37.79

Notes:
(1) 1991: High-low for the year (84.88 / 3.16 = 27)

$\boxed{184}$ (43.75 / 3.16 = 14)

(2) 1991: Earnings per share / Average market price

$$3.16 / [(84.88 + 43.75) / 2] = 4.91\%$$

(3) 1991: Dividend per share / Average market price

$$1.12 / 64.32 = 1.74\%$$

(4) 1991: Dividend per share / Earnings per share

$$1.12 / 3.16 = 35.44\%$$

* 1990 and 1989 results are shown for EPS before effects of divestitures, restructuring, and unusual charges of $2.33 and 2.02 per share respectively.

Higher price earnings ratios brought about by active stock markets benefit a company in many ways; for example, in being able to raise capital inexpensively and in its ability to use common stock as the coin of payment for acquisitions. However, these increasing valuations expose existing and particularly new common stockholders to increasing risks—risks that these rich valuations can be quickly downgraded and reversed. This is so because, unlike in the early stages of the bull market, prices are no longer based on fundamental factors but are based on hope for continuation of the upward price momentum. Thus the stock price includes an evergrowing "enthusiasm component" which, as experience has shown time and again, can be quickly deflated. These considerations, important and crucial as they are for the equity investor in times of euphoric markets, cannot be assessed by means of the analytical tools developed here. They involve a study of market psychology and market cycles. These factors must be given the most serious consideration by the equity investor. The difference between the return a company earns on *its* investment and that which the investors earn on investments is discussed at the end of Chapter 6.

USES OF FINANCIAL STATEMENT ANALYSIS

The foregoing analysis of the financial statements of Campbell Soup Company consists of two major parts: (1) the detailed analysis and (2) the summary and conclusions. As was mentioned earlier, in a formal analytical report the summary and conclusions section may precede the detailed analysis so that the reader is presented with material in the order of its importance to him or her.

The bank loan officer who has to decide on the short-term loan application by the company will normally give primary attention to short-term liquidity analysis and to the funds flow projection, and secondarily to capital structure and operating results.

The investment committee of the insurance company may, in taking a longer-term point of view, pay attention first to capital structure and long-term solvency and then to operating performance, ROI, asset utilizations, and short-term liquidity, and in that order of emphasis.

The potential investor in Campbell shares will, of course, be interested in all the aspects of our analysis. The emphasis may, however, be different again and take the following order of priority: results of operations, ROI capital structure, and long-term solvency and short-term liquidity.

An adequate financial statement analysis (as the Campbell Soup Company analysis illustrates) will contain, in addition to the analysis of the data, enough information and detail so as to allow the decision maker to follow the rationale behind the analyst's conclusions as well as to allow him or her to expand it into areas not covered by the analysis.

QUESTIONS

1. What kind of processes should normally precede an analysis of financial statements?
2. What are the analytical implications of the fact that financial statements are, at best, an abstraction of underlying reality?
3. Name the six major "building blocks" of financial analysis. What does the "building block" approach involve?
4. What are some of the earmarks of a good analysis? Into what distinct sections should a well-organized analysis be divided?
5. What additional knowledge and analytical skills must an analyst bring to bear upon the analysis of enterprises in specialized or regulated industries?

APPENDIX 10

This appendix presents portions from the financial sections of Quaker Oats Company's 1991 annual report which includes Form 10K data. The data in this appendix form the basis for illustrations in the text as well as for questions and problems.

Quaker is a worldwide marketer of consumer grocery products. In the geographic markets in which it competes, Quaker is a major producer of cereals, mixes, grain-based snacks, syrup, corn products, value-added rice and pasta products, chocolates, canned beans, edible oils, thirst-quenching beverages, and pet foods. At the end of fiscal 1991, the company had plant facilities in 16 states in the United States as well as in Western Europe, Canada, and Latin America. Approximately 10,900 of Quaker's 21,000 employees are located in the United States.

The auditor's opinion in the 1991 annual report was unqualified.

The Quaker Oats Company and Subsidiaries

Consolidated Statements of Income

Dollars in Millions (Except Per Share Data)

Year Ended June 30	1991	1990	1989
[1] Net Sales	$5,491.2	$5,030.6	$4,879.4
[2] Cost of goods sold	2,839.7	2,685.9	2,655.3
[3] Gross profit	2,651.5	2,344.7	2,224.1
[4] Selling, general and administrative expenses	2,121.2	1,844.1	1,779.0
[5] Interest expense—net of $9.0, $11.0 and $12.4 interest income	86.2	101.8	56.4
[6] Other expense—net	32.6	16.4	149.6
[7] Income from Continuing Operations Before Income Taxes	411.5	382.4	239.1
[8] Provision for income taxes	175.7	153.5	90.2
[9] Income from Continuing Operations	235.8	228.9	148.9
[10] Income (loss) from discontinued operations—net of tax	(30.0)	(59.9)	54.1
[11] Net Income	205.8	169.0	203.0
[12] Preferred dividends—net of tax	4.3	4.5	—
[13] Net Income Available for Common	$ 201.5	$ 164.5	$ 203.0
Per Common Share:			
[14] Income from Continuing Operations	$ 3.05	$ 2.93	$ 1.88
[15] Income (loss) from discontinued operations	(.40)	(.78)	.68
[16] Net Income	$ 2.65	$ 2.15	$ 2.56
[17] Dividends declared	$ 1.56	$ 1.40	$ 1.20
[18] Average Number of Common Shares Outstanding (in 000's)	75,904	76,537	79,307

See accompanying notes to the consolidated financial statements.

378

Consolidated Statements of Cash Flows		Year Ended June 30	1991	1990	1989
	Cash Flows from Operating Activities:				
	[19]	Net income	$ 205.8	$ 169.0	$ 203.0
		Adjustments to reconcile net income to net cash (used in) provided by operating activities:			
	[20]	Depreciation and amortization	177.7	162.5	135.5
	[21]	Deferred income taxes and other items	45.3	15.2	79.9
	[22]	Provision for restructuring charges	10.0	(17.5)	124.3
		Changes in operating assets and liabilities—continuing operations:			
	[23]	Change in receivables	(97.8)	(55.9)	(77.1)
	[24]	Change in inventories	30.7	(2.2)	(90.3)
	[25]	Change in other current assets	(13.7)	(14.1)	(48.9)
	[26]	Change in trade accounts payable	26.1	31.4	102.2
	[27]	Change in other current liabilities	43.2	83.4	(53.1)
	[28]	Other—net	9.5	0.4	(8.4)
	[29]	Change in payable to Fisher-Price	29.6	—	—
	[30]	Change in net current assets of discontinued operations	66.0	74.9	14.5
	[31]	Net Cash Provided by Operating Activities	532.4	447.1	381.6
	Cash Flows from Investing Activities:				
	[32]	Additions to property, plant and equipment	(240.6)	(275.6)	(223.2)
	[33]	Cost of acquisitions, excluding working capital	—	—	(112.9)
	[34]	Change in other receivables and investments	(10.7)	(22.6)	(5.7)
	[35]	Disposals of property, plant and equipment	17.9	11.9	26.7
	[36]	Other—discontinued operations	(19.8)	(58.4)	(46.7)
	[37]	Net Cash Used in Investing Activities	(253.2)	(344.7)	(361.8)
	Cash Flows from Financing Activities:				
	[38]	Cash dividends	(123.0)	(110.5)	(95.2)
	[39]	Proceeds from issuance of debt for spin-off	141.1	—	—
	[40]	Change in deferred compensation	(0.2)	3.5	(248.4)
	[41]	Change in short-term debt	(265.6)	(7.2)	42.1
	[42]	Proceeds from long-term debt	1.8	252.1	251.2
	[43]	Reduction of long-term debt	(39.7)	(34.8)	(30.1)
	[44]	Issuance of common treasury stock	25.6	12.8	10.1
	[45]	Purchase of common stock	—	(223.2)	(68.5)
	[46]	Issuance of preferred stock	—	—	100.0
	[47]	Purchase of preferred stock	(0.7)	—	—
	[48]	Net Cash Used in Financing Activities	(260.7)	(107.3)	(38.8)
	[49]	**Effect of Exchange Rate Changes on Cash and Cash Equivalents**	(6.0)	1.6	(7.4)
	[50]	**Net Increase (Decrease) in Cash and Cash Equivalents**	$ 12.5	$ (3.3)	$ (26.4)
	[51]	**Cash and Cash Equivalents—Beginning of Year**	$ 17.7	$ 21.0	$ 47.4
	[52]	**Cash and Cash Equivalents—End of Year**	$ 30.2	$ 17.7	$ 21.0

See accompanying notes to the consolidated financial statements.

The Quaker Oats Company and Subsidiaries

Assets			
June 30	1991	1990	1989
Current Assets:			
53 Cash and cash equivalents	$ 30.2	$ 17.7	$ 21.0
54 Short-term investments, at cost which approximates market	—	.6	2.7
55 Receivables—net of allowances	691.1	629.9	594.4
Inventories:			
56 Finished goods	309.1	324.1	326.0
57 Grain and raw materials	86.7	110.7	114.1
58 Packaging materials and supplies	26.5	39.1	39.0
59 Total inventories	422.3	473.9	479.1
60 Other current assets	114.5	107.0	94.2
61 Net current assets of discontinued operations	—	252.2	328.5
62 Total current assets	1,258.1	1,481.3	1,519.9
63 Other Receivables and Investments	79.1	63.5	26.4
64 Property, plant and equipment	1,914.6	1,745.6	1,456.9
65 Less accumulated depreciation	681.9	591.5	497.3
66 Properties—Net	1,232.7	1,154.1	959.6
67 Intangible Assets, Net of Amortization	446.2	466.7	484.7
68 Net Non-current Assets of Discontinued Operations	—	160.5	135.3
69 Total Assets	$3,016.1	$3,326.1	$3,125.9

See accompanying notes to the consolidated financial statements.

Liabilities and Common Shareholders' Equity

June 30		1991	1990	1989
Current Liabilities:				
70	Short-term debt	$ 80.6	$ 343.2	$ 102.2
71	Current portion of long-term debt	32.9	32.3	30.0
72	Trade accounts payable	350.9	354.0	333.8
73	Accrued payrolls, pensions and bonuses	116.3	106.3	118.1
74	Accrued advertising and merchandising	105.7	92.6	67.1
75	Income taxes payable	45.1	36.3	8.0
76	Payable to Fisher-Price	29.6	—	—
77	Other accrued liabilities	165.8	173.8	164.9
78	Total current liabilities	926.9	1,138.5	824.1
79	**Long-term Debt**	701.2	740.3	766.8
80	**Other Liabilities**	115.5	100.3	89.5
81	**Deferred Income Taxes**	366.7	327.7	308.4
82	**Preferred Stock,** no par value, authorized 1,750,000 shares; issued 1,282,051 of $5.46 cumulative convertible shares in 1989 (liquidating preference $78 per share)	100.0	100.0	100.0
83	**Deferred Compensation**	(94.5)	(98.2)	(100.0)
84	**Treasury Preferred Stock,** at cost, 10,089 shares at June 30, 1991	(.7)	—	—
85	**Common Shareholders' Equity:** Common stock, $5 par value, authorized 200,000,000 shares; issued 83,989,396 shares	420.0	420.0	420.0
86	Additional paid-in capital	7.2	12.9	18.1
87	Reinvested earnings	1,047.5	1,164.7	1,106.2
88	Cumulative exchange adjustment	(52.9)	(29.3)	(56.6)
89	Deferred compensation	(168.0)	(164.1)	(165.8)
90	Treasury common stock, at cost, 7,660,675 shares; 8,402,871 shares; and 5,221,981 shares, respectively	(352.8)	(386.7)	(184.8)
91	Total common shareholders' equity	901.0	1,017.5	1,137.1
92	**Total Liabilities and Common Shareholders' Equity**	$3,016.1	$3,326.1	$3,125.9

The Quaker Oats Company and Subsidiaries

Consolidated Statements of Common Shareholders' Equity

		Common Stock Issued	
		Shares	Amount
[93]	Balance at June 30, 1988	83,989,396	$420.0
[94]	Net income		
[95]	Cash dividends declared on common stock		
[96]	Common stock issued for option, stock purchase and profit-sharing plans		
[97]	Repurchases of common stock		
[98]	Current year foreign currency adjustments (net of allocated income taxes of $1.2)		
[99]	Deferred compensation		
[100]	Balance at June 30, 1989	83,989,396	$420.0
[101]	Net income		
[102]	Cash dividends declared on common stock		
[103]	Cash dividends declared on preferred stock		
[104]	Common stock issued for stock purchase and incentive plans		
[105]	Repurchases of common stock		
[106]	Current year foreign currency adjustments (net of allocated income taxes of $6.4)		
[107]	Deferred compensation		
[108]	Balance at June 30, 1990	83,989,396	$420.0
[109]	Net income		
[110]	Cash dividends declared on common stock		
[111]	Cash dividends declared on preferred stock		
[112]	Distribution of equity to shareholders from spin-off of Fisher-Price		
[113]	Common stock issued for stock purchase and incentive plans		
[114]	Current year foreign currency adjustments (net of allocated income taxes of $3.0)		
[115]	Deferred compensation		
[116]	Balance at June 30, 1991	83,989,396	$420.0

See accompanying notes to the consolidated financial statements.

Dollars in Millions

	Additional Paid-in Capital	Reinvested Earnings	Common Stock in Treasury		Cumulative Exchange Adjustment	Deferred Compensation	Total
			Shares	Amount			
	$19.5	$ 998.4	4,593,664	$(132.9)	$(36.5)	$ (17.4)	$1,251.1
		203.0					203.0
		(95.2)					(95.2)
	(1.4)		(601,383)	16.7			15.3
			1,229,700	(68.6)			(68.6)
					(20.1)		(20.1)
						(148.4)	(148.4)
	$18.1	$1,106.2	5,221,981	$(184.8)	$(56.6)	$(165.8)	$1,137.1
		169.0					169.0
		(106.9)					(106.9)
		(3.6)					(3.6)
	(5.2)		(522,110)	21.3			16.1
			3,703,000	(223.2)			(223.2)
					27.3		27.3
						1.7	1.7
	$12.9	$1,164.7	8,402,871	$(386.7)	$(29.3)	$(164.1)	$1,017.5
		205.8					205.8
		(118.7)					(118.7)
		(4.3)					(4.3)
		(200.0)					(200.0)
	(5.7)		(742,196)	33.9			28.2
					(23.6)		(23.6)
						(3.9)	(3.9)
	$ 7.2	$1,047.5	7,660,675	$(352.8)	$(52.9)	$(168.0)	$ 901.0

The Quaker Oats Company and Subsidiaries

Eleven-Year Selected Financial Data

Year Ended June 30	5-Year Compound Growth Rate	10-Year Compound Growth Rate	1991
[118] Operating Results (a)(b)(c)(d)			
Net sales	13.1%	10.7%	$5,491.2
Gross profit	15.3%	14.5%	2,651.5
Income from continuing operations before income taxes	10.0%	11.1%	411.5
Provision for income taxes	9.2%	10.7%	175.7
Income from continuing operations	10.6%	11.4%	235.8
Income (loss) from discontinued operations—net of tax			(30.0)
Income (loss) from the disposal of discontinued operations—net of tax			—
[119] Net income	2.8%	6.9%	$ 205.8
Per common share:			
Income from continuing operations	11.5%	12.5%	$ 3.05
Income (loss) from discontinued operations			(.40)
Income (loss) from the disposal of discontinued operations			—
[120] Net income	3.4%	7.8%	$ 2.65
[121] Dividends declared:			
Common stock	16.5%	14.0%	$ 118.7
Per common share	17.4%	14.6%	$ 1.56
Redeemable preference and preferred stock			$ 4.3
[122] Average number of common shares outstanding (000's)			75,904

(a) Excludes the operating results of businesses reported as discontinued operations (see Note 2)
(b) See Management's Discussion and Analysis for discussion of fiscal 1989 through 1991 restructuring charges and credits.

Dollars in Millions (Except Per Share Data)

	1990	1989	1988	1987	1986	1985	1984	1983	1982	1981
	$5,030.6	$4,879.4	$4,508.0	$3,823.9	$2,968.6	$2,925.6	$2,830.9	$2,172.4	$2,114.7	$1,989.8
	2,344.7	2,224.1	2,111.0	1,751.9	1,299.1	1,174.7	1,085.7	879.1	790.6	683.7
	382.4	239.1	314.6	295.9	255.8	238.8	211.3	180.1	158.9	144.1
	153.5	90.2	118.1	141.3	113.4	110.3	99.0	81.9	68.4	63.7
	228.9	148.9	196.5	154.6	142.4	128.5	112.3	98.2	90.5	80.4
	(59.9)	54.1	59.2	33.5	37.2	28.1	26.4	14.1	26.8	24.8
	—	—	—	55.8	—	—	—	(55.5)	(20.4)	—
	$ 169.0	$ 203.0	$ 255.7	$ 243.9	$ 179.6	$ 156.6	$ 138.7	$ 56.8	$ 96.9	$ 105.2
	$ 2.93	$ 1.88	$ 2.46	$ 1.96	$ 1.77	$ 1.53	$ 1.35	$ 1.19	$ 1.11	$ .94
	(.78)	.68	.74	.43	.47	.35	.32	.17	.34	.31
	—	—	—	.71	—	—	—	(.70)	(.26)	—
	$ 2.15	$ 2.56	$ 3.20	$ 3.10	$ 2.24	$ 1.88	$ 1.67	$ .66	$ 1.19	$ 1.25
	$ 106.9	$ 95.2	$ 79.9	$ 63.2	$ 55.3	$ 50.5	$ 44.4	$ 39.5	$ 35.3	$ 31.9
	$ 1.40	$ 1.20	$ 1.00	$ .80	$ .70	$ .62	$ .55	$ .50	$ .45	$ .40
	$ 3.6	—	—	—	$ 2.3	$ 3.6	$ 3.9	$ 4.1	$ 4.3	$ 4.6
	76,537	79,307	79,835	78,812	79,060	81,492	80,412	79,008	77,820	80,322

(c) Fiscal 1989 net income was decreased by $16 million (after-tax) or $.20 per share due to the adoption of the last-in, first-out ("LIFO") method of valuing inventories.
(d) Per share data reflect the November 1986 and 1984 two-for-one stock splits.

The Quaker Oats Company and Subsidiaries

Eleven-Year Selected Financial Data

Year Ended June 30	5-Year Compound Growth Rate	10-Year Compound Growth Rate	1991
Financial Statistics (a)(b)(c)			
123 Current ratio			1.4
Working capital	2.2%	2.8%	$ 331.2
Working capital turnover (d)			16.3
124 Property, plant and equipment—net	12.3%	8.4%	$1,232.7
125 Depreciation expense	16.2%	14.3%	$ 125.2
126 Total assets	9.2%	8.3%	$3,016.1
127 Long-term debt			$ 701.2
128 Preferred stock net of deferred compensation, and preference stock			$ 4.8
129 Common shareholders' equity			$ 901.0
130 Book value per common share			$ 11.80
131 Return on average common shareholders' equity			24.1%
132 Gross profit as a percentage of sales			48.3%
133 Advertising and merchandising as a percentage of sales			25.6%
134 Research and development as a percentage of sales			.8%
135 Income from continuing operations as a percentage of sales			4.3%
136 Long-term debt ratio (e)			43.6%
Total debt ratio (f)			47.4%
Common dividends as a percentage of income available for common shares			58.9%
Number of common shareholders			33,603
Number of employees worldwide			20,900
137 Market price range of common stock—High			$ 64¾
—Low			$ 41¾

(a) Income-related statistics exclude the results of businesses which have been reported as discontinued operations. Balance sheets and related statistics have not been restated for discontinued operations other than Fisher-Price due to immateriality.
(b) Per share data reflect the November 1986 and 1984 two-for-one stock split-ups.
(c) During fiscal 1991, common shareholders' equity and book value per common share, as well as number of employees worldwide, were reduced by the spin-off of Fisher-Price (see Note 2).

	1990	1989	1988	1987	1986	1985	1984	1983	1982	1981
	1.3	1.8	1.4	1.4	1.4	1.7	1.6	1.6	1.6	1.6
	$ 342.8	$ 695.8	$ 417.5	$ 507.9	$ 296.8	$ 400.7	$ 316.8	$ 261.9	$ 266.6	$ 252.4
	9.7	8.8	9.7	9.5	8.5	8.2	9.8	8.2	8.1	7.7
	$1,154.1	$ 959.6	$ 922.5	$ 898.6	$ 691.0	$ 616.5	$ 650.1	$ 533.0	$ 533.8	$ 552.2
	103.5	94.2	88.3	81.6	59.1	56.3	57.4	40.1	35.2	32.9
	$3,326.1	$3,125.9	$2,886.1	$3,136.5	$1,944.5	$1,760.3	$1,726.5	$1,391.9	$1,383.3	$1,360.3
	$ 740.3	$ 766.8	$ 299.1	$ 527.7	$ 160.9	$ 168.2	$ 200.1	$ 152.8	$ 162.1	$ 164.5
	1.8	—	—		—	37.9	38.5	41.3	45.4	46.7
	$1,017.5	$1,137.1	$1,251.1	$1,087.5	$ 831.7	$ 786.9	$ 720.1	$ 639.4	$ 630.5	$ 612.6
	13.46	14.44	15.76	13.68	10.64	9.76	8.89	8.02	8.04	7.99
	20.8%	12.5%	16.8%	16.1%	17.3%	16.6%	15.9%	14.8%	13.9%	12.7%
	46.6%	45.6%	46.8%	45.8%	43.8%	40.2%	38.4%	40.5%	37.4%	34.4%
	23.8%	23.4%	24.9%	22.9%	21.7%	19.4%	18.4%	18.6%	16.6%	15.3%
	.9%	.8%	.8%	.8%	.8%	.7%	.8%	.8%	1.0%	1.0%
	4.6%	3.1%	4.4%	4.0%	4.8%	4.4%	4.0%	4.5%	4.3%	4.0%
	42.1%	40.3%	19.3%	32.7%	16.2%	16.9%	20.9%	18.3%	19.4%	20.0%
	52.3%	44.2%	33.8%	50.2%	35.7%	28.9%	35.4%	32.9%	32.4%	35.2%
	65.1%	46.9%	31.3%	25.9%	31.2%	33.0%	32.9%	75.8%	37.8%	32.0%
	33,859	34,347	34,231	32,358	27,068	26,670	26,785	27,943	29,552	30,418
	28,200	31,700	31,300	30,800	29,500	28,700	28,400	25,200	26,000	30,900
	$ 68¼	$ 66¼	$ 57⅜	$ 57%	$ 39%	$ 26%	$ 16%	$ 12%	$ 10%	$ 9%
	$ 45%	$ 42%	$ 31	$ 32%	$ 23%	$ 14%	$ 10%	$ 8%	$ 7%	$ 6%

(d) Net sales divided by average working capital

(e) Long-term debt divided by long-term debt plus total equity including preferred stock net of related deferred compensation and preference stock

(f) Total debt divided by total debt plus total equity including preferred stock net of related deferred compensation and preference stock

Management's Discussion and Analysis

[138] Financial Review

On June 28, 1991, the Company completed the distribution of Fisher-Price to its shareholders and Fisher-Price, Inc., an independent, free-standing company, was created (see Note 2). Fisher-Price has been presented as a discontinued operation within these financial statements for all periods shown. Also in fiscal 1991, the Company recorded a $10 million pretax restructuring charge, or 8 cents per share, to close a Golden Grain pasta manufacturing plant.

In fiscal 1990, the Company reassessed a previously announced plan to close two European pet food facilities and invest in a new pet food plant. This reassessment resulted in management's decision to upgrade existing facilities and forego building a new plant. As a result, reserves of $17.5 million, 18 cents per share, charged to fiscal 1989 earnings were reversed in fiscal 1990.

In fiscal 1989, the Company recorded a variety of restructuring charges aimed at improving productivity and lowering costs. The most significant of these related to the closure of its Marion, Ohio Pet Foods Division plant, which resulted in a $70 million pretax charge to income. Also in fiscal 1989, the Company recorded a charge of $20.7 million for the planned consolidation of European pet food facilities (referenced above). In total, these restructuring charges reduced pretax income by approximately $125 million, or $1.00 per share.

[139] Fiscal 1991 Compared with Fiscal 1990
Operations

Fiscal 1991 consolidated sales reached a record $5.5 billion, up 9 percent over fiscal 1990, aided by a solid unit volume increase of 5 percent. U.S. and Canadian Grocery Products sales of $3.9 billion were up 7 percent on a 5 percent volume increase. Most businesses had volume increases, led by *Gatorade* thirst quencher, up over 15 percent. International Grocery Products sales of $1.6 billion were up 15 percent on a 5 percent volume increase. The sales gain was driven by the European and Mexican businesses, due to favorable currency trends and strong volume gains in *Gatorade* and pet foods.

Gross profit margin rose to 48 percent of net sales versus 47 percent in fiscal 1990 due largely to lower commodity and packaging costs in the domestic grocery business.

Selling, general and administrative expenses of $2.1 billion rose 15 percent over fiscal 1990, and were also higher as a percentage of sales versus last year. The increases in both dollar and percentage terms were due to higher planned

advertising and merchandising (A&M) expenditures in the domestic cereals and *Gatorade* businesses as well as the expansion of *Gatorade* thirst quencher in Europe.

[140] Net interest expense declined 15 percent to $86.2 million due primarily to lower financing costs in Brazil due to the hyper-inflationary environment in that country in fiscal 1990.

Fiscal 1991 other expense included foreign exchange gains of $5.1 million compared to losses of $25.7 million in fiscal 1990, due largely to improvement in Brazil. Restructuring items included in other expense were a $10 million Golden Grain plant closing charge in fiscal 1991 and a $17.5 million credit in fiscal 1990.

Consolidated operating income was $533 million compared to $544.2 million last year. Excluding restructuring charges and credits in both years, operating income would have been $543 million in fiscal 1991, or 3 percent higher than the $526.7 million of a year ago. Operating income for U.S. and Canadian Grocery Products for fiscal 1991 was $429 million, up 15 percent from last year's $372.5 million. Excluding the fiscal 1991 restructuring charge of $10 million, operating income rose 18 percent for the year. International Grocery Products operating income in fiscal 1991 was $104 million, versus last year's $171.7 million. The year-to-year comparisons largely reflect the impact of a hyper-inflationary economic environment in Brazil in fiscal 1990 and a downturn in the business in fiscal 1991 because of deteriorating economic conditions in that country, as well as the fiscal 1990 restructuring credit of $17.5 million. The operating income shortfall in Brazil was largely offset by lower financing costs in that country. In addition, significant A&M expenditures were incurred to launch *Gatorade* thirst quencher into Germany, France, Spain and Mexico. A more detailed discussion of operating performance by segment is provided on pages 14 through 32 in the Operations Review section of this report.

Income from continuing operations of $235.8 million increased 3 percent over fiscal 1990. See Note 2 for a discussion of discontinued operations, which include the Company's Fisher-Price business.

In December 1987, the Financial Accounting Standards Board (FASB) issued Statement #96, "Accounting for Income Taxes," which introduces an asset-and-liability approach to financial accounting and reporting for income taxes. This statement has not yet been adopted, although adoption is required by fiscal 1993. Based on preliminary evaluations, Statement #96 is not expected to have a material impact on the Company's financial results.

In December 1990, the FASB issued Statement #106, "Employers' Accounting for Postretirement Benefits Other Than Pensions." This new standard requires that the expected cost of these benefits be charged to expense during the years that the employees render service. This is a significant change from the Company's current policy of recognizing these costs on the cash basis. The Company is required to adopt the new accounting and disclosure rules no later than fiscal 1994, although earlier implementation is permitted. See Note 11 to the consolidated financial statements for a further discussion of Statement #106.

[141] Fiscal 1990 Compared with Fiscal 1989

Operations

Fiscal 1990 sales of $5 billion rose 3 percent above fiscal 1989, driven by solid gains in International Grocery Products. U.S. and Canadian Grocery Products sales of $3.6 billion were essentially even with the prior year, although volumes declined 6 percent.

The gross profit margin increased to 47 percent of net sales versus 46 percent in fiscal 1989 due primarily to sharply higher margins from the Company's Brazilian business. This resulted from aggressive pricing during a period of dramatic inflation in that country and from lower commodity costs, especially oats, in the domestic grocery business. Partially offsetting the benefit of lower commodity costs were charges of approximately $15 million, recorded in fiscal 1990 for oat bran inventory write-downs.

Selling, general and administrative expenses increased 4 percent over fiscal 1989 to $1.8 billion but remained steady with fiscal 1989 as a percent of net sales. The dollar increase was driven by higher advertising and merchandising spending, especially for the expansion of *Gatorade* thirst quencher in Europe.

Net interest expense increased 80 percent to $101.8 million due primarily to higher financing costs in Brazil and, to a lesser extent, domestic interest expense incurred on debt used for the repurchase of the Company's common stock.

Fiscal 1989 other expense included approximately $125 million in restructuring charges.

Operating income increased 56 percent from fiscal 1989. The increase is attributable to the above-mentioned restructuring charges in fiscal 1989 and credits in fiscal 1990 as well as significantly higher operating income from the Brazilian business. The higher Brazilian operating income was achieved in that country's hyper-inflationary environment and was largely offset by accompanying higher financing costs.

Income from continuing operations increased 54 percent over fiscal 1989 due primarily to the restructuring charges in fiscal 1989 and credits in 1990.

[142] Liquidity and Capital Resources

The ability to generate funds internally remains one of the Company's most significant financial strengths. Net cash flow from operations of $532.4, $447.1 and $381.6 million during fiscal 1991, 1990 and 1989, respectively, was well in excess of the Company's dividend and capital expenditure requirements. Capital expenditures for fiscal 1991, 1990, and 1989 were $240.6, $275.6 and $223.2 million, respectively, with no material individual commitments outstanding.

Short-term and long-term debt (total debt) decreased $301.1 million from last year, due primarily to proceeds from debt spun off with the Fisher-Price business. Total debt increased $216.8 million from June 30, 1989 to June 30, 1990, driven primarily by the common share repurchase program (see Note 7). During fiscal 1990, the Company repurchased 3.7 million shares of outstanding common stock as part of a 7 million share repurchase program announced in May 1989. No shares were repurchased in fiscal 1991, because of the impending spin-off of Fisher-Price, leaving 3.3 million shares available to repurchase under this program. The Company's debt to total capitalization ratio was 47.4 percent at June 30, 1991 compared to 52.3 percent and 44.2 percent at June 30, 1990 and June 30, 1989, respectively.

On January 31, 1990, the Company filed a shelf registration with the Securities and Exchange Commission covering $600 million of debt securities. As of June 30, 1991, no securities have been issued under this registration statement.

Commercial paper has been the Company's primary source of short-term financing. Quaker's ratings of "A1" (Standard & Poor's) and "P1" (Moody's) have been maintained throughout the year. The available levels of borrowings are adequate to meet the Company's seasonal working capital needs. The Company maintains domestic and non-U.S. bank lines of credit for future corporate general requirements. For a discussion of these lines of credit, see Note 5.

The Quaker Oats Company and Subsidiaries

Notes to the Consolidated Financial Statements

143 Note 1

Summary of Significant Accounting Policies

Consolidation. The consolidated financial statements include The Quaker Oats Company and all of its subsidiaries ("the Company"). All significant intercompany transactions have been eliminated. Businesses acquired are included in the results of operations since their acquisition date. The Company's toy and juvenile products segment ("Fisher-Price") is reflected in the accompanying financial statements as a discontinued operation (see Note 2). Accordingly, unless otherwise indicated, the following notes relate to continuing operations only.

Foreign Currency Translation. Assets and liabilities of the Company's foreign affiliates, other than those located in highly inflationary countries, are translated at current exchange rates, while income and expenses are translated at average rates for the period. For entities in highly inflationary countries, a combination of current and historical rates is used to determine currency gains and losses resulting from financial statement translation and those resulting from transactions. Translation gains and losses are reported as a component of shareholders' equity, except for those associated with highly inflationary countries, which are reported directly in the Consolidated Statements of Income.

Cash and Cash Equivalents. Cash equivalents are composed of all highly liquid investments with an original maturity of three months or less. All other temporary investments are classified as short-term investments.

Inventories. Inventories are valued at the lower of cost or market, using various cost methods, and include the cost of raw materials, labor and overhead. The percentage of year-end inventories valued using each of the methods is as follows:

June 30	1991	1990	1989
Last-in, first-out (LIFO)	61%	62%	63%
Average quarterly cost	27%	27%	22%
First-in, first-out (FIFO)	12%	11%	15%

If the LIFO method of valuing certain inventories were not used, total inventories would have been $18.9 million, $27.9 million, and $31 million higher than reported at June 30, 1991, 1990 and 1989, respectively.

The Company takes positions in the commodity futures and options markets as part of its overall raw materials purchasing strategy in order to reduce the risk associated with price fluctuations of commodities used in manufacturing. The gains and losses on futures contracts and options are included as a part of product cost.

Properties and Depreciation. Property, plant and equipment are carried at cost and depreciated on a straight-line basis over their estimated useful lives. Useful lives range from 5 to 50 years for buildings and improvements and from 3 to 20 years for machinery and equipment.

Intangibles. Intangible assets consist principally of excess purchase price over net tangible assets of businesses acquired (goodwill).

Goodwill is amortized on a straight-line basis over periods not exceeding 40 years. Accumulated goodwill amortization as of June 30, 1991, 1990 and 1989 is $86.5 million, $71.2 million and $55.6 million, respectively.

Income Taxes. Deferred income taxes are provided when tax laws and financial accounting standards differ in respect to the recording of depreciation, capitalized leases and other items. Federal income taxes have been provided on $96.1 million of the $311.5 million of unremitted earnings from foreign subsidiaries. Taxes are not provided on earnings expected to be indefinitely reinvested. See page 40 for a discussion of SFAS #96, "Accounting for Income Taxes."

Interest Rate Futures, Currency Swaps, Options and Forward Contracts. The Company enters into a variety of interest rate futures, currency swaps, options and forward contracts in its management of interest rate and foreign currency exposures. Realized and unrealized gains and losses on interest rate futures and options are deferred and recognized as interest expense over the borrowing period. Realized and unrealized gains and losses on foreign currency options and forward contracts which hedge operating income are recognized currently in other income and expense. Realized and unrealized gains and losses on foreign currency options that hedge foreign exchange rate exposure on future raw material purchases are deferred and recognized in cost of sales in the period in which purchases occur. Realized and unrealized gains and losses on foreign currency options, currency swaps, and forward contracts which are effective as net investment hedges are recognized in shareholders' equity.

Income Per Common Share. Income per common share is based on the weighted average number of common shares outstanding during the period.

Software Costs. As of July 1, 1989, the Company began deferring significant software development project costs, which had previously been expensed as incurred. Software costs of $12.2 million and $6.8 million were deferred during fiscal 1991 and 1990, respectively, pending capitalization at the projects' completion. In fiscal 1991, $3 million of the deferred costs were capitalized and are being amortized over a three-year period.

[144] **Note 2**
Discontinued Operations

In April 1990, the Company's Board of Directors approved in principle the distribution of Fisher-Price to the Company's shareholders. Accordingly, Fisher-Price has been reflected as a discontinued operation in the accompanying financial statements for all periods presented. The tax-free distribution was completed on June 28, 1991 and Fisher-Price, Inc., an independent free-standing company, was created. The distribution reduced reinvested earnings by $200 million. The $29.6 million payable to Fisher-Price at June 30, 1991 represents an estimate of the final cash settlement pursuant to the Distribution Agreement. Each holder of Quaker common stock on July 8, 1991 received one share of Fisher-Price, Inc. common stock for every five shares of Quaker common stock held as of such date. Fisher-Price, Inc. common stock is publicly traded.

The loss from discontinued operations for fiscal 1990 was $59.9 million, or 78 cents per share, including $25.5 million, or 33 cents per share, for the loss from the first nine months of fiscal 1990 and an after-tax provision of $34.4 million, or 45 cents per share, recorded in the fourth quarter. The third-quarter results included charges of $10.7 million, or 8 cents per share, for the East Aurora, New York manufacturing facility closing and $17 million, or 23 cents per share, for anticipated transaction expenses of the planned spin-off and projected operating losses (including allocated interest expense) through the expected completion date of the spin-off. The fourth-quarter provision included charges of $8.6 million, or 7 cents per share, for the pending closing of Fisher-Price's Holland, New York manufacturing facility and $4.8 million, or 4 cents per share, for costs relating to staff reductions. The fourth-quarter provision also included $25.4 million, or 21 cents per share, for inventory write-downs and the cost of maintaining related trade programs and $18.1 million, or 13 cents per share, for higher projected operating losses through the spin-off date due to lower than previously anticipated sales volumes.

During fiscal 1991, the Company recorded an additional $50 million pretax charge ($30 million after tax), or 40 cents per share to discontinued operations. The charge related primarily to receivables credit risk exposure, product recall reserves and severance costs.

The following summarizes the results of operations for discontinued operations:

Dollars in Millions	1991	1990	1989
Sales	$601.0	$702.6	$844.8
Pretax earnings (loss)	$(50.0)	$(96.2)	$ 89.6
Income taxes (benefit)	(20.0)	(36.3)	35.5
Income (loss) from discontinued operations	$ (30.0)	$ (59.9)	$ 54.1

Fisher-Price operating loss for fiscal 1991 was approximately $35 million.

Fisher-Price operating losses for the fourth quarter of fiscal 1990, including the Holland, New York plant closing and severance charges, were $40 million, including allocated interest expense of $1.2 million. Interest expense of $6.7 million, $7.4 million and $7.1 million was allocated to discontinued operations in fiscal 1991, 1990 and 1989, respectively.

[145] **Note 3**
Accounts Receivable Allowances

Dollars in Millions	1991	1990	1989
Balance at beginning of year	$16.5	$16.5	$18.1
Provision for doubtful accounts	5.8	3.8	2.8
Provision for discounts and allowances	15.8	6.7	7.2
Write-offs of doubtful accounts, net of recoveries	(4.6)	(2.0)	(5.3)
Discounts and allowances taken	(14.8)	(8.5)	(6.3)
Balance at end of year	$18.7	$16.5	$16.5

The Quaker Oats Company and Subsidiaries

146 **Note 4**
Property, Plant and Equipment

Dollars in Millions

1991

	Balance at Beginning of Year	Additions	Retirements and Sales	Other Changes	Balance at End of Year
Gross property:					
Land	$ 31.0	$ .8	$ (.2)	$ (.6)	$ 31.0
Buildings and improvements	395.2	41.5	(4.4)	(5.1)	427.2
Machinery and equipment	1,319.4	198.3	(38.1)	(23.2)	1,456.4
Total	$1,745.6	$240.6	$ (42.7)	$(28.9)	$1,914.6
Accumulated depreciation:					
Buildings and improvements	$ 94.1	$ 13.6	$ (1.8)	$ (1.8)	$ 104.1
Machinery and equipment	497.4	115.0	(23.0)	(11.6)	577.8
Total	$ 591.5	$128.6	$ (24.8)	$(13.4)	$ 681.9

1990

	Balance at Beginning of Year	Additions	Retirements and Sales	Other Changes	Balance at End of Year
Gross property:					
Land	$ 30.6	$ .5	$ (1.1)	$ 1.0	$ 31.0
Buildings and improvements	348.2	36.4	(1.5)	12.1	395.2
Machinery and equipment	1,078.1	238.7	(36.1)	38.7	1,319.4
Total	$1,456.9	$275.6	$ (38.7)	$ 51.8	$1,745.6
Accumulated depreciation:					
Buildings and improvements	$ 80.9	$ 11.3	$ (.7)	$ 2.6	$ 94.1
Machinery and equipment	416.4	95.2	(26.2)	12.0	497.4
Total	$ 497.3	$106.5	$ (26.9)	$ 14.6	$ 591.5

1989

	Balance at Beginning of Year	Additions	Retirements and Sales	Other Changes	Balance at End of Year
Gross property:					
Land	$ 30.1	$ 3.9	$ (3.7)	$ .3	$ 30.6
Buildings and improvements	341.7	36.4	(24.3)	(5.6)	348.2
Machinery and equipment	1,031.3	208.4	(142.5)	(19.1)	1,078.1
Total	$1,403.1	$248.7	$(170.5)	$(24.4)	$1,456.9
Accumulated depreciation:					
Buildings and improvements	$ 75.0	$ 11.1	$ (3.7)	$ (1.5)	$ 80.9
Machinery and equipment	405.6	85.9	(66.2)	(8.9)	416.4
Total	$ 480.6	$ 97.0	$ (69.9)	$(10.4)	$ 497.3

The "Additions" column for fiscal 1989 includes acquisitions made by the Company during that year. Included in the "Other Changes" column for fiscal 1991, 1990 and 1989 are net increases (decreases) of $(18.1), $22.7 and $(13.2) million, respectively, reflecting the effect of translating non-U.S. property at current exchange rates as required by SFAS #52.

147 **Note 5**
Short-term Debt and Lines of Credit

Dollars in Millions

	1991	1990	1989
Notes payable—			
Non-U.S. subsidiaries	$ 67.6	$127.1	$ 49.6
Commercial paper—U.S.			
Dealer-placed on the open market	13.0	216.1	302.6
Commercial paper to be refinanced	—	—	(250.0)
	$ 80.6	$343.2	$102.2
Weighted average interest rates on debt outstanding at end of year—			
Notes payable to banks—non-U.S.	12.1%	17.4%	14.5%
Commercial paper—U.S.	5.9%	8.2%	9.4%
Weighted average interest rates on debt outstanding during the year—			
Notes payable to banks—non-U.S. (computed on month-end balances)	50.7%(a)	76%(a)	50.5%(a)
Commercial paper—U.S. (computed on daily balances)	7.2%	8.5%	8.9%
Average amount of debt outstanding during the year	$263.5	$264.6	$357.7
Maximum month-end balance during the year	$391.4	$355.7	$486.5

(a) The interest rate on debt outstanding was driven principally by periods of high real interest rates in Latin America combined with proportionately lower devaluation of local currencies resulting in high interest rates in dollar terms.

The consolidated balance sheet at June 30, 1989 reflects the reclassification of $250 million of short-term debt, reflecting the Company's intent to refinance this debt on a long-term basis. During fiscal 1990, the Company issued $250 million of medium-term notes. (See Note 6).

The Company has a Revolving Credit Agreement with various banks, which supports its commercial paper borrowings and is also available for direct borrowings. The amount of available borrowings under the agreement was $500 million. The

Agreement, which expires no sooner than June 30, 1996, requires a commitment fee of one-eighth percent per annum, payable on any available and unused portion. There were no borrowings under the Agreement during fiscal 1991, 1990 or 1989. As of July 2, 1991, the amount of available borrowings under the Agreement was reduced to $300 million.

The Company's non-U.S. subsidiaries have additional unused short-term lines of credit of approximately $195 million at June 30, 1991.

Under the most restrictive terms of the various loan agreements in effect at June 30, 1991, minimum working capital of $250 million must be maintained.

**[148] Note 6
Long-term Debt**

Dollars in Millions	1991	1990	1989
Sinking Fund Debentures:			
7.7% due through 2001	$ 16.1	$ 18.5	$ 21.5
8% due through 1999	8.4	9.5	10.6
Industrial Revenue Bonds:			
6%-11.5% due through 2010, tax-exempt	39.0	46.0	46.0
4.5%-8.375% due through 2003, taxable	7.1	8.2	7.4
Non-interest bearing installment note due 2014	3.1	2.7	2.4
7.83% Senior ESOP Notes due through 2002	94.5	98.2	100.0
8.07% Senior ESOP Notes due through 2002	148.2	150.0	150.0
8.75% ESOP installment loan due through 1996	12.2	14.1	15.8
7.2%-7.9% Series A Medium-term Notes due through 2000	119.6	134.6	157.1
5.415% and 6.65% deutsche mark swaps due 1993 and 1998	25.6	27.9	23.8
8.15%-9.34% Series B Medium-term Notes due 1993 through 2020	250.0	250.0	—
Commercial paper to be refinanced	—	—	250.0
Other	10.3	12.9	12.2
	$734.1	$772.6	$796.8
Less: Current portion	32.9	32.3	30.0
Net Long-term Debt	$701.2	$740.3	$766.8

All maturity dates presented refer to fiscal years.

Aggregate required payments of maturities on long-term debt for the next five fiscal years are as follows:

					Dollars in Millions
Year ended June 30	1992	1993	1994	1995	1996
Required Payments	$32.9	$45.3	$48.5	$46.1	$38.9

During fiscal 1990, the Company issued $250 million of Series B Medium-term Notes bearing interest rates ranging from 8.15 percent to 9.34 percent per annum with maturities from 3 to 30 years. The debt issuance was covered under a $250 million shelf registration filed with the Securities and Exchange Commission during March 1987. Although none of these securities were issued as of June 30, 1989, the consolidated balance sheet as of that date reflects a reclassification of $250 million of commercial paper to long-term debt due to the Company's intent to issue the medium-term notes in fiscal 1990.

During January 1990, the Company filed a shelf registration with the Securities and Exchange Commission covering $600 million worth of debt securities. No securities have been issued under the registration statement as of June 30, 1991.

The Quaker Employee Stock Ownership Plan (ESOP) was expanded during fiscal 1989 through two separate transactions:

– In January 1989, the ESOP through a trust issued $150 million Senior ESOP Notes bearing interest at a rate of 8.07 percent per annum. The proceeds from these notes were used to purchase the Company's common stock on the open market.

– In June 1989, the ESOP incurred an additional $100 million of indebtedness through the issuance via a trust of 7.83 percent Senior ESOP Notes. The proceeds from these notes were used to acquire shares of the Company's Series B ESOP Convertible Preferred Stock.

Both issues of Senior ESOP Notes are due through fiscal 2002 and are unconditionally guaranteed by the Company. See Note 8 for a further description of these transactions.

The Quaker Oats Company and Subsidiaries

In July 1987, $25 million of 8.55 and 9.2 percent medium-term notes were issued, completing the $200 million Series A Medium-term Note offering begun in January 1987. The notes mature during fiscal years 1993 and 1998. This note offering was concurrently swapped into deutsche marks at interest rates of 5.415 percent and 6.63 percent. The swap is effective as a net investment hedge.

The non-interest bearing note for $55.5 million (due fiscal 2014) has an unamortized discount of $52.4 million, $52.8 million and $53.1 million as of June 30, 1991, 1990 and 1989, respectively, based on an imputed interest rate of 13 percent.

The 7.7 percent sinking fund debenture requires annual payments of $1.8 million through fiscal 2000 and a final payment of $6.8 million due in June 2001. The 8 percent sinking fund debenture, which is an obligation of Stokely-Van Camp Inc., a subsidiary of the Company, requires annual payments of $1.3 million through October 1997 with a final payment of $5.3 million due in October 1998. Amounts held in treasury for these sinking fund requirements were as follows:

		Dollars in Millions	
June 30	1991	1990	1989
7.7% Sinking Fund Debenture	$6.9	$6.3	$5.1
8% Sinking Fund Debenture	$5.2	$5.2	$5.2

[149] **Note 7**
Capital Stock

In May 1989, the Company announced its intent to repurchase, from time to time, up to seven million shares of its outstanding common stock through open market purchases and privately negotiated transactions. As of June 30, 1991, 3,703,000 shares have been repurchased. In June 1989, the ESOP through a trust issued $100 million of Senior ESOP Notes due through fiscal 2002 and bearing interest at a rate of 7.83 percent per annum. Concurrently, the Company sold 1,282,051 shares of the newly authorized issue of Series B ESOP Convertible Preferred Stock to the ESOP. Each share of the preferred stock, of which 1,750,000 shares are authorized, is convertible into one share of the Company's common stock and pays a dividend of $5.46. The preferred stock will be issued only for the ESOP and will not trade on the open market.

In June 1989, the Company completed the repurchase of two million shares under a program announced in fiscal 1988, and in January 1988 completed a two million share repurchase program (adjusted for the November 1986 stock split-up), announced in fiscal 1986. Repurchased shares are used for general corporate purposes including stock option and incentive plans.

The Company is authorized to issue one million shares of redeemable preference stock and an additional ten million shares of a new class of preferred stock to be issued in series, whose terms will be fixed by resolution of the Board of Directors. As of June 30, 1991, none of the preference stock and 1,282,051 shares of the preferred stock have been issued.

The Dividend Reinvestment and Stock Purchase Plan exists for eligible employees and shareholders. The Plan allows for the use of open market, unissued or treasury shares. The shares used in fiscal 1991, 1990 and 1989 were open market shares.

[150] **Note 8**
Deferred Compensation

The Quaker Employee Stock Ownership Plan (ESOP) was expanded during fiscal 1989 through two separate transactions. In January 1989, the ESOP through a trust issued $150 million Senior ESOP Notes due through fiscal 2002 and bearing interest at a rate of 8.07 percent per annum. The proceeds from the notes, which were received by the trust, were used to purchase 2,813,152 shares of the Company's common stock on the open market. The Senior ESOP Notes are unconditionally guaranteed by the Company.

During May 1989, the Company announced that its Board of Directors authorized the ESOP to incur up to an additional $125 million of indebtedness, which would also be guaranteed by the Company. The Company announced that a new issue of up to $125 million of convertible preferred stock for the ESOP would be purchased with the proceeds of the ESOP debt. In June 1989, the ESOP through a trust issued $100 million of Senior ESOP Notes due through fiscal 2002 and bearing interest at a rate of 7.83 percent per annum. The proceeds from these notes were used to acquire 1,282,051 shares of Series B ESOP Convertible Preferred Stock.

These transactions represent an expansion of the original ESOP, which was adopted during fiscal 1986. The loans from the original and expanded ESOP programs are included as long-term debt on the Company's consolidated balance sheets. Deferred compensation of $262.5 million represents primarily the Company's payment of future compensation expense related to the original and expanded ESOP programs.

As the Company makes annual contributions to the ESOP, these contributions, along with the dividends accumulated on the Company's common and preferred stock held by the ESOP, will be used to repay the outstanding loans. As the loans are repaid, common and preferred stock is allocated to ESOP participants, and deferred compensation is reduced by the amount of the principal payment on the loans.

The following table presents the ESOP loan repayments:

	1991	1990	1989
		Dollars in Millions	
Principal payments	$ 7.4	$ 3.5	$1.6
Interest payments	20.9	17.4	1.5
Total ESOP payments	$28.3	$20.9	$3.1

As of June 30, 1991, 883,395 shares of common stock and 166,470 shares of preferred stock have been allocated to the accounts of ESOP participants.

[15] Note 9
Employee Stock Option and Award Plans

During fiscal 1990, Quaker shareholders approved the adoption of The Quaker Long-Term Incentive Plan of 1990 ("the Plan"). The purpose of the Plan is to promote the interests of the Company and its shareholders by providing the officers and other key employees with additional incentive and the opportunity through stock ownership to increase their proprietary interest in the Company and their personal interest in its continued success. The Plan provides for benefits to be awarded in the form of options, stock appreciation rights, restricted stock (with corresponding cash awards), performance shares, performance units, and other stock based awards. Six million shares of common stock have been authorized for grant under the Plan. Previously, stock options were issued under the 1984 Long-Term Incentive Plan, which expired by its terms on December 31, 1990. Restricted stock awards were previously issued under the 1984 Restricted Stock Plan, which was terminated during fiscal 1990. Officers and other managerial employees may be granted options for the purchase of common stock at a price not less than the fair market value at date of grant. Options are generally exercisable after one or more years and expire no later than ten years from date of grant. As of June 30, 1991, 534 persons held such options. Changes in stock options outstanding are summarized as follows:

	Shares	Options Price (Per Share)
Balance at June 30, 1988	3,226,408	$ 5.64-44.25
Granted	796,820	53.88
Exercised	(651,108)	5.64-44.25
Expired or terminated	(87,633)	10.67-53.88
Balance at June 30, 1989	3,284,487	$ 6.74-53.88
Granted	809,300	57.00
Exercised	(535,194)	6.74-53.88
Expired or terminated	(103,356)	6.74-57.00
Balance at June 30, 1990	3,455,237	$ 7.08-57.00
Granted	781,100	49.50
Exercised	(600,065)	7.08-57.00
Expired or terminated	(210,554)	28.69-57.00
Balance at June 30, 1991	3,425,718	$ 8.30-57.00

During July 1991, the number and exercise price of all options outstanding at the time of the Fisher-Price spin-off (see Note 2) were adjusted to compensate for decreases in the economic value of the options as a result of the distribution to shareholders. This adjustment increased the number of options outstanding by 293,241 and decreased the exercise price of the options outstanding by approximately 8 percent.

At June 30, 1991, options for 2,664,490 shares were exercisable. As of June 30, 1991, the average per share option price of unexercised options expiring during the period January 13, 1992 to January 9, 2001 was $43.46.

Since fiscal 1977, the stock option plans have provided for the granting of stock appreciation rights in tandem with the granting of stock options. At June 30, 1991, 42,156 stock appreciation rights were attached to outstanding options.

Restricted stock awards grant shares of the Company's common stock to key officers and employees. These shares are subject to a restriction period from the date of grant, during which they may not be sold, assigned, pledged or otherwise encumbered. The number of shares of the Company's common stock awarded were 172,700, 3,700 and 10,200 in fiscal years 1991, 1990, 1989, respectively. Restrictions on these awards lapse after a period of time designated by the Plan committee. In addition, participants may receive a cash award at the end of the restricted period not to exceed 200 percent of the current market value of the shares received as designated by the committee.

The Quaker Oats Company and Subsidiaries

[152] Note 10
Shareholder Rights Plan

The Company's Shareholder Rights Plan, adopted July 9, 1986 and amended July 12, 1989, is designed to deter coercive or unfair takeover tactics and to prevent a person or group from gaining control of the Company without offering a fair price to all shareholders.

Under the terms of the plan, all common shareholders of record on July 30, 1986 received for each share owned one "Right" entitling them to purchase from the Company one one-hundredth of a newly issued share of Series A Junior Participating Preferred Stock at an exercise price of $300.

The Rights become exercisable (1) ten days after a public announcement that a person or group has acquired shares representing 20 percent or more of the voting power of the Company's capital stock, (2) ten business days following commencement of a tender offer for more than 20 percent of such voting power, or (3) ten business days after a holder of at least 15 percent of such voting power is determined to be an adverse person by the Board of Directors. The time periods can be extended by the Company. Unless the Board of Directors has made a determination that any person is an adverse person, the Company can redeem the Rights for $.05 per Right at any time prior to their becoming exercisable. The Rights will expire on July 30, 1996 unless redeemed earlier by the Company.

If after the Rights become exercisable the Company is involved in a merger or other business combination at any time when there is a holder of 20 percent or more of Quaker's stock, the Rights will then entitle a holder, upon exercise of the Rights, to receive shares of common stock of the acquiring company with a market value equal to twice the exercise price of each Right. Alternatively, if a 20 percent holder acquires the Company by means of a reverse merger in which the Company and its stock survive, or if any person acquires 20 percent or more of the Company's voting power or acquires 15 percent of the Company's voting power and is determined by the Board to be an adverse person, each Right not owned by such 20 percent shareholder or adverse person would, upon exercise of the Right, entitle the holder to common stock of the Company (or in certain circumstances other consideration) having a market value equal to twice the exercise price of the Right. The rights described in this paragraph shall not apply to an acquisition, merger or consolidation which is determined by a majority of the Company's independent directors, after consulting one or more investment banking firms, to be fair and otherwise in the best interest of the Company and its shareholders.

[153] Note 11
Pension Plans and Other Post-Employment Benefits

The Company has various pension plans covering substantially all of its domestic and certain foreign employees. Plan benefits are based on years of service and earnings. Company policy is to make contributions to its U.S. plans within the maximum amount deductible for federal income tax purposes. Plan assets consist primarily of equity securities as well as government, corporate and other fixed-income obligations.

The components of net pension cost for defined benefit plans are detailed below:

Dollars in Millions	1991	1990	1989
Service cost (benefits earned during the year)	$28.5	$26.7	$22.7
Interest cost on projected benefit obligation	39.7	36.5	34.1
Actual return on plan assets	(70.5)	(66.7)	(51.6)
Net amortization and deferral	9.8	10.6	(3.3)
U.S. and Canadian pension cost	7.5	7.1	1.9
Multi-employer plans	.7	.8	.7
Foreign plans	3.2	.6	3.7
Net pension cost	$11.4	$ 8.5	$ 6.3

Reconciliations of the funded status of the Company's defined benefit plans to the accrued pension asset (liability) included in the consolidated balance sheets are as follows:

Dollars in Millions	Overfunded			Underfunded		
	1991	1990	1989	1991	1990	1989
Vested benefits	$363.6	$336.8	$307.7	$43.6	$42.8	$37.8
Non-vested benefits	8.1	12.9	10.5	.2	.6	.3
Accumulated benefit obligation	371.7	349.7	318.2	43.8	43.4	38.1
Effect of projected future salary increases	54.2	61.7	56.7	5.4	11.8	7.1
Projected benefit obligation	425.9	411.4	374.9	49.2	55.2	45.2
Plan assets at market value	588.2	543.7	499.3	28.0	26.7	25.5
Projected benefit obligation less (greater) than plan assets	162.3	132.3	124.4	(21.2)	(28.5)	(19.7)
Unrecognized net (gain)	(81.3)	(39.5)	(12.4)	(14.1)	(5.7)	(6.3)
Unrecognized prior service cost	10.4	9.1	9.5	5.6	6.3	1.6
Unrecognized net (asset) liability at transition	(83.8)	(90.8)	(109.0)	5.6	6.3	7.1
Prepaid (accrued) pension costs (in the Balance Sheet)	$ 7.6	$ 11.1	$ 12.5	$(24.1)	$(21.6)	$(17.3)

Assumptions:
Weighted average discount rate: 9%
Rate of future compensation increases: 6%
Long-term rate of return on plan assets: 9%

Foreign pension plan assets and accumulated benefit obligations are not significant in the aggregate. Therefore, SFAS #87 disclosures have not been presented for these plans.

In addition, the Company provides certain health care and life insurance benefits to its retired employees. A substantial number of the Company's domestic employees and certain employees in foreign countries become eligible for these benefits if they meet retirement age and service requirements while still working for the Company. These costs are expensed as incurred and amounted to $7.4 million, $6.9 million and $6.4 million in fiscal 1991, 1990 and 1989, respectively.

In December 1990, the Financial Accounting Standards Board issued Statement #106, "Employer's Accounting for Postretirement Benefits Other Than Pensions." This new standard requires that the expected cost of these benefits be charged to expense during the years that the employees render service. This is a significant change from the Company's current policy of recognizing these costs on the cash basis. The Company is required to adopt the new accounting and disclosure rules no later than fiscal 1994, although earlier implementation is permitted. The Company may adopt the new standard prospectively or via a cumulative catch-up adjustment.

The Company has not decided when it will adopt the new standard or if it will adopt the new accounting method prospectively or by recording a cumulative catch-up adjustment in the year of adoption. Because of the complexities of the new standard, management has not yet determined the effect that the change in accounting will have on the Company's reported financial position and results of operations. However, management expects that the annual postretirement benefit expense computed in accordance with the new standard will be significantly greater than the annual cash payments.

[154] Note 12
Leases and Other Commitments

Certain equipment and operating properties are rented under non-cancellable operating leases that expire at various dates through 2002. Total rental expense under operating leases was $44.5 million, $44.3 million and $42.4 million in fiscal 1991, 1990 and 1989, respectively. Contingent rentals and subleases are not significant. Capital leases, which are included in fixed assets, and minimum lease payments under such leases are not significant.

The following is a schedule of future minimum annual rentals on non-cancellable operating leases, primarily for sales offices, warehouses and corporate headquarters in effect at June 30, 1991:

Dollars in Millions	1992	1993	1994	1995	1996	Later	Total
Total payments	$16.5	$16.5	$15.7	$15.2	$15.0	$66.8	$145.7

[155] Note 13
Supplementary Expense Data

Dollars in Millions	1991	1990	1989
Advertising, media and production	$ 277.5	$ 282.8	$ 256.5
Merchandising	1,129.9	912.5	886.2
Total advertising and merchandising	$1,407.4	$1,195.3	$1,142.7
Maintenance and repairs	$ 96.1	$ 96.6	$ 93.8
Depreciation expense	$ 125.2	$ 103.5	$ 94.5
Research and development	$ 44.3	$ 43.3	$ 39.3

[156] Note 14
Interest (Income) Expense

Dollars in Millions	1991	1990	1989
Interest expense on long-term debt	$ 43.3	$ 38.3	$25.7
Interest expense on short-term debt and other	60.5	84.7	52.4
Interest expense capitalized—net	(1.9)	(2.8)	(2.2)
Total interest expense	101.9	120.2	75.9
Interest income on securities	(5.5)	(7.2)	(7.3)
Interest income, other	(3.5)	(3.8)	(5.1)
Total interest income	(9.0)	(11.0)	(12.4)
Net interest allocated to discontinued operations	(6.7)	(7.4)	(7.1)
Total net interest expense	$ 86.2	$101.8	$56.4

The Quaker Oats Company and Subsidiaries

157 Note 15
Other (Income) Expense

Dollars in Millions	1991	1990	1989
Foreign exchange (gains) losses—net	$(5.1)	$25.7	$14.8
Amortization of intangibles	22.4	22.2	18.2
Losses (gains) from plant closings and operations sold or to be sold—net	8.8	(23.1)	119.4
Miscellaneous—net	6.5	(8.4)	(2.8)
Net other expense	$32.6	$16.4	$149.6

158 Note 16
Provision for Income Taxes

Provisions for income taxes applicable to continuing operations were as follows:

Dollars in Millions	1991	1990	1989
Currently payable—			
Federal	$103.0	$72.7	$12.7
Non-U.S.	36.6	44.3	26.9
State	21.8	17.9	10.0
Total currently payable	161.4	134.9	49.6
Deferred—net			
Federal	6.7	13.4	30.8
Non-U.S.	4.1	5.4	8.2
State	3.5	(.2)	1.6
Total deferred—net	14.3	18.6	40.6
Total income tax provision	$175.7	$153.5	$90.2

158A
The components of the deferred income tax provision were as follows:

Dollars in Millions	1991	1990	1989
Accelerated tax depreciation	$ 8.4	$14.5	$15.0
Receipt of tax benefits	(1.3)	(2.8)	(2.1)
Long-term tax liability	—	—	18.2
Tax benefits—ANC(a)	—	—	(1.7)
Other—net	7.2	6.9	11.2
Total deferred income tax provision	$14.3	$18.6	$40.6

158B
The sources of pretax income from continuing operations were as follows:

Dollars in Millions	1991	1990	1989
U.S. sources	$328.7	$265.2	$162.2
Non-U.S. sources	82.8	117.2	76.9
Total income before taxes	$411.5	$382.4	$239.1

A reconciliation of the statutory federal income tax rate to the effective income tax rate follows:

158C

Dollars in Millions	1991		1990		1989	
	Amount	% of Pretax Income	Amount	% of Pretax Income	Amount	% of Pretax Income
Tax provision based on the federal statutory rate	$139.9	34.0%	$130.0	34.0%	$81.3	34.0%
State and local income taxes, net of federal income tax benefit	16.7	4.1	11.9	3.1	7.7	3.2
ANC benefit(a)	—	—	—	—	(1.7)	(.7)
Repatriation of foreign earnings	4.3	1.0	4.8	1.3	(2.1)	(.9)
Non-U.S. tax rate differential	8.2	2.0	9.8	2.5	8.8	3.7
U.S. tax credits	(.2)	(.1)	(.1)	—	(.7)	(.3)
Miscellaneous items—net	6.8	1.6	(2.9)	(.8)	(3.1)	(1.3)
Actual tax provision	$175.7	42.7%	$153.5	40.1%	$90.2	37.7%

(a)In fiscal 1989, the Company recognized $1.7 million of tax benefits in its provision for income taxes related to Alaskan Native Corporation (ANC) agreements. The ANC agreements granted the Company the right to utilize net operating losses of the ANC's for tax purposes during fiscal 1987 and 1988. At June 30, 1991, $67.8 million relating to these agreements are included in deferred taxes.

Note 17
Supplemental Cash Flow Information

Dollars in Millions	1991	1990	1989
Interest paid	$101.7	$96.8	$73.8
Income taxes paid	$88.7	$90.7	$140.0

Interest paid and income taxes paid include amounts related to Fisher-Price. The Company assumed liabilities in conjunction with acquisitions in fiscal 1989 of $13.6 million.

Note 18
Financial Instruments

Foreign Currency Forward Contracts. At June 30, 1991, the Company had forward contracts for the purchase and sale of European and Canadian currencies to hedge foreign exchange operating income and balance sheet exposure, purchases totaling $47.2 million and sales totaling $148.9 million. While the contracts generally mature in less than 12 months, the total sales include obligations to sell $8.2 million in British pounds in fiscal 1998 and $7.6 million in Canadian dollars in fiscal 1994.

Deutsche Mark Swap. During fiscal 1988, the Company swapped $25 million for deutsche marks in two separate transactions. The Company is committed to re-exchange 18.5 million deutsche marks for $10 million in August 1992 and 27.9 million deutsche marks for $15 million in August 1997. The Company is also committed to make semi-annual interest payments of 1.4 million deutsche marks through August 1992 and, thereafter, 0.9 million deutsche marks through August 1997.

Note 19
Litigation

On December 18, 1990 Judge Prentice H. Marshall of the United States District Court for the Northern District of Illinois issued a memorandum opinion stating that the Court would enter judgment against the Company in favor of Sands, Taylor & Wood Co. The Court found that the use of the words "thirst aid" in advertising *Gatorade* thirst quencher infringed the Plaintiff's rights in the trademark THIRST-AID. On July 9, 1991 Judge Marshall entered a judgment of $42.6 million, composed of $31.4 million in principal, plus prejudgment interest of $10.6 million, and fees, expenses and costs of $0.6 million. The order enjoins use of the phrase "THIRST-AID" in connection with the advertising or sale of *Gatorade* thirst quencher in the United States. The Company and its subsidiary, Stokely-Van Camp, Inc., ceased use of the words "thirst aid" in December 1990. The Company on the advice of inside and outside counsel, strongly believes that it will prevail in an appeal of the judgment. Therefore, no provision for loss has been made in the accompanying financial statements.

The Company is not a party to any other pending legal proceedings which it believes will have a material adverse effect on its financial position or results of operations.

Note 20
Quarterly Financial Data (Unaudited)

Year Ended June 30

Dollars in Millions (Except Per Share Data)

1991	First Quarter	Second Quarter(a)	Third Quarter	Fourth Quarter(b)
Net sales	$1,326.5	$1,293.8	$1,334.6	$1,536.3
Cost of goods sold	685.2	689.0	682.3	783.2
Gross profit	$641.3	$604.8	$652.3	$753.1
Income from continuing operations	$33.2	$33.1	$63.1	$106.4
(Loss) from discontinued operations, net of tax	—	(30.0)	—	—
Net income	$33.2	$3.1	$63.1	$106.4
Per common share:				
Income from continuing operations	$0.42	$0.43	$0.82	$1.38
(Loss) from discontinued operations	—	(0.40)	—	—
Net income	$0.42	$0.03	$0.82	$1.38
Cash dividends declared	$0.39	$0.39	$0.39	$0.39
Market price range:				
High	$50⅝	$53	$60⅝	$64¼
Low	$41⅛	$42⅛	$47⅛	$55¼

(a) Includes a provision for discontinued operations of $30 million after-tax ($.40 per share) for Fisher-Price receivables, credit risk exposure, product recall reserves, and severance costs.
(b) Includes a charge of $6.6 million after-tax ($.08 per share) for the closing of a Golden Grain pasta manufacturing facility. Also includes a $4.2 million after-tax ($.05 per share) credit for favorable LIFO price variances that were not projected in the prior fiscal 1991 quarters.

Appendix

THE AUDITOR'S OPINION— MEANING AND SIGNIFICANCE

An entity's financial statements are the representations of its management. Management bears a primary responsibility for the fairness of presentation and the degree of informative disclosure in the financial statements it issues to interested parties, such as present and potential owners, creditors, and others. It has, however, become generally accepted that there is a need for an independent check on management's financial reporting.

The profession that serves society's need in this respect by performing the attest function is the public accounting profession. It may be readily observed that the more developed a country's economy and the more diverse, free, and mobile its capital and money markets, the stronger and the more important its public accounting profession is likely to be. Surely, the United States experience supports this conclusion, for the public accounting profession here is perhaps the world's largest and most vital.

Some states recognize and license "Public Accountants" and "Licensed Accountants," and the requirements for practice under these titles vary from strict to feeble. However, there is another title that has the most consistent significance—that of "Certified Public Accountant." It can be acquired only by those who have passed the CPA examination, a rigorous series of tests that are uniform in all states and that are graded centrally under the auspices of the American Institute of Certified Public Accountants (AICPA). While no profession can ensure uniformity of quality among its members, the successful completion of these examinations does ensure that the candidate has demonstrated a sufficiently acceptable knowledge of accounting and auditing principles and practices.

Since the CPAs represent by far the most important segment of public accounting practice in the United States, our consideration of the auditor's opinion will be confined to that issued by the CPA and governed by the various pronouncements issued by their professional association, the AICPA.

Author's Note: Women have been analysts and auditors for years, and their numbers are growing. In this book masculine pronouns are often used for succinctness and are intended to refer to both males and females.

In spite of the many real and imagined shortcomings of the auditor's work, and, as this book illustrates, there are many of both varieties, the auditor's function is of critical importance to the financial analyst. While improvements are needed in many areas of the auditor's work, his or her attestation to the fair presentation of the financial statements greatly increases their reliability to the analyst as well as the degree and quality of disclosure provided in them.

As in many areas of endeavor, so in the analysis of financial statements, partial or incomplete knowledge can be more damaging than a complete lack of it. This truth applies to the analyst's understanding and knowledge of the auditor's work and the significance of his opinion.

WHAT THE ANALYST NEEDS TO KNOW

In relying on the auditor's opinion, which covers the financial statements subject to review, the analyst must—

1. Learn as much as possible about the auditor upon whom reliance is placed.
2. Understand fully what the auditor's opinion means and the message it is designed to convey to the user.
3. Appreciate the limitations to which the opinion is subject, as well as the implications that such limitations hold for the analysis of financial statements covered by the opinion.

Knowing the Auditor

The possession by the auditor of the CPA certificate does assure the analyst of a reasonable qualification for practice as an auditor. However, as is the case in other professions, differences in ability, competence, and qualifications can be considerable.

The relationship between the auditor and those who rely on his opinion differs markedly from that existing in other professional relationships. While the auditor has both an obligation and a concurrent responsibility to users of his opinion, he is in most cases neither appointed nor compensated by them. He must look mostly to management for both recommendation for his appointment and the determination of his fee. When management's desires with respect to financial reporting are in conflict with the best interests of the outside users of financial statements, the auditor's integrity and independence are put to a stern test. Thus, one criterion of the auditor's reliability is his reputation for integrity and independence in the community at large and among respected members of the financial community. Whatever else the auditor must have, and his qualifications and skill must be considerable, without these attributes nothing else counts for very much. The reputation of an auditor for competence and for knowledge of his work can be established in a variety of ways. The auditor's professional credentials, including the length, breadth, and quality of his experience, are one element; his membership and standing in state and national accounting associations another; and his participation in professional organizations yet another factor to be assessed by the analyst. An auditing firm's activities and past performance are usually well known in the community in which it operates.

Finally, the analyst from his own experience is often able to form a judgment about the auditor's reputation for quality work. Since there exists considerable leeway in adherence to audit standards and in the application of accounting principles, an audit firm's "track record" of actual level of performances in these critical areas provides a firsthand guide to its reliability and integrity. The analyst would do well to note instances in which a CPA firm (1) has accepted the least desirable acceptable accounting principle among the available alternatives, (2) has equivocated unnecessarily in its opinion, or (3) was found wanting in adherence to auditing standards.

Good sources of information on the reputation and the capabilities of an audit firm include local bankers, investment bankers, attorneys, and particularly numerous findings and orders concerning auditor performance issued by the SEC.

The Auditor's Opinion

The auditor's opinion is the culmination of a lengthy and complicated process of auditing and investigation. It is here, and only here, that the auditor reports on the nature of his work and on the degree of responsibility he assumes. While his influence may be indirectly felt throughout the financial statements by the presentation, description, and footnote disclosure that he may have suggested or insisted upon, the opinion, and the opinion alone, remains his exclusive domain. Thus, the opinion and the references to the financial statements which it contains should always be carefully read. To ignore the auditor's opinion, or to assume that it does not mean what it says, or that it means more than it says, is unwarranted.

The auditor's responsibility to outsiders whom he does not know and who rely on his representations is considerable, and his exposure to liability arising therefrom is growing. Thus, the obligations that the standards of his profession impose on him, while extensive, are at the same time defined and limited. Consequently, no analyst is justified in assuming that the association of the auditor's name with the financial statements goes beyond what the auditor's opinion says, or is a form of insurance on which the analyst can rely to bail him out of bad decisions.

The accounting profession has increasingly had to cope with an "expectations gap," a gap between the responsibility it wants to assume as reflected by professional standards and the responsibility the public thinks is assumed by the auditor in his attesting opinion. In general terms that responsibility was clearly stated by Chief Justice Burger in a unanimous decision of the U.S. Supreme Court in March 1984:

> ... By certifying the public reports that collectively depict a corporation's financial status, the independent auditor assumes a *public* responsibility transcending any employment relationship with the client. The independent public accountant performing his special function owes ultimate allegiance to the corporation's creditors and stockholders, as well as to the investing public. The "public watchdog" function demands that the accountant maintain total independence from the client at all times and requires complete fidelity to the public trust.
>
> It is not enough that financial statements *be* accurate; the public must also *perceive* them as being accurate. Public faith in the reliability of a corporation's financial statements depends upon the public perception of the outside auditor as an independent professional ... if investors were to view the auditor as an advocate for the corporate client, the value of the audit function itself might well be lost.

The court's definition of the independent auditor's public responsibility laid down the general expectations the public is entitled to have with regard to his opinion, but the application of this doctrine to specific cases remains difficult and controversial. For example, does the financial failure of an enterprise shortly after an unqualified opinion has been rendered mean that the auditors fell short in their reporting responsibility? The answer to that question is complex and depends on many attending circumstances, all weighed by a public that believes the auditor's report (opinion) is in the nature of a guarantee of accuracy.

AUDITOR'S REPORT

To narrow the gap between the responsibility auditors intend to assume and the responsibility the public believes them to assume, the Auditing Standards Board (ASB) has revised language for the audit report. The language is intended to be less technical and to more explicitly address the responsibility the auditor assumes, the procedures which he performs, and the assurance which he provides. To this end the report:

1. States that the financial statements were *audited,* which is hoped will be a more descriptive term than the word *examined* used previously.
2. States specifically that the financial statements are the responsibility of *management* and that the auditor's responsibility is to express

an opinion on the financial statements, thus giving readers a clearer notice of the responsibilities assumed by each party.

3. States in the scope paragraph that the audit was conducted in accordance with generally accepted auditing standards and as such is designed to obtain reasonable assurance that the financial statements are free of *material misstatement.*

4. States that the steps the auditor takes to achieve *reasonable* assurance that the financial statements are free of material misstatement include *(a)* examining on a *test basis* evidence that supports the amounts and disclosures in the financial statements, *(b)* assessing the accounting principles used and estimates made by management, and *(c)* evaluating the overall financial statement presentations.

5. Indicates that the financial statements present fairly in all material respects the financial position, results of operations, and cash flows of the company for the period reported upon.

The Scope of the Audit

The introductory and scope paragraphs of the auditor's report set forth the financial statements examined, the period of time that they cover, and the scope of the audit to which they and the underlying records have been subjected.

The standard terminology refers to an audit made in accordance with "generally accepted auditing standards" (GAAS). This is "shorthand" for a very comprehensive meaning that is elaborated upon in the profession's literature and particularly in *Statements on Auditing Standards* and subsequent codifications. These auditing standards are broad generalizations classified under three headings: (1) general standards, (2) standards of fieldwork, and (3) standards of reporting.

General standards define the personal qualities required of the independent CPA. They are:

1. The examination is to be performed by a person or persons having adequate technical training and proficiency as an auditor.
2. In all matters relating to the assignment an independence in mental attitude is to be maintained by the auditor or auditors.
3. Due professional care is to be exercised in the performance of the examination and the preparation of the report.

Standards of fieldwork embrace the actual execution of the audit and cover the planning of the work, the evaluation of the client's system of internal control, and the quality and sufficiency of the audit evidence obtained. *SAS 1* enumerates them as follows:

1. The work is to be adequately planned and assistants, if any, are to be properly supervised.
2. There is to be a proper study and evaluation of the existing internal

control as a basis for reliance thereon and for the determination of the resultant extent of the tests to which auditing procedures are to be restricted.
3. Sufficient competent evidential matter is to be obtained through inspection, observation, inquiries, and confirmations to afford a reasonable basis for an opinion regarding the financial statements under examination.

Reporting standards govern the preparation and presentation of the auditor's report. They are intended to ensure that the auditor's position is clearly and unequivocally stated and that the degree of responsibility he assumes is made clear to the reader. These standards are:

1. The report shall state whether the financial statements are presented in accordance with generally accepted accounting principles.
2. The report shall identify those circumstances in which such principles have not been consistently observed in the current period in relation to the preceding period.
3. Informative disclosures in the financial statements are to be regarded as reasonably adequate unless otherwise stated in the report.
4. The report shall either contain an expression of opinion regarding the financial statements, taken as a whole, or an assertion to the effect that an opinion cannot be expressed. When an overall opinion cannot be expressed, the reasons therefore should be stated. In all cases where an auditor's name is associated with financial statements, the report should contain a clear-cut indication of the character of the auditor's examination, if any, and the degree of responsibility he is taking.

Audit standards are the yardsticks by which the quality of audit procedures are measured.

Auditing Procedures   The scope section describes auditing procedures as were considered necessary in the circumstances.

These encompass the wide sweep of auditing theory brought to bear on the particular examination, as well as the professional discretion the auditor uses in the performance of his work.

The subject of auditing is, of course, a discipline in itself requiring for successful mastery a period of study and practical application. Thus, while we obviously cannot go with any degree of detail into what constitutes the process of auditing, it behooves all who use its end product to have a basic understanding of the process by which the auditor obtains assurance about the fair presentation of the financial statements as to which he expresses an opinion.

A basic objective of the financial audit is the detection of errors and irregularities, which if undetected would materially affect the fairness of presentation of financial summarizations or their conformity with GAAP. Errors are distinguished from irregularities in the latter result from *intentional* misconduct.

To be economically feasible and justifiable, auditing can aim only at a reasonable level of assurance in this respect about the data under review. This means that under a testing system, assurance can never be complete, and that the final audit conclusions are subject to this inherent probability of error.

The Importance of Internal Control or Control Structure   After ascertaining, by means of investigation and inquiry, what management's plan and design for a system of internal control is, if any, the auditor proceeds to test the system in order to ascertain whether it is in existence and is, in fact, being implemented as intended. This testing is called compliance testing or Control-Risk-Assessment Procedures.

If after application of compliance testing, the control structure is found to be well conceived and in proper operation, the amount of testing to which income statement items or individual assets and liabilities will be subjected can be significantly reduced. The latter type of testing, which is called substantive testing, or Tests of Financial Statement Balances, will have to be increased significantly if compliance testing reveals the control structure to be deficient or not operational.

This method of evaluating the system and then performing additional sample tests on the basis of this evaluation does, of course, leave room for a great deal of professional discretion, for "corner-cutting," and for a variety of qualities of judgment. Hence, this method is subject to the risk of failure. However, an examination conducted in accordance with GAAS should be designed to detect material misstatements that affect the financial statements.

From the above discussion it should be clear that reliance on an audit must be based on an understanding of the nature of the audit process and the limitations to which it is subject.

The Opinion Section

The auditor's opinion deals with:

1. The fairness of presentation of the financial statements.
2. Their conformity with GAAP. (These two points are interrelated as many believe GAAP include a requirement for the disclosure needed to ensure that the financial statements are not misleading.)
3. Disclosure when a material change in accounting principle(s) has occurred.

"Fair Presentation"

One of the great debates among auditors and between auditors and society in general, particularly in the courts, concerns the meaning of the phrase "present fairly" which is found in the auditor's report. Most auditors maintain that financial statements are fairly presented when they conform to GAAP and that "fairness" is meaningful only when measured against some established standard such as GAAP.

Yet, clearly, in quite a number of cases reaching the courts, financial statements that, according to expert testimony were prepared in accordance with GAAP, were nevertheless found to be misleading in an overall sense. This became particularly apparent in the landmark *Continental Vending* case where the lack of disclosure of certain highly dubious transactions was defended as not being, at that time, required by GAAP. In refusing to instruct the jury that conformity with GAAP was a complete defense to the charge of fraud, the trial judge maintained that the critical question was whether Continental's financial statements, taken as a whole, "fairly presented" its financial picture. He found that while conformity with GAAP might be very persuasive evidence of an auditor's good faith, it was not necessarily conclusive evidence.

The auditors, in an attempt to respond to a clear divergence between their and society's views of what is meant by "present fairly," issued a statement maintaining that "fairness" must be applied within the framework of GAAP, and that "fair presentation" within that framework requires that—

a. The accounting principles selected and applied must have general acceptance.[1]
b. The accounting principles must be appropriate in the circumstances.
c. The financial statements must be "informative of matters that may affect their use, understanding, and interpretation."
d. The information must be presented and summarized "in a reasonable manner, that is, neither too detailed nor too condensed."
e. The financial statements must reflect "the underlying events and transactions" in a way that states the results within "a range of acceptable limits that are reasonable and practicable."

As part of the accounting profession's periodic attempts at self-examination and assessment, especially in the face of congressional and public scrutiny and criticism, an AICPA-appointed Commission on Auditor's Responsibilities issued its "Report, Conclusions, and Recommendations" in 1978. Only a few of the Commission's recommendations were adopted.

In 1987 the Report of the National Commission on Fraudulent Financial Reporting (the Treadway Commission) included recommendations on the audit report. The ASB in issuing its *Statement on Auditing Standards (SAS)* on "Reports on Audited Financial Statements" was guided by many of these pressures, ideas, and recommendations.

---

[1] *SAS 69* (1992) "The Meaning of Present Fairly in Conformity with Generally Accepted Accounting Principles in the Independent Auditor's Report" details a hierarchy of Generally Accepted Accounting Principles.

Modification of the Opinion

The standard short-form report may contain a "clean opinion"; that is, the auditor had no qualifications to record as to any of the criteria enumerated above. Any modifications of substance in the language of the auditor's opinion paragraph is, technically speaking, considered to be a qualification, a disclaimer, or an adverse opinion. Not all modifications are, of course, of equal significance to the user. Some deviations in language are explanatory in character reflecting matters that the auditor wishes to emphasize and may not affect the auditor's opinion significantly. References to the work of other auditors is not regarded as a qualification but rather an indication of divided responsibility for the financial statements. Other explanatory comments may not carry over to affect the auditor's opinion and, at times, one may wonder why mention of them is necessary. On the other hand, certain qualifications or disclaimers are so significant as to cast doubt on the reliability of the financial statements or their usefulness for decision-making purposes.

Let us then examine the major categories of the auditor's explanatory language, qualifications and disclaimers, the occasions on which they are properly used, and the significance which they hold to the user of financial statements.

CIRCUMSTANCES GIVING RISE TO EXPLANATORY LANGUAGE, QUALIFICATIONS, DISCLAIMERS, OR ADVERSE OPINIONS

There are four main categories of conditions that require explanatory language, qualifications, adverse opinions, or a disclaimer of opinion:

1. Limitations in the scope of the auditor's examination affected by *(a)* conditions that preclude the application of auditing procedures considered necessary in the circumstances or *(b)* restrictions imposed by the client.
2. The financial statements do not present fairly the financial position and/or results of operations because *(a)* they fail to conform with GAAP or *(b)* they do not contain adequate disclosure.
3. There exist uncertainties about the future resolution of material matters, the effect of which cannot presently be estimated or the outcome of which cannot reasonably be determined. This includes concerns regarding the enterprise's ability to continue in existence.
4. Inconsistent application of GAAP.

Before we consider the variety of conditions that call for qualified opinions, let us examine the major types of qualifications that the auditor may express.

QUALIFICATIONS—"EXCEPT FOR"

These qualifications express an opinion on the financial statements except for repercussions stemming from conditions that must be disclosed. They may arise from limitations in the scope of the audit which, because of circumstances beyond the auditor's control or because of restrictions imposed by the audited company, result in a failure to obtain reasonably objective and verifiable evidence in support of events which have taken place. They may arise from a lack of conformity of the financial statements to GAAP.

When there are uncertainties about future events that cannot be resolved or the effect of which cannot be estimated or reasonably provided for at the time the opinion is rendered, such as one due to operating losses or serious financial weakness that calls into question the fundamental assumption that an entity can continue to operate as a going concern, a separate paragraph should refer the reader to the note to the financial statements that provides data about the uncertainty. In cases of pervasive uncertainty that cannot be adequately measured, an auditor may, but is not required to, issue a disclaimer of opinion rather than merely call the reader's attention to the uncertainty.

ADVERSE OPINIONS

An adverse opinion should be rendered in cases when the financial statements are not prepared in accordance with GAAP, and this has a significant effect on the fair presentation of those statements. An adverse opinion results generally from a situation in which the auditor has been unable to convince his client to amend the financial statements so that they reflect the auditor's estimate about the outcome of future events or so that they otherwise adhere to GAAP. The issuance of an adverse opinion must always be accompanied by a statement of the reasons for such an opinion.

DISCLAIMER OF OPINION

A disclaimer of opinion is a statement of inability to express an opinion. It must be rendered when, for whatever reason, insufficient competent evidential matter is available to the auditor to enable him to form an opinion on the financial statements. It can arise from limitations in the scope of the audit as well as from the existence of uncertainties, the ultimate impact of which cannot be estimated. Material departures from GAAP do not justify a disclaimer of opinion.

Adverse Opinions versus Disclaimers of Opinion

The difference between adverse opinions and disclaimers of opinion can be best understood in terms of the difference that exists between exceptions that affect the quality of the financial statements, on one hand, and those that express uncertainties affecting the auditor's opinion, on the other. Thus, a situation that may call for an "except for" opinion may at some point result in such a degree of pervasive or material disagreements with management that it will require an adverse opinion.

THE FORM OF THE REPORT

Whenever the auditor expresses a qualified opinion, he must disclose in a middle paragraph, or in a footnote that is referred to in that paragraph, the substantive reasons for the qualification. The explanatory paragraph should disclose the principal effects of the subject matter of the qualification on financial position, results of operations, and changes in cash flows, if reasonably determinable.

All qualifications must be referred to in the opinion paragraph, and a qualification due to scope or lack of sufficient evidential matter must be also referred to in the scope paragraph. Thus, a mere explanatory statement should not be referred to in either the scope or the opinion paragraphs.

Having covered the various types of opinions an auditor can express, let us now turn to the various conditions that call for qualifications in such opinions.

LIMITATIONS IN THE SCOPE OF THE AUDIT

A limitation in the scope of the auditor's examination, that is, an inability to perform certain audit steps that he considers necessary, will, if material, result in a qualification or disclaimer of his opinion.

Some limitations in the scope of the auditor's examination arise from an inability to perform certain audit steps because of conditions beyond the auditor's and the client's control, for example, an inability to observe the opening inventory where the audit appointment was not made until the close of the year. Other limitations may result from a client-imposed restriction on the auditor's work. Whatever the reason for an incomplete examination, the auditor must report the inadequacy of the examination and the conclusions that flow from such an inadequacy.

The accounting profession has given special status to procedures with respect to observation of inventories and the confirmation of accounts receivable. If these steps cannot be reasonably or practically performed, the auditor must, in order to issue an unqualified opinion, satisfy himself about the inventories and accounts receivable by alternative means. For ending inventory in the balance sheet there are no alternative procedures to making or observing some counts of inventory items.

FAILURE OF FINANCIAL STATEMENTS TO CONFORM TO GENERALLY ACCEPTED ACCOUNTING PRINCIPLES

The auditor brings to bear his expertise in the application of auditing techniques and procedures to satisfy himself about the existence, ownership, and validity of presentation of the assets, the liabilities, and net worth as well as the statement of results. As an expert accountant, the auditor judges the fairness of presentation of financial statements and their conformity with GAAP. The latter judgment is one of the most important functions of the auditor's opinion.

Fair presentation is, to an important extent, dependent on the degree of informative disclosure provided. This is consistent with GAAP, which requires adequate disclosure. *Opinions* of the APB and *Statements* of the FASB enjoy, by definition, authoritative support. If the accountant concurs in a company's use of an accounting principle which differs from that approved by an authoritative body but which he believes enjoys the support of other authoritative sources, he need not qualify his opinion, but he must disclose that the principle used differs from those approved by such authoritative body. This, of course, puts the onus on the auditor in justifying the departure from a principle which enjoys authoritative approval.

If, because of lack of adequate disclosure or the use of accounting principles that do not enjoy authoritative support, the auditor concludes that the financial statements are not fairly presented, he must qualify his opinion or render an adverse opinion. The decision of whether to make his opinion an "except for" type, which is a qualified opinion, or to render an adverse opinion, which states that the "financial statements do not present fairly . . ." hinges on the materiality of the effect of such a deficiency on the financial statements taken as a whole. The concept of materiality in accounting and auditing is, however, very vague and remains so far unquantified.

It is obvious that a qualification due to a lack of disclosure or a lack of adherence to GAAP is the result of the auditor's inability to persuade his client to modify the financial statements. Thus, an "except for" type of opinion is not proper, and an adverse opinion is called for together with a full description of the shortcomings in the financial statements as well as their total impact thereon.

The following are pertinent excerpts from an opinion qualified because of lack of adherence to GAAP:

As explained in Note A, the year 3 financial statements include interest expense that has not been capitalized as required by *SFAS 34.*

In our opinion, except that in year 3 interest expense has not been capitalized as described in the preceding paragraph . . .

FINANCIAL STATEMENTS SUBJECT TO UNRESOLVED KNOWN UNCERTAINTIES

In cases where uncertainties about the future cannot be resolved, or their effect cannot be estimated or reasonably provided for at the time of the issuance of the auditor's opinion, an unqualified opinion with a required explanatory paragraph is called for. Such uncertainties may relate to lawsuits, tax matters, or other contingencies, the outcome of which is dependent upon decisions of parties other than management. Or the uncertainties may relate to the recovery of the investment in certain assets through future operations, or through their disposition.

Hitherto, a material uncertainty may have resulted in an uncertainty qualification. Under the *SAS,* "Reports on Audited Financial Statements," the qualification is replaced by explanatory language that discloses the uncertainty.

The practical effect of explanatory language because of uncertainty is to state the auditor's inability to assess the impact of the contingency, or the likelihood of its occurrence, and to pass on to the reader the burden of its evaluation.

One variety of explanatory language relates to the question of whether the going-concern assumption in accounting (see Chapter 3) is justified. This question may arise when a company is incurring continued operating losses, deficits in the stockholders' equity, working capital insufficiencies, or defaults under loan agreements or litigation. In such cases, the auditor expresses his doubt about the propriety of applying practices implicit in the going-concern concept such as the valuation of fixed assets at cost.

The following is an example of the pertinent portion of an auditor report relating to uncertainties. The explanatory language follows the opinion paragraph:

> The accompanying financial statements have been prepared assuming that Company Y will continue as a going concern. As discussed in Note X to the financial statements, Company Y has suffered recurring losses from operations and has a net capital deficiency that raise substantial doubt about the entity's ability to continue as a going concern. Management's plans in regard to these matters are also described in Note X. The financial statements do not include any adjustments that might result from the outcome of this uncertainty.

Inconsistent Application of GAAP   When there has been a material change between periods in accounting principles or in the method of their application, the auditor should refer to the change in explanatory language which follows the opinion paragraph.

SPECIAL REPORTS

In certain cases the standard report of the auditor is not appropriate because of special circumstances or because of the limited scope of the examination that the auditor is requested to undertake. It is particularly important that the analyst read such reports carefully so that he is not misled into believing that the auditor is assuming here his ordinary measure of responsibility. The following are some types of special reports that the reader may encounter:

1. Reports by companies on a cash, modified cash, or tax basis of accounting.
2. Reports by regulated organizations using regulatory accounting practices.
3. Reports prepared for limited purposes. Such reports usually deal with certain aspects of the financial statements (such as computations of royalties, rentals, profit-sharing arrangements, or compliance with provisions of bond indentures, etc.).

In *FRR* No. 1 Section 304, the SEC has called for the auditor's "association" with published interim reports based on performance of a limited review.

REPORTS ON "COMPILED" AND "REVIEWED" FINANCIAL STATEMENTS

The AICPA has made available to "nonpublic entities" compilation and review services that, while falling short of a full audit, provide the reader with lower defined levels of assurance.

Compiled financial statements are accompanied by a report that indicates that a compilation has been performed and that such a service is limited to presenting, in financial statement format, information that is the representation of management or owners. The report should also state that the financial statements have not been audited or reviewed; thus no opinion or any other form of assurance is expressed on them. No reference is made to any other procedures performed before or during the compilation engagement.

Reviewed financial statements are accompanied by a report that indicates that a review was performed in accordance with AICPA standards. The report describes a review engagement, states that the information in the financial statements is the representation of management (or owners), and disclaims an opinion on the financial statements taken as a whole. The report should state that: "The accountant is not aware of any material modifications that should be made to the financial statements in order for them to be in conformity with generally accepted accounting principles, other than those modifications, if any, indicated in his report." No reference is made to any other procedures performed before or during the review engagement.

THE SEC'S IMPORTANT ROLE

The SEC has in recent years moved particularly forcefully to monitor auditor performance as well as to strengthen the hands of auditors in their dealings with managements.

Disciplinary proceedings against auditors were expanded by means of innovative remedies in consent decrees to include requirements for improvements in internal administration procedures, professional education, and a review of a firm's procedures by outside professionals, known as "peer review."

SEC *FRR* No. 1 Section 603, in moving to strengthen the auditor's position, requires increased disclosure of the relationship between auditors and their clients, particularly in cases where changes in auditors take place. Disclosure must include details of past disagreements, including those resolved to the satisfaction of the replaced auditor, as well as footnote disclosure of the effects on the financial statements of methods of accounting advocated by a former auditor but not followed by the client.

The SEC has also moved to discourage "opinion shopping," a practice under which companies canvass audit firms to gain acceptance of accounting alternatives they desire to use.

IMPLICATIONS FOR ANALYSIS

Auditing as a function and the auditor's opinion as an instrument of assurance are widely misunderstood. The responsibility for this lack of communication cannot be all laid at the auditor's door, for the profession has published a number of pamphlets in which it has endeavored to explain its function. Nor should the readers of financial statements bear the full responsibility for this state of affairs, because the accounting profession's message in this area is often couched in technical and cautious language and requires a great deal of effort and background information for a full understanding.

A useful discussion of the implications of the current state of auditing to the user of audited financial statements may be presented in two parts:

1. Implications stemming from the nature of the audit process.
2. Implications arising from the professional standards which govern the auditor's opinion.

Implications Inherent in the Audit Process

Auditing is based largely on a sampling approach to the data under audit. Statistical sampling uses a rigorous approach to this process, which lends itself to a quantification of conclusions. Nevertheless, many audit tests are based on "judgmental samples" of the data, that is, samples selected by the auditor's intuition, judgment, and evaluation of many factors. Often the size of the sample is necessarily limited by the economics of the accounting practice.

The reader must realize that the auditor does not aim at, nor can he ever achieve, complete certainty. Even a review of every single transaction—a process that would be economically unjustifiable—would not achieve a complete assurance.

Auditing is a developing art. Even its very basic theoretical underpinnings are far from fully understood or resolved. There is, for instance, no clear relationship between the auditor's evaluation of the effectiveness of the control structure and the extent of audit testing and the nature of audit procedures employed. If we add to that the fact that the qualities of judgment among auditors do vary greatly, we should not be surprised to find that the history of auditing contains many examples of significant failure. On the other hand, as is the case with the risk of accidental death in commercial aviation, the percentage of failure to the total number of audits performed is very small indeed. Thus, while the user of audited financial statements can, in general, gain some reassurance about the overall results of the audit function, he must remember that there is substantial risk in reliance on its results in specific cases. Such risks are due to many factors, including the auditor's inability and/or unwillingness to detect fraud at the highest level and the application of proper audit tests to such an end (*McKesson and Robbins* case through the *Cenco, Inc.,* case and all the way to the *Equity Funding, ESM Government Securities, ZZZ Best, Regina,* and *Lincoln Savings* cases), the auditor's inability to grasp the extent of a deteriorating situation (the *Yale Express* case), the auditor's conception of the range of his responsibilities to probe and disclose (the *Continental Vending, National Student Marketing,* and *Bank of Credit and Commerce International* cases), and the quality of the audit (*Bar Chris Construction, U.S. Financial, Whittaker Corporation,*

Mattel, McCormick Company, Saxon Paper, and the multitude of Savings and Loan Associations cases.)

Thus, while the audit function may generally justify the reliance that financial analysts place on audited financial statements, such a reliance must be a cautious and informed one. The analyst must be aware that the entire audit process is a probabilistic one subject to many risks. Even its flawless application may not necessarily result in complete assurance, and most certainly cannot ensure that the auditor has elicited all the facts, especially if there is high-level management collusion to withhold such facts. Finally, the heavy dependence of the auditing process on judgment will, of necessity, result in a wide range of quality of performance.

An insight into what can be missed, and why, in the internal and external audit of a large corporation can be obtained from a reading of the *Report of the Special Review Committee of the Board of Directors of Gulf Oil Corporation* (the McCloy report—December 1975). In searching for reasons why Gulf's internal financial controls, its internal auditors, and its external auditors failed to detect or curb the expenditure of large amounts of corporate funds through "off the books" bank accounts for unlawful purposes, the review committee concluded that internal control committees chose not to control, that the corporate comptroller did not exercise the control powers vested in him, that the internal auditing department (reporting to the comptroller rather than to an audit committee of the board) lacked independence and stature, and that while it is clear that the external auditors had some knowledge of certain unusual transactions, the extent of their knowledge could not be determined.

To provide the reader with insights into how wrong things can go in the "audit" of a major corporation, let us focus on the landmark *Equity Funding* case.[2] This case includes expected elements such as human greed and shortcomings (see also discussion in Chapter 3), and the resulting fraud and deception and audit failure. This case also includes a more unusual element in that public accountants have been charged with knowing complicity in a fraud extending over many years.

THE EQUITY FUNDING CASE. The Equity Funding Corporation of America (EFCA) was an organization which sold mutual fund shares and used these as security against which the investor could borrow moneys for the payment of life insurance premiums on his or her behalf (the "funding" concept). From its inception as a public company in 1964, the major holders of its stock were obsessed with a desire to keep aloft the market price of its stock by fraudulently inflating reported earnings. As the fraud progressed and grew, vanity, pride, and the fear of being discovered provided added incentives to keep the fraud going.

---

[2] Most of the public documents as well as commentaries on this case are contained in L. J. Seidler, F. Andrews, and M. J. Epstein, *The Equity Funding Papers: The Anatomy of a Fraud* (New York: John Wiley & Sons, 1977).

An amazing aspect of this case is the relatively crude and unsophisticated design and execution of the fraud which relied on fictitious manual accounting entries lacking any real support.

In its early stages, the fraud consisted of recording nonexistent commission income with the charge (debit) going to a greatly inflated "Funding Loans Receivable" asset, supposedly representing borrowings by customers for life insurance premiums, and so on. Over the years, $85 million in such bogus income was recorded. As is true with most frauds, the fictitious entries involved do not, of course, create cash. Thus, to provide cash and at the same time keep the mushrooming "Funding Loans Receivable" in check, the conspirators borrowed money (on the basis of glowing earning results), and instead of booking the corresponding liabilities, credited the Funding Loans Receivable account. Other complicated shams involved foreign subsidiaries.

As the cash-hungry fraud monster grew, the expanding circle of fraud participants, now including senior as well as lower-management levels, had to invent new cash raising schemes. This led to the involvement of Equity Funding Life Insurance Company (EFLIC), a unit involved in reinsurance, that is, in the sale to others of insurance risks in force. Starting with intermediate, less crass and ambitious steps, there ultimately evolved a practice of creating totally fictitious products (insurance policies) that were sold to unsuspecting reinsurers who provided significant cash inflows. The process involved the "creation" of all needed documentation and related fictitious records. But, it also created the need for EFLIC to remit increasing amounts of cash to these reinsurers representing the premium payments which the company presumably collected from the fictitious policyholders. This created monumental documentation problems as well as severe cash flow problems (in 1972 reaching $1.7 million in cash flow deficit). These ever-growing fictions and problems that fed on themselves created a "house of cards" that would have collapsed of its own weight even without the whistle-blowing of a disgruntled dismissed employee in early 1973.

The sheer size of the deception as well as its duration should give pause to any analyst. From 1964 through 1972, at least $143 million in fictitious pre-tax income was reported in EFCA's financial statements. During the same period, the net income reported by the company amounted to about $76 million. Thus, this company whose reported success captured the imagination of Wall Street, in fact never earned a dime.

The bankruptcy proceedings and investigation which started in 1973 also revealed that:

Latecomers to the fraud benefited from and were motivated by prestigious and well-paying positions. This in turn led to a climate of dishonesty which included theft, expense account padding, and other manifestations of a breakdown of restraint and morality.

The small audit firm performed its audit during 1961–70 with such manifest incompetence that it could only be explained by a knowledge of the fraud. A larger successor audit firm that purchased the practice of the smaller firm changed practically nothing in the sloppy and uncoordinated audit approach.

The "big 8" audit firm of EFLIC failed to review internal controls and based its audit conclusions almost solely on internal records, thus omitting the crucial audit steps of independent outside verification.

The auditors had to settle for about $39 million in damages.

Rigorous financial analysis should have revealed the propensities of the defrauders if not the specific elements of the fraud. Thus, a comparison of quarterly reports in 1971 would have revealed that derived fourth-quarter income was inflated while the related expenses were understated in relation to the revenue amounts. The EFCA fraud holds many important lessons about the dynamics of a fraudulent process as well as the weak points that can be revealed to a trained and inquisitive eye.

Consider the case of ZZZ Best Company, a carpet cleaning company run by a 20-year-old. It received a clean audit opinion after booking fictitious receivables and revenues from nonexistent fire damage restoration contracts. The fraud included the renting by ZZZ Best of a building for a weekend for the sole purpose of persuading the auditors that work on a fictitious contract was in fact proceeding.

In relying on audited financial statements, the analyst must be ever aware of the risks of failure inherent in an audit; he must pay attention to the identity of the auditors and to what their record has been; and armed with a knowledge of what auditors do and how they do it, he must himself assess the areas of possible vulnerability in the financial statements. This brings us to the concept of audit risk.

Audit Risk and Its Implications

Audit risk, while related, is of a different dimension and represents, as a study of some of the above-mentioned cases will reveal, an equally clear and present danger to lenders and investors who rely on audited financial statements.

It is impossible for the analyst to substitute his judgment for that of the auditor. However, armed with an understanding of the audit process and its limitations, he or she can, through identification of special areas of vulnerability, make a better assessment of the degree of audit risk present in a given situation. The following are circumstances that can point to such areas vulnerability:

Glamour industry and company with need for continuing earnings growth to justify high market price or to facilitate acquisitions.

Company in difficult financial condition requiring credit urgently and frequently.

Company with high market visibility issuing frequent progress reports and earnings estimates.

Managements dominated mostly by one or a few strong-willed individuals or consisting mostly of financial people including CPAs.

Management compensation or stock options importantly dependent on reported earnings.

Managements that have displayed a propensity for earnings maximization and manipulation by various means.

Indications of personal financial difficulties by members of the senior management team.

Deterioration in operating performance.

Deterioration in liquidity or long-term solvency.

A capital structure far too complex for company's operations or size.

Problem industry displaying weaknesses in such areas as receivable collection, inventories, contract cost overruns, dependence on few products, and so forth.

Dealings with insiders or related parties, stockholder lawsuits, frequent turnover of key officers, legal counsel, or auditors.[3]

Audit conducted by a firm that has, for whatever reason, experienced a higher than normal incidence of audit failures.

While none of the above situations can be relied on to indicate situations of higher audit risk, they have been shown by experience to have appeared in a sufficient number of problem cases to warrant the analyst's close attention.

IMPLICATIONS STEMMING FROM THE STANDARDS THAT GOVERN THE AUDITOR'S OPINION

In relying on the auditor's opinion, the analyst must be aware of the limitations to which the audit process is subject, and this was the subject of the preceding discussion. Moreover, he or she must understand what the auditor's opinion means and particularly what the auditor himself thinks he conveys to the reader by means of his opinion.

Let us first consider the unqualified opinion or the so-called clean opinion. The auditor maintains that he expresses an opinion on *management's* statements. He is very insistent on this point and attaches considerable importance to it. This assertion means that normally he did not prepare the financial statements nor did he choose the accounting principles embodied in them. Instead, he reviews the financial statements presented to him by management and ascertains that they are in agreement with the books and records that he audited. He also determines that generally acceptable principles of accounting have been employed in the preparation of the financial statements, but does not claim to represent that they are the *best* principles that could have been used. It

---

[3] The SEC, in *FRR* No. 1 Section 603, required increased disclosure of relationships between registrants and their independent public accountants, including disputes, particularly in cases where changes in accountants occur.

is a well-known fact that management will often rely on the auditor, as an expert in accounting, to help them pick the principle that, while still acceptable, will come nearest to meeting their reporting objectives. Finally, the auditor will determine that the minimum standards of disclosure have been met so that all matters essential to a fair presentation of the financial statements are included in them.

One might well ask what difference it makes whether the auditor prepared the statements or not, so long as he expresses an unqualified opinion on them. The accounting profession has never clearly explained what the implications of this really are to the user of the financial statements. However, a number of such possible implications should be borne in mind by the analyst:

1. The auditor's knowledge about the financial statements is not as strong as that of the preparer who was in more intimate contact with all the factors which gave rise to the transactions. He knows only what he can discern on the basis of a sampling process and may not know all that he should know.

2. Since many items in the financial statements are not capable of exact measurement, he merely reviews such measurements for reasonableness. His are not the original determinations, and unless he can successfully prove otherwise (as, for example, in the case of estimates of useful lives of property), management's determination will prevail. Thus, the auditor's opinion contains no reference to "present exactly" or "present correctly" but rather states that the statements "present fairly."

3. While the auditor may be consulted on the use of accounting principles, he, as auditor rather than as preparer of such statements, does not select the principles to be used. Moreover, he cannot insist on the use of the *best* available principle any more than he is likely to *insist* on a degree of disclosure above the minimum considered acceptable at the time.

4. The limitations to which the auditor's ability to audit are subject have never been spelled out by the accounting profession. Knowledgeable auditors do, of course, know about them; but there seems to be a tacit agreement, of doubtful value to the profession, not to discuss them. For example, is the auditor really equipped to audit the value of complex technical work in progress? Can he competently evaluate the adequacy of insurance reserves? Can he estimate the value of problem loans? Can he second-guess the client's estimate of the percentage of completion of a large contract? While such questions are rarely raised in public, let alone answered, they cannot be unequivocally answered in the affirmative.

5. While the preparer must, under the rules of double-entry bookkeeping, account for all items, large or small, the auditor is held to

less exacting standards of accuracy in his work. Thus, the error tolerances are wider. He leans on the doctrine of materiality that in its basic concept simply means that the auditor need not concern himself, in either the auditing or the reporting phases of his work, with trivial or unimportant matters. What is important or significant is, of course, a matter of judgment, and so far the profession has neither defined the concept nor set limits or established criteria to govern the overall application of the concept of materiality. This has given it an unwarranted degree of reporting latitude.[4]

It is important to understand, from the point of view of accounting and audit risk, that new industries and new practices (such as novel financial instruments) spawn abuses that are not foreseen or that auditors refuse to address in the absence of specific professional guidelines. Such guidelines will generally be issued as a result of the publicity attending the next transgression or accounting or audit failure. By that time it will be too late to reverse the adverse consequences which the analyst must face.

Auditors even as a profession, in contradistinction to a business, must pay attention to the economics of their function and to the limits of the responsibilities they can assume. Thus, whether the foregoing limitations on the auditor's function and responsibility are justified or not, the analyst must recognize them as standards applied by auditors and evaluate his reliance on audited financial statements with a full understanding of them.

The auditor's reference to "generally accepted accounting principles" in his opinion should be well understood by the user of the financial statements. Such reference means that the auditor is satisfied that such principles, or standards, have authoritative support and that they have been applied "in all material respects." Aside from understanding the operation of the concept of materiality, the analyst must understand that the definition of what constitutes "generally accepted accounting principles" is often vague and subject to significant latitude in interpretation and application. For example, an *SAS* issued in 1975 states that "when criteria for selection among alternative accounting principles have not been established to relate accounting methods to circumstances (e.g., as in case of inventory and depreciation methods) the auditor may conclude that more than one accounting principle is appropriate in the circumstances."

Similarly indeterminate are present-day standards relating to disclosure. While minimum standards are increasingly established in

---

[4] See Leopold A. Bernstein, "The Concept of Materiality," *The Accounting Review,* January 1967; and Sam M. Woolsey, "Approach to Solving the Materiality Problem," *Journal of Accountancy,* March 1973. The FASB has published a *Discussion Memorandum* on the subject and held public hearings on it. The FASB has no present intention to issue pronouncements on the subject beyond what is already skimpily covered in its statements.

professional and SEC pronouncements, accountants have not always adhered to them. The degree to which the lack of disclosure impairs the fair presentation of the financial statements remains subject to the auditor's judgment and discretion, and there are no definite standards that indicate at what point lack of disclosure is material enough to impair fairness of presentation thus requiring a qualification in the auditor's report.

THE AUDIT FUNCTION AS PERCEIVED BY THE AUDITOR

The auditor's misperception of his function is a major problem area for the analyst and the general user of financial statements.

Take the question of who the client is, or who the auditor is working for. Despite the 1984 decision of Chief Justice Burger, cited earlier, many auditors still consider their relationship with the companies they audit as amounting to a privileged attorney-client relationship where everything can be kept private. Some auditors even believe that they are entitled to determine when revelations of fraud or irregularities should be disclosed so as to forestall what they view as unfavorable economic or other adverse effects that could result from such disclosure.

ILLUSTRATION 1.   In 1990 the auditors gave the Bank of Credit and Commerce International a clean opinion. The auditors later admitted that at the time the opinion was issued they had knowledge of the presence of serious fraud or irregularities, the extent of which was not yet determined. The auditor's senior partner in London defended its actions by stating: "You simply can't go around qualifying the accounts of a bank without creating all sorts of problems, without the whole thing collapsing." Must users of audited financial statements now consider whether other considerations may have priority over their right to know the whole and unvarnished truth?

This confusion about auditor role and function manifests itself in other areas. Auditing, the major public franchise of the profession and the reason for its existence, often takes a back seat, sometimes as loss leader, to such tangential services as headhunting, system design, and other types of consulting.

The auditing profession did not fare well in the 1980's savings and loan debacle. In his decision re the *Lincoln Savings and Loan* vs. *Office of Thrift Supervision* case, Judge Stanley Sporkin noted that the audit partner in charge of the failed audit left his audit firm in order to assume a high-paying position with Lincoln, his former client and beneficiary of favorable reports. This, in the judge's view, certainly raised questions about the auditor's independence. In his summation of this case of substantial audit failure the judge concluded "What it is hoped the accounting profession will learn from this case is that an accountant must not blindly apply accounting conventions without ... determining whether a transaction makes any economic sense ... and without finding that the transaction is realistic and has economic substance...."

Qualification, Disclaimers, and Adverse Opinions

When the auditor qualifies his opinion, the analyst is faced with an additional problem of interpretation, that is, what is the meaning and intent of the qualification and what effect should such qualifications have on his reliance on the financial statements? The usefulness of the qualification to the analyst depends, of course, on its clarity, its lack of equivocation, and on the degree to which supplementary information and data enable an assessment of its effect.

An additional dimension of confusion and difficulty of interpretation is introduced when the auditor includes explanatory information in his report, merely for emphasis, without a statement of conclusions or of a qualification. The analyst may in such situations be left wondering why the matter was emphasized in this way and whether the auditor is attempting to express an unstated qualification or reservation.

ILLUSTRATION 2.   In 1981, Manville Corporation stated that it had substantial defenses to legal actions. In 1982, it declared bankruptcy because of asbestos-related law suits.

Up to the first quarter of 1991, Columbia Gas failed to disclose its take-or-pay contracts to buy gas at fixed prices which proved to be far above market when gas prices declined. The subsequent sharp decline in the company's stock took many analysts by surprise.

As discussed in an earlier part of this chapter, generally when an auditor is not satisfied with the fairness of presentation of items in the financial statements, he issues an "except-for" type of qualification, and when there are uncertainties that he cannot resolve, he adds explanatory language after the opinion paragraph. At some point, the size and importance of items under qualification must result in *adverse opinions* or *disclaimers of opinion,* respectively. Where is this point? At what stage is a specific qualification no longer meaningful and an overall disclaimer of opinion necessary? Here again, the analyst won't find any explicit quantitative guidelines by turning to the auditor's own professional pronouncements or literature.

ILLUSTRATION 3.   Language of a qualification:

As more fully described in Note X to the financial statements, the Company has excluded certain lease obligations from property and debt in the accompanying balance sheets. In our opinion, generally accepted accounting principles require that such obligations be included in the balance sheets.

In our opinion, except to the effect of not capitalizing certain lease obligations as discussed in the preceding paragraph. . . .

Explanatory Language for Uncertainties. When the auditor cannot assess the proper carrying amount of an asset or determine the extent of a possible liability or find other uncertainties or contingencies that cannot be determined or measured, he will describe such uncertainties in his report and refer the reader to the relevant notes to the financial statements. The analyst using financial statements that contain such explanatory language is, quite bluntly, faced with a situation where the auditor has passed on to him the uncertainty described and, consequently, the task of evaluating its possible impact. The analyst should recognize the situation for what it really is and not assume that he is dealing with a mere formality designed only for the auditor's self-protection. Moreover, the auditor's efforts to estimate future uncertainties cannot normally be expected to exceed those of management itself. As an *SAS* issued in 1974 put it, "The auditor's function in forming an opinion on financial statements does not include estimating the outcome of future events if management is unable to do so."

In those cases where explanatory language is inserted because of uncertainties that cannot be resolved, it is hard to blame the auditor for shifting the burden of evaluation on to the reader. At the same time, it must be remembered that as between the reader and the auditor, the latter, due to his firsthand knowledge of the company's affairs, is far better equipped to evaluate the nature of the contingencies as well as the probabilities of their occurrence. Thus, the analyst is entitled to expect, but will unfortunately not always get, a full explanation of all factors surrounding the uncertainty.

Lest the absence of explanatory language because of uncertainty in the auditor's report lull the analyst into a false sense of security, it must be borne in mind that there are many contingencies and uncertainties that do not call for explanatory language but that may nevertheless have very significant impact on the company's financial condition or results of operations. Examples of such contingencies or possibilities are:

1. Obsolescence of a major product line.
2. Loss of a significant customer.
3. Overextension of a business in terms of management capabilities.
4. Difficulty of getting large and complex production units on-stream on time.

These matters may, however, affect a company's ability to continue as a going concern. They must, moreover, be discussed by management in the SEC-mandated "Management's Discussion and Analysis of Financial Condition and Results of Operations" (see Chapter 7).

From the above discussion it should be obvious that the analyst must read with great care the auditor's opinion as well as the supplementary information to which it refers. While the analyst can place some reliance on the auditor, he must maintain an independent and open-minded attitude towards the assurances which the auditor's report convey.

QUESTIONS

1. In relying on an auditor's opinion, what should the financial analyst know about the auditor and his work?
2. What are "generally accepted auditing standards"?
3. What are auditing procedures? What are some of the basic objectives of a financial audit?
4. What does the opinion section of the auditor's report usually cover?
5. Which are the four major categories of conditions that require of the auditor explanatory language, qualifications, disclaimers, or adverse opinions?
6. What is an "except-for" type of audit report qualification?
7. What is a *(a)* disclaimer of opinion and *(b)* an adverse opinion? When are these properly rendered?
8. What is the practical effect of explanatory language because of uncertainty in an auditor's report?
9. How does the auditor report on an inconsistency in the application of GAAP?
10. What are the major disclosures required by SEC's *FRR* No. 1, Section 603, on the relationship between auditors and clients?
11. What are some of the implications to financial analysis which stem from the audit process itself?
12. The auditor does not prepare the financial statements on which he expresses an opinion but instead he samples the data and examines them in order to render a professional opinion on them. List some of the possible implications of this to those who rely on the financial statements.
13. What does the auditor's reference to "generally accepted accounting principles" mean to the analyst of financial statements?
14. Of what significance to the financial analyst is explanatory language because of uncertainty?
15. What are some of the circumstances which can point to areas of higher audit risk?

Index